Global System Change

We the People Achieving True Democracy, Sustainable Economy And Total Corporate Responsibility

Frank Dixon

TCR® (Total Corporate Responsibility) is a registered trademark of Frank Dixon. TCR is a system change-based approach to corporate responsibility and socially responsible investing.

Library of Congress Control Number 2017932841

ISBN 978-0-9986138-3-3 (e-book)
ISBN 978-0-9986138-4-0 (paperback)

First Edition: 2017

Publisher

Global System Change
PO Box 41
Middle Grove, NY 12850

www.GlobalSystemChange.com

Dedication

Founders of the United States – George Washington, Benjamin Franklin, Thomas Jefferson, James Madison and James Wilson. Their wise, enlightened ideas and actions hugely inspired and guided this book.

Our Children and Future Generations. Protecting future generations was the primary concern of the US Founders. It also is the primary purpose of this book.

Acknowledgment

Rosalind Morley, my dear friend who provided extensive editing and inspirational support throughout this whole system exploration and adventure.

Francis J. Dixon, Jr. and Carol J. Dixon, my wonderful parents.

William B. Dixon and Kathleen Gavigan, my wise and supportive uncle and aunt.

Evelyn Brandin, my lifelong friend whose love, prayers and encouragement helped to sustain me while writing a whole system series of books.

Robert and Gloria Fox, my good friends whose long-term support and encouragement helped me to complete this whole system assessment of human society.

Table of Contents

Global System Change

We the People Achieving
True Democracy, Sustainable Economy
And Total Corporate Responsibility

INTRODUCTION

Industrialization and technological development cause many people to believe that human society is advanced and sophisticated. But all of our life support systems are in rapid decline, with some regional exceptions. In addition, there is widespread poverty, hunger, suffering, political turmoil, unemployment, inequality and other economic, political and social problems around the world. This is not what an advanced and sophisticated society looks like. Instead, it reflects a civilization in rapid decline.

We have developed great power to dominate nature and other people. But widespread and expanding environmental and social degradation show that we have not developed the wisdom needed to use this power wisely. If we truly were wise and sophisticated, nearly all humans on Earth would be living satisfying, prosperous lives, and we would not be doing anything that inhibits the ability of humanity to survive and prosper over the very long term.

The root cause of environmental and social degradation, and essentially all other major problems facing humanity, is our flawed ideas and systems. Flawed economic and political systems compel all businesses, without exception, to degrade the environment and society. If companies attempted to act in a fully responsible manner by voluntarily eliminating all negative environmental and social impacts, they would put themselves out of business. This largely is a system problem, not a company problem. But the corporate responsibility, socially responsible investing (SRI) and sustainability movements are focused mainly on company-level changes. To achieve sustainability and real prosperity, we must substantially shift this focus to system change.

Flawed systems result from flawed thinking and ideas. The primary thinking problem is shortsightedness or myopia. We usually focus narrowly on the well-being of individual persons, companies or countries, instead of the whole system that enables individuals to survive and prosper. Everything in human society is connected. The economic is not separate from the political, social, environmental, or even psychological, spiritual and religious. But the conscious human mind has difficulty considering the whole Earth system, and its sub-element human society, at once. As a result, we often break society down into

1

parts (economic, political, social) and study them without adequate reference to the whole system that contains them, a process known as reductionism. This produces unintended consequences, such as widespread environmental and social degradation, because major, relevant aspects of reality are ignored when developing human systems.

As Einstein implied, the solution to myopia is whole system thinking. To resolve the major challenges facing humanity and achieve sustainability and real prosperity, we must exit the ivory tower of reductionism and begin reality-based, whole system thinking.

This book is a summary of a whole system book (*Global System Change: A Whole System Approach to Achieving Sustainability and Real Prosperity*) that illustrates one way to do this. In the whole system book, all major physical (economic, political, social, environmental) and nonphysical (psychological, spiritual, religious) aspects of human society are discussed as parts of one whole system. This perspective illuminates root causes and effective systemic solutions. The book provides detailed descriptions of the many economic, political and social system changes needed to achieve sustainability and real prosperity. The proposed changes minimize unintended consequences because all major aspects of reality are integrated and taken into account.

In the environmental area, the whole system book discusses root causes, public deceptions and systemic solutions for major issues, including climate change, chemicals, genetic engineering, nanotechnology and nuclear power. In the social area, extensive analysis and systemic solutions are provided for important issues, such as population growth, education, food production, crime, privacy and terrorism prevention. Vested interest strategies for misleading and disempowering citizens also are thoroughly examined.

All actions begin in the mind. To change our physical world, we must change the way we think about it. To facilitate this, the whole system book extensively discusses psychology, spirituality and religion. Collaboration and other processes for implementing systemic changes also are thoroughly described. This summary book and the whole system book are intended for business, political and civil society leaders, as well as average citizens – the ultimate leaders of society. Information is presented in ways that all levels of readers can easily understand.

In addition to being published in the whole system book, the last three chapters of that book are being published separately as this book – *Global System Change: We the People Achieving True Democracy, Sustainable Economy and Total Corporate Responsibility.* The whole system book is about ten times longer than this book. Several sections from it are being published as separate books.

Positions and conclusions in the whole system book are extensively supported with logic, references and examples. The book has over 3,000 endnotes. Many positions taken in the whole system book are summarized here. Frequent references to earlier sections in the whole system book show where more detailed and fully referenced discussions can be found. The table of contents of the whole system book is shown in the appendix.

This summary book (i.e. We the People book) emphasizes important actions needed to achieve sustainability and real prosperity. Chapter Seven (the first chapter of this book) discusses how We the People can unite and establish true democracy in United States and other countries. In the US Constitution, the Founders gave all ultimate power to We the People (all citizens collectively). But in his Farewell Address, George Washington warned that vested interests would use political parties to divide the people and suppress their ability to rule themselves. This is exactly what happened.

Dividing the people into conservatives and liberals inhibits their ability to attain the majorities needed to take back control of government and compel it to serve all citizens equally and fairly. During the Civil War, President Lincoln warned that wealthy business owners had gained stronger control of government and would use this influence to unfairly concentrate public wealth in their own hands. Especially since the 1980s, business-controlled government has facilitated concentration of wealth at the top of society, while life became more difficult for nearly everyone else.

The division of the US into two major political parties is a sham that has existed since the founding of this country. Virtually everyone wants a strong economy, prosperous society and stable life support systems. Dividing the people into conservatives and liberals prevents them from working together in their massive areas of common interest and agreement. To achieve sustainability and real prosperity, we must end the civil war between conservatives and liberals. This book describes how to unite citizens under a We the People movement, the name given to us by our Founders. Once united, we can take back control of government, establish true democracy and use the public wealth to equally and fairly benefit all citizens.

Shifting the focus of the corporate responsibility, SRI and sustainability movements from company change to system change also is discussed. Chapter Eight summarizes the Total Corporate Responsibility (TCR®) approach. TCR provides a practical and profitable way for businesses and financial institutions to engage in system change. This is by far the most important sustainability issue. Therefore, companies that aggressively promote system change at the sector-level and overarching economic and political system-level are the true sustainability leaders. Investment funds developed with the TCR model have the potential to drive far greater positive environmental and social impacts than any other SRI approach, while providing superior investment returns.

Chapter Nine further describes the We the People movement and summarizes many of the problems and systemic solutions discussed in the whole system book. A major emphasis is placed on implementing sustainable economic and financial systems. Current systems concentrate wealth at the top of society, produce widespread unemployment and under-employment, drive declining quality of life for the vast majority of citizens, and severely degrade environmental life support systems. Clearly these systems are not sustainable, fair or even rational.

The main Founders of the US, except Alexander Hamilton, strongly opposed a highly centralized, speculative economy. They knew that it would produce the unjust, destructive results we see today. President Franklin D. Roosevelt strongly advocated a just economy that strives to meet the needs of all citizens. His policies produced widespread economic prosperity and the largest middle class in the world. Building on the suggestions of great US leaders, Chapter Nine summarizes many of the critical actions needed to implement sustainable, fair, efficient and highly productive economic and financial systems.

This book concludes by discussing the destiny of humanity. We are surrounded by nearly infinitely greater technological sophistication, coordination, sustainability and prosperity in nature and our own bodies. We are part of nature. Therefore, we have the innate potential to display the vastly higher levels of sophistication, coordination and widespread prosperity seen in nature.

Emulating nature is one of the most important actions needed to achieve sustainability and real prosperity. Solutions to nearly all of the major challenges facing humanity are modeled or implied there. Nature produces no waste, equitably distributes resources among individuals and generations, lives on renewable resources, decentralizes production, and enables nearly all individuals to reach their fullest potential.

As discussed, there is an imbalance between power and wisdom in human society. Rapid environmental and social degradation show that we lack the wisdom needed to use our abundant power wisely. Perhaps the most important aspect of emulating nature is increasing wisdom in human society. The imbalance between power and wisdom reflects the imbalance between men and women. Men innately manifest greater physical strength, aggressiveness and other aspects of power than women. In our competitive society, power is honored. As a result, men often have higher status than women.

But excessive competition is degrading life support systems and society. Limited competition occurs in nature at the individual level. But the overwhelming force in healthy natural systems and nature overall is cooperation. In the same way that men innately manifest more power, many studies show that women innately manifest greater cooperation, empathy, whole system thinking ability and other aspects of wisdom. As we elevate and honor wisdom and cooperation in human society, it naturally will elevate those who manifest more of these characteristics (women) a position of true equality with men.

We have free will. Virtually every major problem facing humanity results from our ideas and actions. Except for natural disasters, nothing is imposed on us. We caused the problems. Therefore, we can create the solutions. Destiny is not predetermined. We choose it. Whatever actions we choose will be our destiny.

Essentially everyone wants current and future generations to survive and prosper. With free will, we can choose this outcome. We have the desire, power and innate wisdom needed to attain it. This book and the whole system book from which it comes take the position that the destiny of humanity is to manifest the wisdom of nature in human society, reach our fullest potential, and achieve sustainability and real prosperity. The books describe the whole system thinking, systemic changes and implementation processes needed to achieve this destiny.

CHAPTER SEVEN – EMPOWERMENT AND DEMOCRACY

Chapters One through Six of the whole system book extensively describe the major economic, political and social system changes needed to achieve sustainability and real prosperity. These concluding three chapters (Seven through Nine) summarize many problems and systemic solutions that are discussed in the whole system book as well as describe the processes needed to implement effective system change.

Non-judgment is an essential system change principle. Flawed economic and political systems put companies in fundamental, systemically-mandated conflict with society. These systems myopically focus on maximizing economic growth and shareholder returns, instead of the actual well-being of society. When there are conflicts between shareholders and employees, customers, communities, the environment or anything else, as there frequently are, business leaders and politicians who accept money from them often are compelled to put shareholder returns first. They essentially are forced by flawed systems to oppose anything that threatens ever-increasing shareholder returns, including democracy and fair use of the public wealth. Inappropriate government influence and public deception frequently are used to protect financial returns. As noted, flawed systems suppress democracy, concentrate public wealth at the top of society and severely degrade life support systems.

Wealthy citizens who benefit from flawed systems and politicians who accept money from them are not the enemies. These leaders virtually always intend to benefit, not harm society. In a sense, they are cogs in a wheel. Replacing business and political leaders who unintentionally degrade the environment and society often would have little impact. Flawed systems frequently would compel their replacements to take similar harmful actions.

Environmental and social degradation largely is not caused by greed, immorality or bad people. It mainly is caused by flawed systems that compel good, well-meaning leaders to take actions that harm society. These systems, and the myopic ideas and thinking that created them, are the true enemies of humanity.

The purpose of this book is not to criticize individual companies or leaders. It is to analyze and suggest improvements for our flawed systems. Therefore, when negative actions are attributed to individuals or companies, names rarely are used.

Effective change of economic and political systems is complex. It only can be achieved through collaboration. Business and political leaders are important participants in this collaboration. They frequently have the power to facilitate system change. Judging, criticizing or demonizing politicians, business leaders, wealthy citizens or anyone else who benefits from current systems can severely inhibit collaboration and effective system change. Therefore, this book does not do it. Whenever attention is placed on those who benefit from current systems, the intention always is to criticize systems. It never is to criticize companies, individuals or groups of people.

Economic, political and other human systems are not sacred. Life, families, communities and the environment are sacred (in part because there is no life without the environment). Our allegiance should not be to ideas, philosophies or human systems. These simply are tools. Ensuring the long-term survival and prosperity of humanity requires that we open our minds and become willing to question and change these tools when they no longer serve us, and especially when they threaten our survival. Our allegiance should be to life and doing whatever is necessary to protect it, including improving our flawed systems.

Effective system change requires whole system thinking. Incremental change of current economic, political and other systems almost certainly will not provide the pace and scale of change needed to resolve the major environmental, social and economic problems facing humanity. Whole system thinking involves stepping back and seeing the big picture. This greatly facilitates system change because it provides a clear, inspirational goal. Achieving sustainability and real prosperity is a high level goal for society that virtually all sane people would support. The term means that humanity survives and truly prospers over the very long term (at least thousands of years). Real prosperity means meeting all physical and nonphysical human needs.

This book also refers to achieving sustainability and real prosperity as humanity reaching our highest potential, manifesting the wisdom of nature in human society, and creating Heaven on Earth. Clarifying an inspirational goal is the first and most important system change action. Doing this upfront helps to overcome resistance to system change. As discussed in the Misleading the Public section, businesses and their allies often attempt to block changes that benefit society but threaten shareholder returns by arguing that change would be too difficult, expensive and/or disruptive. This technique for protecting shareholder returns could be referred to as Putting the How before the What.

Putting the what before the how (i.e. identifying the goal before figuring out how to achieve it) helps to overcome resistance to change. For example, achieving sustainability and real prosperity essentially means ensuring that our children and future generations survive and prosper. Companies sometimes argue that system changes needed to achieve this goal would be too difficult. Whole system thinking shows that companies taking this position effectively are saying, we must continue to harm or kill our children because not harming or killing them would be too difficult. Establishing the goal first (i.e. putting the what before the how) will greatly reduce the ability of vested interest to block changes that are essential for the survival and real prosperity of humanity.

Regarding priorities and goals, as discussed in the Well-Being of Society section, the survival of current generations is the first priority (because future generations will not survive if we do not). After that, the survival and prosperity (i.e. comfort and well-being) of future generations is the next highest priority. The prosperity of current generations is the lowest priority. The survival of future generations obviously takes priority over our prosperity. The prosperity of future generations also should take priority over our own prosperity. Our Founders sacrificed greatly for us. We should do the same if necessary for future generations.

Giving up some comforts, such as wasteful lifestyles, might not be easy. But it usually produces a richer, more truly satisfying and meaningful life. We have no right to degrade or destroy environmental life support systems with our gluttony and ignorant extravagance. (Ignorant because people often seek satisfaction through overconsumption. But it rarely satisfies because they are attempting to fulfill nonphysical needs with material consumption.) True life satisfaction largely does not result from material abundance. Once basic needs are met, the greatest joy and meaning in life come from nonphysical factors, such as love, friendship, helping others and reaching one's fullest potential.

Focusing on the goal first also facilitates system change by emphasizing the positive. A fulfilling, positive vision of the future can inspire people to work for it. Focusing on the positive does not mean ignoring problems or the negative. Problems are addressed through the process of attaining the compelling vision. Emphasizing problems first can be depressing and overwhelming, especially considering the scale of problems facing humanity. This can reduce motivation to change. Emphasizing the positive usually is more effective.

Achieving sustainability and real prosperity means that we figure out how to provide far more fulfilling and meaningful lifestyles for nearly everyone, while ending the degradation of life support systems and society. Humans are part of nature. We implicitly have access to the virtually infinite implied intelligence and wisdom seen in nature. We definitely have the ability to achieve sustainability and real prosperity. This section discusses how we can make the systemic changes needed to achieve these goals.

This book has extensively discussed systemic problems and solutions in virtually every major area of human society. The root cause of essentially all major environmental, social, economic and political challenges facing humanity is our flawed ideas and systems. Therefore, the primary, foundational solution to these challenges is improving ideas and systems. Primary flawed ideas relate to reductionism and individualism. Economic theory often discusses the 'rational actor' who seeks to maximize their own well-being. This might make sense from the perspective of the individual. But the individual perspective is not the rational perspective for promoting individual well-being. Focusing on the individual is unintentionally suicidal. Suicide clearly is not rational.

Einstein said that we must think at a higher level to solve our most complex challenges. As discussed in Chapter One, this higher level is whole system thinking. Focusing on the individual level would be rational if we each were individual self-sustaining entities floating out in space. But we are not. We are parts of one interconnected whole system. None of us can survive in outer space (without a simulated Earth). We are as much a part of the Earth as the hand is of the body. If a cell in the body sought to maximize its own well-being without regard for the larger body that supports it, we would not call this rational. It would be called irrational, suicidal or cancerous.

In the same way, seeking to maximize individual well-being without regard for the larger environmental and social systems that enable individuals to survive and prosper is not rational. This once again shows the grossly flawed, myopic nature of economic and other systems. The individual perspective is an irrational, ivory tower, fantasy perspective. Humans do not exist in isolation. Therefore, considering the individual in isolation is irrational. In reality, we are parts of a larger system. The reality-based perspective is this whole system perspective.

From this perspective, one sees that the so-called 'rational actor' of modern economic theory actually is an irrational, unintentionally suicidal actor. The true rational actor is one who understands that they cannot survive or prosper apart from larger social and especially environmental systems. The actor who actually is rational understands that cooperating or helping others ultimately is the same as helping oneself, in the same way that the rational cell implicitly understands that cooperating with other cells is the only way that the body (and therefore cells) can survive and prosper.

The individual, reductionistic perspective or consciousness of many humans has placed us in rapid suicide mode. Environmental life support systems are being quickly degraded, while inequality and other social problems are rapidly increasing. The ultimate solution is to adopt higher level ideas or perspectives. In other words, to truly prosper, we must evolve our consciousness to a higher level.

As discussed in the Women's section, traditional psychology often considers the most evolved psychological state to be individuation. In this state, one establishes themself as a separate, autonomous individual. But a higher, more accurate perspective shows this supposedly evolved state to be unintentionally suicidal. A more accurate model of human development would show individuation to be one step along the path of full human development. The ultimate goal could be referred to as conscious unity. In this state, people understand that they are interconnected parts of one whole system. From this perspective, one recognizes that it is not rational to consider one's own well-being apart from the well-being of others and society as a whole. It especially is not rational to increase one's own well-being by degrading the well-being of others or the whole system.

Our flawed economic, political and other systems result from flawed, myopic ideas. The most important action needed to evolve our systems into sustainable forms is to evolve our ideas into rational, reality-based forms. The primary idea evolution needed is to move from illusion (separation) to reality (interconnectedness and unity). The illusion of separation has produced irrational ideas, such as the 'rational' (i.e. irrational) actor theory in economics. Moving into the reality of the whole system perspective does not require that each person experience the reality of interconnectedness (or Nirvana) on an inner level. The whole system perspective can be understood on an intellectual level. Rational thought shows that none of us can survive in outer space. Therefore, protecting the environment that keeps us alive is highly rational.

A whole system perspective provides many other benefits beyond showing the reality of our interconnectedness. For example, it illuminates the most effective ways to evolve our systems into sustainable forms. There is growing awareness among businesses and larger society that system change is essential for achieving sustainability. As discussed in Chapter Three, mid-level and high-level system change are important corporate and financial sector issues. Mid-level system change involves changes at the sector, stakeholder or environmental/social issue levels. High-level system change refers to evolving overarching economic, political and social systems into sustainable forms.

Mid-level and especially high-level system change only can be achieved through collaboration (in part because no individual, group or segment of society is powerful enough to change overarching systems). As a result, many consulting firms, NGOs and other groups are promoting and helping with collaborative system change. For example, the consulting firm Blu Skye has effectively facilitated mid-level system changes in the apparel, dairy and waste management sectors.

But the ability of collaborative processes to achieve high-level system change of economic and political systems is limited. Two reasons for this include the scope of collaboration and vested interest efforts to block change. To illustrate, the purpose of economic and political systems in a true democracy is to support and benefit each citizen and society in general. Therefore, each person has a right to participate in the evolution of these systems. But managing the input of about 300 million citizens in the US, for example, would be difficult or impossible.

In addition, current systems inhibit system change. Flawed economic and political systems essentially compel publicly traded companies, and their political and media allies, to oppose actions that threaten short-term shareholder returns. As discussed in many sections, the most important high-level system change needed in the business area is to hold companies fully responsible for negative environmental and social impacts. This makes acting sustainably and responsibly the profit-maximizing strategy. But holding companies fully responsible often would restrict short-term shareholder returns. As a result, flawed systems frequently compel businesses and business leaders to vigorously oppose efforts to hold them responsible.

Business largely controls government and society in the US and many other countries. As a result, large companies and their wealthy owners have great power to block high-level system change efforts. Enlightened collaborative approaches, such as David Cooperrider's Appreciative Inquiry and Otto Scharmer's U Process, can help business executives to evolve their views and support system change. But the ability of enlightened leaders to make a difference is severely constrained by current systems.

As discussed in Chapters Three and Eight, companies very generally can mitigate about 20 percent of their negative environmental and social impacts in a profit-neutral or profit-enhancing manner. This is the realm within which enlightened leaders can operate. They can move their companies closer to 20 percent impact mitigation. Mid-level or sector-level system change can help companies to move further along the impact mitigation spectrum. But overarching systems often will prevent them from mitigating many, if not the large majority, of negative impacts without putting themselves out of business.

System change has little to do with morals, ethics or good intentions. Even the best, most enlightened and committed business leaders cannot get anywhere near sustainability without killing their companies. The requirement to maximize short-term shareholder returns frequently requires companies, even the best and most enlightened companies, to oppose system change efforts that threaten shareholder returns or business existence. Enlightened companies (i.e. those which understand that acting in a fully responsible manner ultimately is the only way that businesses can succeed) frequently will get involved in system change. But the requirement to maximize shareholder returns often will compel them to delay or limit system change efforts.

The main economic and political systems functioning on this planet massively violate the laws of nature and reality. As a result, they absolutely will change. They are in the process of changing now. A whole system perspective shows that high-level system change is inevitable. It will occur through voluntary or involuntary means. High-level system changes, such as the fall of communism in the Soviet Union and end of slavery in the US, usually occur in a highly disruptive manner. A whole system perspective makes it clear that if we do not evolve our systems into sustainable forms voluntarily, reality and nature will do it for us in a highly disruptive, perhaps humanity destroying, manner. This perspective shows that we do not have a choice. We must make high-level system change happen, before it happens to us.

A whole system perspective also shows how to achieve high-level system change voluntarily. It makes clear that the most powerful force in society is society (i.e. all citizens). When the people understand their collective best interests (such as the survival of current and future generations) and act in a coordinated manner to achieve them, no government, business or any other force or entity can stand in their way. Probably only the collective power of the people can drive successful, voluntary high-level system change. This illustrates that perhaps the most important high-level change needed is to enlighten and empower citizens.

A whole system perspective also illuminates the second most important action needed to achieve voluntary high-level system change – establish democracy. Most of the high-level system changes needed to achieve sustainability and real prosperity only can be implemented by government. For example, only government can hold businesses fully responsible for negative impacts, and thereby make acting responsibly the profit-maximizing strategy. As discussed in the Time Value of Money section, only government can nullify suicidal time value of money concepts and ensure that business and society treat future generations and the resources that will keep them alive as if they were at least as valuable as current generations and resources. As discussed in the Externalities section, only government can ensure that all real external costs are integrated into prices, and thereby enable markets to function in a beneficial rather than destructive manner. As discussed in the Advertising, Media and Culture section, only government can compel advertising and media to put the well-being of society ahead of the well-being of shareholders.

In a democracy, government is supposed to be the agent of the people. This is what the US Founders intended. But as President Washington warned, vested interests have divided the people and stolen their wealth and power. Large companies and their wealthy owners largely have taken over government and removed the people's ability to rule themselves. They have turned government into their agent. This abusive, business-focused government only can continue as long as the people remain deluded and divided, for example, into conservatives and liberals.

Once the people are empowered to see through deception, they can reclaim control of government. Government is supposed to be the expression of the people's collective will and power to protect their best interests. As the people wake up, see their collective interests and take back control of government, they can compel their servant to implement the high-level system changes needed to achieve sustainability and real prosperity.

Empowering citizens and establishing democracy address the two main barriers to collaborative system change discussed above – the large number of people involved and business resistance to system change. Empowered citizens understand their best interests and collaboratively act to achieve them through their servant government. The people use their collective power to overcome business resistance to system change. Businesses are compelled to act responsibly. In so doing, they maximize their long-term well-being. Voluntary high-level system change probably only can be achieved in this truly democratic environment.

This section discusses the most important actions needed to achieve sustainability and real prosperity (empowering citizens and establishing democracy). It also discusses other important actions that will be strongly facilitated by empowered citizens and democracy, such as collaborative system change, improving businesses and strengthening communities.

EMPOWER CITIZENS

Democracy is the ultimate collaborative form in human society. It implicitly includes the needs and desires of every citizen. All citizens deserve a say in high-level system change (i.e. evolving economic, political and other systems into sustainable forms). As a result, democracy implemented through democratic government probably is the best, and perhaps only, way to effectively and voluntarily achieve high-level system change.

The people (all citizens) are the most powerful force in human society. Nothing is powerful enough to hold the people down, except the people. Citizens do this mainly by implicitly choosing to not think for themselves. Instead, they essentially let other people do their thinking for them. This occurs primarily by blindly believing economic, political, religious and other dogma and philosophies. Blindly believing other people's ideas without thinking them through rationally is the main reason why citizens in the US and many other countries are deceived, divided, conquered and controlled by a small group of wealthy citizens.

It is not surprising that this occurs. Authoritarian society has existed in various forms since the agricultural revolution. As discussed in the Education section, forced education indoctrinates young people to believe prevailing ideas, rather than think for themselves. Rational thought was elevated during the 1700s Enlightenment and formation of the US. But vested interests largely have tricked citizens into not thinking for themselves again. As a result, we have descended into a New Dark Age. The people largely have been intellectually enslaved and neutered through authoritarian education and society.

But this is voluntary. No force or group suppresses the people. We voluntarily suppress ourselves by abdicating our ability to think for ourselves. No one holds us down but us. Do we want to be held down? Do we want trillions of dollars of our wealth stolen every year through corporate welfare? Do we want our ability to rule ourselves to be taken away? Do we want a small group of citizens to suppress us and treat us like ignorant fools? Virtually all citizens would emphatically answer no to these questions. Okay then. Let's go. We can end it. The power to end these injustices lies in our own hands. We are disempowered only because we allow ourselves to be disempowered.

Empowering citizens requires enlightenment. People must be taught and encouraged to think for themselves, rather than blindly believe vested interests and authoritarian leaders. As discussed in the Education section, replacing forced education with freedom-based education will empower young people to think for themselves. But we do not have time to wait for empowered young people to grow up, take control of society and resolve major challenges. We also must empower current adults. This will enable us to make the system changes needed to avoid great disruption.

Education is a main vehicle for empowering young people. But most adults are out of school. They often do not have the time or money needed to go back to school. Instead, many adults get most of their ongoing 'education' from media. But as discussed extensively throughout this book, media is rife with deception and dishonesty. The main goal of for-profit mainstream media is not to enlighten and empower citizens. It is to increase the wealth of media and other business owners. To learn the truth about what is happening in society, citizens often must take the time to extensively research various issues. But many people do not have the time needed to do this. It frequently is easier and faster to simply trust biased vested interest information.

As a result, much greater efforts are needed to help citizens more easily understand what is happening in society. There are thousands of excellent, honest and accurate websites and other information sources. These often focus on specific issues or areas. But in reality, none of these economic, political, environmental or social issues are separate or isolated. They all are interconnected. One of the most important ways to help citizens understand what is happening in society is to provide information in an integrated, whole system manner.

This book illustrates one way to do this. But there is no one 'right' way. Much greater efforts are needed in this area. This book is intended to make it vastly easier for average, non-expert citizens to understand what is happening in society. Tens of thousands of articles, reports, studies, websites, books and other information sources were analyzed to produce this book. The book is intended to provide citizens with critical information that they might learn from getting bachelors, masters and doctorate degrees in many economic, environmental, social, political, psychological and comparative religious areas.

Citizens also will learn extensive information that they often would not learn in higher education because higher education largely is reductionistic. As discussed throughout this book, economic and other theories often produce harmful, unintended consequences because they were developed in a theoretical vacuum that ignores much of reality (i.e. reductionism). By stepping back and viewing society from a big picture, whole system perspective, this book strives to show citizens the linkages and interconnected nature of human society.

Adopting a whole system perspective often is more complex. But it also can facilitate learning because the functioning of society is made clearer. For example, studying the economy in isolation can be difficult and confusing because many of the major forces that form and control the economy are ignored. But by considering the whole system, citizens understand the environmental, social, psychological and other factors that enable and control the economy. This often produces 'Ah-ha!' moments because things suddenly become clearer when one steps back and sees the big picture. This book attempts to help citizens better understand society in an integrated manner by condensing nearly all major issues into one book. It also strives to protect citizens from vested interest deceptions by extensively discussing deception techniques and specific deceptions.

A major goal of this book is to help citizens clearly understand what is happening in society in a relatively short period of time. Reviewing the tens of thousands of sources analyzed to produce this book would take citizens many years of full-time, difficult work. By reading a volume that is the length of about five nonfiction books, and written in a manner that is intended to be easy for non-expert citizens to understand, people can greatly reduce study time. This book is not meant to be a panacea. It simply is one way to present a whole system view of human society. There are many other equally valid ways to present this information. As discussed in the Education section, it would greatly benefit society to quickly expand whole system approaches in education and society in general.

Enlightenment requires rational, objective thinking. Readers are encouraged to think for themselves and question everything said in this book. The book strives to provide logic and facts, and then draw rational conclusions based on them. But people should critically examine the logic and facts presented, and then draw their own conclusions.

If positions in this book threaten vested interests, they might attempt to mislead citizens by using the deception techniques discussed in the Misleading the Public section. For example, vested interests might employ the One Wrong Equals All Wrong deception technique. If they find one point that seems illogical or incorrect, they might imply that the whole book is illogical, and therefore should be ignored.

Readers might disagree with conclusions drawn about religious and other issues in this book. But it would be illogical to dismiss other issues because of this. For example, positions taken about government corruption, business degradation of society, and the negative impacts of advertising and media are strongly supported with logic, facts and examples. It would not be logical to dismiss these positions because one did not agree with religious or spiritual positions taken in this book. Enlightenment requires open-mindedness. Good, useful information is available nearly everywhere. Enlightenment is strongly facilitated by objectively considering all positions, utilizing those that are helpful, and discarding or ignoring the rest.

This book attempts to illustrate the application of rational thought and intuitive wisdom to virtually all major aspects of human society. Several issues discussed in this book should be main components of citizen empowerment efforts. These include replacing blind faith with rational thought, seeing the big picture, raising public awareness, increasing cooperation in society, changing the definition of success, helping each citizen to understand that they are important, encouraging people to identify and be their authentic selves, and showing citizens what actions they can take to quickly and effectively drive necessary system changes.

Replacing blind faith with rational thought is a major theme of this book. Instead of blindly believing economic, political, religious and other dogma, citizens should be encouraged to rationally and objectively consider these ideas and determine if they are useful or harmful. Vested interests often encourage citizens to blindly support or reject certain philosophies, such as capitalism, socialism, communism and libertarianism. As discussed, philosophies or dogma frequently interfere with rational thought. People often are encouraged to believe someone else's views rather than reach their own conclusions.

Vested interests frequently use emotionally deceptive practices to encourage people to let others think for them. As noted, among non-expert citizens, it often is best to throw philosophies and 'ism' words in the garbage can. Citizens should demand that leaders and media figures explain what they mean in a particular situation, rather than using 'ism' words.

To illustrate, as discussed in the Libertarianism section, the emphasis on small government is an ignorant, irrational way to promote the well-being of society. Focusing on the Libertarian philosophy of small government is putting the how before the what. The priority is the well-being of society, not the size of government. But suicidal businesses are required to grow forever. Encouraging citizens to rationally determine if the well-being of society is maximized by using business or government in a particular situation often would limit business growth. Right-wing libertarians and other business allies implicitly encourage citizens to blindly assume that business always is better than government. This irrational philosophy often maximizes the short-term well-being of business, but severely degrades society.

Beyond economic and political dogma, blind faith in religious dogma also can be destructive and disempowering. As discussed in the Education section, some Christian sects and other religious groups say that humans are inherently flawed and bad. Without God, we will succumb to our flawed nature and live unproductive and unsatisfying lives. These dogmatic views are irrational. They are not based on reality. In reality, probably over 99 percent of human interactions are kind or civilized. This strongly implies that the inherent nature of humanity is the same as every other creation of nature. We are inherently good and beautiful.

To support their dogmatic view that humans are innately flawed, some religious leaders might say that people act in a civilized manner because laws compel them to do so. This also is not logical. Many offensive, uncivilized actions are legal, such as rude language, driving or other behaviors. Yet even when people are free to act in an offensive, uncivilized manner, the vast majority of people choose to be kind or civilized most of the time. This once again indicates that the inherent nature of humanity is goodness, kindness and cooperation.

Some religious leaders might continue to disagree and say that religion compels people to overcome their flawed nature and act in a civilized manner. It is true that religions often encourage civilized, kind behavior. However, rather than helping to overcome the supposedly flawed nature of humanity, religions in a sense create or promote it. To illustrate, with the best of intentions, some dogmatic religions teach young people that they are inherently flawed, bad or fallen. Some interpretations of Christian dogma say that humans are unworthy (due to our flawed nature or past mistakes). But magnanimous God loves us, in spite of our unworthiness.

Dogmatic religious ideas sometimes say that people are unable to accurately discern God's will on their own because their flawed thinking or evil influences will deceive them. Instead, strict Christian and other dogma sometimes say that people only can reliably know the will of God through religion. In other words, religions sometimes imply or claim that they are the best or only reliable mediator with God. These religions attempt to insert themselves between individuals and God (or people's inner wisdom). Of course, religious leaders who promote this disempowering dogma are good people who mean well. But as is so often the case with blind faith in dogma, good intentions frequently produce harmful results.

Teaching children, teenagers and adults that they are inherently flawed and unworthy is unintentionally abusive, harmful and disempowering. If people are frequently reminded that they are flawed and unworthy, they often will live down to these low expectations. In addition, teaching people that they cannot reliably access God (or their own inner wisdom) without religion is severely disempowering. As parts of nature, we all have access to the implied infinite wisdom and intelligence of nature through the intuitive function (i.e. intuitive wisdom). But people often are taught to not trust their own inner wisdom and guidance. They are taught to not trust the actual inner word of God (or intuitive wisdom). Instead, they are encouraged to blindly believe someone else's opinions about God.

Economic and political dogma suppress rational thought by encouraging people to blindly believe irrational concepts, such as the ideas that putting economic growth before all else maximizes the well-being of society and business always is better than government. But religious dogma might be the most destructive and disempowering type of dogma because it not only suppresses rational thought. It also suppresses intuitive wisdom. In other words, it inhibits or blocks access to the infinite wisdom and intelligence of nature. Empowering citizens requires encouraging them to not blindly believe religious or any other dogma. People should be taught and strongly encouraged to use their gifts of rational thought and intuitive wisdom.

One of the most important aspects of replacing blind faith with rational thought relates to the vested interest and media manufactured civil war between conservatives and liberals. This manufactured war is one of the most important and destructive deceptions in modern society. As George Washington warned in his Farewell Address, political parties are used to fracture society into debating, acrimonious factions. Emotionally charged, blind faith deceptions are used to deceive, divide and conquer the people.

Virtually all people agree on nearly all major aspects of society. All sane people want a strong economy, good jobs, strong families and communities, low crime, a clean environment, efficient and effective government, high-quality education and good international relations. If people look at the big picture more, they also would realize that they largely agree on how to achieve these goals. And yet, in spite of these huge areas of common interest and agreement, vested interests (mainly wealthy business owners and their media and political allies) have successfully fostered extreme division and even hatred in society. Average citizens are tricked into blaming the other team or party for their increasingly difficult lives, while the actual causes, such as corporate welfare and business control of government, largely are ignored.

If we do not stop irrationally blaming each other, society will collapse. Then we will be forced to work together. The solution is to start thinking rationally. Instead of blindly believing radical media announcers who continuously blame the other side for problems, think for oneself. Consider alternative opinions and views. Try to see beyond the emotions and lies to what really is happening in society.

Ending the civil war between conservatives and liberals is the heart or essence of empowering citizens. We cannot exercise our great collective power unless we begin to work together. Ending the war between conservatives and liberals might be the most important collective action needed in society. As a result, we must vastly increase efforts in this area. Extensive NGO and other programs should be launched to promote the unification of society. Enlightened business, political, media, sports and entertainment leaders should use their fame and influence to promote this most important issue. As discussed in the Misleading the Public section, the Fairness Doctrine should be quickly re-established. This will minimize the ability of businesses and their allies to deceive and divide citizens for the purpose of taking their wealth and power. It will help to ensure that citizens get honest, balanced information from Media. (Ending the civil war between conservatives and liberals is further discussed in the We the People section of Chapter Nine.)

Encouraging citizens to see the big picture and think from a whole system perspective is another critical aspect of empowering citizens. At humanity's currently low level of intellectual development (compared to the vastly greater implied intelligence of nature), we often incorrectly focus on the individual perspective. Enlightenment includes expanding our perspective out to the whole system. Wealthy business owners, large companies, politicians who accept money from them and other business allies often argue that we must balance environmental and social concerns with economic and business needs. But this is a myopic, unintentionally destructive viewpoint.

There is no human life without an environment that is clean and stable enough to support it. Individuals generally cannot prosper if the environment and society in which they live are not at least stable, and preferably thriving. The economy should not be balanced with environmental and social concerns. This is unintentionally suicidal. We must abide by the hierarchy of needs dictated by reality and nature. The environment obviously takes priority over all else because all else is irrelevant (or dead) without it. After the environment, society as a whole takes priority. The economy is a servant of society. It must be adapted and molded to conform to the needs of society. We should not trade off the environment against the economy. To achieve sustainability and real prosperity, we should set absolute standards by which the economy must abide, such as environmental and social protection. Then we should intelligently develop an economy that efficiently operates within these constraints.

Raising public awareness is another essential component of achieving sustainability and real prosperity. This is facilitated by seeing the big picture. Many people focus mainly on their immediate environments and communities. They often do not see the vast and growing human driven environmental degradation occurring on this planet. They also frequently do not see the widespread and growing hunger, inequality, suffering and other social problems. Citizens must be made aware of these huge problems. The environment and society are being widely and rapidly degraded. It is in the collective best interests of all citizens to resolve these problems. But adequate public demand to resolve them will not manifest if the people are not fully informed.

In addition, citizens must be made aware of the main cause of environmental and social degradation and the primary action needed to resolve it. The main cause is our flawed ideas and systems. The main solution is evolving ideas and systems into sustainable forms. People must be made aware of the grossly flawed and myopic nature of current systems and the essential need to improve them. But citizens often are indoctrinated to believe that these suicidal systems are sound and admirable. To combat this suicidal, rational thought-suppressing indoctrination, we must greatly increase public awareness efforts that enlighten citizens (i.e. illuminate reality in part by exposing public deceptions and myopia).

Promoting increased cooperation in society also is a critical aspect of empowering citizens. Emphasizing the individual perspective, as modern society largely does, creates widespread fear in society. People often feel isolated or separate. They frequently worry that their needs will not be met. This often causes them to hoard resources. There is no shortage of resources on this beautiful and abundant planet. We could meet the physical needs of virtually all people, as the infinitely greater intelligence of nature does on a regular basis.

In reality, we are part of one interconnected system. Achieving sustainability and real prosperity requires that we begin to act this way more. It requires that we emulate the overwhelming cooperation seen in nature. As discussed in Chapter One, limited competition occurs in nature at the individual level. But the overwhelming force in healthy natural systems and nature overall is cooperation. Indigenous societies often were based on cooperation with nature and each other. These societies frequently survived and prospered for thousands of years. Cooperation will greatly reduce fear and increase joy in society. In many indigenous societies, people did not worry about having their needs met. High status in the community was obtained by helping others. Those with greater capability understood that it was their responsibility to help those with less ability or those in need.

This is how humanity is meant to operate on this planet. This is what reaching our highest potential and creating Heaven on Earth looks like. This is how human society will function when we begin to manifest the nearly infinitely greater intelligence and wisdom of nature. Increased cooperation will greatly reduce fear and hoarding in society. We will learn how to meet human needs without degrading the life support systems that future generations will need to survive and prosper.

This illustrates another important aspect of empowering citizens – changing the definition of success. As discussed in the Advertising, Media and Culture section, prior to widespread media and advertising, the most admired people in society usually were those who did the most to help their families and communities. As with many indigenous societies, high status usually was obtained through helping others. However, to promote increased sales and consumption, advertising and media largely have changed the definition of success. They often imply that high status is attained by beating, rather than helping, other people. The implied goal is to have the best wealth, possessions or appearance. This creates widespread senses of emptiness and inadequacy in society. It causes us to rapidly degrade life support systems while over-consuming in a fruitless effort to find life satisfaction.

Empowering citizens partly involves changing this destructive and inaccurate definition of success. As we begin to cooperate and act like the one interconnected system that we already are in reality, definitions of success will evolve into more useful, effective and accurate forms. The most admired people in society once again will be those who give, rather than get, the most. People who devote their lives to helping others will be the most admired and respected. We will change advertising and media in part by beginning to honor and promote the action that produces true prosperity at the individual and societal levels – cooperation.

Another critical aspect of empowering citizens is to help each person understand that they are unique and important to society. Authoritarian society, as we have in the US, often elevates and honors a few leaders and wealthy citizens, while implicitly demeaning or marginalizing most citizens. This is the expected outcome in a plutocracy (i.e. society and government controlled by a small group of wealthy citizens). Empowering citizens requires replacing plutocracy with democracy. Every person is absolutely equal, from the most depraved criminal in jail to the President of the United States. In a true democracy, all citizen/leaders are valued equally. Citizens are the ultimate leaders in a democracy. Freedom-based education will teach our children that they each are unique and equally important.

Adults who have been degraded by forced education and authoritarian society might have a harder time believing that they are important and relevant. Our rude, often highly critical culture frequently makes needy or troubled citizens feel as if they are a burden or drag on society. This demeaning of needy citizens facilitates cutting social welfare programs and increasing corporate welfare. This must end. In reality, every person is absolutely equal, regardless of the good or bad that they have done in life. One might ask, does that mean that Hitler is equal to Mother Teresa? Obviously, in terms of actions, they are not equal. They reflect the best and worst of humanity. However, in terms of inherent, basic value, every human being is equal. But our harmful, disempowering culture creates fear and degrades many people. This contributes to genocides and other abominations in human society.

In our deeply flawed society, there are many wounded people. They often have difficulty getting by on their own. The solution is not to insult them and push them aside. It is to help them. People who are lucky enough to have high talent and self-esteem have an obligation (in rational, sustainable society) to help the less fortunate. By truly helping those in need, we build them up and greatly increase the chances that they will stand on their own. The current social welfare system in the US often belittles aid recipients. Radical media frequently makes them feel vile and useless. This greatly increases the likelihood that they never will stand on their own.

One of the most important actions needed to empower citizens is to encourage and help them to identify their authentic selves. Our disempowering authoritarian society often fills people with conscious and unconscious beliefs of inadequacy. Business-controlled divisive media pits us against each other. This causes many people to feel alone, isolated and afraid. Advertising constantly tells us that we are not good enough. Media often teaches us that 'real' men are rude and aggressive. This promotes further fear and isolation. Forced education constantly makes children and teenagers feel inadequate during the most important psychologically formative years of their lives. Wounded insecure parents often hit or shame their children. This causes children to become wounded, insecure adults, like their parents. These and many other factors produce overwhelming senses of inadequacy, fear and isolation in society. Making citizens feel afraid and inadequate is a foundation of authoritarian society. Vested interests can easily control and take wealth from the public when citizens feel afraid, inadequate, divided and disempowered.

The psychological damage caused by our divisive, individualistic culture is massive. Many people have thoughts of inadequacy and self-judgment floating around in their minds. Not liking oneself often causes people to project this onto others. In other words, people frequently assume that other people do not like them, in the same way that they do not like themselves. They interpret other people's actions in ways that support their inadequacy. They often incorrectly assume that other people are challenging or questioning them. This severely degrades quality of life. Many people feel that they are at odds with others. But they really are at odds with themselves. Not liking themselves causes them to misinterpret others' words and actions. They push other people away. Their often unconscious belief that they are inadequate and unworthy of love and respect from others becomes a self-fulfilling prophecy.

This book has extensively discussed many ways to overcome the inadequacy imposed by our divisive, authoritarian society. One of the most effective methods is to learn to live in the presence of one's authentic self, or to manifest one's authentic self. As discussed in the Life Satisfaction and Meditation sections, people often are not mentally present in the moment. Instead, their minds think or obsess about slights from others, fears of the future, regrets about the past and other ideas that pull them away from the present. Mindfulness and other types of meditation help people to exit their mental chatter and ground themselves in the present. They might focus on their breath or feel the weight of their bodies in their particular location at the particular moment. They realize that no one is attacking or criticizing them in the moment. Mostly people attack and criticize themselves in their minds. In many cases, individuals are their own worst abusers. Grounding in the present and focusing on the physical helps people to let go of the illusory, fantasy nature of the mind, where most fears never manifest in the physical world.

Once people are physically grounded in the present, perhaps focusing on their breath or bodies, they can begin to contemplate their authentic selves. The authentic self is the essence, foundation or core of who we really are. We are not the incessant mental chatter, often about inadequacy. Inadequacy is an irrational human phenomenon. Plants and animals do not feel inadequate. Everything in nature is innately beautiful and precious. It is absurd to think that humans could be the only inadequate parts of nature. Thoughts of inadequacy are an irrational waste of time. As people let go of disempowering beliefs and focus on the present moment, they are able to clearly perceive reality and enjoy the beauty present in each moment.

Self-love (not selfishness or self-centeredness) is a critical aspect of being one's authentic self. We all are innately valuable and worthy of love. It is highly rational to grant oneself the love and acceptance that every other aspect of reality deserves. Selfishness usually indicates lack of self-love. People are seeking external sources of satisfaction. But true life satisfaction only can come from within. It results in large part from accepting and loving oneself as they are. Self-acceptance empowers people to change. Self-condemnation usually keeps people locked into harmful behaviors, patterns and beliefs. Addictions and other destructive behavior often are used to suppress the negative emotions resulting from self-condemnation.

As people contemplate who they really are at the deepest level, they frequently realize that their primary purpose for being on this planet is to help other people. In reality, we literally and truly are parts of one interconnected system. Therefore, it should not be surprising that our deepest nature and desire is to help others because we really are helping ourselves. Living a life of service produces the most meaningful and satisfying life because it aligns us with who we really and authentically are.

The ideal form of service varies from person to person. For many people, service involves being a good, loving parent, friend or neighbor. There is no one right way. The beauty of humanity is that we are all different. The key to living a rich, fulfilling life is to find out who we authentically are, and then live according to this reality. This means that people learn to stand in their authentic selves. They no longer obsess or focus on how other people are treating them.

As said in the St. Francis Prayer, people focus on giving, rather than receiving. Those who display anger or inappropriate criticism are seen as wounded and worthy of compassion. Rather than feeling hurt by inappropriate treatment, the empowered person who is standing in their authentic self feels compassion and a desire to help. Other people's actions do not disrupt their inner peace because they love and accept themselves. They understand that our divided, individualistic world often wounds and isolates people. They further understand that their role is to heal division and promote cooperation. They of course do not naïvely allow themselves to be hurt physically. But most wounding in society is psychological. The wise, empowered person understands that all psychological wounding is voluntary. Other people's words and usually actions rarely hurt another person directly. People usually cannot be hurt by someone else's words unless they agree with the words. An empowered person knows the truth about themself. They know that they are worthy. Therefore, words to the contrary have no impact on them.

As discussed throughout this book, an essential part of being one's authentic self is to seek, trust and utilize one's intuitive wisdom. The intuitive gives us access to infinite knowledge and wisdom. Intuition is the path to our authentic selves. In this case, utilizing intuition partly involves discerning one's bliss, passion or excitement. True deep passion or excitement (i.e. not distraction or compulsive behavior) helps people to identify what they are meant to do in life, and thereby be authentic. At the collective level, ending the war between conservatives and liberals probably is the most important action needed to empower citizens. At the individual level, the most important action often is to learn to be and stand in one's authentic self.

In addition to the above actions, empowering citizens also includes teaching them how they can promote system change and make a difference in society. People can get involved and make a difference at all levels of society, including the community, national and international levels. High-level system change will require extensive citizen involvement and action at the national level. Extensive high-level system change efforts should be initiated and coordinated by government, NGOs and other groups. As noted, probably the most important action needed to achieve successful high-level system change is to end the civil war between conservatives and liberals. Once the people are united and focusing on their abundant common interests, they can demand that government implement high-level system change.

Many actions will be needed to achieve this unification and effective coordination of the people. For example, forums might be convened that bring together liberal and conservative leaders, critically examine philosophies, reveal extensive common ground, and build commitment to work together. As this occurs, liberal and conservative citizens can work together in a coordinated manner. They can demand that their political servants begin to serve all citizens equally and fairly (instead of primarily serving those who give large amounts of money to politicians). Research and experimentation are needed to identify and develop additional effective ways to unite citizens and help them to utilize their great collective power. Uniting and empowering citizens is further discussed in the We the People section of Chapter Nine.

IMPLEMENT DEMOCRACY

Democracy is the ultimate form of collaboration. Democratic government is the main vehicle through which citizens collaborate. It is the expression of the people's collective will and power. Citizens use democratic government to protect and promote the long-term well-being of individuals and society. The two most important phrases in the US Constitution are "We the People" and "promote the general Welfare". We the People clarifies that the people (all citizens) established the US Constitution and government. As a result, all of the power of government derives from the people. The government has no power apart from the people. Promote the general welfare clarifies that the overarching purpose of the US Constitution and government is to ensure the general well-being of all citizens and society. In other words, every citizen equally controls government and government is required to equally serve every citizen.

As discussed in the Influencing Government section, some delegates to the Constitutional Convention of 1787 argued that only wealthy people or landowners should be allowed to vote, which was the practice in most states and England at the time. But Benjamin Franklin and other wise delegates successfully argued that citizens should have equal influence over government, regardless of wealth. These delegates prevailed. Our Constitution does not say that only wealthy people can vote. No restrictions based on wealth were placed on voting, beyond those imposed by the states. The US government was established to serve citizens equally and fairly. (Allowing all white men to vote was an enlightened approach at the time, compared to allowing only wealthy white men to vote. Obviously, enlightenment further expanded by allowing all adults to vote.)

As discussed in the Tenth Amendment and Libertarianism sections and as shown in Article I, Section 8 of the US Constitution, the Founders gave the US government nearly unlimited power to promote the general welfare. In other words, the people empowered their agent to do whatever was necessary to promote the general welfare. But as discussed throughout this book, a small group of wealthy business owners largely has taken control of the US government. They are using the great power of government to benefit themselves in ways that frequently harm the large majority of citizens. As a result, the US government is doing the opposite of what it was intended to do. Instead of promoting the general welfare, it largely is degrading it.

Vested interests have done exactly what President Washington said they would do in his Farewell Address. They used political parties to divide the public and build a spirit of vengeance and hatred in society. In addition, wealthy business owners have done exactly what President Lincoln said they would do during the Civil War. They used their influence of government to gain even greater influence. For example, by giving money to politicians, they compelled the appointment of radical pro-business Supreme Court justices. These justices are doing the opposite of what the Founders intended. They are saying that all citizens should not have equal influence over government. Instead, they implicitly are saying that wealthy citizen should have far greater influence and control.

Business influence and control of government have substantially increased since the 1980s. However, democracy never has fully existed in the US. As discussed in the Government and Elections section, before President Washington completed his first term in office, wealthy business and bank owners had established the first political party. This gravely concerned Presidents Washington, Adams, Jefferson and Madison. In his Farewell Address, President Washington strongly warned us about political parties. He called them the worst enemy of elected governments. He said that vested interests would use political parties to take control of government away from the people. He was correct. This is exactly what has happened. As discussed in the Political Parties section, the two major political parties in the US largely are controlled by wealthy business owners. The parties are used to fracture the people. Once divided, the people often are unable to gain the majorities needed to take control of government (perhaps for the first time).

Political parties violate our Constitution. Party leaders are not appointed or controlled by the people. Parties are not required to nominate the candidate who gets the most votes from citizens. Political parties sit above politicians and tell them how to vote. Every party line vote is a violation of our Constitution. The people should be controlling politicians and telling them how to vote. But this largely does not occur. Republican and Democratic politicians often do what their business-controlled parties tell them to do.

Citizens are tricked into thinking that they have two options, Republican or Democrat. But this largely is an illusion. Both parties are controlled by a small group of wealthy citizens. Regardless of which party wins, this small group wins. This is shown by the rapid income growth of the small group controlling government since the 1980s, regardless of which party was in power, while income for nearly all other citizens has grown much more slowly or declined. The political party system perfectly supports plutocracy. Citizens are tricked into thinking that they will benefit if their party wins. But nearly all citizens lose, regardless of which party wins. As President Washington warned, political parties enable vested interests to essentially steal the people's wealth and power to rule themselves.

As discussed extensively, the suicidal requirement to put shareholder returns before all else is causing large companies to rapidly degrade life support systems and society. Businesses are unable to voluntarily stop this degradation. If companies voluntarily reduce negative environmental and social impacts beyond a certain point, they will put themselves out of business. But companies will not voluntarily go out of business. Therefore, it is absolutely essential that companies be compelled to act responsibly. This is the only way that society and business can survive and prosper over the long-term. Only government can hold businesses fully responsible for negative impacts. But this cannot and will not occur if a small group of wealthy business owners largely control government.

Achieving sustainability and real prosperity requires that democracy be implemented. In other words, the people must take control of government from big business. Once the Constitution is enforced and the people control government, the people's servant will compel businesses to act in a fully responsible manner. Companies will be held responsible for all negative impacts.

As discussed in the Misleading the Public section, the Founders' greatest concern about democracy was the ease with which non-expert citizens could be misled. Right-wing libertarianism and other deceptive philosophies and dogma have been used to mislead and harm citizens. They often have been turned against government and regulations. They have been tricked into allowing large companies and their wealthy owners to control government and not be held responsible for negative impacts. All rational people understand that individuals must be held fully responsible for negative impacts on society, such as murder, assault and robbery. But citizens frequently have been deceived into thinking that corporations should not be held responsible for all negative impacts. We allow structures such as limited liability that enable businesses and their owners to avoid being held responsible. Not holding businesses responsible creates a situation where companies must degrade the environment and society to survive. When companies are not held fully responsible for negative impacts, voluntary corporate responsibility ultimately equals voluntary corporate suicide.

Once the people are empowered and united, we can take control of government and use it to implement the high-level system changes needed to achieve sustainability and real prosperity. This book has extensively discussed the many actions needed to implement democracy in the US.

One of the easiest and most important actions is to make the Supreme Court accountable to the people by implementing the changes discussed in the Judicial Branch section, including imposing term limits, improving the judicial appointment process, and restricting judicial review (i.e. the power to interpret the Constitution and void laws that violate it). Lifetime judicial appointments make the Judicial branch unaccountable to the people. No other country allows lifetime appointments to their highest court.

The Constitution does not clearly define judicial terms, as it does for the Legislative and Executive branches. Instead, the Constitution gives Congress broad authority to structure and regulate the Judicial branch. As a result, Congress can impose judicial term limits. Article III, Section 2 gives Congress clear authority to restrict and regulate the Supreme Court in appellate jurisdiction cases (i.e. nearly all Supreme Court cases). The Constitution does not give the Supreme Court the power of judicial review. The Supreme Court unconstitutionally gave itself this power in 1803. Through unconstitutional fiat, it placed itself above the Legislative and Executive branches. It made itself the highest authority in the US. The Supreme Court placed itself above the true highest authority, which is shown in the first three words of the Constitution, "We the People".

Through legislation, Congress can quickly impose term limits on the federal courts and remove or restrict the power of judicial review. The President and Senate also could unilaterally agree to implement a bipartisan, objective process for appointing Supreme Court and other federal court judges. The goal would be to appoint judges with high judicial competence, strong commitment to upholding the Constitution, and little or no tendency to let political views interfere with upholding the Constitution and promoting the general welfare. Several suggestions for modifying judicial review and the judicial appointment process are discussed in the Judicial Branch section. No constitutional amendments are required to make these changes. They could (and should) be implemented immediately.

Supreme Court justices are human beings, not gods or oracles. Every human being is vulnerable to hubris and corruption. As Thomas Jefferson strongly warned, lifetime appointments create a very dangerous situation. All government officials must be held accountable to the people. There must be consequences for failing to uphold the Constitution. But lifetime appointments with limited ability to remove justices from office removes consequences.

With Citizens Divided and other cases discussed in this book, the effectively business appointed radicals on the Supreme Court have made a mockery of our Constitution. It is absurd to allow wealthy individuals and corporations to spend unlimited amounts of money on political campaigns. As discussed in the Campaign Finance section, this obviously gives wealthy people much greater influence over government than citizens who do not give money to politicians. The effectively business appointed Supreme Court radicals implemented the minority view held during the Constitutional Convention. They essentially are saying that wealthy people largely should control government. The radicals are violating the intentions of the Founders and changing the meaning of the Constitution.

(As discussed in the Influencing the Supreme Court section, the name of the Supreme Court case *Citizens United* is extremely misleading. Allowing corporations to spend unlimited amounts of money on elections will increase the use of attack ads and other negative political ads. This will further divide and disempower citizens. Therefore, to promote clarity and honesty, this book colloquially refers to the *Citizens United* case as Citizens Divided.)

As discussed in the Judicial Branch section, The Supreme Court radicals are acting like tyrants. Lifetime appointments enable them to give wealthy citizens nearly complete control of government without consequences. They can do whatever they want. Their actions do not have to be fair, logical or constitutional. They are free to disregard the Constitution and take irrational positions. For example, the radicals say that directly and indirectly giving large amounts of money to politicians is free speech. However, common sense shows that this action is bribery. The business appointed radicals clearly are freely exercising their power to ignore the Constitution. It is time to put an end to this gross subversion of democracy and our Constitution. We should not be letting pro-business radicals effectively amend our Constitution to benefit those who effectively paid to appoint them. We the People must demand that aristocracy be replaced with democracy in the US Judicial branch of government.

Fortunately, in this case, the solution is easy. We simply demand that our political servants adopt an objective, transparent, bipartisan judicial appointment process and use legislation to impose judicial term limits and restrict the power of judicial review.

Beyond making these changes in the Judicial branch, the Influencing Government, Government and Elections, and other sections describe many other actions needed to implement democracy in the US. These include imposing term limits on Congress, requiring popular election of the President, publicly funding political campaigns, redefining corporations as artificial citizens that are held fully responsible and prohibited from influencing government (as occurred in the early US), do everything possible to ensure that every adult citizen votes including removing unnecessary voting restrictions and maximizing voting options and times, require voting district structures that fairly segment society rather than protect political parties, require TV stations to provide free airtime during elections, provide extensive debates and discussions of issues rather than 30-second soundbites, prohibit deceptive political ads, limit referendums, and greatly restrict political parties.

These are main actions needed to achieve democracy in the US. We the People have the power to implement these changes in government. They already are common practice in many other countries. The well-being of our children and ourselves demand that we impose these changes on our supposed servant – the US government. Implementing good government is further discussed in Chapter Nine.

Another important aspect of implementing democracy involves re-establishing the status and dignity of working in government. To protect shareholder returns, businesses and their allies have been castigating government and those who work in it since the 1980s. This frequently made pursuing a career in government less appealing. But libertarian and other business characterizations of government are harmful deceptions. In reality, there would be no civilized society without government. In spite of vested interest influence, the excellent government established by our Founders enabled the US to grow into one of the greatest countries in human history. Virtually every major accomplishment of the US would not have been possible without government. Without the US government, there would be no US. The business driven castigation of government is harmful and inaccurate. We must reverse business deceptions intended to protect shareholder returns and re-establish the dignity and honor of working in government.

As discussed, living a life of service often provides the most filling and meaningful life. The purpose of government is to serve society (all of society, not just wealthy business owners). People who work in government are public servants. This can be a highly rewarding profession. Implementing democracy also requires that we make sure that government employees understand that they are servants. They are given power to serve society. Strong mechanisms must be put in place to quickly remove any government employee who abuses their power over citizens. One honest minor mistake might be acceptable, if it is quickly rectified. But a second abuse of power probably should result in quick termination. The priority of government should be serving the people well, not job retention.

In general, implementing democracy is essential for achieving sustainability and real prosperity. We the People must be able to exercise our collective power to protect our common present and future interests. The US Constitution is based on the principle of democracy. But democracy largely does not exist in the US. The US is an authoritarian plutocracy. This is rapidly degrading our country. We the People must stand up, work together and exercise our right to rule ourselves.

SUSTAINABLE SYSTEMS IMPLEMENTATION

Once the people are united and democratic government is established, virtually all other high-level system changes needed to achieve sustainability and real prosperity can be implemented. This book provides a detailed description of system changes needed in nearly all major areas of society. Chapter Five describes many high-level economic, political and social system changes needed to achieve sustainability and real prosperity. Chapter Six discusses more specific system changes needed in major environmental and social areas, including chemicals, energy, food production, population control, crime, privacy and education.

Global System Change is a whole system strategy for implementing necessary system changes and achieving sustainability and real prosperity. This book extensively describes the content and process aspects of Global System Change. Total Corporate Responsibility (TCR) is an element of Global System Change that is designed for the corporate and financial sectors. The TCR model includes a specific process for organizing and implementing high-level system change efforts, called Sustainable Systems Implementation (SSI). Aspects of SSI include barriers to system change, system change principles, SSI structure and participants, focus of SSI efforts, and SSI work areas. These aspects are summarized below. TCR is further discussed in the next chapter.

Collaborative system change efforts should consider and address barriers to system change. These include low public awareness, public deception, corrupted government, failure to take a whole system view, complexity, inertia, fear of change and lack of business involvement. Failure to take a whole system view is one of the most important system change barriers. For example, many people see the benefits of current economic systems, but fail to see the environmental and social degradation caused by these systems. Adopting a whole system view facilitates developing systems that do not have unintended consequences because all relevant factors are taken into account. It also can reduce complexity and raise public awareness by making root causes and most effective solutions more apparent. In addition, adopting a whole system view can help people to overcome fear of change, inertia and complacency with current systems by illuminating the mechanics and benefits of system change.

Regarding principles, many system change principles have been discussed throughout this book. Using these principles as foundations for SSI and other collaborative system change efforts will help to overcome barriers and greatly facilitate successful change. Important system change principles include empower citizens, implement democracy, think systemically, emulate nature, increase cooperation in society, require full responsibility, understand the inevitability of system change, seek evolution not revolution, be willing to question everything, make change easy for citizens, be practical, practice non-judgment and expand existing system change efforts.

As discussed, voluntary high-level system change probably only can be achieved by united citizens working through their servant democratic government. Thinking at a higher, whole system level is essential for improving our flawed, myopic systems. Emulating nature and abiding by its laws also are essential for achieving sustainability and real prosperity. The answers to nearly all major challenges facing humanity are modeled or implied in the virtually infinitely greater sophistication of nature. Probably the most important aspect of emulating nature is increasing wisdom and cooperation in human society, in large part by making our economic, political, social and education systems more cooperative.

As discussed in Chapter Eight, holding businesses and all other organizations fully responsible for negative environmental, social and economic impacts is the most important overarching system change required in the business area. Understanding that nature and reality absolutely will change our flawed systems increases motivation to improve them voluntarily before they collapse involuntarily. Seeking to evolve systems voluntarily will minimize disruption and lower the risk of revolution that might result from system collapse.

Human systems and processes tend to evolve over time in an uncoordinated, non-systemic manner. As a result, they usually contain extensive inefficiency, redundancy and irrational components. Effectively evolving these systems into sustainable forms requires open-mindedness and a willingness to question everything. Blindly or stubbornly adhering to dogmatic economic, political and other ideas will severely impede or block system change.

Many people are struggling to survive in our grossly flawed and inequitable society. It is unrealistic to expect that citizens will make lifestyle changes that are more difficult or expensive. Some people will. Most will not. As a result, making life easier and less expensive for citizens should be an essential component of collaborative system change efforts.

Practicality is an important requirement for effective collaborative system change. Collaborative efforts should identify the needs of all stakeholders and strive to meet them to the greatest extent possible. For example, structuring system change efforts in ways that enable businesses to enhance financial performance and competitive position will greatly facilitate business participation. However, as discussed, the priority is maximizing the well-being of society, not the well-being of business. Therefore, it sometimes will not be possible to fully meet the needs of businesses and other stakeholders. Achieving long-term prosperity probably will require some short-term sacrifices.

Judgment, criticism and condemnation will greatly impede system change efforts. As discussed extensively throughout this book, virtually all business and political leaders are good people who intend to benefit, or at least not harm, society. Our grossly flawed systems compel these good people to take actions that degrade society. These degradations largely are the unintended consequences of being compelled to place short-term shareholder returns before all else. Judgment and criticism will make collaborative system change efforts nearly impossible. This does not mean that leaders and companies should not be held responsible. However, we should hold them responsible in ways that recognize the unintended, systemically mandated causes of environmental and social degradation. Acknowledging the good intentions of leaders (and all other people) while minimizing judgment will greatly facilitate collaborative system change efforts.

Another critical aspect of implementing sustainable systems is recognizing that we already know virtually everything needed to achieve sustainability and real prosperity. Throughout the world, there are many experts, organizations and collaborative efforts that are making large positive contributions to society. In addition, much, if not nearly all, of the technology needed to achieve sustainability and real prosperity has been developed. We largely know what to do and how to do it. We have nearly all the tools, technologies and processes needed to achieve our goals. Therefore, a major focus of collaborative system change efforts should be to scale up the many good ideas and efforts already in existence.

To illustrate, the New Economics Foundation (NEF) and its partners have been developing and promoting sustainable economic ideas and models for decades. Integrating the practical experience of NEF and many other organizations into collaborative system change efforts could greatly accelerate the implementation of sustainable systems.

Regarding structure and participants, citizens working collectively through their servant government ultimately can and should be the main force driving high-level system change. However, initial collaborative system change efforts could be established by environmental and social NGOs and foundations, proactive businesses, business consultants, and other civil society organizations. Government also could initiate and/or support these efforts. All relevant stakeholder groups should be represented. Businesses can and should play a major role in these efforts. Various system changes will modify business operations. Business involvement can minimize disruption and ease the transition to sustainable business.

However, the systemically mandated requirement to oppose actions that threaten shareholder returns should be identified and managed up front. Businesses and their allies must not be allowed to block or delay necessary system changes to protect shareholder returns. This problem can be minimized by initially inviting the most proactive and enlightened companies to participate in collaborative system change efforts. Companies such as these understand the need for system change. They often will proactively help to develop system change strategies that lower negative impacts, while still providing reasonable investor returns.

Regarding focus, the SSI collaborative system change approach can be applied at all levels, including local, regional, national and global. However, the most important collaborative high-level system change efforts generally would be focused on the national level. As discussed, high-level system change involves evolving overarching economic, political and social systems into sustainable forms. These systems largely are established and controlled at the national level. Nationally-focused

SSI efforts generally would be the most effective way to drive rapid high-level system change. However, countries operate in and often are constrained by global economic and political systems. Therefore, once national SSI efforts are established, these groups could and should begin to collaborate on achieving global system change.

Regarding SSI work areas, these could be generally segmented into three areas – framing, quick wins and longer-term system change efforts. Framing involves establishing a whole system view and understanding the context of system change. Establishing a compelling vision of a sustainable country or world is an essential component of SSI and other high-level system change efforts. The vision promoted in this book is described as achieving sustainability and real prosperity, manifesting the wisdom of nature in human society, reaching our fullest potential and creating Heaven on Earth. A compelling vision provides the clarity and motivation needed to guide and sustain collaborative system change efforts.

Additional critical framing actions include understanding current realities (i.e. declining environmental and social conditions), identifying barriers to system change, and developing short-term and long-term strategies for overcoming barriers and achieving sustainability goals.

Focusing initially on achieving quick wins is essential for building enthusiasm and commitment to high-level system change. Potential quick wins include streamlined regulations that enable businesses to improve environmental and social performance. Longer-term SSI efforts include the many mid-level and high-level system changes described in this book.

Beyond the SSI approach for managing collaborative high-level system change, many experts and organizations have developed processes for managing collaborative efforts, including collaborative system change. Leaders in this field include Peter Senge – Founder of the Society for Organizational Learning, David Cooperrider – developer of the Appreciative Inquiry process, Otto Scharmer – developer of the U Process, and Jib Ellison – Founder of Blu Skye Consulting. These and many other experts and organizations have proven track records of facilitating successful collaborative efforts.

Extensive system change content and process expertise strongly indicates that humanity has all the resources, talent and know-how needed to improve systems and achieve sustainability and real prosperity. As the people acting through their servant government employ these resources, systems can be quickly evolved into sustainable forms.

One of the most important aspects of sustainable systems implementation is shifting the focus from maximizing the short-term well-being of business and the economy to maximizing the long-term well-being of society. To survive, citizens often are required to work long, difficult, boring jobs for reduced pay and benefits. This is the inevitable result of focusing primarily on maximizing shareholder returns. As we begin to abide by our Constitution and focus on promoting the general welfare, quality of life for the vast majority of citizens can be substantially improved.

As discussed in Chapter Nine, sustainable systems will focus on meeting the needs of all citizens in the most efficient and effective manner. Instead of continuously ratcheting up prices so that investors can make more money, we will focus on continuously reducing prices while increasing quality and service. We will have more people working easier, shorter, more fulfilling jobs. Citizens will have more time to spend with their family and friends and do what they love in life. Rather than using our intelligence to enrich shareholders, we will figure out how to truly enrich (i.e. in mostly nonphysical ways) the lives of virtually all citizens. We are smart enough to do this. It is time to make it happen.

Achieving these goals requires implementing the many system changes discussed in this book. Critical systemic changes include improve measurement (i.e. by mainly measuring the goal or endpoint – social well-being, not the means to the end – economic growth), implement accurate pricing and markets (by including all real costs in prices), establish democracy (through the government changes noted above), hold companies fully responsible (by eliminating limited liability and other mechanisms that compel companies and investors to act irresponsibly), end public deception (by requiring media to provide honest, accurate and balanced information), pursue balance instead of never-ending growth, accurately value and strongly protect future generations and resources (by replacing myopic time value of money concepts with reality-based approaches), and limiting emotionally deceptive advertising that makes people feel inadequate.

As discussed in the Well-Being of Society section, replacing economic growth with a more accurate measure of social well-being is extremely important. What gets measured gets managed. Economic growth mainly measures the financial well-being of the small group of wealthy citizens who own most business assets. Using this implied measure of social well-being compels us to manage business, government and society in ways that maximize the wealth of this small group. Economic growth is a secondary indicator. It does not directly measure the well-being of society. Social well-being only can be measured accurately by using a suite of direct or primary indicators. These indicators relate to environmental conditions, labor, crime, education and other important aspects of social well-being.

Another problem with economic growth is that it is a macro-level indicator. A single number supposedly measures the well-being of over 300 million citizens in the US. This is grossly simplistic. Massive amounts of information are lost in this aggregation. As discussed in Chapter Nine, the income of a small group of already wealthy citizens is rising rapidly while income for the vast majority of citizens is rising slowly, flat or declining. Rapid income growth of wealthy people often increases overall economic growth. This implies that society is improving. But in reality, it is not. While economic growth rises, quality of life for many, if not the large majority, of citizens is declining. Refocusing society on the well-being of society instead of business means in large part that we begin to accurately measure the well-being of society. These and many other system changes discussed in this book can be implemented by a united people working through their servant government and collaborative processes.

The concept of reengineering can be useful in collaborative system change efforts. Reengineering is an organizational improvement process that is based on systems thinking. As noted, organizations, governments and even countries often evolve in an uncoordinated manner. As result, they frequently contain extensive inefficient, redundant and counterproductive operations. Reengineering involves stepping back and looking at the big picture. Overarching goals are identified. Then one imagines how the organization would be designed to achieve these goals if they could start with a clean slate. This helps to clarify the optimal organizational structure and strategy. Once these are clear, a rational plan is designed to evolve the current inefficient structure into the optimal form. This enables organizations to achieve their goals more efficiently and effectively.

This type of approach is needed at the societal level. It can be used at the local, regional, national and even international levels. As noted, high-level system change requires efforts like this at the national level because many economic, political and social systems are established and controlled at this level. These types of higher-level changes probably only can be achieved by the people working through truly democratic government. The reengineering process at the national level starts by putting the what before the how. In other words, higher-level goals are identified upfront. In the case of the US, this is easy. Our Constitution specifies our highest-level goal – promote the general welfare. This implies protecting and meeting the needs of current and future citizens to the greatest extent possible.

The initial phase of reengineering (stepping back and seeing the big picture – thinking systemically) illuminates irrational ideas and actions that cause extensive environmental, social and economic problems. A whole system perspective shows that we run our country based on the intensely myopic idea that growing the economy always will promote the general welfare. This is irrational dogma. It often is accepted blindly. But rational thought quickly illuminates the grossly destructive and inaccurate nature of this dogmatic economic idea. This irrational, myopic idea causes us to send millions of manufacturing and other jobs overseas. From 2000 to 2010, real manufacturing output in the US declined by 11 percent. One-third of US manufacturing jobs (over 5 million jobs) were lost during this period.[1]

The requirement to put shareholder returns and economic growth before all else is the main cause of US manufacturing decline. Investment returns implicitly are considered to be more important than jobs for US citizens. As a result, jobs frequently are automated or sent away. As discussed in Chapter Five, the form of capitalism operating in the US is unfair and grossly unsustainable. It is not remotely close to what capitalism was meant to be. Our so-called capitalistic system is socialist on the downside because taxpayers frequently are compelled to act like the owners of business. They often are required to cover the losses of wealthy, speculative investors while getting none of the financial upside. The system puts financial returns to wealthy people ahead of employees, children, the environment and the survival of humanity.

People in the future (assuming there are any) will look back on the current form of capitalism the way we look back on witch burning and slavery. The economic system operating in the US is hugely myopic and destructive. But people often do not see this because we are too close to it. Our lives frequently depend on this system that ultimately and ironically might take our lives if we do not change it. It is not appropriate to call the US economic system capitalistic. In spite of the name, capitalism is meant to benefit all citizens, not just capital (i.e. business owners).

As we reengineer US society, we will employ rational thought. We will stop blindly believing irrational economic dogma, such as the idea that putting the economy before all else will maximize the well-being of society. As we employ rational thought and think systemically, we will take advantage of the many good, sustainable ideas, models and systems all around us in nature and human society. For nearly all of human history, humans implicitly used sustainable economics that were similar to the economics of nature. As discussed in the Environmental Sustainability Principles section, economic principles or laws implied in nature include equitable resource distribution, equally valuing current and future generations, producing zero waste, seeking balance instead of growth, living off of current solar energy (i.e. instead of fossil fuels, which represent past solar energy), and enabling each individual to reach their fullest potential. As discussed in the Sustainable Economy section, these are the principles that should be guiding our economy, not the suicidal, reality-ignoring requirement to seek infinite economic growth in a finite system.

Once the people understand the extremely destructive nature of current economic and political systems, they will demand that their servant government change them. We will refocus our economy and society on promoting the well-being of all citizens, not just wealthy citizens. Providing high quality jobs often will be given higher priority than achieving ever-increasing shareholder returns. This means that we will not require US citizens to compete with people in developing countries who are willing to work for one dollar per day. It means that we probably will restrict imports in some cases so that we can rebuild our manufacturing base. At times, prices might go up and product selections might go down. But having a job and being able to feed one's children are more important than price and product selection. As we implement democracy, we will require that businesses be primarily focused on maximizing the well-being of society. Adequate shareholder returns will result from doing this well.

The US is a truly blessed and gifted nation. We have done great things in human society. We have tremendous physical and intellectual resources. We do not have to tolerate the destructive, reality-ignoring systems functioning in our society. We definitely have the ability to evolve them into sustainable forms. It is time to make this happen.

IMPROVE BUSINESS

Improving business is a critical aspect of achieving sustainability and real prosperity. In a democracy, citizens would not allow the existence of business and economic structures that were not primarily focused on maximizing the well-being of society, unless they were misled or did not see the big picture. Current business structures not only are not focused on maximizing the well-being of society. They are in fundamental, systemically mandated conflict with it. Forcing companies to focus primarily on shareholder returns and not holding them responsible for negative impacts compels them to degrade the environment and society. If companies do not do this, they will die. Of course no one intended that companies would degrade society. The current suicidal structure of businesses results from myopia.

Focusing primarily on shareholder returns and not holding companies fully responsible for negative impacts degrades society in many ways. For example, companies often are required to use chemicals and other materials and processes that degrade environmental life support systems. They degrade families and communities by forcing down wages and benefits and sending jobs overseas. Current business structures place shareholders in inevitable conflict with customers. Customer value frequently is degraded so that shareholder value can be continuously increased.

For example, in mature or slow growth markets, to provide ever-increasing profit growth, companies regularly reduce product sizes, raise prices and/or reformulate products in ways that cause them to be consumed more quickly. To illustrate, orange juice in the US was sold in half-gallon (64 ounce) containers for decades. Most major brand orange juice containers were reduced to 59 ounces. In a few years, package sizes probably will be further reduced so that shareholders can continue to make more money. This occurs with many, if not the large majority, of products. To reduce customer losses, companies often try to minimize price increases and quality or quantity reductions. Nevertheless, customers regularly experience smaller quantities, rising prices and/or declining quality.

Many companies emulate competitors' price, volume and/or quality changes. As a result, customers often have few alternatives. They frequently experience continuously declining value. This is the inevitable result of flawed systems which essentially require that a small group of wealthy citizens extract ever-increasing amounts of wealth from society. Companies obviously try to increase customer value while increasing shareholder value. These win-win situations sometimes occur. But many times, the only way to increase shareholder value is by reducing customer value.

As discussed in the Improve Business Education section, improving business requires shifting the focus of companies from maximizing shareholder returns to maximizing the well-being of customers and society in general. Several simultaneous actions are needed to achieve this transition from suicidal to sustainable business operations. For example, under current systems, no company could consistently put the well-being of customers and society ahead of shareholder returns and survive. Overarching economic and political systems establish unintentionally destructive incentives and operating principles for business. These must be changed.

The previous section discussed the need for collaborative system change and the importance of involving business in it. Getting businesses involved in system change requires raising business awareness about the benefits of it. Chapter Three discussed the business case for system change. In summary, in a closed system, such as the Earth, negative environmental and social impacts return to hurt companies, often in the form of lawsuits, market rejection, reputation damage, difficulty attracting and retaining talented employees, poor community relations, difficulty citing new facilities, increased regulatory scrutiny and reduced earnings. As the human economy expands in the finite Earth system, feedback loops are accelerating. This means that companies feel the negative effects of their negative environmental and social impacts more quickly. This in turn makes reducing negative impacts more financially relevant and important. Growing financial relevance is the main reason why corporate responsibility and sustainability have become mainstream business practices.

However, as discussed in Chapters Three and Eight, companies only can voluntarily mitigate about 20 percent of their negative environmental and social impacts. As businesses continue to produce systemically required negative impacts, these impacts will return to hurt them. For their own well-being, companies must figure out how to go beyond 20 percent impact mitigation. The only way to do this is through collaboration and system change. As discussed, companies can move further along the impact mitigation spectrum through mid-level or sector-level system change. But most negative impacts only can be mitigated when overarching economic and political systems are changed (i.e. high-level system change).

Chapters Three and Eight discuss a corporate responsibility approach called Total Corporate Responsibility (TCR®). TCR combines leading-edge corporate responsibility with collaborative mid-level and high-level system change. The approach provides a practical and profitable way for companies to get involved in system change. TCR is based on eliminating conflicts between business and society. As the name implies, the most important aspect of this is enabling companies to act in a fully responsible manner by eliminating all negative environmental, social and economic impacts. Current economic and political systems do not allow this. TCR helps companies to work with others to evolve systems in ways that make TCR (full impact mitigation) the profit-maximizing strategy. (The next chapter provides a more detailed description of the TCR approach.)

Corporate responsibility has evolved over the past 20 years. Originally, it was seen as a risk mitigation activity that increased costs. Now it largely is seen as a way to add business value, for example, through the development of environmentally and socially responsible products and services as well as through proactive management of environmental and social risks and opportunities. Corporate responsibility is on the verge of a new evolution or transition. The most advanced corporate responsibility approaches recognize that impact mitigation beyond a certain point is not possible without mid-level and high-level system change. Therefore, the new corporate responsibility leaders proactively engage in system change efforts. As discussed, leaders such as Blu Skye help companies to engage in mid-level system change. But there are few opportunities, forums and vehicles for engaging in high-level system change. These activities must be quickly and substantially increased. A main purpose of this book is to facilitate rapid expansion of collaborative high-level system change efforts. It does this in part by describing the business case for system change and providing extensive information about how systems can be improved in virtually all major areas of society.

Facilitating business involvement in collaborative system change requires helping businesses to publicly discuss it. Currently, capital markets probably would punish business leaders who suggest that the primary focus of their company should be on something other than shareholder returns. As a result, awareness raising is needed in the capital markets. (This also is discussed in more detail in the next chapter.) Perhaps no CEO could publicly suggest that their company would shift its primary focus from shareholders to the well-being of society. But business leaders as a group, along with other thought leaders, could publicly explain how current systems compel companies to degrade society, which ultimately degrades business. This shows the essential need for system change. As a group, leaders could promote the critical need for evolving systems in ways that benefit shareholders and society. Systems that put shareholders in conflict with society will end by voluntary or involuntary means. It will be much better for shareholders and society to end (i.e. evolve) systems through voluntary means.

As the people direct their servant government to evolve systems, often through collaborative efforts, new, sustainable business structures will emerge. Many of these structures already are functioning successfully around the world. For example, as discussed in the Misleading the Public section, in large German companies, labor representatives often hold half of Board of Directors seats. This ensures that companies are adequately focused on sharing success with the people who largely made it possible – employees. This is a more balanced and effective structure than the shareholder-dominated structure of US companies. As noted, Germany has been a global manufacturing leader for many years, while US manufacturing has declined substantially.

As the US evolves from plutocracy to democracy, business will assume its rightful place as the servant of society. Businesses have no inherent right to exist. The priority of society should be the well-being of society. Businesses and business sectors should expand or contract based solely on what maximizes the well-being of society. Citizen/taxpayers never should cover the downside óf business, for example, through limited liability and other structures. The focus of companies should shift to maximizing the well-being of all stakeholders, including customers, employees and future generations. Shareholders would be rewarded when companies efficiently and effectively meet stakeholder needs without degrading society in any way.

As the focus of society shifts from maximizing the well-being of business to maximizing the well-being of society, technology will be used to maximize social well-being. To illustrate, as discussed in the Privacy section, the largely for-profit Internet system in the US is focused mainly on benefiting business. The goal of a for-profit Internet system is to provide continuously increasing profits to Internet companies. As a result, the Internet is being segmented. People and companies that pay more often get better service. Vested interests are attempting to eliminate net neutrality so that companies that give more money to Internet companies (and politicians) can get better Internet service. As discussed in the Public Internet and Online Services section below, this for-profit Internet structure provides increasingly expensive, low-quality service (compared to many other countries).

An efficient, fast, open, fair Internet is essential for the well-being of business and society, as public highway and regional road systems are. Imagine the impact on society if public roads were privatized and for-profit road companies were allowed to limit access to roads for low-income citizens and companies that did not pay enough money. The same severe degradation of society will occur to a growing degree with a for-profit Internet system. As discussed in the Privacy section, a public

Internet system would hugely benefit business and society, as public road systems currently do. Some for-profit Internet companies might shrink or go out of business. But this is how democracy and capitalism are intended to function.

The priority is not that businesses survive. The priority is that society survives and prospers. Wealthy investors seeking high returns should bear the risk of their investments. They have no right to have their downside covered by average citizens through limited liability, bailouts or any other means. As discussed in the Corporate Welfare section and Public Wealth section below, at least several trillion dollars of public wealth are transferred to wealthy citizens every year through many forms of corporate welfare. As democracy is implemented in the US, corporate welfare will be ended. Then the wealth of this great nation can be used to establish a social safety net that is comparable to other developed countries. When the wealth of society is used to benefit all citizens, not just wealthy campaign donors, people will not become destitute due to the natural expansion and contraction of businesses and the economy.

This shift in business focus from the well-being of business to the well-being of society is essential for achieving sustainability and real prosperity. The transition is not possible without high-level system change. Therefore, it is critical that high-level system change quickly become a mainstream business activity. It took over 20 years for corporate responsibility to evolve from marginal to mainstream. The mainstream business focus on high-level system change should occur far more quickly.

STRENGTHEN COMMUNITIES

Helping communities to become more self-sufficient and truly prosperous is an important component of achieving sustainability and real prosperity. Emulating nature is perhaps the most important sustainability principle and strategy. Nature mainly is organized into local, largely self-sufficient communities. Humanity functioned this way for nearly all of human history. This largely decentralized approach produces the most rigorous and stable economic system. Problems in one area usually have little impact on other areas.

But the emphasis on providing ever-increasing shareholder returns has rapidly expanded the big company economy. This in turn has severely degraded local economies. The requirement to grow forever often causes large companies to open stores, restaurants and other operations that underprice and shut down local businesses. Replacing local businesses with large company chains and operations degrades communities in many ways. For example, wealth is removed from the community as profits are sent to distant owners. Large businesses frequently pay low wages and provide part-time jobs so that they can avoid paying healthcare, pensions and other benefits. Also, large companies based outside of communities frequently have little or no commitment to the local environment, citizens and community. If profits are inadequate, they often shut down local operations, which degrades families and communities.

Large companies also often degrade communities by increasing prices and lowering product and service quality. For example, national drugstore chains frequently open stores and sell products at lower prices than local drugstores. This often causes local drugstores to go out of business. Once this occurs, large chain drugstores frequently raise prices substantially. Local citizens often wind up paying higher prices and receiving lower quality products and services when big companies come to town. Large companies also degrade communities by playing states and communities against each other. They often demand reduced taxes, development funding and other inducements to locate in certain areas. This frequently shifts the tax burden to local citizens and businesses.

Many actions are required to strengthen communities. These could be broadly segmented into higher-level and local. Higher-level actions include many of the economic, political and social system changes discussed in this book. For example, as discussed in the Trade, Scale and Competitive Advantage section, once all real environmental, social and economic costs are included in prices, local businesses often would provide the lowest cost products and services. Also, large companies should not be allowed to evade taxes by giving money to politicians and engaging in other inappropriate government influence. Furthermore, as corporate welfare is ended and public wealth is used to benefit all citizens, a strong social safety net will be established. As a result, citizens will not become destitute when large companies leave. A strong social safety net also will reduce the ability of large companies to demand tax breaks and other concessions from states and communities (because citizens will not be dependent on large companies for healthcare, retirement security and other basic needs that are provided by government in most other developed countries).

At the local level, several actions could be taken to strengthen communities. One of the most important is to employ a whole system approach. Citizens could discuss their short-term, mid-term and long-term goals for the community. Many communities probably would decide that the most important goal is to maximize the well-being and quality of life of local citizens in the short-term and long-term. Numerous communities around the world are well down this path. They have chosen to become more sustainable and improve quality of life. Many consultants, NGOs and other organizations help communities to become sustainable and truly prosperous, such is the Business Alliance for Local Living Economies. Therefore, one of the most efficient and effective strategies is to not reinvent the wheel. Communities can learn from others' experience. They can take advantage of the abundant resources available for strengthening communities.

There are a wide variety of strategies to employ, based on communities' goals and cultures. For example, some communities seek to lower the cost of living and improve quality of life. This can be done through bulk purchasing, sharing cars and other items, and building cluster housing.

One of the most important strategies for strengthening communities is to develop collectively owned or cooperative businesses and banks. These organizations direct profits back to employees, customers and the community in general. They often provide better, more fulfilling jobs. They also have stronger commitments to the local environment and citizens. There are many successful cooperative businesses functioning around the world that communities could use as models. There also are extensive resources and many organizations available to help communities establish cooperative businesses, such as the National Cooperative Business Association.

Another important aspect of strengthening communities involves discussing and possibly evolving cultures. As discussed in the Advertising, Media and Culture section, our advertising and media driven culture is highly competitive and disempowering. Communities might discuss becoming more cooperative. Increased cooperation reduces fear and hoarding of resources. It builds trust and helps people to redefine the meaning of success. Our disempowering culture often compels people to buy trophy homes, cars and other possessions. But these frequently do not provide satisfying lives. Redefining success at the community level often involves considering what actually produces meaningful and satisfying lives, and then refocusing communities on strengthening these factors. As this occurs, the means of attaining respect and status in communities might change from having the best possessions to helping others.

In general, strengthening communities involves emulating the resilience and brilliance seen in nature at the local level. In nature, local communities implicitly are managed in ways that enable each community member, present and future, to reach their fullest potential. We are part of nature. Therefore, we have the ability to implement the same level of brilliance and beauty seen in nature.

In summary, achieving sustainability and real prosperity requires implementing the many individual, community, societal, national and international level system changes and other actions discussed in this book. In the US, two of the most important actions are empowering citizens and establishing democracy. Under the category of empowering citizens, the most important action almost certainly is ending the civil war between conservatives and liberals. As our wise President Washington warned, vested interests have taken advantage of the ease with which non-expert citizens can be misled. Conservatives and liberal citizens agree on nearly all major issues. Yet large companies, wealthy business owners and their political and media allies have used deception and emotional manipulation to falsely divide US citizens and pit us against each other. As discussed in the Public Wealth section below, while we irrationally fight each other, vested interests unfairly take trillions of dollars of public wealth every year through many forms of corporate welfare. By dividing us, they have ended democracy in the US.

It is essential that we wake up. We must put rational thought ahead of blindly believing irrational dogma. Thinking about what radical media says, instead of blindly believing it, will enable us to see through the lies and deceptions intended to protect shareholder returns. Once we realize that we all have nearly the same goals at the societal level, we will work together to achieve these goals. Probably the most important work is to do what our Founders intended – rule ourselves. We must end authoritarianism and plutocracy in the US and establish democracy.

Once we are united and ruling ourselves through democratic government, we will make the changes needed to protect our children and ourselves. We will use collaboration to evolve our systems into sustainable forms. We will emulate nature by establishing a far more decentralized, rigorous, stable and productive economy, in large part by strengthening communities. We also will evolve businesses into sustainable forms. Currently, there often is great stress, sadness and boredom in business. The current suicidal, infinite growth business model regularly extracts wealth from employees, customers, life support systems and society in general so that shareholder returns can grow continuously. Managers are forced to make the lives of their employees more difficult. Human values of compassion and fairness are forced out of our myopic business structures. These suicidal structures ultimately do not work for anyone, including those who unfairly profit from them.

Suicidal business structures that seek never-ending growth in a finite system kill us physically and spiritually. They kill us physically by rapidly destroying all life support systems on this planet. They kill us spiritually and psychologically by creating extensive and unnecessary fear and suffering in human society. It is time to end this madness. Whole system thinking shows our suicidal systems to be no more intelligent than witch burning. In reality, they are far worse because witch burning only killed a relatively few unfortunate people (but terrorized many others). However, our current flawed business, economic, political and other structures literally are killing much of the life on this planet, including human life.

None of this is necessary. We the People must use our gifts of rational thought and intuitive wisdom more effectively. Virtually every problem in human society was caused by humans. This means that we have the power to solve these problems. But this requires that we use our power. No beings will come from outer space to rescue us from our unintentionally destructive ways of living on this planet. No Savior will come from Heaven to save us. If God exists, we are the hands of God. We must save ourselves. We will rescue ourselves or we will suffer the consequences of our failure to abide by the laws of nature. There is no escape from reality. In reality, we are interconnected components of one interdependent system. This is obvious from a whole system perspective. It is time for us to do what we clearly are capable of doing. It is time to achieve what we all want – sustainability and real prosperity.

CHAPTER EIGHT – TCR: CORPORATE AND FINANCIAL SECTOR SYSTEM CHANGE STRATEGIES

As discussed in chapter One, system change could be broadly segmented into four levels – low-level, mid-level, high-level and global. Low-level system change mainly refers to internal organizational changes. Mid-level system change involves systemic changes at the sector, stakeholder or environmental/social issue levels. High-level system change refers to evolving overarching economic, political and social systems into sustainable forms.

Global system change involves evolution of the largest whole system that humans influence – the whole Earth system and its sub-element human society. This whole system book provides a detailed description of the major intellectual and physical aspects of global system change. Chapter Three and this chapter discuss mid-level and high-level system change because these are most relevant to the corporate and financial sectors. This book largely does not discuss low-level system change (i.e. organizational change) because there already is an abundance of excellent material written on this subject. However, the whole system thinking discussed and modeled throughout this book could greatly facilitate organizational change.

As discussed Chapter Seven, achieving sustainability and real prosperity is not possible without high-level system change. The corporate and financial sectors cannot drive it on their own. No segment of society is powerful enough to do this. In addition, current systems severely constrain the ability of businesses and financial institutions to promote high-level system change. System change probably only can be achieved by united citizens working through truly democratic government.

However, this is an ultimate or overarching solution. Under the umbrella of democratic society and government, many simultaneous actions are needed to successfully achieve high-level system change. Large companies and their wealthy owners are not powerful enough to evolve economic and political systems into sustainable forms. Nevertheless, they are very powerful, in part because they largely control government in the US and some other countries. As a result, there is much that businesses and investors can do to promote system change on their own and in collaboration with others.

As discussed in Chapters Three and Seven, the Total Corporate Responsibility model (TCR®) was developed to help the corporate and financial sectors promote system change in a practical and profitable manner. This chapter summarizes the evolution of socially responsible investing and corporate responsibility, and shows how TCR is the next logical step in this evolution. It then describes how TCR can be used to develop investment products, funds and strategies that engage the capital markets in promoting system change. It also discusses how companies can use TCR as a roadmap for leading-edge corporate responsibility and mid-level and high-level system change.

SOCIALLY RESPONSIBLE INVESTING AND CORPORATE RESPONSIBILITY

Socially responsible investing (SRI) involves taking environmental, social and governance issues (ESG) into account when making investment decisions (social includes labor, product safety, stakeholder relations, supply chain and international operations). A main goal of SRI is to produce environmentally and socially beneficial results, for example, through shareholder activism and investments in companies and sectors that produce positive environmental and social impacts, such as energy efficiency and renewable energy. Corporate responsibility (CR) strategies involve companies acting in an environmentally and socially responsible manner, in large part by minimizing negative environmental and social impacts.

The earliest SRI occurred hundreds of years ago as religious groups avoided investments in areas that were not aligned with their beliefs. Modern SRI began in the 1970s. A primary concern was avoiding investments in companies that supported apartheid in South Africa.[2] From the 1970s to the 1990s, SRI mainly utilized ethical investing or negative screening. This involves avoiding investments in companies or sectors to which one is ethically opposed, such as gambling, armaments, nuclear power or genetic engineering. Negative screening can reduce diversity in investment portfolios, increase risk and lower return potential.

In the 1990s, a New York-based company, Innovest Strategic Value Advisors, pioneered a new approach to SRI. (The author of this book was the Managing Director of Research at Innovest from 1998 to 2006.)

Mainstream investors and financial institutions traditionally believed that SRI violated their fiduciary responsibility to maximize investor returns by taking nonfinancial issues into account. Innovest argued the opposite. It said that environmental and social issues were increasingly financially relevant. Therefore, failing to take them into account when making investment decisions violates the fiduciary responsibility to maximize returns, in the same way that ignoring any other financially relevant factor would.

Innovest utilized a more rigorous research approach. Up to that point, companies that provided ESG research gathered their data mainly by sending questionnaires to companies. This was problematic because companies often did not respond. When they did, the information was biased. There frequently was no way to verify accuracy. Innovest gathered data from many sources, including government, NGO and other databases. It reviewed company, academic and other literature. And it conducted in-depth interviews with senior corporate executives. This enabled Innovest to gather far more accurate and detailed information.

Probably the most important aspect of Innovest research was the focus on financial performance. Traditional ESG research companies simply provided ESG performance information. But Innovest focused its analysis on how CR/ESG performance affected financial performance. The company analyzed and rated the world's 2,000 largest companies in over 50 industry sectors. Innovest's main work involved producing best-in-class ESG ratings as well as company, sector and sustainability issue reports.

Innovest developed rigorous rating models that focused on three general performance categories – risk, opportunity and management. The models had core elements that were common to all sectors. Customized metrics were added for each sector. Metrics in the risk area assessed exposure relative to peers on factors such as pollution, product safety, and relations with employees, communities, and domestic and foreign governments. Opportunity metrics examined the degree to which companies were developing and selling environmentally and socially responsible products and services. The greatest model weightings usually were applied to management metrics. These assessed the degree to which management was effectively managing financially relevant environmental and social factors on the downside and upside.

In all high environmental impact sectors (i.e. petroleum, electric utilities, mining, chemicals, pulp and paper) and nearly all other sectors, Innovest found that companies with above average CR ratings, taken as a group, outperformed companies with below average ratings in the stock market, usually by 300 to 3000 basis points (3 to 30 percentage points) over the short to longer-term. Innovest provided extensive evidence which showed that superior CR performance strongly promotes superior financial performance. The company also thoroughly explained the link between CR and financial performance, for example, by clarifying why taking CR into account when making investment decisions was increasingly important.

In the 1990s and early 2000s, many factors were causing environmental and social issues to become more financially relevant for companies and investors. For example, increasing regulations frequently were holding companies more responsible for negative environmental and social impacts. Growing shareholder activism and governance concerns were affecting corporate reputations and market perceptions. Increased information transparency was exposing negative corporate impacts. Rising demand for environmentally and socially responsible products, services and corporate behavior made CR performance more financially relevant. Changing pension fund laws in Europe and evolving interpretations of fiduciary responsibility compelled increased investor focus on CR performance. Growing awareness among companies that superior CR performance could be used to build competitive advantage and improve financial performance further increased investor awareness and focus on CR performance.

Probably the most important factor driving increased financial relevance for companies and investors was the rapid expansion of the human economy in the finite Earth system. Rising population, resource consumption, pollution and waste generation were rapidly degrading environmental life support systems and causing many social problems. Seeking infinite growth in a finite system was accelerating feedback loops. Companies were receiving pushback for their negative environmental and social impacts more quickly and strongly. This often took the form of market rejection, lawsuits, reputation damage and difficulty expanding domestic and foreign operations.

Innovest's financially focused CR/ESG research helped investors to minimize risk and improve returns in many ways. For example, traditional financial reporting often does not disclose substantial financial risks related to the environment, labor, community relations, product safety and other factors. Innovest research helped investors to quantify these risks relative to peers, and adjust investments accordingly. Also, the collapse of the energy company Enron showed that internal unethical behavior could substantially harm investors. But it often is difficult to determine the presence of internal unethical management behavior because it obviously is not disclosed. Innovest research assessed ethical performance relative to peers on many external environmental and social issues. Assessment of external ethical performance can be used to strongly imply the possible presence of internal ethical problems.

Innovest research and reports helped investors to understand that many companies were gaining substantial competitive and financial benefits by implementing proactive CR and sustainability strategies. Benefits included enhanced corporate reputation and brand value, increased market share through development of more appealing products and services, reduced materials, energy and waste management costs, streamlined project development through improved community relations, facilitated access to natural resources and new markets, increased productivity through improved employee morale, and greater ability to attract and retain a high quality workforce.

Probably the most important way that Innovest research helped investors to increase financial returns was by providing a strong indicator of management quality. Many financial analysts would agree that management quality is the most important determinant of financial performance. It affects nearly all aspects of companies' operations and performance. But management quality is intangible. It cannot be measured directly. Some experts say that financial performance is a good indicator of management quality. But there are many factors that affect financial performance over which management has little or no control, such as unexpected external events or mergers of competitors.

One way to gauge management quality is to assess performance on a highly complex issue. If management is able to perform well in complex areas, it implies that they have the ability and sophistication to perform well in other operating areas. As discussed in Chapter Three, sustainability is one of the most complex challenges facing companies. Management must effectively address many different stakeholder groups, complex environmental and social issues, intangible, long-term, nonfinancial measurement factors, and high levels of technical, market and regulatory uncertainty. Performing well in this highly complex area strongly implies that management has the ability to succeed in other areas, and thereby earn superior returns.

As discussed in the Finance and Capital Markets section, intangible value has become increasingly important in the capital markets. It is the difference between the market value of outstanding shares and tangible assets (i.e. property, plant, equipment). Intangible value as a percentage of market capitalization of the S&P 500 grew from 17 percent in 1975 to about 85 percent today. Intangible value includes assets such as intellectual property, reputation and brand value.

Management quality probably is the most important aspect of intangible value. It strongly affects innovation capacity, product development, stakeholder relations, and ability to adapt to rapidly changing markets and other conditions. Companies with superior CR and sustainability performance generally are more forward-looking, strategic, agile and adaptable. They tend to be better managed in general. The strong link between sustainability performance and management quality probably is the main reason why Innovest research showed that sustainability leaders outperformed laggards, on average, in nearly all sectors.

Innovest did not blindly assume that all environmental and social issues were important for companies. Instead, it assessed which factors had the greatest financial impact in various sectors. These factors usually were given higher weightings in rating models. However, the company also did not ignore environmental and social factors that appeared to be less relevant. Many factors have little financial relevance in the short-term, but can become more relevant over the mid to longer-term. These factors usually were given lower model weightings. In rankings of the ESG research providers, Innovest usually was ranked number one in the world.

As a pioneer in the 1990s and early 2000s, Innovest senior executives (including the author) spoke at many mainstream business and financial sector conferences, sometimes to skeptical audiences. As noted, the prevailing mainstream view was that SRI reduced investment returns. But Innovest was providing compelling logic and evidence which showed that the opposite was true. Over time, the tide began to turn. As discussed throughout this book, reality always prevails. In reality, environmental and social issues are increasingly financially relevant for companies. It was only a matter of time before the corporate and financial sectors adapted to reality. Many of the world's largest financial institutions began purchasing Innovest research and integrating it into their investment strategies. Some of these institutional investors also invested in Innovest. Innovest research was being used for nearly all types of SRI strategies, including negative and positive screening, impact investing, shareholder activism, best-in-class investing, and integration with conventional financial analysis. It was used to develop enhanced index, active equity, debt and other types of SRI products.

Growing investor awareness of the financial benefits of superior corporate sustainability performance compelled many companies to improve in this area. Large companies often sought to get higher Innovest and other ESG ratings, in part because this could put upward pressure on stock prices. Implementing proactive CR strategies also enabled companies to take advantage of previously ignored financial and competitive benefits. Growing corporate and financial sector awareness of the financial relevance and importance of sustainability shifted the prevailing view about CR. As noted, CR formerly was seen largely as a risk mitigation activity that increased costs. But experience was proving that effective CR strategies could substantially enhance competitive position and shareholder value.

A watershed moment occurred in the CR area in 2005 when Walmart implemented a highly proactive and effective CR strategy. As much as anything else, this signaled that CR and sustainability had gone mainstream. Since 2005, and especially in the past five years, large, prestigious business schools, consulting firms and investment banks have published reports about the financial and competitive benefits of CR and SRI. These mainstream institutions now are making the same arguments that Innovest made 15 to 20 years before them. Innovest was a pioneer in promoting the idea that CR performance was a strong indicator of stock market potential. Now, many other organizations advocate and utilize similar approaches.

This evolution of business thinking and behavior occurs regularly. A few pioneers promote new approaches. As the benefits of these approaches become obvious, large businesses and financial institutions adopt them. As pioneering approaches become mainstream, pioneers often get acquired by large companies. Innovest was acquired by RiskMetrics in 2009, which subsequently was acquired by a Morgan Stanley spinoff (MSCI) in 2010.

REFOCUSING CR AND SRI ON SYSTEM CHANGE

As the largest and often top ranked corporate sustainability research company in the world, Innovest was in a good position to define leading-edge CR. Developing CR ratings first requires defining superior CR performance. Innovest models essentially defined the most advanced CR performance in each sector by including all aspects of it as metrics in rating models. Through its successful rating business, Innovest established itself as a world-leading judge of CR performance.

As the head of research at Innovest, the author of this book oversaw the in-depth environmental and social performance analysis of the world's 2,000 largest companies for many years. This provided a very clear understanding of the extent to which companies could mitigate negative environmental and social impacts without violating their fiduciary responsibility to maximize shareholder returns. After a while, it became clear that no company could come remotely close to full impact mitigation without putting itself out of business. Based on extensive expert analysis, the author estimated that, on average, companies could mitigate roughly 20 percent of their environmental and social, tangible and intangible, short-term and long-term negative impacts in a profit-neutral or profit-enhancing manner. If companies attempt to voluntarily mitigate impacts beyond this point, costs usually would go up relative to peers. If they continued down this path, they would put themselves out of business.

As discussed extensively throughout this book, this situation exists due to flawed, myopic systems that fail to hold businesses fully responsible for negative impacts. Under these flawed systems, companies must degrade the environment and society to survive. Our flawed systems unintentionally create a situation where being in business and acting in a fully responsible manner are mutually exclusive. Without exception, it is not possible for any company in the modern world to act in a fully responsible manner and remain in business.

The focus of Innovest was on rating CR performance and providing this information to the financial community. The author saw that this work could greatly benefit society by compelling companies to act more responsibly. (That is why he began working with Innovest.) However, after a few years, he realized that more work was needed, work that was beyond the scope of Innovest. It appeared that nearly 100 percent of CR and SRI efforts were focused on about 20 percent of the problem (i.e. negative impacts that could be unilaterally mitigated by companies). Achieving sustainability and real prosperity required a major shift in the CR and SRI movements. Roughly 80 percent of the unsustainability problem was caused by flawed systems, not irresponsible corporate behavior. As a result, the emphasis on system change had to be greatly increased in the CR and SRI areas.

As the head of research at Innovest, the author developed and refined rating models, oversaw CR/ESG analysis and approved final ratings. Having essentially been the chief judge at the largest company in the world rating CR performance for many years, he was in a good position to define the next level of CR and SRI. As part of advisory work separate from his Innovest role, the author developed the TCR model in 2003. As noted, TCR is intended to provide a practical and profitable way for companies and investors to engage in system change. The author developed the terms mid-level system change and high-level system change to help differentiate the challenges and optimal strategies needed in each area. Since 2000, he has been advocating the need to greatly increase the focus on system change in the CR and SRI areas by publishing articles, launching websites, speaking at universities, and presenting at corporate and financial sector conferences. Writing this book is a major project intended to facilitate an increased focus on system change and promote achieving sustainability and real prosperity in general.

Many actions are needed at the individual, company, regional, national and global levels to achieve a sustainable and truly prosperous human society. However, great opportunity for rapid, positive change lies in the corporate and financial sectors. Business is powerful and innovative. It exerts strong influence over citizens, government and society. We can harness the power of business to produce huge, positive changes in society.

To achieve this, we must remember what business is, and what it is not. Corporations are tools designed to do certain things. Like washing machines, automobiles and other tools, they have no consciousness or morality. Morality does not apply to non-living entities. Currently, we myopically design corporations to frequently put shareholder returns before the environment, customers, employees and broader society. When there are conflicts between shareholder returns and these factors (as there often are), flawed systems often compel corporations to put shareholder returns first. Widespread environmental and social degradation largely is not caused by lack of morality or poor management. Managers and companies do what they are incentivized and designed to do. Economic and social degradation largely are caused by flawed systems and myopic corporate designs, which in turn result from flawed, myopic thinking.

This situation illustrates the need for a major refocusing of the CR and SRI movements. As noted, these movements largely are focused on unilateral, voluntary corporate action. But companies cannot mitigate roughly 80 percent of their negative environmental and social impacts without putting themselves out of business. In other words, nearly 100 percent of the focus of CR and SRI is on about 20 percent of the problem. Eliminating impacts that cannot be unilaterally mitigated requires system change. To achieve sustainability and real prosperity, the focus of the CR and SRI movements largely must be shifted to improving flawed economic, political and other systems.

The business case for system change is strong and clear. Flawed systems compel companies to degrade the environment and society. This ultimately degrades businesses and investors. As the human economy and society expand in the finite Earth system, negative corporate impacts return more quickly to harm companies, often in the form of reputation damage, boycotts and rising mitigation costs. Proactively reducing negative impacts and preventing problems frequently is less expensive than cleaning up problems and suffering reputation and other damage. Companies have a strong and growing incentive to do all they can to minimize negative environmental and social impacts. System change is the *only* way to fully mitigate impacts, and thereby maximize the well-being of business and society.

How do we shift the focus of the CR and SRI movements to system change? The most efficient and effective means probably is to use existing mechanisms. ESG ratings are one of the most important mechanisms and activities in the CR and SRI areas. The ESG rating process is a primary driver of CR and SRI. Many companies and NGOs provide ESG ratings. As noted, to produce ratings, organizations first must develop rating models. Developing models requires defining leading-edge corporate sustainability or CR performance. Key aspects of superior CR are used as metrics or measurement points in ESG rating models. The model and its metrics serve as a roadmap for companies. They identify which actions and structures are needed to achieve superior CR performance. The financial community uses ESG ratings to develop high-performance SRI products and funds. This puts pressure on companies to achieve superior ESG ratings. High ratings can provide several corporate benefits, including enhanced reputation and stock price (through increased inclusion in SRI funds).

In summary, ESG ratings define leading CR. This mechanism can be used to strongly promote system change. Current ESG ratings mostly focus on voluntary impact mitigation (about 20 percent of the problem). System change is the most important sustainability issue. It allows the remaining 80 percent of negative impacts to be mitigated. To achieve sustainability, ESG definitions and rating processes must be expanded to include a heavy focus on system change. This is exactly what the TCR approach does.

TOTAL CORPORATE RESPONSIBILITY

TCR identifies and measures important corporate system change activities. The approach represents the next generation of corporate sustainability ratings. It evolves the ESG rating process into a form that has the potential to achieve sustainability (i.e. by enabling 100 percent impact mitigation). The name Total Corporate Responsibility emphasizes the importance of fully mitigating all negative impacts (i.e. acting in a fully responsible manner).

The TCR approach defines and measures two broad levels of system change – mid-level and high-level. Over the past 10 years, a growing number of companies have gotten involved in mid-level system change. Walmart, for example, has worked extensively with suppliers, NGOs and other stakeholders to reduce negative environmental and social impacts in several industry sectors. Mid-level system change is important. But high-level system change is by far the most important sustainability issue.

Myopic economic and political systems essentially force companies to rapidly degrade the environment and society. These systems grossly violate the laws of nature. They absolutely will change. Not changing it is not an option. Reality and nature will not allow flawed human systems to exist indefinitely. The American and French revolutions, end of slavery in the US, collapse of communism in the Soviet Union and many other large-scale system changes throughout human history show that all human systems that violate the laws of nature (including the natural laws of equality and fairness) end, usually by collapsing.

Our only options are voluntary or involuntary system change. Involuntary change (i.e. collapse) would cause unprecedented suffering and disruption because human society is larger and more interconnected than ever. Voluntary high-level system change is the most important action needed in human society. It is the only way to reverse rapid environmental and social degradation and achieve sustainability and real prosperity.

TCR is based on whole system thinking. It seeks to promote an evolution in business consciousness. The model is based on three principles – interconnectedness, actualization and posterity. Interconnectedness emphasizes the reality that companies are parts of larger environmental and social systems. They ultimately cannot prosper if these larger systems are not stable and healthy. Actualization emphasizes that the primary purpose of business in a democracy should be to promote the well-being of society. Reasonable investor returns result from doing this well. Posterity emphasizes that the most important goal of current generations is to ensure the survival and prosperity of future generations. From a business perspective, this means that companies should limit any activity that threatens future generations.

Rating corporate system change performance is far more complex than rating corporate responsibility performance. As noted, conventional CR and ESG rating mostly measures voluntary, unilateral impact mitigation. System change rating largely assesses the degree to which companies are working unilaterally and collaboratively to evolve sectors and overarching systems in ways that enable further, ultimately total, impact mitigation.

To assess the effectiveness of impact mitigation, analysts must understand companies' negative impacts. This enables them to determine if mitigation efforts are effectively focused on the most important impact areas. To enhance their reputations, companies sometimes engage in greenwashing (i.e. portraying themselves as proactive on sustainability, when they actually are not). Understanding impacts enables analysts to see through greenwashing and identify the extent to which companies are effectively mitigating impacts, for example, by selling low impact products, taking better care of employees and reducing pollution. The frame of reference for conventional CR and ESG rating mainly is companies' negative impacts and effectiveness in mitigating them. Leading CR largely involves voluntarily, proactively and effectively mitigating the most important impacts. This is the standard against which companies are rated.

The frame of reference for system change rating is vastly larger. To adequately assess system change activities, analysts must understand which system change actions are necessary. This requires far more than an understanding of companies' negative impacts. It ultimately requires an understanding of the whole Earth system and its many environmental and human subsystems. This enables identification of the most important system changes needed, including those that allow full impact mitigation.

Without this understanding, analysts might be fooled by system change greenwashing. As it becomes more widely known that system change is by far the most important sustainability action, companies might attempt to enhance their reputations by portraying themselves as system change leaders. Understanding the most important system changes enables analysts to see through system change greenwashing and accurately assess system change performance. Leading system change performance largely involves focusing unilateral and collaborative system change actions on the most relevant and important system changes needed. This is the standard against which companies are rated.

Beyond system change relevance, focus is another critical aspect of system change rating. The vast majority of system change efforts focus on single issues or components of society. For example, many system change efforts focus on resolving climate change and other environmental and social problems. Many other efforts focus on establishing a sustainable economy, or improving specific economic system components, such as measurement of success or money creation. Narrowly focused system change efforts have produced some benefits. But they have not reversed rapid environmental and social degradation. Myopia is the main reason for this ineffectiveness.

Nothing occurs in isolation in the interconnected whole Earth system and human society. Root causes and most effective solutions often lie outside the issue-specific area. As a result, narrowly focused system change efforts frequently are ineffective because they are not addressing root causes and promoting the most effective solutions. To illustrate, as discussed in the Climate Change section, the root cause of global warming is not burning fossil fuels and other human activities that cause atmospheric and ocean warming. The root causes are the flawed ideas and systems that drive these unsustainable human actions. Extensive fossil fuel consumption results from flawed economic and political systems that do not hold companies fully responsible for negative impacts. Evolving these systems into sustainable forms will drive rapid reduction in fossil fuel use.

A whole system perspective reveals that the root causes of virtually all major environmental, social, economic and political problems facing humanity are flawed ideas and systems. Going beyond specific issues to address root causes is a hugely efficient and effective process. It can provide substantial progress, not only on the specific issues being addressed, but also on nearly all other major problems facing humanity. In other words, one meta-solution (i.e. evolving overarching ideas and systems into sustainable forms) can provide huge benefits in nearly all areas of human society.

Through a whole system approach, many problems would be resolved with little or no issue specific action. For example, if economic systems were evolved into reality-based pricing (i.e. incorporating all real, actual, relevant costs into prices), the climate change issue largely would resolve itself. Fossil fuel consumption would plummet in a reality-based pricing environment, while lower impact technologies rapidly expand.

Using a whole system approach does not mean doing everything at once. This would be impractical and ineffective. A whole system approach greatly increases practicality and effectiveness because it identifies root causes, most effective solutions and key leverage points for system change. In nearly all cases, effective system change requires a whole system focus. Therefore, whole system focused system change efforts generally would receive higher TCR ratings than narrowly focused efforts.

TCR combines the most advanced ESG metrics with extensive measurement of mid-level and high-level system change activities and results. The ESG component evaluates management of risks, opportunities and impact mitigation in areas including the environment, product safety, labor, customers, suppliers, communities, government relations and foreign operations. The TCR model assesses the presence of superior CR strategies. Leading-edge CR strategies include a focus on adding financial and competitive value, senior management commitment, integrating CR into the core business, developing environmentally and socially responsible products and services, identifying and quantifying negative impacts, establishing impact measurement and management systems, prioritizing and aggressively mitigating impacts, and fully and accurately disclosing sustainability performance.

The mid-level and high-level system change components of TCR assess unilateral and collaborative system change actions, as well as the relevance, focus and results of system change efforts. It is not enough to assess involvement in various system change activities. Additional assessment questions include, are system change efforts strongly promoting sustainability and focused on the most important system changes needed (relevance)? Are they narrowly focused on single issues or broadly focused on the whole system (focus)? And are system change efforts enabling further impact mitigation and providing other environmental and social benefits (results)?

Mid-level system change analysis determines the extent to which companies are working alone or with suppliers and other stakeholders to achieve sector-level, stakeholder-level, and environmental and social issue-level changes. High-level system change analysis measures how companies are interacting with broader society and working alone or with others to evolve overarching systems into sustainable forms.

Assessment questions might include, are companies using campaign finance and lobbying to remove regulations that protect the environment and society, but inhibit ever-increasing shareholder returns? Or are they seeking economic and political changes that require responsible corporate behavior, and thereby make acting responsibly the profit-maximizing strategy? Are companies working with industry groups and others to mislead the public about climate change and other issues that threaten short-term shareholder returns? Or are they using advertising and media to raise public awareness about issues that threaten the environment and society?

A major TCR analysis and rating focus area is the degree to which companies are proactively involved in mid-level and high-level system change efforts. As discussed, the main overarching system flaw in the corporate area is the failure to hold companies full responsible for negative impacts. This creates conflicts between business and society. It causes a situation where companies must degrade the environment and society to survive. In other words, not holding companies fully responsible for negative impacts is unintentionally suicidal. Given the extreme importance of holding companies fully responsible for negative impacts, TCR analysis and ratings are strongly focused on the degree to which companies work unilaterally and in collaboration with others to evolve systems in ways that require fully responsible behavior.

No company is powerful enough to change overarching systems. Voluntary high-level system change only can be achieved through collaboration. Therefore, TCR extensively analyzes the degree to which companies work with government, civil society and other groups to evolve industry sectors and overarching systems into sustainable forms. Various NGOs, academic leaders and other experts have been advocating economic and political reform for decades. But there is a severe lack of collaborative mechanisms and efforts through which companies and financial institutions can engage in high-level system change. To promote the development of collaborative system change efforts, TCR thoroughly assesses the degree to which companies help to establish and support these efforts.

High-level system change is a young field. We are in the early, pioneering stage of evolving our economic, political and social systems into sustainable forms. The means to achieve necessary system changes often are not clear. Experts have provided numerous suggestions about how to evolve systems into sustainable forms. Many of these system changes are successfully operating on a smaller scale. But large-scale whole system change still eludes us. The main reason for this is the failure to think from the whole system perspective. Many economic, political and social system change ideas do not fully address the whole system. As a result, they often have limited success and sometimes produce unintended consequences. Successful system change requires a whole system approach, such as TCR.

TCR utilizes best-in-class rating. The model contains numerous metrics that assess system change actions, relevance, focus and results. Many metrics apply to all sectors. Sector-specific metrics are added to assess sector-related risks, opportunities and necessary system changes.

As noted, a growing number of companies are involved in mid-level system change. But few companies are engaged in collaborative high-level system change. Companies with the highest TCR ratings are not perfect. They simply are leading their sectors on conventional and advanced (i.e. system change-focused) CR. A best-in-class rating approach can drive sector-wide improvement in sustainability performance, in part by raising awareness in the financial community and broader society about critical sustainability issues, especially system change. As companies improve sustainability and system change performance, the standards for achieving high TCR ratings become more stringent. This can promote continuous, sector-wide improvement.

GLOBAL SYSTEM CHANGE

One of the most difficult and important aspects of TCR (and system change rating in general) is establishing standards for superior system change performance. This is highly complex because it ultimately requires a whole system perspective. Adequately assessing system change performance requires an understanding of the end state (i.e. a truly sustainable and prosperous human society), major system changes needed to achieve it, barriers to change, and the most effective ways to overcome barriers and achieve successful system change.

The book, *Global System Change: A Whole System Approach to Achieving Sustainability and Real Prosperity*, summarizes and links together virtually all major issues and aspects of human society, including economic, political, social, environmental, psychological, spiritual and religious. The book puts major environmental, social, economic and political problems in a whole system context, and suggests effective systemic solutions for them.

Global System Change serves as a companion to TCR. By clarifying virtually all major system changes needed to achieve a sustainable and truly prosperous human society, the book helps to establish standards for superior system change performance. This facilitates the production of accurate and effective system change ratings.

Not all necessary system changes are relevant for each company and industry sector. But a whole system perspective nevertheless is necessary to accurately identify the most relevant, sector-specific system changes and leverage points. Focusing only on a particular sector almost certainly would result in failing to identify root causes, optimal solutions and key leverage points that lie outside the sector, but nevertheless are highly relevant to sector-wide sustainability performance.

Beyond overarching system changes, *Global System Change* extensively describes the most important system changes needed in many sectors, including food production, chemicals, energy, pharmaceuticals and education. By clearly and comprehensively describing important overarching and sector-specific system changes, *Global System Change* provides a roadmap for mid-level and high-level system change. It also provides the framework and reference points needed for effective TCR and other types of system change rating.

Over the past 50 years, there have been few efforts to link all physical aspects of society (environmental, social, economic, political) and nonphysical aspects (psychological, spiritual, religious) in a clear, detailed, actionable, whole system manner. But this type of work is essential for implementing the system changes needed to achieve sustainability and real prosperity. Without this broader, whole system perspective, we will not be able to voluntarily evolve our grossly flawed, myopic, unsustainable systems into sustainable forms. They will evolve themselves by collapsing. Instead of evolution, we will have revolution and probably great suffering among humanity. *Global System Change* is intended to model and promote the whole system thinking needed to voluntarily evolve our systems into sustainable forms and maximize the long-term well-being of human society.

Some of the most important systemic solutions discussed in *Global System Change* include holding companies fully responsible, establishing true democracy and emulating nature. As noted, from a business perspective, the most important overarching economic and political system flaw is the failure to hold companies fully responsible. This is the mechanism that puts businesses in conflict with society. Failing to hold companies fully responsible for negative impacts makes it impossible to fully mitigate impacts voluntarily. *Global System Change* describes the major economic and political system components that fail to hold companies responsible. The book explains how TCR and other approaches can be used to evolve systems in non-disruptive ways that hold companies fully responsible, and thereby make acting in a fully responsible manner the profit-maximizing strategy.

Our myopic systems often focus on business well-being apart from the well-being of society. This is unintentionally suicidal. It would be like cells in a body focusing on maximizing their own well-being without regard for the larger body that sustains them. When cells in the body do this, the body often is dying of cancer. When businesses seek to maximize their own well-being without regard for the well-being of larger environmental and social systems, it causes humanity to act like a cancer on this planet. We unintentionally kill ourselves. In reality, businesses are parts of one interconnected whole system. It is not rational to consider the well-being of business apart from the well-being of society. Like individuals, businesses should be free to do whatever they want, provided that they do not degrade society or harm anyone in any way. Evolving systems into forms that hold companies fully responsible for negative impacts will compel companies to act on the reality-based idea that their well-being ultimately is not separate from the well-being of society.

A critical aspect of voluntary high-level system change involves harnessing the power of the people. Corporations are powerful. But all power ultimately resides with citizens collectively. Vested interests often manipulate public opinion in ways that divide and disempower citizens.

This can protect short-term profitability and shareholder returns. But it ultimately degrades businesses and society over the mid to long-term, and increasingly in the short-term. An effective whole system approach requires not only suggesting specific economic, political and social system changes. It also requires describing how to unite citizens and establish true democracy. This will enable citizens to exercise their ultimate authority and drive high-level system changes that protect business and society over the long-term. *Global System Change* extensively describes the major actions needed to unite citizens, establish true democracy and evolve human society into a sustainable form.

Perhaps the most important system change principle and overarching solution discussed in *Global System Change* is emulating nature. Nature displays nearly infinitely greater technological sophistication, coordination, efficiency and prosperity than human society. As noted, nearly all of the systemic solutions needed to achieve sustainability and real prosperity are modeled or implied in nature.

The essentially infinitely greater sophistication of nature shows the vast, untapped potential of humanity. We are part of nature. Therefore, we have the innate potential to achieve the same high level of sophistication and coordination seen in nature. Humanity can be nearly infinitely more sustainable and prosperous than we are now. We only have reached the tiniest fraction of our potential. But myopia often makes it difficult to see this. We compare ourselves to past societies and say that we are advanced and sophisticated. But compared to nature, our supercomputers and other inventions are little more sophisticated than a caveman's club. *Global System Change* uses whole system thinking to show how humanity can attain our fullest potential, and explains this in ways that can be easily understood by average, non-expert citizens.

TCR BENEFITS

Effective communication is a major benefit of TCR. Business leaders who discuss high-level system changes could put their careers and companies at risk. For example, a CEO who discusses the need to shift the measured and managed focus of society from maximizing economic growth to maximizing the actual well-being of society could raise concerns among investors about achieving ever-increasing shareholder returns. This could lower stock prices and cause CEOs to lose their jobs.

Effectively encouraging the corporate and financial sectors to embrace system change requires using the right language and arguments. In reality, flawed systems pose major threats to businesses and investors. But discussing how to evolve these systems into sustainable forms could raise concerns that short-term interests might be threatened. TCR provides language and system change business cases that minimize these concerns. The approach helps corporate and financial sector parties to see that system change is inevitable. It is far better to have a seat at the system change table and help to control the process, rather than have unanticipated changes ruin companies and investments.

It is widely known that proactive sustainability strategies provide many benefits to companies and investors. The same rationale applies to system change. Companies that are proactively involved in mid-level and high-level system change gain many potential financial and competitive benefits. As it becomes known that system change is the most important aspect of sustainability and CR, system change leaders (i.e. those with high TCR ratings) will be seen as the true corporate sustainability leaders and pioneers. They often will attain all the benefits that accrue to current sustainability leaders, such as enhanced reputation, market share and profitability.

One of the most important aspects of TCR is the proxy value for management quality. Extensive research by Innovest Strategic Value Advisors and other organizations shows that corporate sustainability leaders often outperform in the stock market. The main reason for this probably is superior management quality. Effectively addressing sustainability is a difficult and complex management challenge. Success in this area implies management has the ability to succeed in other areas, and thereby earn superior returns.

System change represents an even more complex challenge for management. No company can unilaterally change overarching systems. Successful system change performance requires superior collaboration, public relations and other skills. As a result, system change performance potentially provides an even better indicator of superior management quality and stock market potential than conventional sustainability performance.

The systemic focus of TCR helps businesses to better understand their true self-interests and achieve long-term prosperity. Looking at the big picture clarifies that negative environmental and social impacts will come back to harm companies to a rapidly growing degree. Therefore, minimizing these impacts to the greatest extent possible will help to maximize business well-being.

Through the use of TCR ratings, financial institutions can develop SRI products with high outperformance potential. At the same time, TCR products and funds can drive far greater positive environmental and social impacts than any other SRI approach. This occurs because the focus of TCR is on system change, by far the most important sustainability issue. Beyond system change analysis, TCR helps investors to increase returns by providing information about financially relevant issues, including undisclosed liabilities, environmental and social risk exposure, development of environmentally and socially responsible products and services, and management of the environmental and social upside and downside.

Investors and other parties who are interested in using the TCR approach can employ the model in-house to enhance existing research or develop new ratings. Alternatively, production of TCR research and ratings can be subcontracted to ESG research providers.

Through the same mechanism as CR/ESG ratings, TCR ratings can be used to strongly promote superior CR and system change performance in the corporate sector. As Innovest research and ratings became widely used in the financial sector, many companies strove to improve their Innovest ratings. This could help them to get into SRI funds, increase demand for their stocks, and potentially raise stock prices and shareholder returns. As institutional investors and other capital market parties better understand that our grossly flawed economic and financial systems absolutely, inevitably will change, they will realize the importance of voluntary system change. This will produce far more favorable results than pretending that current systems are fine and do not need major revisions. This reality-ignoring approach inevitably will produce highly disruptive changes, and perhaps financial and economic system collapse.

As the financial sector realizes that system change is inevitable and voluntary system change is far better than involuntary change, financial institutions will work to promote voluntary system change. Using TCR and similar system change-based approaches is one of the most effective ways for investors to drive system changes that protect the financial sector, economy and society over the mid to longer-term. As financial institutions integrate TCR research and ratings into investment decisions, it will put pressure on companies to improve CR and system change performance. (Financial institutions can use TCR to broadly promote the system changes discussed throughout this book, including financial sector changes. The Finance and Capital Markets section and Sustainable Finance section below discuss many specific systemic changes needed in the financial sector.)

From a whole system perspective, it is obvious that system change is the most important, but most neglected aspect of CR and SRI. As noted, system change represents roughly 80 percent of the sustainability problem and solution. But it gets relatively little attention, compared to conventional CR. From a higher perspective, it becomes clear that mid-level system change and especially high-level system change are essential for achieving sustainability and real prosperity. This shows that a new leading-edge is required in the CR and SRI areas. TCR and other system change-based CR approaches are the new leading-edge in CR and SRI. TCR shifts the focus from the 20 percent (negative impacts that companies can unilaterally mitigate) to the 80 percent (negative impacts that cannot be mitigated without system change). To avoid system collapse and achieve sustainability and real prosperity, we must evolve CR into TCR.

SYSTEM CHANGE ANALYSIS

The following discusses the analysis of corporate system change efforts. As noted, Walmart implemented a proactive sustainability strategy in 2005. As a retailer, Walmart recognized that about 90 percent of its negative environmental impacts occur in the supply chain. To mitigate these impacts, Blu Skye Consulting helped Walmart to establish Sustainable Value Networks in several areas, including seafood, food and agriculture, electronics, chemicals, operations, fleet, packaging and China. Within the networks, Walmart works collaboratively with suppliers, NGOs and other parties to reduce negative impacts throughout the supply chain. Each of these networks is a mid-level system change effort.

Through these collaborative processes, Walmart is able to reduce negative impacts more than it could on its own. As a result of this proactive system change work, Walmart almost certainly would receive superior TCR rankings in the mid-level system change area. The overall TCR rating also would include assessment of negative environmental and social impacts, conventional CR and high-level system change performance relative to peers.

Another important example of corporate system change activities involves B Corporations. In 2006, the NGO B Lab was established to facilitate the development of B Corporations. Under traditional corporate structures, corporations are under strong pressure to focus mainly on maximizing the financial returns of shareholders. Investors often can sue board members if companies fail to do this. The B Corporation (Benefit Corporation) structure allows companies to focus on maximizing benefits to many stakeholders, including employees, suppliers, communities, the environment and shareholders. B Lab certifies B Corporations. To become a B Corporation, companies must submit to annual audits and meet rigorous standards in areas including environmental and social performance, accountability and transparency. There are over 1,200 certified B Corporations in more than 30 countries. Over 25 states have passed legislation that allows B Corporations.[3]

The B Corporation represents an important system change. It establishes the idea and legal option that corporations do not have to focus primarily or exclusively on shareholder returns. As discussed extensively throughout this book, this change in business structure is essential for achieving sustainability and real prosperity. As servants of interconnected society, corporations should focus primarily on maximizing the well-being of society. Superior shareholder returns would result from doing this well.

The B Corporation structure substantially advances system change by changing the exclusive focus on shareholder returns. However, far more system change work is needed to achieve sustainability and real prosperity. The B Corporation strategy and structure falls mainly within current CR because it is based on voluntary action. Companies are not required to become B Corporation. They voluntarily choose to do so. Companies also are not required to eliminate all negative environmental and social impacts. To achieve B Corporation certification, they usually must go beyond current regulations that do not require full impact mitigation. They achieve superior CR performance, but often are not required to fully mitigate negative impacts.

As noted, under current flawed systems, no company could fully mitigate negative impacts and survive. B Corporations must compete in markets, often against companies that are exclusively focused on maximizing shareholder returns. Under current CR, companies have developed thousands of strategies for reducing negative environmental and social impacts in ways that enhance or do not harm financial returns. B Corporations essentially must employ the same creative strategies. They have more flexibility to benefit all stakeholders. But if costs become too high, they might not be able to compete or attract investors and customers.

The impact of B Corporations could be limited for several reasons. For example, many current corporations, especially large ones, would have difficulty converting to B Corporations. Investors provided funds with the expectation that companies would focus on maximizing shareholder returns. Changing to a B Corporation might violate this legal commitment made when shareholders invested. Also, as shown by Innovest, B Corporations, like other companies, can use leading CR performance to achieve superior financial performance. But, there is a limit to this. Beyond a certain point, further impact mitigation often increases costs and reduces profits. Focusing on maximizing the well-being of all stakeholders could reduce shareholder returns. Some investors would accept reduced returns in exchange for environmental and social benefits. But many others would not. As a result, B Corporations frequently could have a substantially smaller pool of potential investors.

The B Corporation structure is a significant improvement over current corporate structures. But it still is based on voluntarily acting responsibly. As noted, beyond a certain point, voluntary corporate responsibility absolutely cannot work. No company can voluntarily mitigate all negative impacts and remain in business. This once again shows the essential need for high-level system change. The most important overarching change in the business area is holding companies fully responsible for all negative environmental and social impacts. When this occurs, even current corporations that are exclusively focused on benefiting shareholders will fully mitigate negative impacts because this will be the profit-maximizing strategy.

Under the TCR rating approach, B Corporations almost certainly would get superior CR ratings (i.e. unilaterally mitigating negative impacts). The B Corporation structure facilitates mid-level system changes, such as working with suppliers. Therefore, B Corporations also probably often would get superior mid-level system change scores. However, the most important action needed to achieve sustainability and real prosperity is high-level system change. Changing corporate structures is important. But the far more important system change work involves improving the overarching economic and political systems that largely constrain and control the actions of corporations. As a result, high-level system change would be heavily weighted in the TCR model. To achieve high overall TCR ratings, companies, including B Corporations, would have to be supporting and/or engaging in collaborative high-level system change.

Blu Skye Consulting and other organizations are helping many companies to implement collaborative mid-level system change strategies in several industry sectors. But there are limited opportunities and vehicles for companies to engage in high-level system change. As noted, organizations such as the New Economics Foundation have been promoting the implementation of sustainable economic systems for decades. Corporate and financial sector support of organizations such as these is one element of high-level system change. But far more high-level system change vehicles and opportunities must be established. Collaborative high-level system change efforts that bring together business, political and civil society leaders are essential.

As discussed in Chapter Seven, probably the most important actions needed to facilitate system change are empowering citizens and establishing democracy. Corporate and financial sector support of efforts in these areas is a critical component of high-level system change. As a result, these types of activities would be heavily weighted in TCR ratings. High-level system change is the most important action needed to achieve sustainability and real prosperity. Therefore, companies that strongly promote high-level system change are the true sustainability leaders. They deserve the highest TCR ratings.

Many system changes are needed to achieve sustainability and real prosperity. As discussed, in the business area, holding companies fully responsible for negative impacts is the most important system change. It makes full impact mitigation (TCR) the profit-maximizing strategy. Holding companies fully responsible through laws, regulations and other mechanisms is the most fair and effective approach. It levels the playing field for all companies. No company gets an unfair advantage. However, companies that proactively mitigate impacts in excess of regulatory requirements often will gain competitive advantages as regulations increase.

The main system change being suggested for companies (i.e. full responsibility) is fair because it is the same standard that is applied to individuals. Citizens are held fully responsible for negative impacts on society, but companies frequently are not. As discussed, it is far more important to hold companies responsible. Individuals can and usually do voluntarily act responsibly. But publicly traded companies often cannot act in a fully responsible manner. Flawed systems often force them to act irresponsibly. Therefore, it is essential that we evolve systems in ways that require fully responsible corporate behavior.

Whole system thinking and public awareness raising efforts will help the corporate and financial sectors to understand that system change is inevitable. This will help them to realize that it is better to have a seat at the system change table, rather than oppose system change efforts. Opposition ultimately is futile. Companies are fighting reality. Reality always wins. Companies will be severely harmed or put out of business if they are not ready for system change. By proactively getting involved in system change, businesses can help to guide the process in ways that protect shareholders and other stakeholders. They also can more effectively prepare for inevitable system changes.

TCR and similar approaches are the logical next step in the evolution of CR and SRI because system change is inevitable and essential for achieving sustainability and real prosperity. Partial corporate responsibility must be replaced with total corporate responsibility. As discussed, sustainability cannot be achieved until we evolve CR into TCR.

High-level system change is difficult and complex. It usually happens involuntarily in a highly disruptive manner, as occurred with the end of slavery in the US and the fall of the Soviet Union. Involuntary high-level system change in modern human society would cause unprecedented pain and suffering. It is essential that We the People (not just in the US, but all of human society) work together to achieve high-level system change. TCR is intended to facilitate this in the corporate and financial sectors. The approach utilizes market mechanisms and is based on widely used investment strategies.

Through TCR and the many other changes and approaches discussed in this book, we can achieve sustainability and real prosperity. Millions of people are focused on making our unsustainable systems work. If we refocus this attention on sustainable systems, we can make them work too. We have all the resources, tools and know-how needed to evolve our systems into sustainable forms and achieve sustainability and real prosperity.

As economic and political systems are evolved into sustainable forms, the business case will change. Making the business case (for increased profits and shareholder returns) is a central component of business. Businesses are structurally precluded from taking actions that threaten shareholder returns. As a result, encouraging and empowering them to take certain actions usually requires making the business case for those actions. Innovest was a pioneer in making the business case for sustainability. The company provided extensive research, evidence and logic which showed that acting more responsibly and sustainably often could enhance financial and competitive performance.

But the need to make the business case reflects the grossly flawed structure of businesses and overarching economic and political systems. Activists and other sustainability advocates often must show companies how acting more responsibly can help shareholders. As discussed in the environmental sections, corporate pollution and other negative impacts sicken and kill millions of people. In effect, sustainability advocates must make the business case for not killing children or harming society in other ways.

When viewed from this larger perspective, having to make the business case for acting responsibly seems insane. Sustainability advocates should not have to make the business case for protecting life support systems and the health and lives of citizens. These actions should be automatic on the part of companies. Failing to hold businesses fully responsible for negative impacts creates the situation where they must try to figure out how to voluntarily mitigate impacts in ways that do not violate their obligation to protect shareholders. As noted, companies generally cannot mitigate roughly 80 percent of negative impacts without reducing profits. When systems are evolved into forms that require fully responsible corporate behavior, it no longer will be necessary to make the business case for acting responsibly. Acting in a fully responsible manner will be a requirement for business survival. The business case always will be obvious and automatic – act responsibly or cease to exist.

CHAPTER NINE – ACHIEVING SUSTAINABILITY AND REAL PROSPERITY

A main purpose of this book is to help business, political and civil society leaders, as well as citizens (the ultimate leaders of society) to better understand how humanity might reach our fullest potential. The limited human perspective often misleads us into thinking that we are advanced. Compared to past human civilizations, we often are. But compared to nature, we are not. Virtually every aspect of nature is nearly infinitely more sophisticated than humanity. Nature displays vastly superior technology, cooperation, coordination, symmetry and implied wisdom. Measured against this standard, we only have reached the tiniest fraction of our potential. We have the potential to be nearly infinitely more sophisticated, coordinated and sustainable than we are now. We have the potential to end hunger and nearly all suffering on this planet. We can learn to live in balance with nature and each other, and thereby enable humanity to exist and truly prosper over the very long term on Earth.

We often imagine that we are the most advanced creatures on this planet. But in some ways, we are near the least advanced. When measuring the sophistication of a particular species, the most important requirement is survival. If a species cannot survive, everything else ultimately is irrelevant. Indigenous spiritual and other beliefs frequently put humans in harmony with nature and others in their communities. This enabled us to survive for thousands of years. Early human spiritual beliefs often saw the divine in nature, and thereby revered it. From a practical perspective, these belief systems were highly logical. Nature is the actual, immediate, reality-based source and sustenance of human life. Therefore, from a whole system perspective, respecting and protecting nature essentially is the same as respecting and protecting human life.

As discussed in the Well-Being of Society section, humanity's slide into ignorance, myopia and unsustainability began with the agricultural revolution. Around this time, we ideologically separated ourselves from nature. We began to abandon old spiritual views of reality that had worked for thousands of years. In a sense, our increased ability to think made us less intelligent. We often seemed to lose the implicit awareness that we were an integrated part of nature. Other creatures rely on intuition or instinct. They do not appear to have the ability to think or reflect as humans do. They essentially are guided by the wisdom of nature. This implied wisdom coordinates other creatures and lifeforms in ways that produce nearly infinite sophistication, coordination and beauty. When our spiritual beliefs put us in harmony with nature and fellow community members, we also largely displayed the coordination and sustainability of nature.

But as the intellect began to ascend over the intuitive, we seemed to lose awareness of our interconnectedness with nature. Our consciousness or focus, at least in terms of spiritual beliefs, seemed to move from the collective to the individual. We seemed to over-rely on our five senses and under-rely on intuition. This made us myopic. Our five senses told us that we were separate from each other and nature. This sense of isolation often produced fear. Around this time, new spiritual ideas were developed. We created religions that placed humans above nature, other creatures and often other humans. The genesis of these religious ideas was fear, myopia and the belief in separation. We seemed to lose touch with the intuitive knowledge that we were one with nature and each other.

As our intuitive wisdom declined, we replaced it with intellectual concepts. We made up invisible Gods. This made it more difficult to question the existence of a particular version of God. One can point to a statue and say that is not God. But it is not possible to point to an invisible God and say it is not God. People were encouraged or coerced into blindly believing these stories about God. The gods often were angry and punishing. If we did not do what these human created gods wanted, we might burn for eternity in hell, according to many human created stories about God.

People who feel alone and isolated in the world often are afraid. It is logical that this myopic, fearful perspective or consciousness would produce angry, restricting, dogmatic religions. Fear and the sense of separation from each other and nature led to the belief that we must compete for scarce resources. In this competitive environment, power (and those who innately manifest more of it – men) was valued and elevated. Justified and encouraged by our new myopic religions, we developed ideas and systems for dominating other people and nature. Those with more power often took control of society. Fear, coercion, religious dogma and violence frequently were used to subdue and subjugate others. We developed economic, political and social systems based on these myopic ideas of separation and domination.

Since then, humanity has evolved through a series of authoritarian ideas, systems and structures. This is all coming to a head now. As discussed in Chapter Six, every life support system is in rapid decline. Pollution, inequality, hunger, poverty and many other major problems are growing rapidly. Humanity is quickly approaching a wall. The dominant economic and political ideas on this planet are based on flawed premises. They are bound to fail. We live in a time of accelerating consequences. We are being pushed. We can go in two basic directions – extinction or wisdom.

The loss of wisdom, started thousands of years ago, put us on the path to extinction. Reality and nature are teaching us in an increasingly powerful manner that our ideas about separation and domination are wrong. We will not be allowed to continue on this path much longer. We are being presented with a choice. We can cling to our intellectually driven sense of isolation from each other and nature, and thereby continue down the accelerating path to extinction.

Or we can wake up from our delusion. We can free ourselves from religious and economic dogma, from the mindset of separation and domination. The key to this awakening or enlightenment is humility. Observations of reality show the vastly superior technology, sophistication and coordination all around us in nature and in our own bodies. Observations of reality also show the vast and accelerating environmental and social problems and dangers facing humanity.

As we free ourselves from blind faith in dogma, we can base our ideas and actions on reality. Reality shows that we are infinitely less sophisticated than nature and we are killing ourselves. From a rational, reality-based, whole system perspective, it is not possible to conclude that our current systems are intelligent. Destroying our life support systems and creating vast, unnecessary suffering among humanity is not intelligent.

Humility strongly promotes enlightenment. Once we lose the arrogance and realize that the current human intellect is not the genius we think it is, we can move forward very quickly. We are all geniuses. We all have access to infinite intelligence and the wisdom of nature. But we have stifled our intuitive genius with myopic intellectual concepts and dogma.

One might ask, what is the point of all this? Why are we choking out human and other life on this planet and creating massive pain and suffering? If we once were sustainable and had spiritual ideas that worked in the real world, why did we abandon them? One possibility is that, on a higher, unconscious level, we chose to experience and endure separation so that we could experience the joy of awakening and integration. If we had not endured psychological separation, we could not have experienced reintegration. From a physical perspective, we always have been connected. None of us can survive in outer space. Separation always was an illusion, a psychological trick of the mind. Our experience of reality largely is determined by perceptions or psychology, not reality itself. We have been living in the illusion of separation for millennia. It has brought us near the point of collective death.

As discussed throughout this whole system book, waking up requires re-establishing the authority of wisdom. This requires humbly making the intellect a servant to something infinitely wiser. We no longer arrogantly and ignorantly claim to be the greatest intelligence on this planet. Instead, we use the intellect to observe that the implied intelligence all around us in nature essentially is infinitely greater than our own conscious intelligence. This places the conscious mind in a state of receptivity to infinite wisdom and intelligence.

Massive and growing environmental and social problems reflect humanity's abundance of power and lack of wisdom. This imbalance mirrors the imbalance between men and women. As noted, men innately manifest greater physical strength, aggressiveness and other aspects of power, in the same way that women innately manifest greater cooperation, empathy, whole system thinking and other aspects of wisdom. In our fear-filled consciousness of separation, power, aggression and those who manifest more of it (men) are honored. As we recognize the need for greater cooperation, wisdom and whole system thinking, those who manifest more of these qualities (women) will be honored and elevated to a position of true equality with men.

Achieving sustainability and real prosperity requires balancing power with wisdom. Power without wisdom is destructive, as we see in the world today. Wisdom teaches us, through enlightened ideas and inner and outer experience, that we are in reality parts of one interconnected system. This wise inner awakening will guide us to cooperate more with nature and each other. As this occurs, we will experience the reality and joy of interconnectedness. This is our natural state. It is our destiny. The cells in the body thrive when they cooperate and act as the one interconnected, healthy organism that they are in reality.

It is the same for us. Why did we create separation and suffering for so long? Perhaps so that we could experience integration and joy for vastly longer. Why did we forget that we are one? Perhaps so that we could have the experience of remembering it. This conscious recognition of our already existing oneness in reality could be thought of as reaching our fullest potential or creating Heaven on Earth. As this awakening or consciousness raising occurs, human society will begin to experience and display the vibrant health, brilliance and joy of nature.

This book has extensively discussed the flawed ideas and systems that create the vast problems facing humanity. This concluding chapter summarizes the degradation caused by these flawed ideas and systems, restoration through implementation of enlightened ideas and systems, and achieving sustainability and real prosperity by uniting and empowering citizens under a We the People movement.

DEGRADATION

Flawed ideas and systems are causing huge, ultimately suicidal problems for humanity. The US is a world leader in modeling and promoting these flawed ideas and systems. As discussed in the Economic Growth section, one of the main system flaws is seeking infinite growth in a finite system. Myopic economic theories and business structures seek never-ending growth of the economy and investor returns. This requirement is relatively new in human society. For nearly all of history, businesses did not labor under these reality-ignoring, ultimately suicidal growth requirements. This is another example of humans becoming less intelligent when we thought we were getting smarter. Like many other flawed ideas and systems, suicidal growth requirements result from myopia, or failing to think from a whole system perspective. Irrational growth theories result from focusing on individual persons, companies and countries, rather than the whole systems that contain them.

If we looked at the whole system of nature (of which human society is a sub-element), we would realize that seeking never-ending growth is the same as cancer in the human body. The failure to think systemically is causing humanity to act like a cancer on this planet. As we increase wisdom in human society and emulate the infinitely more intelligent master all around us, we will end our suicidal, cancerous ways. Like nature, we will seek balance, not growth. We will strive to maximize the well-being of human society, instead of economic growth.

When implementing suicidal economic systems, such as those functioning on the Earth now, there often is room to benefit multiple segments of society, at first. But after a while, the suicidal requirement to provide ever-increasing economic growth and shareholder returns ultimately pushes everything else aside.

The US provides a perfect example of this. From 1945 to 1975, the US economy and worker pay doubled. After World War II, more than one-third of US private sector workers were unionized. One middle-class working parent often could buy a home and raise a family, while the other parent stayed home and raised children. The US produced the largest middle class in the world.[4] Top marginal tax rates ranged from 70 percent to over 90 percent. The US was investing in infrastructure, K-12 education and public higher education. We were the world's largest economy, exporter and creditor. Social Security, Medicare and other social well-being programs substantially reduced poverty and increased quality of life for the large majority of US citizens. To illustrate, the poverty rate among elderly citizens is about 10 percent. Without Social Security, it would be 54 percent.[5]

But the measured and managed focus of the US economy and society was not on strengthening the middle class or promoting the general welfare, as our Constitution requires. It largely was on achieving never-ending economic growth. Economic growth mostly measures the growth and well-being of business. Most business assets are owned by a small group of wealthy people. As a result, the actual measured and managed focus of the US economy and society mainly was on ensuring that a small group of wealthy citizens gets continuously wealthier.

After several decades of growth that benefited the large majority of citizens, our suicidal systems began to push everything else aside. In the early 1980s, things began to change for average citizens in the US. As our suicidal systems continued to seek ever-increasing wealth for the small group at the top of society, it became increasingly difficult to provide increasing wealth to the rest of society. The vast majority of citizens were forced to sacrifice so that the wealthy could get continuously wealthier.

If we had been thinking systemically in the 1970s, we could have foreseen the inevitable decline of US society that began in the 1980s. Had we done this, we could have modified our systems in ways that enabled the vast majority of citizens to prosper. But we did not think systemically. As a result, US society has been declining in many ways since the 1980s. This is indicated by growing plutocracy, inequality, stock market values, labor degradation, poverty, public deception and retirement problems.

Plutocracy

Providing increased prosperity and well-being for nearly all citizens (i.e. promoting the general welfare) interfered with the measured and managed focus of US society – ensuring that a small group of wealthy citizens gets continuously wealthier. To minimize this interference, business control of the US government appeared to increase in the early 1980s. In other words, plutocracy (control of government and society by a small group of wealthy citizens) increased. Laws and government programs were changed in ways that transferred substantially more public wealth to the wealthy citizens who largely were controlling the US government and society.

As shown through many examples in this book, beginning in the 1980s, many social welfare programs were reduced, while corporate welfare was substantially expanded. Wealthy citizens no longer were required to pay their fair share for benefits derived from the society that enabled them to become wealthy. Instead, business-influenced politicians reversed the flow of funds. Trillions of dollars of public wealth were transferred to the small group that largely controls government. Mechanisms that facilitate transferring wealth from average citizens to wealthy citizens relate to taxes, trade agreements, military spending, privatization, legal protections and campaign finance.

Taxes. In 1981, the top marginal income tax rate was cut from 70 percent to 50 percent. Estate, corporate and capital gains taxes also were reduced. In 1988, the top marginal tax rate was further reduced to 28 percent, the lowest level since the early 1920s.[6] As discussed in the Taxes section, one study found that the wealthiest US citizens avoid as much as $3 trillion of taxes per year – more than twice the cost of Social Security and Medicare. Wealthy citizens avoid taxes through factors including special deductions, exemptions, credits, loopholes, tax havens, tax underpayments, capital gains tax subsidies, regressive payroll taxes, the absence of taxes on financial transactions, and low corporate taxes. From 2008 to 2012, the actual federal income tax rate paid by corporations averaged 10 percent, even though profits had doubled in less than 10 years.[7] Corporate taxes actually paid are near the lowest rate in 60 years, despite record profits.[8] Many large, profitable corporations pay little or no income tax.

The top marginal tax rate has been below 40 percent for nearly 30 years, less than half the 1950s rate. About 75 percent of dividend and capital gains subsidies go to the wealthiest one percent of citizens in the US.[9] Financial speculation by wealthy citizens is taxed at a low rate, while hard-working average citizens are taxed at far higher rates. Many billionaires pay lower tax rates than average citizens. The wealthiest 400 individual taxpayers in the US paid average income tax of less than 20 percent, substantially less than millions of people who earn far less money.[10]

Vested interests often argue that wealthy citizens pay most of the taxes in the US. However, when federal, state and local taxes are taken into account, the wealthiest one percent of citizens paid about 20 percent of taxes and earned about 20 percent of income.[11] This is not progressive or fair. As discussed, no one gets wealthy on their own. Wealthy citizens have an obligation to support the society that enabled them to become wealthy.

Trade Agreements. Several trade agreements have been implemented or are being negotiated that strongly benefit the wealthiest citizens in the US, but degrade the lives of many other citizens. For example, the North American Free Trade Agreement caused a net loss of about 1 million US jobs.[12] Potential trade agreements with Asia (Trans-Pacific Partnership) and Europe (Transatlantic Trade and Investment Partnership) will strongly benefit wealthy business owners, but degrade society in many ways.

Trade agreements usually are negotiated in secret, even though they substantially affect the lives of hundreds of millions of citizens in the countries involved. Like already implemented trade agreements, the agreements being proposed often will place corporations above democratically elected governments. Companies will be able to sue governments for restraint of trade and force the weakening or removal of environmental, food safety and other laws and protections. These rulings frequently are decided by trade panels comprised of corporate lawyers. Citizens and communities have no standing in these proceedings. Rulings cannot be appealed. These undemocratic, strongly corporate-influenced panels often have the effective power to overturn rulings of parliaments, legislatures and supreme courts.[13]

Existing and proposed trade agreements show the suicidal nature of our flawed systems on a global scale. Anything that interferes with ever-increasing shareholder returns, such as the will of the people and democratic government, must be suppressed.

Military Spending. Military expenditures further illustrate how the business-controlled US government inappropriately utilizes public wealth to benefit wealthy campaign donors. As discussed in the Governance section, total US military expenditures, including Homeland Security, Veterans Affairs and interest on the military portion of national debt, are about $1 trillion per year. This is about the same as the military expenditures of all other countries combined. About 40 percent of US military expenditures are used to support approximately 850 military facilities in over 40 countries and US territories.

The US is bordered by two friendly countries and two very large oceans. Much of foreign military expenditures are not needed to protect national security. It appears that these military operations are intended in large part to protect the expansion of US businesses overseas. The US does not need to spend as much as the rest of the world combined on military to protect national security. As discussed in several sections, extensive military activities overseas often cause animosity toward the US, increase the demand for terrorism and apparently make the US less secure. Also, diverting public wealth to extensive military operations reduces the ability to provide social well-being enhancement programs that are taken for granted in nearly all other developed countries, such as healthcare, secure retirement, daycare and low-cost higher education.

Privatization. Extensive privatization of government services represents another major transfer of public wealth to wealthy citizens. As discussed in the Education, Crime, Healthcare and other sections, privatization often substantially degrades society. Business-influenced politicians frequently privatize government services in ways that substantially benefit the corporations and citizens who gave them large campaign contributions. For-profit companies often can cut costs by laying off employees or reducing wages and benefits. However, these actions frequently raise total costs to society because laid-off employees utilize social welfare programs and tax revenues decline.

In addition, the requirement to provide ever-increasing shareholder returns often compels companies to raise prices and reduce service quality. As a result, citizens frequently wind up paying higher prices for lower quality services. The primary focus of organizations providing healthcare, incarceration, education and other human-related services should be on maximizing the well-being of the people receiving the services and society overall. But the primary focus on maximizing shareholder returns frequently puts companies in systemically-mandated conflict with service recipients and society. Through this structural flaw, privatization often benefits wealthy business owners, but degrades society, especially over the mid to longer-term.

Legal Protections. Business influence of the judicial system represents another means of transferring public wealth to wealthy citizens. As discussed in the Judicial Branch, Crime, Education, environmental and other sections, wealthy citizens and corporations strongly influenced the appointment of many radically pro-business federal and state judges. These judges frequently reduced class action and other legal protections for citizens. For example, essentially business appointed judges have ruled that corporations are equivalent to human citizens and therefore deserve Bill of Rights protections. In several cases, business biased judges have ruled that government cannot require warning labels on food and other products because it violates corporations' supposed First Amendment free speech rights. The dairy industry, for example, has used this argument to block disclosure of the use of synthetic bovine growth hormone in the production of milk products.[14]

The focus on providing ever-increasing shareholder returns often compels companies to reduce product and service quality. As citizens are harmed by inferior or harmful products and services, their ability to hold companies responsible and receive restitution is being reduced by strong business influence of the judicial system.

Campaign Finance. This represents one of the most important mechanisms for increasing plutocracy and transferring public wealth to wealthy citizens. As discussed in the Campaign Finance, Judicial Branch and other sections, strongly pro-business judges essentially made bribery legal in the US. Nearly all campaign funding and funding for 'independent' campaign ads comes from the top 10 percent of society.[15]

Allowing wealthy citizens and corporations to spend unlimited amounts of money on political campaigns gives them vastly greater control of government than citizens who give little or no money to politicians. Politicians essentially become the paid servants of wealthy citizens. They do their master's bidding by essentially stealing trillions of dollars from average citizens and transferring it to the wealthy corporations and citizens who paid to put them in office.

Inequality

Beginning in the early 1980s, inequality in the US grew rapidly due in large part to the shift in focus of the US government, economy and society from maximizing the well-being of all citizens to maximizing the well-being of the wealthy citizens who were controlling government. From the 1930s to the 1970s, the financial markets were strongly regulated, tax rates on wealthy citizens were high, wages were rising and public and private debt were relatively low. However, beginning in the 1980s, as business control of government increased, the financial markets were deregulated, taxes on wealthy citizens declined, wages stagnated, and private and public debt increased.[16]

Wealthy citizens often prefer to loan money to government, rather than pay tax rates that cover the large benefits they received from the society that enabled them to become wealthy. By loaning money to government, wealthy citizens can get a return on their investment and compel low and middle-income citizens to pay back much of the debt through taxes. As tax rates began to decline on wealthy citizens and corporations in the 1980s, national debt increased substantially. To support ongoing economic growth, citizens were encouraged to buy on credit. Expansion of public and private debt contributed to substantial growth in the financial sector. In 1980, the financial sector represented 7 percent of US corporate profits. This increased to 40 percent by 2006.[17]

As the US began to switch from democracy to plutocracy in the 1980s, inequality rose. Prior to 1980, economic growth usually increased the incomes of the majority of citizens more than the wealthiest people in society. But beginning in the 1980s, most of the benefits of economic growth went to the wealthiest citizens.[18] From 1948 to 1973, the average income of the bottom 99 percent of society rose by 102 percent, while income for the top one percent rose by 46 percent. From 1973 to 2012, income for the top one percent rose by 187 percent, while income for the bottom 99 percent was flat (i.e. zero income growth).[19]

From 1900 to 1980, worker productivity and wages roughly rose together. Productivity continued to increase after 1980. But wages remained nearly flat as more wealth was transferred to wealthy citizens. From 1949 to 1979, productivity rose by 98 percent, while worker income rose by 94 percent. From 1980 to 2010, productivity rose by 87 percent, but worker income rose by only 4 percent.[20] The minimum wage peaked in 1968. It has lagged behind inflation and especially productivity ever since.[21] In 2015, the federal minimum wage was $7.25 per hour. If the minimum wage had kept pace with inflation since 1968, it currently would be over $21 per hour. Only 22 percent of the working age population today makes more than the equivalent of the 1968 full-time minimum wage.[22]

As discussed in the Finance and Capital Markets section, beginning in the 1980s, business-controlled government removed many of the financial sector regulations that were put in place after the 1929 stock market crash. Deregulation facilitated extensive speculation in real estate, derivatives, commodities and other areas. Deregulation and speculation were main causes of the 2008 stock market crash. Business-influenced politicians used potentially $6-12 trillion of taxpayer wealth to bail out mainly wealthy speculators who had made highly risky investments. This contributed to inequality growth after the 2008 recession.

From 2009 to 2013, US wealth grew by 53 percent from $47 trillion to $72 trillion. About 95 percent of this new wealth went to the top one percent of society. The remaining 5 percent went to the top 2-10 percent of society. The bottom 90 percent of society received none of the post-recession wealth growth.[23] Most of the wealth increase resulted from stock market growth, rather than new job creating business ventures.[24] High-speed trading and sophisticated investment strategies, such as hedge fund and private equity, enable sophisticated, wealthy investors to capture much of the stock market gains, often at the expense of average, middle-income investors.

By 2014, US wealth grew further to $82 trillion. Nearly 40 percent ($33 trillion) is owned by the top one percent of society. However, this understates the wealth of the top one percent. One study estimated that the wealthiest one percent of households in the US have an additional $12 trillion hidden in tax havens and possibly over $5 trillion in the shadow financial market (discussed in the Finance and Capital Markets section). In total, the top one percent of US society potentially has over $50 trillion of wealth.[25] Inequality is rising even in the top one percent. The top 0.01 percent of society (the top one percent of the top one percent – individuals with over $100 million of wealth) own about one-third of the wealth in the top one percent.[26]

Thirty-five years of corporate welfare and business-controlled government have caused the US to have near the highest wealth and income inequality in the world. A study of 141 countries found that only Russia, Ukraine and Lebanon have higher income inequality than the US.[27] The 30 wealthiest citizens in the US own as much wealth as the bottom 50 percent of society.[28] The middle class in the US has fallen to near the lowest level in the developed world. A study of 20 developed countries found that the US had the second lowest median wealth (net worth). However, the US has 42 percent of the world's millionaires and 49 percent of people with over $50 million in assets.[29] We also have by far the highest number of billionaires (571 in 2014, China was second with 190).[30]

Further indicating growing inequality in the US, in 1977, the top 0.1 percent of society owned 7 percent of US wealth. This rose to 22 percent in 2014. As business-controlled government continues to transfer trillions of dollars of corporate welfare each year from low and middle-income citizens to wealthy citizens, average citizens are getting poorer. In 1980, the bottom 90 percent of society owned 36 percent of US wealth. By 2014, this had fallen to 23 percent.[31]

The US economic strategy since the 1980s has been referred to as trickle-down economics. The idea is that if wealthy citizens are made wealthier, for example through lower taxes and other forms of corporate welfare, they will invest in society. This will cause the economy to grow and benefit all citizens. But this is an irrational, myopic and obviously incorrect philosophy. The obvious main driver (and creator) of the economy is demand for products and services, not investments by rich people.

When demand for products and services is high, wealthy citizens and business owners do not need extra cash from taxpayers. They usually can raise debt and equity financing because they have attractive value propositions for lenders and investors. Giving wealthy citizens corporate welfare when the economy is down largely will not help the economy. Business owners will not build factories and create jobs if demand for products and services is low. Instead, they often will squirrel away their taxpayer subsidies in foreign accounts.

Stock Market Growth

Stock market growth reflects the increasingly inequitable state of US society. Since the 2008 recession, the stock market has grown rapidly and reached several record highs. But this growth largely does not result from creating true value that widely benefits society. It mostly results from speculation and actions that degrade society. As discussed in the Labor section, about 75 percent of S&P 500 profit growth from 2000 to 2007 resulted from cutting employee wages and benefits. As a result, US labor compensation as a percentage of GDP is at the lowest level in 50 years.[32]

Business-controlled government has removed labor, environmental and many other protections for society. This makes it much easier to transfer the wealth of society to the small group of wealthy citizens who are controlling government. About 91 percent of US stocks and mutual funds are owned by the top 10 percent of society. The remaining 9 percent is owned by the 11-40 percent wealth bracket. The bottom 60 percent of society owns virtually none of the stock market.[33] Stock market growth largely does not show that the US economy and society are improving. It mainly represents already wealthy citizens prospering at the expense of the rest of society.

Much of the stock market growth results from cutting wages and benefits and selling more expensive, lower quality products and services. This degrades society, but enriches wealthy business owners. US corporations are sitting on about $2 trillion of cash, in large part because they are swimming in corporate welfare.[34] They could afford to build factories and create jobs. But this does not make sense in the face of weak demand. Transferring trillions of dollars of wealth from low and middle-income citizens substantially suppresses demand for products and services by impoverishing average citizens. Instead of creating jobs, corporations often are using their abundant corporate welfare generated cash to buy back stock. This further inflates the stock market and creates the illusion of prosperity and widespread value creation.

Corporate profits are at the highest level in 85 years. But corporations largely are not investing profits into higher wages, equipment, product development and other areas that would tangibly benefit broader society. Instead, in 2014, about 95 percent of the profits of S&P 500 companies were used to buy back stocks.[35] This inflates stock market values and benefits the small group of wealthy citizens who own most of the nation's wealth. But it does little to help average citizens.

Many politicians and economic experts argue that the economy is improving because it is growing. They imply that this broadly benefits society. But this is deceptive. As noted, economic growth mostly measures the financial well-being of a small group of wealthy citizens. The economy is growing in large part because extensive wealth is being transferred from low and middle-income citizens to wealthy citizens. As a result, while the economy grows, the lives of hundreds of millions of average citizens become more difficult. In other words, due to our flawed, myopic economic and political systems, as the economy gets 'better', society often gets worse.

The stock market is going up while quality of life for the large majority of citizens is going down. This occurs mainly because providing ever-increasing shareholder returns is the measured and managed focus of corporations and politicians who accept money from them. Focusing on pushing the stock market up is degrading the general welfare. Our flawed, myopic systems are doing the opposite of what the Constitution requires.

Labor Degradation

The emphasis on shareholder returns has substantially degraded labor and manufacturing in the US since the 1980s. An excellent article by Tom Hartman and Sam Sacks, called *How America Is Turning into a Third World Nation*, describes the decline of US manufacturing and labor.[36] In 1791, Alexander Hamilton, the first US Treasury Secretary, developed a plan to protect US manufacturing. For nearly the next 200 years, the US protected the manufacturing sector with import tariffs and support for domestic industries. This provided high-paying jobs and enabled the US to develop the largest middle class in the world.[37]

Prior to 1980, US corporations had relatively little debt. Earnings often were reinvested in new plant and equipment, research and development, and increased wages and benefits. As the financial sector was deregulated in the 1980s, corporate debt increased substantially. Instead of using debt to reinvest in workforces and product development, it often was used to buy other companies and load them up with debt. Earnings frequently were used to buy back stock and inflate share prices, rather than reinvest in companies. To pay rising debt costs, companies often laid off workers, cut wages and benefits, shifted production overseas and replaced full-time employees with part-time or temporary workers.[38]

In the early 1980s, the focus of the US shifted from protecting manufacturing, jobs, small businesses and society overall to protecting the financial wealth of large corporations and wealthy citizens who gave large amounts of money to politicians and inappropriately influenced government in other ways. The emphasis on protecting large companies instead of small ones contributed to the rate of new business formation falling by about 50 percent since 1980.[39]

To facilitate ever-increasing shareholder returns, unions and other protections for labor have been weakened since the 1980s. As discussed in the Labor section, companies have great power over employees. Unions protect employees by balancing the power between labor and management. Weakening or eliminating unions enables companies to force down wages, benefits and working conditions. In the mid-1970s, 25 percent of the private sector workforce was unionized. This has fallen to 7 percent.[40] The decline of unions coincides with substantial labor degradation since the 1980s.

The decline of manufacturing in the US contributed to labor degradation by eliminating many high quality jobs. As the US focus shifted in the 1980s from benefiting all citizens to mainly benefiting wealthy citizens, manufacturing declined. The strategy of protecting manufacturing, maintained since the founding of our country, largely was abandoned. Instead, the US adopted free trade agreements, such as GATT, NAFTA and the WTO. Wealthy citizens often can make more money by sending jobs overseas. As a result, business-influenced politicians implemented policies that facilitated shutting down extensive manufacturing in the US and shifting production to other countries. From 2000 to 2012, over 50,000 manufacturing plants were shut down and more than 5 million manufacturing jobs were lost.[41]

In the 1950s, manufacturing represented about 25 percent of GDP. This is down to about 10 percent. In the 1960s, one-third of jobs in the US were manufacturing. This has fallen to about 10 percent. In the 1970s, the US was the world's largest creditor, importer of raw materials and exporter of manufactured goods. However today, we are the world's largest debtor, importer of manufactured goods and exporter of raw material.[42]

In spite of extensive degradation of labor and manufacturing, our flawed, myopic, suicidal systems never will be satisfied. Business-influenced politicians (mostly Republicans) continue to try to weaken or eliminate protections put in place from 1930 to 1980 for labor and the middle class, such as a minimum wage, 40-hour work week, child labor laws and workplace safety laws.

Many foreign manufacturers are opening facilities in the US. They are attracted in large part by low wages and weak labor protections. For example, IKEA pays workers in Sweden $19 per hour and provides five weeks of vacation. However, in their Virginia plant, the company pays workers $8 per hour and provides about two weeks of vacation. In Germany, Volkswagen employees are unionized, have board representation, and receive high wages and benefits. But at the Volkswagen plant in Tennessee, US employees have no union protection, no board representation and receive far lower pay and benefits.[43]

Placing shareholder returns before all else is driving development in reverse. The US is becoming like an industrialized Latin American country, such as Brazil or Mexico, that has an ultra-wealthy minority, widespread poverty and a small middle-class. In effect, the US is undeveloping. As discussed in the article above, the middle class devolved into the working class. The working class is further devolving into the working poor. High quality manufacturing and other jobs frequently have been replaced by low-paying service jobs. As a result, the US middle class has been severely degraded. To illustrate, fast food jobs used to be dominated by teenagers. But adults who cannot find better jobs increasingly are forced to work poverty level retail sector jobs to survive. As a result, the percentage of 25-54 year olds working in fast food grew to 36 percent in 2014.[44]

In an effort to provide ever-increasing shareholder returns, new financial structures have been developed, such as private equity. These often further degrade labor and manufacturing. As discussed in the Finance and Capital Markets section, private equity firms frequently acquire companies, load them up with debt, lay off workers and shift production overseas. This is the expected outcome of placing shareholder returns before the well-being of society. It severely degrades labor and society. About 70 percent of people in the US hate, dislike or do not feel committed to their jobs. The US ranks last among developed countries on the Social Progress Index and the UN Happiness Index.[45]

In the mid 1980s, as protections for manufacturing were being removed, the US trade deficit began to increase. Since 2000, the trade deficit has been consistently high. In 2011, the US trade deficit was $560 billion. Year after year, large amounts of wealth are being removed from the US. This degrades the US economy and society. But unfortunately, the US is not focused on maximizing the well-being of society.

As discussed in the Labor section, the well-being of labor is a more accurate measure of social well-being than GDP. The majority of citizens in the US are employees or dependents of employees. GDP mostly measures the financial well-being of a small group of already wealthy people. Labor metrics assess the well-being of a much larger number of people, including many who are near or below the poverty line. Unfortunately, our flawed systems are not focused on the well-being of employees, their dependents and other average citizens. They are focused on ensuring that a small group of wealthy citizens gets continuously wealthier. These flawed systems drive ongoing labor degradation. Ever-increasing shareholder returns are achieved in large part by suppressing unions, wages and benefits. They also are achieved by sending jobs overseas, automating jobs and laying people off for other reasons. Layoffs often result in companies having fewer employees who are expected to work harder.

As discussed in the Misleading the Public section, the US government misleads the public about the actual unemployment levels in the US. Since the 1980s, several changes to the official method of calculating unemployment resulted in substantial undercounting of it. There are far more people seeking work than there are available jobs. As a result, many people are unable to find jobs, regardless of how long or hard they look. People who are willing and able to work, but have stopped looking because they could not find a job, no longer are considered to be unemployed, according to deceptive US unemployment definitions. People who have not looked for a job in the past four weeks are referred to as discouraged workers. These unemployed, willing to work people deceptively are not considered to be unemployed.

The participation rate (i.e. the percentage of adults in the labor force) helps to indicate the actual level of unemployment in the US. The participation rate (63 percent) is at the lowest level since 1978. However, this is misleading because more women work outside the home now. The participation rate for men is at the lowest level since 1948.[46] Part of the lower participation rate results from an aging population and more people retiring. But 70 percent of people not in the labor force are under 55 years old. Three-fourths of people under 55 who drop out of the workforce do so because they cannot find jobs.[47]

As discussed in the Labor section, another deceptive aspect of the official unemployment measure involves people with part-time jobs who want full-time jobs. Until the 1990s, these people were included in the official unemployment number. Excluding them substantially lowered the reported level of unemployment. To avoid paying benefits and thereby increase profits, many companies hire temporary or part-time workers. Over 20 million people in the US want full-time jobs, but cannot find them.[48]

Indicating the difficult and declining state of labor in the US, the working age population is 213 million. But there are only 118 million full-time jobs and 28 million part-time jobs. In addition, 47 percent of full-time workers and nearly all part-time workers make less than $35,000 per year. As discussed below, these people usually are not earning enough to meet basic needs.[49]

When discouraged workers and part-time employees seeking full-time work are included, the actual level of unemployment in the US is about 23 percent.[50] As discussed in the Misleading the Public section, reporting the actual high levels of unemployment and under-employment in the US would increase public demand to protect US jobs, for example, by limiting imports and providing tax penalties (instead of the current tax incentives) for sending jobs overseas. But protecting US jobs would limit short-term growth of shareholder returns. Misleading the public into believing that unemployment is much lower than it actually is helps the

US to achieve its primary objective – ensuring that wealthy people get continuously wealthier.

The unemployment situation in the US inevitably will get worse. Current systems are not focused on maximizing the well-being of average citizens and seeking full employment. The primary focus on maximizing shareholder returns puts publicly traded companies in systemically-mandated conflict with labor. Companies often are compelled to maximize shareholder returns by degrading labor.

Recessions facilitate the degradation of labor. They often enable companies to lay off higher paid employees and replace them with lower wage workers. To illustrate, low-income jobs represented 20 percent of the jobs lost after the 2008 recession, but 60 percent of the jobs regained.[51] Further indicating the inevitable decline of labor under current systems, about 45 percent of US jobs are estimated to be automated over the next 20 years.[52] In addition, of the ten fastest growing jobs in the US, eight are service sector jobs that pay $15 per hour or less.[53]

Business control of government strongly drives the degradation of labor in the US. As discussed in the Taxes section, through deferred tax loopholes and other mechanisms, the US tax code strongly incentivizes laying off employees in the US and shifting jobs overseas. Since 2000, nearly every large US multinational corporation has created more jobs overseas than in the US.[54] Germany and other countries use their tax codes to incentivize keeping jobs at home. But these countries are more focused on the well-being of all citizens than the US. Sending jobs overseas greatly benefits the small group of wealthy citizens who control government, but greatly harms millions of US citizens and families.

As is the case in nearly all other areas of US society, business-controlled politicians degrade the lives of millions of average citizens so that they can help wealthy campaign donors. Quality of life for the large majority of employees and other average citizens inevitably will get worse until we switch the focus of our economic and political systems from maximizing the financial well-being of wealthy citizens to maximizing the total well-being of all citizens.

Poverty

Transferring trillions of dollars of public wealth to wealthy citizens is substantially reducing the middle class and increasing poverty in the US. From 2007 to 2013, median family wealth fell from $99,000 to $56,000.[55] From 2000 to 2011, the number of people living below the official poverty level increased by 25 percent. An excellent book by David DeGraw, called *The Economics of Revolution*, extensively discusses rising poverty and declining quality of life for the vast majority of US citizens.[56]

The book explains how the US government grossly understates the actual level of poverty in the US. The official Census Bureau poverty rate is 15 percent. But the methodology for calculating the federal poverty rate is based on 1960s living standards. It substantially undercounts the actual costs of living in modern society, in part by ignoring widely varying costs of living in many different cities and regions. The poverty rate is based on the Consumer Price Index (CPI). As discussed in the Misleading the Public section, the CPI does not accurately measure inflation. Many changes have been made to the CPI methodology since 1980. These changes mislead citizens into thinking that inflation is lower than it actually is. To illustrate, the current CPI inflation rate is about 2 percent. But if inflation were calculated using the same method that was used in 1980, the current inflation rate would be about 10 percent.[57] This is obvious to many citizens. The costs of food, housing, healthcare, education and many other products and services often are rising faster than the CPI.

The official US poverty rate is more accurately described as an extreme poverty rate. A more accurate definition of poverty is inability to meet basic needs. On average, individuals and families need an income that is about twice the official poverty level to meet basic needs. When poverty is defined as inability to meet basic needs, the poverty level rises from 15 percent to 47 percent of the US population.[58] Misleading the public into believing that poverty is much lower than it actually is helps to protect the status quo of corporate welfare and business control of government. Honestly admitting that about 150 million people in the US cannot afford to meet basic needs (i.e. actually are living in poverty) would greatly increase public pressure to end the theft of the people's wealth and power.

Several studies indicate that the actual poverty rate in the US is higher than 47 percent. For example, one study estimated that the average person must earn at least $35,000 per year to cover the cost of basic necessities. Only about 30 percent of the working age population and 20 percent of the overall population have an income of over $35,000 per year.[59]

In other words, about 70 percent of the working age population does not earn enough to meet basic needs. These citizens often are compelled to take on increasing debt to survive. As a result, household debt is rising rapidly in the US. We are on the verge of another debt crisis. About 40 percent of US home mortgages are underwater or nearly so. Many interest-only second mortgages will be resetting to include principal payments over the next several years. This will cause rising defaults.[60] The large majority of average citizens are facing nearly flat or declining wages, rapidly rising living expenses, and rising debt. This is a formula for disaster. If these trends continue, as much as 90 percent of the US population could be heading for insolvency.[61]

Wages, benefits, unions, job quality and often job availability are being forced down so that a small group of wealthy citizens can get continuously wealthier. This is making life increasingly difficult for millions of hard-working average citizens. Many people are working two or more jobs, but still not earning enough to live a comfortable lifestyle, or even meet basic needs. Millions of citizens are receiving declining wages while facing rapidly rising healthcare, higher education, home rental/ownership, and other costs. Job security largely is a thing of the past. Companies often quickly jettison workers when ever-increasing shareholder returns are threatened.

Millions of citizens are taking less vacation time and experiencing higher stress, mental illness and other problems caused by our failure to focus on promoting the general welfare. Sixty-five percent of working families are living paycheck to paycheck. They usually do not have enough savings to handle emergencies or plan for the future.[62] Sixty-two percent of US families could not afford to pay a $500 repair bill.[63] US families have an average debt of over $200,000.[64] Fifty-six percent of citizens have subprime credit.[65] Thirty-five percent of adults in the US have debt in collections. This usually means that the debt has been outstanding for over six months and has been reported to credit bureaus.[66]

The US emphasis on ensuring that wealthy citizens get continuously wealthier is making life particularly difficult for many young adults. People born in the 1980s (millennials) are falling behind on nearly every adult milestone.[67] As discussed in the Higher Education section, large and often growing numbers of people in their 20s and 30s are moving home to live with parents and delaying getting married, having children and buying homes. They often have high student loan and other debt levels and face higher unemployment and under-employment. In spite of higher college education rates, young adults aged 25 to 34 were doing substantially worse in 2013 than the same age group in 1989. Medium income declined by 20 percent, home ownership fell by 3 percent and net worth was 56 percent lower.[68]

Many young adults would like to have children, but cannot afford them. The cost of raising children has risen rapidly. The estimated cost for a middle-income couple to raise a child born in 2013 to the age of 18 is projected to be about $245,000. This does not include savings for college. Working parents often cannot afford the rapidly rising costs of childcare. Center-based care for a single infant costs more than median rent levels in nearly half of states.[69] Childcare for an infant in Massachusetts, for example, costs more than $16,000 per year.[70]

Many developed countries provide childcare for working parents. But the US focus on helping wealthy citizens instead of all citizens makes it increasingly difficult for young adults who would like to start and raise families. Protecting children and helping young adults to achieve adequate or better lifestyles are primary obligations of society. But the structural requirement to put shareholder returns and economic growth before all else is causing gross failure to fulfill these obligations.

Contrasting the responses to the 1929 and 2008 stock market crashes illustrates the great extent to which business controls government in the US. After the 1929 crash, the US made extensive infrastructure investments, strengthened unions and took several other actions that enabled the US to become a global economic leader with the largest middle class in the world. In 1929, the top one percent of society had 23 percent of US income. This fell to 9 percent by the late 1960s.[71] As discussed in the Finance and Capital Markets section, by 2006, the share of US income of the top one percent had risen back to 23 percent.

Following the 2008 crash, we largely are doing the opposite of what was done in 1929. Instead of helping average citizens and rebuilding the middle class, we are accelerating its decline. Rather than reducing inequality, it is expanding rapidly. We are not aggressively investing in infrastructure, public education and job creation. Instead, infrastructure is crumbling, public education is in free fall, and job quality and labor well-being are declining.

Instead of shrinking 'too-big-to-fail' banks that drove the $6-12 trillion bailouts, we allowed banks to use taxpayer funds to acquire other banks. Now several of the too-big-to-fail banks are even larger. Knowing that they are too big to fail empowers banks and other financial institutions to continue highly risky investment strategies. If things go well, they earn very high returns. If they get in trouble, Democratic and Republican politicians who accept large amounts of money from the financial community probably will use taxpayer funds to bail out the banks again.

In the post-2008 environment, the focus of business-controlled government continues to be on helping wealthy citizens, not all citizens. This is reflected in government actions related to unemployment benefits, hunger and homelessness. Food Stamp and other social welfare programs keep many people above the poverty level. Without these programs, the official poverty rate would be twice as high.[72] But many politicians are working aggressively to reduce unemployment benefits and other social welfare programs that benefit average citizens.

To illustrate, in December 2013, Republicans in Congress voted to end unemployment benefits for citizens who had been out of work for over six months. By June 2014, 3 million unemployed citizens, including 300,000 veterans, lost unemployment benefits.[73] The large majority of these people could not find jobs in our shareholder-focused economy. Cutting benefits causes destitution, hunger and suffering among millions of US citizens. Rather than reducing obscenely high levels of corporate welfare in the US, political puppets made millions of average citizens destitute so that they could protect their wealthy masters.

The same thing occurred with Food Stamps. From 2008 to 2013, the number of citizens who lacked sufficient food increased by 30 percent. But Republicans voted to substantially cut food assistance programs.[74] Politicians who accept money from business gladly use taxpayer funds to essentially buy caviar for billionaires. But these supposed servants of the Constitution allow children to go hungry.

Dealing with homelessness illustrates the often cruel and ignorant nature of our shareholder-focused systems. Transferring trillions of dollars of public wealth to wealthy citizens is increasing homelessness in the US. It lowers the quality and often availability of jobs, reduces affordable housing and other programs that prevent homelessness, and increases stress and mental illness. All of these factors cause growing homelessness.

It is difficult to estimate the number of homeless people. One study estimated that there are over 600,000 homeless people in the US.[75] However, another study estimated that about 1.3 million K-12 students were homeless during the 2012-13 school year. This represents an 8 percent increase from the prior year. It was the highest level of K-12 student homelessness ever recorded in the US. But this probably undercounts the number of homeless young people. Many students hide their homelessness from school officials due to fear that they might be taken from their parents.[76] As a result, the actual number of homeless children and adults in the US could be substantially higher than estimated in the above studies.

Many cities and towns are criminalizing homelessness. They increasingly are making it illegal to sit or lie in public places for too long, camp in parks, sleep in cars and feed homeless people. About 44 percent of homeless people are employed, but do not earn enough to pay rent and buy food and other necessities.[77] Putting homeless people in jail and giving them criminal records reduces their ability to find jobs or retain existing ones. It often is less expensive and more beneficial to help homeless people, for example by providing affordable housing, than to incarcerate them and incur other criminal enforcement expenses. This once again reflects growing division and hatred in society. As discussed in the Crime section, we often appear to be unwilling to spend relatively small amounts to help people. But we spend much more to punish.

Criminalizing homelessness violates international human rights treaties. The UN Committee on Human Rights has condemned this practice in the US. Leaders in many other countries find it incomprehensible that we criminalize homelessness.[78] We implement economic and political systems that inevitably will produce large and growing numbers of homeless people. We reduce or eliminate social welfare programs that prevent homelessness. And then we make homelessness illegal. It seems insane. It is a sign of an angry, ignorant, myopic and declining society. It seems as if we are telling homeless people to go off into the woods and die. What do we expect them to do? Many homeless people are mentally ill. We are punishing and abandoning the most severe casualties of our flawed systems, while we lavish wealthy citizens with trillions of dollars of corporate welfare.

Helping average citizens, instead of giving corporate welfare to wealthy citizens, is the obviously superior strategy. It will increase demand for products and services, strengthen the economy, improve quality of life for the vast majority of citizens, and strongly position the US for long-term prosperity. Helping all citizens would reduce inequality and poverty. But it also might inhibit growth of shareholder returns in the short-term. As a result, our flawed systems and business-controlled politicians degrade the lives of the vast majority of citizens so that a small group of wealthy people can get continuously wealthier.

Public Deception

Public deception is a main cause of the degradation of society. In some ways, it is the main cause. As discussed in Chapter Seven, the people are the most powerful force in society. They would not allow a small group of wealthy citizens to essentially steal their wealth and power unless they were deceived. This book extensively discusses how citizens are misled and how they can overcome this deception. The main deception strategy is to divide citizens into debating, acrimonious factions. Radical media strongly promotes this division by providing a nearly nonstop invective about how the other side (liberals or conservatives) is destroying society. This drives ongoing anger, hatred and fear in society.

The business and media manufactured war between conservatives and liberals is working. Several studies have shown that society is becoming more divided along ideological lines. To illustrate, 50 percent of Republicans and 35 percent of Democrats say that it is important to live in a place where most people have similar political views. About 63 percent of conservatives and 49 percent of liberals say that most of their friends share the same worldviews. About 36 percent of Republicans and

27 percent of Democrats think the opposing party is a threat to the nation's well-being.[79] Further indicating that division and distrust is growing in the US, the belief that most people can be trusted dropped from 77 percent in the 1960s to 37 percent in the 2000s.[80]

The US Congress is more divided, acrimonious and unproductive that at any time in the past 150 years. Fewer laws were passed in 2012 than in any Congress since 1861.[81] The issue of division and gridlock in Congress is complex and deceptive. It appears that there are vast ideological divides between Republicans and Democrats. These differing worldviews supposedly make it difficult for the two parties to work together and pass legislation.

But as discussed in Chapter Seven, the idea that Republicans and Democrats have large ideological divides mostly is an illusion or deception. Politicians from both parties often work aggressively to benefit the wealthy citizens and corporations who paid to put them in office. The actual ideology or philosophy being implemented by both parties largely is to increase the wealth of a small group of already wealthy citizens. Republicans usually are more honest than Democrats about the actual strategy being implemented. They often make it clear that they believe that helping large companies and wealthy business owners is the best way to maximize the well-being of society. Democrats largely implement the same strategy because, like Republicans, most of their campaign funding comes from wealthy citizens and large corporations. But Democrats generally are not as forthcoming about this being their primary agenda. Instead, they frequently speak about helping average citizens, but then duplicitously take actions that subvert these goals.

Several studies have shown that senators and representatives from both parties consistently do what wealthy campaign donors want and ignore the requests and needs of lower income constituents (the obvious and expected outcome). For example, one study of five Congresses found that Senators consistently supported the needs and requests of wealthy citizens. The needs of lower income citizens appeared to have no impact on senators' voting. The tendency to support wealthy citizens was even stronger when Democrats controlled the Senate.[82]

A study by Princeton and Northwestern Universities found similar results. Senators and representatives from both major political parties respond to the policy demands of wealthy citizens and large corporations (i.e. those who spend the most on lobbying and campaign finance). The preferences of average citizens appeared to have a near-zero, statistically insignificant impact on public policy. The study analyzed data from 1981 to 2002. Since then, Citizens Divided and other pro-business Supreme Court decisions have given wealthy citizens even greater control of government. As a result, the miniscule impact that the requests of average citizens had on the voting of Republican and Democratic politicians probably has gotten even smaller.[83]

Several polls have found that over 60 percent of citizens support protecting Social Security and Medicare, ending corporate welfare, protecting worker rights, raising wages, reducing military spending, getting money out of politics, and requiring wealthy citizens and corporations to pay fair tax rates that reflect the large benefits they receive from society. But senators and representatives from both parties frequently vote against these and other issues that are widely supported by citizens in both parties.[84]

To illustrate, 88 percent of citizens oppose cuts to Social Security and Medicare. About 75 percent of Republicans and 91 percent of Democrats said that they would be willing to pay more taxes to support Social Security. About 62 percent of Republicans and 84 percent of Democrats said that Social Security benefits should be increased. But many Republican and Democratic politicians are supporting cuts to these and other social welfare programs.[85]

This shows that the ideological divide largely is an illusion. When we allow politicians to indirectly accept large amounts of money from wealthy citizens and corporations, they become the political servants of these people and companies. Democratic and Republican politicians mainly do what they are paid to do – help wealthy campaign donors.

While the ideological divide largely is an illusion, it is essential for maintaining the status quo of corporate welfare and business control of government. Continuing to take the people's wealth and power requires that citizens' attention be turned away from the real causes of their increasingly difficult lives. Warring political parties create convenient false enemies. Citizens are deceived into disliking or hating their fellow citizens in the other political party. They are misled into focusing on a false enemy and ignoring the real enemies (ultimately flawed ideas and systems).

As noted, Republican politicians often are more honest than Democrats. They are more likely to disclose that their primary focus is on helping corporations and wealthy citizens. They frequently argue that this is the best way to help the economy and society. But this honesty is creating a problem for the Republican Party. Honestly admitting that they are the big business party alienates many low and middle-income citizens, especially minority citizens. This does not bode well for the Republican Party as the percentage of white citizens in the US population continues to decline. (About **88** percent of Republican voters in the 2012 presidential election were white.[86])

To offset unfavorable demographics, many Republican politicians have promoted actions that primarily suppress Democratic votes. To illustrate, for many years, Republicans frequently have promoted voter roll purges, made online and other voter registration more difficult, aggressively promoted voter ID laws, and taken other actions that mainly suppress minority and Democratic votes. The justification given for these actions usually is to prevent voter fraud (i.e. the impersonation of a voter by another person). But this is deceptive. As discussed in the Government and Elections section, voter fraud is extremely rare. There is no evidence of systemic voter fraud anywhere in the US.[87] Federal courts have found that voter fraud is virtually non-existent.[88]

Common sense shows that voter fraud is unlikely. As discussed in the Elections section, people presumably only would engage in voter fraud and risk criminal prosecution if they believed it would influence election results. Individuals or small groups voting fraudulently usually would have little or no impact on elections, especially at the state level. Voter fraud generally only could be effective through the coordinated efforts of many people. It is highly unlikely that large, coordinated voter fraud efforts would go undetected. Rather than preventing voter fraud, it appears that Republicans often are using the voter fraud excuse to perpetuate election fraud (i.e. preventing people from voting or manipulating elections in other ways). If voter identification, voter registration and other restrictive voting requirements suppressed mainly

Republican votes, Republican politicians obviously would not be aggressively promoting them.

As discussed in the Elections section, the US has near the lowest voter turnout in the world. About 93 million people (43 percent of eligible voters) did not vote in the 2012 elections.[89] We should be taking actions that greatly increase voter participation, rather than aggressively working to reduce our already near worst in the world performance. But increasing voter participation would favor Democrats, mainly because they often are more successful at deceiving average citizens into believing that their primary focus is on serving average citizens, rather than wealthy campaign donors.

Allowing either party to get too powerful would threaten ever-increasing shareholder returns. If the Republican or Democratic Party substantially dominated government, the focus on the controversy or beating the other side would be greatly reduced. As citizens in the dominant party no longer had to focus on their false enemy (the other party) because it was so weak, they might focus more on real enemies. Perpetuating the status quo requires that the two parties remain about equal. This maintains bitter rivalries and even hatred in society. Dividing and disempowering the people enables wealthy citizens to continue stealing the people's wealth and power.

Republicans are more honest than Democrats about their strong focus on helping wealthy citizens. But Republicans cannot be completely honest. If Republicans acknowledged that they are almost completely focused on helping wealthy campaign donors get continuously wealthier (as Democrats are), only wealthy citizens would vote Republican. Republicans more obviously oppose Social Security, Medicare and other social welfare programs that benefit the vast majority of average citizens. As a result, they often must employ different deceptions than Democrats to get votes. The Democratic deception strategy is simpler and more straightforward. Democratic politicians often claim that they will protect the environment, labor, children, Social Security, Medicare and other social welfare programs. Then they frequently vote to weaken these groups and programs.

Republicans have a more difficult public deception job. It is difficult for Republicans to argue that they support average citizens when they so vigorously and obviously attack Social Security, Medicare and other programs that hugely benefit average citizens, while strongly supporting low taxes and other corporate welfare for wealthy citizens and corporations. As a result, Republicans often must employ more sophisticated public deceptions. This frequently involves fomenting anger and hatred for Democrats and liberals. When people are whipped up into an emotional frenzy, it is much easier to suppress rational thought. Republican citizens can be tricked into not focusing on how Republicans strongly support wealthy citizens and take actions that harm average citizens. Instead, the focus becomes defeating the evil liberals who are destroying society.

Religious, racist, entitlement and poverty deceptions frequently are used to turn Republican citizens against Democrats and prevent them from seeing the true big business focus of the Republican Party. In the religious area, Republicans often use abortion, same-sex marriage and other religious issues to mislead citizens into voting against their self-interests. To illustrate, 9 of the 10 poorest states are in the South. These states mostly are controlled by Republicans. Poor Southern states frequently reject Medicaid expansion, oppose early education expansion, pass anti-union laws, cut food assistance programs and take many other actions that make life more difficult for middle and low-income citizens. At the same time, they implement generous corporate tax breaks and other corporate welfare programs. This degradation of average citizens is a main reason why these states are so poor.[90]

Southern states also generally are highly religious, compared to other states. Republican politicians often utilize this strong religious inclination to mislead citizens into voting against their best interests. The Republican strategy mainly is to help wealthy citizens get continuously wealthier by removing labor, environmental and any other protections that interfere with ever-increasing shareholder returns. This strategy is emphasized to wealthy campaign donors. But it usually would not work with average citizens.

Instead, to hide their primary emphasis on helping wealthy citizens, Republicans often emphasize religious issues. When devout, good religious citizens vote against abortion and same-sex marriage, for example, they also often are supporting programs that will make their lives substantially more difficult, stressful and painful. Citizens are tricked into placing what unknown adults are doing in the privacy of their bedrooms ahead of being able to feed their children and live a reasonable quality of life.

To illustrate, Alabama and Mississippi are the two most religious states in the country (in terms of the percentage of citizens who say that religion is very important in their lives – about 75 percent). More than 30 percent of the children in these states live in extreme poverty.[91] This is unchristian. Ensuring that children do not go hungry and families can meet basic needs is vastly more important than legislating how women use their bodies or which adults are allowed to marry. Republican politicians may or may not care about abortion and same-sex marriage. But this is not what they are paid to care about. They mostly are paid (i.e. bribed) to protect the financial interests of wealthy campaign donors. They often use religion to essentially steal wealth from good, religious average citizens and transfer it to their wealthy masters.

In addition to religion, racism also is used to mislead Republican citizens. As discussed in the Crime section, radical media and Republican politicians often state or imply that social welfare recipients mainly are lazy, immoral African American and Hispanic people who want to live off of hard-working white citizens. This breeds anger and hatred among whites at people who they incorrectly believe are responsible for their increasingly difficult lives. This makes it much easier to cut social welfare programs. White citizens are misled into believing that cutting social welfare reduces the unfair theft of their wealth by lazy people of color.

This deception truly is tragic. Two-thirds of people using social welfare programs are white.[92] In addition, nearly all of the people on social welfare programs are using them legitimately. As discussed, many people cannot find jobs in our shareholder-focused economy, regardless of how long or hard they look. Also, the distinction between middle-class and poor is rapidly declining. Hard-working citizens often face declining wages, rising expenses and little or no job security. Social welfare programs strongly benefit hard-working white and other citizens who are struggling to make ends meet. Racist characterizations of social welfare recipients frequently mislead Republican citizens into voting to reduce social welfare. This often makes their lives more difficult, but enables

Republican politicians to fulfill their primary goal – transferring more public wealth to wealthy campaign donors.

Entitlement deceptions also are used to mislead Republican citizens. Social Security, Medicare and other social welfare programs often are characterized as entitlement programs. The term entitlement frequently is used in a derogatory way. It implies that lazy people feel entitled to something that they do not deserve or did not earn. This negative characterization of social welfare programs makes it easier to mislead citizens into supporting cuts to social welfare programs and increasing corporate welfare. But this is a grossly unfair and inaccurate characterization of social welfare programs. Social Security and Medicare, for example, are public insurance programs that people pay for through taxes over the course of their careers. Characterizing Social Security and Medicare as benefits that people do not deserve or did not earn would be like putting money in a savings account throughout one's career. Then when people seek to withdraw the money during retirement, the bank manager says, what makes you think that you deserve the funds in this account?

We the People formed the US in part because we each could achieve far more successful lives by working together and pooling our wealth and power. As discussed in the Misleading the Public section, each citizen cannot afford to buy their own aircraft carrier for self-defense. Using public wealth to ensure that basic needs are met is an appropriate use of public funds in a civilized society. People have a right to this protection in a prosperous and wealthy country, such as the US. In this sense, average citizens are entitled to Social Security, Medicare and other social welfare programs.

The true entitlement unfairness and deception relates to corporate welfare, not social welfare. Our flawed systems imply that wealthy citizens should not have to pay for the resources and services that enabled them to become wealthy or be held responsible for negative impacts that they impose on society. Wealthy citizens do not deserve corporate welfare. They have not earned it. They are not entitled to it. Flawed systems compel wealthy citizens and corporations to essentially steal trillions of dollars of corporate welfare from average citizens every year. Corporate welfare is the true entitlement crisis that must be resolved.

Poverty deceptions are among the most tragic and reprehensible. Many Republican politicians and conservative groups argue that poor people in the US have better lives than poor people in India and China, for example. Therefore, people in the US should not complain. The ignorance and heartlessness of this position is stunning. Costs of living in developing countries usually are far lower than in the US. Therefore, the difference in quality of life often is lower than argued by Republican politicians. But the major deception is the implication that it is acceptable for people to be struggling and suffering in this wealthy country because people struggle and suffer in much poorer countries.

We could easily end poverty and hunger in the US. The simple solution is to end welfare for wealthy people. But Republican (and Democratic) politicians are not paid by wealthy citizens to do this. Instead, they seem to often argue that poor people should accept their lot in life and tolerate the ongoing theft of their wealth and power.

Another poverty deception that is used to cut social welfare and increase corporate welfare involves claiming that welfare is a disincentive for work. This implies that people on social welfare programs are lazy. They could work. But they are taking advantage of social welfare and choosing not to work. Republicans sometimes paternalistically (and ignorantly) use a tough love approach to social welfare. They effectively are saying to poor people, we are helping you by taking away your social welfare benefits. It might be hard for you at first. But it will force you to do the right thing and become a better person. You will thank me later for being tough on you now. This further reflects extreme ignorance and heartlessness. The conservative politicians and media personalities who make this argument fail to see reality.

For example, two-thirds of people using food stamps are children, elderly or disabled.[93] The vast majority of the remainder are legitimately unemployed or under-employed. Probably only a tiny fraction of people using food stamps and other social welfare programs are using them fraudulently or inappropriately. Our shareholder-focused economy creates vast and unnecessary unemployment. There are far more unemployed people who are willing to work than there are available jobs.

The ignorant fools who promote the tough love approach to social welfare imply that eight-year-old children, 88-year-old adults and quadriplegic people should get jobs if they wish to avoid going hungry. They further imply that working age adults who are willing to work, but cannot find jobs, should wave a magic wand and create jobs out of thin air. The obvious solution is to use the public wealth to meet basic needs and minimize suffering in the US, instead of giving trillions of dollars of public wealth to wealthy campaign donors. But Republican and Democratic politicians are not paid to promote the general welfare. They are paid to promote corporate welfare.

As noted, Republicans have a more difficult public deception challenge. It is difficult to argue that they are helping average citizens because they take so many actions that harm average citizens. As discussed in the Misleading the Public section, the Rule of Dumb deception technique often is used to distract citizens from these harmful actions. Rule of dumb involves using anger, rudeness or condescension to compel people to blindly believe myopic or irrational ideas. In an angry and irrational manner, Republican politicians and radical media figures often use religious, racist or other irrational arguments to mislead Republican citizens into voting against their best interests.

The point here is not to promote the Democratic or Republican Party. Both parties are heavily focused on taking trillions of dollars of wealth from average citizens and transferring it to wealthy campaign donors. A main suggestion of this book is to greatly weaken the political party system and implement the government developed by our Founders. The two-party system misleads citizens into thinking that they have a choice between two competing ideologies. But they do not. There essentially is only one ideology functioning in the US – putting shareholder returns and economic growth before all else.

An excellent article by Chris Hedges, called *Totalitarianism, American Style*, explains how business influence of government has compelled the Democratic Party to adopt essentially the same strategies as the Republicans.[94] In the 1990s, under a Democratic President, Democrats implemented a more conservative strategy than previous Republicans in many ways. They expanded free trade, cut welfare for low-income citizens, deregulated the financial sector and greatly increased incarceration. As Chris Hedges points out, the Democratic Party transformed into the Republican Party. This forced the Republican Party to move to the extreme right.

The conservative strategies implemented in the 1990s by a Democratic President were continued in the 2000s by a Republican President and largely were continued by President Obama. Under his administration, civil rights were severely repressed and energy exploration was substantially increased. The Republicans and Democrats essentially are doing the same things (i.e. whatever large corporations and wealthy campaign donors tell them to do).

To illustrate, Republicans often deny climate change, and then do nothing about it. Democrats frequently acknowledge the reality of climate change, but then promote nonbinding agreements that have little or no impact (i.e. they essentially do nothing, like Republicans).[95] Differences between the two parties largely are an illusion. Democrats often pretend to protect the environment and society, but then protect wealthy campaign donors instead. As noted, Republicans frequently attempt to distract citizens from their focus on helping wealthy campaign donors by using right-wing religious, racist and other irrational arguments.

The Democratic Party used to protect average citizens. From the 1930s to 1970s, the party promoted extensive, major environmental and social protection legislation. But no major environmental and social protections have been implemented since the 1970s.[96] President Obama's Affordable Care Act prevented thousands of deaths by providing health insurance to uninsured citizens. But the act is a huge giveaway to the healthcare sector. It often will increase healthcare company revenues and profits, but do little to reduce extremely high healthcare costs. We are not emulating the vastly more effective and less expensive healthcare approaches of every other developed country, largely because this would reduce the shareholder returns of wealthy campaign donors.

Both the Democratic and Republican parties have become the big business parties. This must end. Citizens should have the option to vote for candidates who will put citizens first and uphold the Constitution. But the political party system takes this option away. Regardless of which party citizens vote for, they are voting to put the financial interests of wealthy citizens ahead of the survival and other interests of the vast majority of citizens. (The We the People section below discusses providing a voting option that truly is focused on benefiting all citizens, not just wealthy citizens.)

Differing ideologies exist in the US for public deception purposes. But when focusing on what actually is happening in reality, it becomes clear that one ideology or strategy overwhelmingly dominates everything else. This is strongly indicated by the fact that income for the small group of wealthy citizens who give large amounts of money to politicians has risen rapidly since the 1980s, while life became more difficult for nearly all other citizens, regardless of which party was in power.

Retirement Crisis

The looming retirement crisis in the US provides one of the best examples of how public deception degrades society. Since the 1980s, corporate welfare and business control of government have made life more difficult for the large majority of US citizens, including elderly citizens. The situation for elderly citizens is poised to get much worse over the next 20 years as a growing number of people retire and face rising expenses and declining retirement benefits. The percentage of the US population over 65 years old is projected to increase from 14 percent in 2013 to 21 percent in 2035.[97]

A study of US households aged 25 to 64 found that people are not saving nearly enough for retirement. Ninety-two percent of working households do not meet conservative retirement savings targets for their age and income. The US retirement savings deficit is between $7-14 trillion.[98] Two-thirds of working citizens will not be able to maintain their standard of living when they retire. Many will be forced to live at poverty or near poverty levels.[99] The average Social Security benefit is about $1,300 per month. For one-third of senior citizens, Social Security is their only income. For another third, Social Security represents over half of income.[100]

As noted, beginning in the early 1980s, social welfare programs often were cut while corporate welfare was increased. In 1983, to reduce Social Security costs, the age at which citizens received full Social Security benefits was raised from 65 to 67. Social Security, public pensions and several other social welfare programs are tied to the CPI, which substantially undercounts actual inflation. Social Security benefits have risen more slowly than the rate of inflation. As a result, inflation adjusted benefits have declined by 24 percent since 1983.[101] The large majority of elderly citizens have been forced to endure a steadily declining quality of life since the 1980s so that wealthy citizens could get continuously wealthier.

As discussed in the Finance and Capital Markets section, some wealthy citizens and politicians paid by them are attempting to mislead citizens into believing that the Social Security program is in crisis and will hurt the economy to a growing degree going forward. As a result, they often suggest that Social Security should be reformed, for example, by privatizing it and putting retirement funds into 401(k) type accounts. This would provide huge benefits, fees and growth opportunities for the financial community. But it would be a disaster and tragedy for elderly citizens and society in general.

Social Security is one of the most successful government programs in US history. As noted, the elderly poverty rate would be about five times higher without it. Contrary to financial community deceptions, the Social Security program is stable and well funded. It has a $2.5 trillion surplus. The program can meet all needs through 2033. Beyond that, it will be solvent through 2084 with minor changes of about 0.3 percent of GDP. Social Security provides guaranteed benefits. Senior citizens do not have to worry that they will receive lower or no benefits if the stock market declines. In addition, Social Security is extremely efficient. Administrative costs are less than one percent. Over 99 percent of the funds are paid out as benefits.[102]

To get a sense of the degradation that would be caused by privatizing Social Security, one could consider the degradation that was caused by converting defined benefit to defined contribution pensions. Under defined benefit plans, employees who had worked for many years received a secure retirement. Their guaranteed retirement income did not fluctuate based on the stock market or other factors. With defined benefit plans, companies assume the risk of providing guaranteed retirement income. This substantially limited the ability to provide ever-increasing shareholder returns. A 1981 tax ruling greatly facilitated defined contribution pension plans. Under this approach, retirement risk is transferred from companies to employees. It also often greatly reduces costs and funding requirements. Shifting retirement costs and risks to employees makes it much easier to provide ever-increasing shareholder returns.

With defined contribution plans, such as IRA and 401(k) plans, employees often had to develop financial management skills or rely on financial advisors. Their ability to be comfortable or meet basic needs in retirement frequently was dependent on capital market growth. This indicates perhaps the greatest business benefit of defined contribution plans. These plans caused millions of citizens to invest retirement savings in the capital markets. This drove substantial capital market growth and financial community fees.

The top 10 percent of society owns about 91 percent of US stocks and mutual funds. Compelling average citizens to put retirement savings in the capital markets provided substantial downside protection for wealthy investors. Previously, wealthy investors often were required to bear the losses of risky investments. However, average citizens frequently cannot afford to lose retirement savings. To protect the approximately 9 percent of the stock market that is owned by the bottom 90 percent of society, corrupted politicians often bailed out companies and provided other types of downside protection.

As discussed, stock market growth frequently is based on speculation, extracting wealth from employees and other actions that degrade society. From the perspective of wealthy citizens, converting defined benefit to defined contribution pension plans was a stroke of genius. By making retirement security dependent on stock market growth, average citizens became cheerleaders for a system that frequently impoverishes average citizens. The need to protect the retirement security of average citizens often compelled politicians to provide downside protection for wealthy speculators.

Defined contribution pension plans provide huge fees to the financial community. One study found that a two-earner, medium income household would pay $150,000 in 401(k) fees over their lifetimes.[103] Another study assessed the costs of putting $1,000 per year for 30 years into a so-called no fee 401(k) fund, and then holding the accumulated sum for another 20 years. At an industry average fee of 1.3 percent, 40 percent of the earnings on the investment in the 'no-fee' fund would be taken as fees.

Loopholes in current regulations do not require financial advisors to abide by the fiduciary standard in many cases. In other words, financial advisors usually are not required to put their clients' interests ahead of their own. Financial advisors can put clients' money in high risk, high fee funds that might not be appropriate for clients. Advisors often are not required to disclose commissions and other conflicts of interest to clients. New regulations have been proposed that would require financial advisors to put client interests ahead of their own. Financial institutions have aggressively opposed abiding by the fiduciary standard. By giving money to politicians and influencing government in other ways, they have been able to block regulations that protect clients, but limit ever-increasing shareholder returns.[104]

Average citizens usually do not have the time or interest needed to become investment experts. They often rely on financial advisors. Elderly people frequently experience cognitive impairment or dementia. They are dependent on financial advisors. Not requiring financial advisors to put the well-being of clients ahead of their own financial well-being is grossly wrong.

Another example of opposing regulations that protect clients and citizens, but limit shareholder returns, involves post-2008 financial regulations. Prior to the 2008 collapse, financial institutions frequently sold risky loan products to unsophisticated investors, charged high fees and took advantage of citizens in other ways. To limit this abuse, the Consumer Finance Protection Bureau and other financial regulations were established after the 2008 crash. The financial community and conservative groups vigorously opposed these consumer protection regulations. They spent over $1.3 billion on lobbying and other government influence activities to block them.[105] While they failed to block the regulations, the financial community and conservative groups are working aggressively to repeal post-2008 financial sector regulations. Opposing regulations that protect average citizens but threaten ever-increasing shareholder returns once again shows the grossly flawed, suicidal nature of our economic and political systems.

Pushing to privatize Social Security also shows the suicidal nature of our systems. Suggesting that citizens should give up guaranteed retirement benefits, base their retirement security on wealthy people getting continuously wealthier (i.e. the capital markets going up), and putting retirement savings in high fee, often high risk products is insane. But the goal of billionaires and political puppets pushing Social Security privatization is not to help elderly citizens. It is to help wealthy citizens get continuously wealthier.

The solution to Social Security is not to shrink or privatize the program. It is to expand it. Social Security costs about $900 billion per year. As noted, wealthy citizens avoid as much as $3 trillion in taxes per year. This is not even the largest form of corporate welfare. As discussed in the Corporate Welfare section, externalized negative environmental and social impacts probably are. Reducing corporate welfare could fund a doubling of Social Security benefits. In addition, benefits should be increased at the actual rate of inflation and the full-benefit retirement age should be lowered to 62. This is what true Social Security reform can and should look like. It would provide vast stability and benefits to society. It would greatly alleviate poverty, stimulate the economy, and improve the quality of life of many average citizens, not just elderly citizens (partly because working citizens would face less pressure to support their retired parents). Increasing Social Security is an appropriate use of the public wealth. Giving trillions of dollars per year to wealthy citizens is not.

Another action needed to raise Social Security benefits and ensure that the program remains well-funded is to raise or eliminate the cap on income subject to the Social Security payroll tax. Currently, income only is taxed up to $118,500 per year. This means that someone who makes $1 billion per year pays the same as someone earning $118,500. This is another example of wealthy citizens not paying the full cost for benefits derived from society. As discussed in the Public Wealth section below, no one gets wealthy on their own. People need employees, customers, infrastructure, and legal and other government services to become wealthy. About 90 percent of Democrats and 73 percent of Republicans support raising the cap on Social Security taxes.[106] But in spite of overwhelming public support for expanding Social Security, many politicians who accept large amounts of money from wealthy citizens and corporations are advocating cutting benefits or privatizing the program.

Defined contribution pension plans give the financial community great power over society. Average citizens with 401(k) and other plans become dependent on the capital markets and financial community for retirement security. The goal of the financial community is to maximize the well-being of the financial community, not society. They extract huge fees from citizens and fight efforts to put client well-being ahead of their own. It might be appropriate for wealthy citizens to utilize the financial community to manage retirement and other assets. But the retirement security of average citizen should not be dependent on the financial sector. Average citizens would be better off putting their wealth, for example through taxes and savings, in government programs that provide guaranteed benefits and have vastly lower fees.

Significantly expanding Social Security would substantially benefit corporations. Reducing the need to provide retirement funding would make US companies more competitive globally. It also would greatly facilitate capitalism. Basing retirement security on stock market growth often compels taxpayers to cover the downside of business and investing. This is socialism. Greatly reducing citizens' dependence on corporations for retirement security would substantially lower pressure to bail out companies. Businesses would be required to succeed or fail on their own, without taxpayer subsidies. This would be true capitalism.

Also, substantially increasing Social Security would vastly improve the efficiency and effectiveness of the retirement system. As noted, Social Security administrative costs are less than one percent. With commissions, fees and other costs, private sector retirement plans, such as 401(k)s, cannot come close to matching the low cost and high efficiency of Social Security. They are orders of magnitude more expensive and less efficient. Social Security channels virtually all retirement funds to citizens. As shown with 40 percent fees on 'no-fee' 401(k) funds, private sector retirement funds channel a very large percentage of funds to the financial community.

Funding shortfalls in state public pensions illustrates public deception in the retirement area. The 2008 financial collapse contributed to states' pension fund assets being about $1.4 trillion less than needed to pay retirement benefits over the next 30 years. This shortfall is less than 0.2 percent of projected gross state product over the same period.[107] Many politicians are arguing that pension benefits should be reduced. These positions involve extensive deception and dishonesty. To support pension cuts, politicians and radical media figures, frequently state or imply that retired public workers are greedy and do not deserve the benefits that they were promised.

This is truly tragic. It shows how flawed systems often compel good people to do bad things. State and other public employees often sacrificed higher private sector wages in return for guaranteed retirement security. These people worked hard and did their jobs for decades. They enabled states and communities to function. Promises made to these hard-working public servants essentially are sacred. We have an obligation to fulfill them.

The state pension shortfall is about $46 billion per year. Corporate tax loopholes cost states about $40 billion per year. In addition, states, cities and towns provide about $80 billion per year in subsidies to corporations.[108] These two types of corporate welfare are nearly three times higher than the annual state pension shortfall. Rather than reducing corporate welfare and fulfilling their sacred obligation to retired public employees, business-influenced politicians are disparaging public employees and often forcing them to accept lower retirement benefits than they were promised. This is another abomination resulting from government corruption. Political puppets will not bite the hand that feeds them by lowering corporate welfare. Instead, they force retired public servants to suffer a reduced quality of life.

The 2015 federal budget further illustrates government actions that benefit wealthy campaign donors, but harm retired workers. The budget act states that pension funds with more than one employer, such as union pension funds, can be scaled back to pay financial sector creditors. The government's Pension Benefit Guarantee Corporation was established to protect pension benefits. But the 2015 budget act circumvents this and allows benefits to be cut.[109]

Many pensions are underfunded, in large part because employers often were not required to put enough money in to pay benefits. Instead, pension funds attempted to accumulate necessary assets through investing. But as discussed above with individual investors, the financial institutions that managed pension funds were not required to put the interests of pension funds ahead of their own (i.e. abide by the fiduciary standard). Pension funds often were managed in ways that provided huge fees and profits to financial institutions, but losses or little growth to the funds. To illustrate how financial institutions sometimes benefited themselves at the expense of pension funds, one large financial institution regularly placed opposing bets. On a given day, one bet might be that a stock or bond would go up, and the other bet would be that it would go down. At the end of the day, the winning bet was put in the financial institution's account, while the losing bet went into the pension fund account.[110]

The focus on benefiting wealthy campaign donors is illustrated by another provision of the 2015 budget act. Under the act, taxpayers often essentially are required to guarantee bank trades in derivatives. As discussed in the Finance and Capital Markets section, derivatives are complex, often risky financial instruments. Speculation in derivatives was a main cause of the 2008 financial collapse and potentially $6-12 trillion bank bailouts. Derivatives often have two sides, a winner and a loser. The budget act essentially says that taxpayers frequently will cover the downside if banks lose on derivative trades.[111]

This once again illustrates the tragic and suicidal nature of our flawed systems. Under the budget act, taxpayers often will bail out wealthy speculators who lose money on risky investments. But we will not bail out pensions to ensure that retired workers receive the benefits they were promised. This of course is not surprising. It is the expected outcome of our flawed systems. Many Republican and Democratic politicians supported the budget. They voted to bail out the wealthy speculators who paid to put them in office. But they are not protecting retired citizens who worked hard to get a secure retirement, but often will not receive it due to business control of government.

As discussed in the Advertising, Media and Culture section, treatment of the elderly reflects a society's level of wisdom and maturity. The declining quality of life for elderly citizens in the US is a tragedy. It shows the increasingly immature, divisive and selfish nature of US society. Declining Social Security benefits, pensions and social welfare programs are making it difficult or impossible for millions of elderly citizens to survive and meet basic needs.

To survive, a growing number of senior citizens have essentially been forced to become elderly migrant workers. They often live in cramped recreational vehicles (RVs) and travel around the country seeking temporary or seasonal work. The need to survive forces them to work difficult jobs, such as cleaning toilets at campgrounds, walking miles in warehouses to fill orders, or harvesting crops. They frequently work 12-

hour days outdoors in hot or cold weather. Elderly migrant workers often take pain medication to keep going. Sometimes their RVs become coffins.[112]

The treatment of elderly citizens in this country is revolting. How can we look at ourselves in the mirror? We have vastly more wealth than is needed to ensure that every elderly citizen lives a comfortable and dignified retirement. The so-called retirement crisis at the federal and state levels is a deception. There is no retirement crisis. We have a corporate welfare crisis. Money is being stolen from retired citizens who worked hard and earned a secure retirement so that wealthy citizens can get continuously wealthier.

The retirement/corporate welfare crisis in the US once again shows the destructive nature of our flawed systems. Forty to sixty years ago, wealthy investors often took high risks and sometimes earned high returns. Hard working average citizens frequently earned wages that provided a decent standard of living and received a secure retirement. In other words, they pursued a lower risk lifestyle and received lower returns. But over time, the need to provide ever-increasing shareholder return pushes everything else aside, including living wages and retirement security. Today, wealthy investors often earn even higher returns, while much of the risk has been shifted to employees and other average citizens. To provide higher returns, employees often are forced to accept lower wages, little or no job security, and greatly reduced retirement security. This is another tragic, grossly unfair and yet inevitable result of our flawed systems. Ending disrespect for elderly citizens is another major reason why our flawed systems must be improved and made fair and sustainable.

Global Degradation

The US is a world leader in putting economic growth and shareholder returns before all else, and in suffering the inevitable environmental and social degradation that results from this myopic approach. Similar approaches are being implemented in many other countries. They also are experiencing inevitable degradation. As noted, plutocracy has been rising in the US as business control of government increased since the 1980s. Increased control of government by a small group of wealthy citizens is occurring in many other developed and developing countries, including Thailand, Ukraine and Egypt.[113]

Flawed systems frequently require that the large majority of citizens sacrifice so that a small group for wealthy citizens can get wealthier. As discussed in the Privacy section, as wealthy citizens in the US essentially steal the people's wealth and power, business-controlled government is protecting the status quo by more severely suppressing dissent. It often is being criminalized and excessive police force is being used to suppress peaceful protests. As plutocracy increases around the world, the tendency to criminalize and severely suppress dissent also is increasing.[114] Suppression of dissent is high in Russia and China. It also is growing in countries that formally allowed more peaceful protests and dissent. Stealing the people's wealth and power and then using frequently violent government force to suppress opposition to this theft is severely degrading society around the world.

As occurs in the US, rising plutocracy in other countries is producing growing inequality. As wealthy citizens gained control of government, they implemented tax and other policies that transferred wealth from low and middle-income citizens to wealthy citizens. To illustrate, an Oxfam report on global inequality found that tax rates for wealthy citizens have fallen since the late 1970s in 29 of 30 countries for which data was available.[115] In addition, business-controlled governments implemented tax loopholes that enabled wealthy citizens to avoid paying taxes. It is estimated that the wealthiest individuals and companies around the world are hiding $21 trillion in tax havens, and thereby avoiding paying taxes on the funds.[116] The large majority of stimulus efforts around the world following the 2008 recession were focused on helping wealthy people. They did little to help average citizens.[117]

Global wealth doubled from 2000 to 2012. But much of this wealth growth was due to speculation, rather than job creation and other actions that benefit average citizens. As in the US, much of the global wealth growth over the past 10 years went to already wealthy citizens.[118] As a result, inequality has been rising around the world. From 1980 to 2012, the top one percent of society increased their share of income in 24 of 26 countries for which data was available. As a result, nearly half of the world's wealth is owned by the top one percent of society. The world's 85 wealthiest individuals have the same wealth as the bottom half of the world's population (i.e. over 3.5 billion people).[119]

As occurs in the US, implementing economic policies that are focused on helping wealthy citizens instead of all citizens is degrading job quality and often job availability. Global unemployment has risen since the 2008 recession and is projected to continue rising. The problem is particularly severe among young people. Global youth unemployment (age 15 to 24) is three times higher than adult unemployment. It is especially high in the Middle East, North Africa and Latin America.[120] High levels of youth unemployment cause rising frustration and anger. This contributes to social unrest, violent protests and political upheaval. The World Economic Forum found that high and rising global inequality and resulting social unrest represent the greatest threats to the global economy over the next 10 years.[121]

In the US prior to 1980, increased prosperity and economic growth widely benefited many citizens. But as business increased control of government, prosperity was concentrated at the top of society, while quality of life for the vast majority of citizens declined. The same degradation is occurring around the world. A study of the US and other countries that represent over half of the world's population and nearly 60 percent of global GDP found that GDP tripled in these countries on average from 1950 to 2003. Social well-being, as measured by the Genuine Progress Indicator (GPI), rose with GDP from 1950 to 1978. But beginning in 1978, social well-being in these countries began to decline while GDP continued to increase.[122] (The GPI measures several aspects of environmental and social performance and well-being.)

This is the obvious and expected outcome (when one adopts a whole system perspective). Myopically focusing on ensuring that a small group of wealthy citizens gets continuously wealthier inevitably will degrade the quality of life for the vast majority of citizens. If we wish to maximize the well-being of all current and future citizens, we must focus measurement and management on this objective. Maintaining flawed, myopic economic and political systems will accelerate environmental and social degradation around the world.

This systemically driven degradation is occurring in parts of Europe. European countries generally have been more proactive than the US in using the public wealth to fairly benefit all citizens. They often compelled wealthy citizens to pay fair tax rates and thereby were able to implement a strong social safety net. However, flawed economic systems like those operating in the US also operate in much of Europe. These systems often seek never-ending growth of the economy and shareholder returns. This creates pressure to reduce taxes for wealthy citizens, increase other types of corporate welfare and reduce social welfare programs.

Rather than compelling wealthy citizens to pay their fair share and reducing other forms of corporate welfare, several European countries are implementing austerity programs. These deceptive programs often are used to facilitate ever-increasing shareholder returns. In Greece, for example, strict austerity programs were implemented between 2008 and 2012. Politicians argued that sacrifice was needed to improve the financial condition of Greece. But a much heavier burden was imposed on average citizens than on wealthy citizens. Low-income citizens lost 86 percent of their income while wealthy citizens lost about 20 percent. Taxes on low-income citizens were increased by 337 percent, while taxes on wealthy citizens only were increased by 9 percent.[123] Rather than cutting corporate welfare and requiring wealthy citizens to pay fair taxes, business-influenced politicians often cut social welfare programs and raised taxes on average citizens.

This is making life increasingly difficult for millions of people in Europe. This in turn often is increasing anger at immigrants, racism and radical politics. As in the US, average European citizens are being deceived into not focusing on the main causes of their increasingly difficult lives. Rather than focusing on business control of government and corporate welfare, they often blame immigrants and low-income people on social welfare programs for their problems. The theft of the people's wealth and power frequently is causing growing division and anger in Europe, as it is in the US. European and other countries will continue to decline until we change our flawed economic and political systems that put the financial well-being of wealthy citizens ahead of all else.

United States Decline

Flawed systems have driven extensive public deception and degradation in the US since the early 1980s. The US has nearly the highest inequality in the world. Regardless of which party was in power, quality of life for the vast majority of citizens has gotten worse since the 1980s, due in large part to flat wages and rising costs. Throughout this time, income for the small group of wealthy citizens who are controlling government rose rapidly. Beyond rising inequality, many other factors illustrate the decline of US society.

An analysis of 132 developed and developing countries found that, while the US has the largest economy, it ranked 70th on health, 69th on ecosystem sustainability, 39th on basic education, 34th on access to water and sanitation, 31st on personal safety and 23rd on Internet access.[124] A study of the 20 advanced democracies in the OECD found that the US had the highest rates of mental illness, child and adult poverty, infant mortality, obesity, personal bankruptcy due to medical expenses, homicide and incarceration. The study also found that the US had the worst gender inequality, child welfare, social mobility and life expectancy.[125] Out of 188 countries in the world, only eight do not provide paid maternity leave, the US and seven small developing countries.[126]

Over 170 studies worldwide have linked income inequality to health outcomes. As inequality rises, health usually declines, in part because high inequality often creates high stress for average citizens. Over the past 25 years, as inequality in the US rose, health performance relative to other developed countries declined. In 1990, the US ranked 20th on life expectancy among 34 industrialized nations. This fell to 27th by 2013.[127]

Several studies also have linked so-called conservative government policies to higher suicide rates. Conservative policies, such as austerity programs being implemented in several European countries, often reduce social welfare programs and transfer more public wealth to already wealthy citizens. This increases stress for average citizens and contributes to rising suicides. For example, as inequality rose in the US from 2004 to 2013, the suicide rate increased by 23 percent.[128] About 40,000 people commit suicide each year in the US. Suicide is the second highest cause of death among 15-34 year olds.[129]

The fact that a Democratic president and Democrat-controlled Senate were in office during much of this time largely is irrelevant. As discussed, both parties are primarily focused on helping wealthy campaign donors to get continuously wealthier. Both parties essentially are implementing conservative (i.e. big business-focused) policies. Since the 1980s, Democratic and Republican politicians frequently have deregulated the financial sector, cut social welfare programs, privatized public services, and cut or maintained low taxes for wealthy citizens. In other words, Democrats and Republicans largely are implementing the same so-called conservative, big business-focused economic approaches.

Virtually all advanced democracies allocate the public wealth more equitably and fairly than the US. Citizens in most other developed countries have a higher quality of life in part because public wealth is used to implement a strong social safety net. In the US, business-controlled Democratic and Republican politicians transferred and continue to transfer trillions of dollars of public wealth to wealthy citizens. This substantially increases stress, illness and suicide among average citizens.

Public deception is a main cause of US decline. Large businesses and their media and political allies have mastered the art of public deception. The first political party in the US, the Federalist Party, was established by bankers and businessmen. It lost appeal with average citizens and disappeared after 25 years. In the late 1800s and early 1900s, large business trusts were abusing labor, unfairly shutting down small businesses and harming society in other ways. Growing public opposition lead to the breaking up of several business trusts.

But improved public deception techniques and control of media have enabled large companies and their wealthy owners to steal trillions of dollars of wealth from average citizens for many years. As noted, the primary deception strategy is to divide the public into debating, acrimonious factions. Another critical deception strategy is turning citizens against government. As discussed in the Suppressing Critical Thinking section, right-wing libertarianism and similar philosophies were used to turn citizens against government. Democratic government is supposed to be the agent of the people and protector of their rights, wealth and power. But Democratic government interferes with wealthy citizens getting continuously wealthier. To reduce this interference, citizens were turned against government. As protections for average citizens were removed, it became much easier to steal the people's wealth and power. Right-wing libertarianism, *Atlas Shrugged* and other irrational dogma often deceived citizens into believing that unemployed people and other citizens using social welfare programs were stealing public wealth. Social welfare recipients often were referred to as parasites and takers.

This is a truly tragic and sad public deception. Citizens were tricked into taking food out of the mouths of hungry children so that the public wealth could be used to essentially buy more mansions, yachts and luxury cars for billionaires. Using the language of right wing libertarianism, the actual parasites and takers in the US are the small group of wealthy citizens who control government and steal trillions of dollars of public wealth from average citizens every year. However, this book does not suggest using this type of derogatory language. The wealthy citizens who essentially steal the people's wealth and power are no better or worse than anyone else. Their intention often is to benefit society. As discussed extensively, the real enemies are not people. They are ideas or low levels of consciousness. Myopic ideas produce flawed systems that frequently compel good, well-intentioned people to take actions that degrade society.

A main system flaw is placing ever-increasing shareholder returns and economic growth before all else. Politicians who accept large amounts of money from businesses frequently remove regulations that restrict ever-increasing shareholder returns. Anti-government rhetoric, dogma and deception often are used to facilitate this shareholder-enhancing deregulation.

An example in Tennessee shows the hypocritical nature of the anti-government deception. Businesses usually promote less regulation because this helps shareholders and facilitates corporate welfare. The public argument used to support less regulation usually emphasizes that big government is bad. But this is a deception. The priority is not the size of government. It is ever-increasing shareholder returns. When reducing regulations or the size of government enhances shareholder returns, businesses and their allies usually support it. But when government is needed to protect ever-increasing shareholder returns, businesses and their allies usually support increased government regulations.

To illustrate this hypocrisy, a public utility in Chattanooga Tennessee provides among the fastest Internet access speeds in the US, often for lower prices than major telecommunications companies. To protect shareholder returns and limit competition, large companies hypocritically reversed their typical arguments. They normally argue that the private sector is more efficient than the public sector. Therefore, privatizing public services will benefit society. But in this case, large companies argued that the public sector has inherent advantages against which the private sector cannot compete. By giving money to politicians and inappropriately influencing government in other ways, telecommunications companies encouraged 20 states to pass laws that limit the ability of public utilities to compete with private sector companies.[130]

Businesses and their allies generally use whatever arguments or deceptions are necessary to protect shareholder returns. When regulations limit shareholder returns, companies oppose big government. However, when public sector competition limits shareholder returns, companies seek big government (i.e. regulations that suppress public sector competition).

One of the largest and most harmful examples of this deception is in the healthcare area. As discussed in the Healthcare section, under the Affordable Care Act, inappropriate influence of government enabled the healthcare sector to retain its monopoly on serving working age citizens in the US. Our flawed systems place ever-increasing shareholder returns ahead of the lives and health of US citizens. As with the Internet access example above, citizens are forced to pay more money for lower quality service. US citizens pay 200-300 percent more for healthcare than citizens in most other developed countries. In return, they receive the worst coverage in the developed world, unnecessary death or illness due to inadequate healthcare, mediocre results, cancelled policies, administrative hassles, medical bill driven bankruptcies and many other problems that do not occur under public healthcare systems.

Public deception enables this degradation of society. The manufactured war between conservatives and liberals builds anger and hatred. Emotions often overwhelm logic. People frequently blindly believe radical media announcers without thinking for themselves. Critical thinking and public literacy are declining. Only six percent of citizens read at least one book per year. Sixty percent of citizens have not read a book since leaving school.[131] Low public literacy, anger and hatred for the other side, suppress rational thought and increase stress among average citizens. This strongly facilitates authoritarianism.

Public deception and theft of citizens' wealth and power are degrading US society and pushing us towards collapse. An analysis of human society over the past 5,000 years found that the rise and collapse of civilizations occurs regularly. The primary factors driving the collapse of societies are environmental degradation and unequal wealth distribution. Unsustainable resource exploitation reduces ecological carrying capacity. This often makes it difficult for average citizens to meet basic needs. Wealthy citizens frequently are insulated from the pain felt by average citizens. As a result, they often continue business as usual and fail to recognize the looming collapse of society.[132]

Near the end of the Roman Empire, wealth inequality was high and rising, government legitimacy was declining, materialism and distraction dominated culture, wealthy citizens had virtually no concern for the well-being of average citizens, and military expenses and commitments were unsustainable.[133] All of these conditions exist in the US.

Inequality and environmental degradation are growing around the world. Human society is at a turning point. We can use a rational whole system perspective, learn from history's mistakes and change our direction. The collapse of human society, if it occurs, will be voluntary. It is not inevitable. If we fail to change our flawed ideas and systems, nature and reality will force system change, probably through collapse. But we can choose to change our ways. In this sense, a collapse of human society would be voluntary (i.e. we had the ability to change, but chose not to use it).

In the US in particular, we have overwhelming evidence that our current economic, political and social systems are grossly flawed, unsustainable and destructive. Since the 1980s, Republicans and Democrats have implemented a big business-first philosophy. Placing the financial well-being of wealthy citizens before all else has severely degraded life support systems and society. It no longer is a matter of opinion or philosophy. Reality has spoken. We have several decades of hard numbers, evidence and experience. Reality shows that placing shareholder returns and economic growth before all else severely degrades society and ultimately is suicidal.

Wealth has been concentrated at the top of society, life has become more difficult for most citizens and life support systems are being severely degraded. One definition of insanity is doing the same thing and expecting different results. Maintaining our current systems and expecting that things will turn around is magical, childish, irrational, insane thinking. If we want different results, we must take different actions. The next two sections – Restoration and We the People – discuss these actions.

RESTORATION

Restoring the degradation caused by our flawed ideas and systems requires adopting a whole system perspective and implementing enlightened ideas and systems. In reality, everything in the whole Earth system, including human society, is connected. No major aspect of society can be studied in isolation if one wishes to develop solutions that work in the real world.

As discussed in the Education section, sustainability could be seen as the meta-discipline. Everything in human society, without exception, is part of sustainability. To operate effectively in the whole system and achieve long-term prosperity, we must teach people to think from the whole system perspective. Sustainability education can and should be a main vehicle for teaching whole system thinking. Sustainability or whole system thinking can be the overarching framework for converting education and society in general from reductionistic, reality-ignoring thinking to interconnected, reality-based thinking.

Whole system thinking greatly increases complexity in terms of the number of issues considered and addressed. But in another sense, it lowers complexity by making reality clearer and easier to understand. One no longer is living in an ivory tower ignoring 90 percent of reality. Instead, they see the linkages and overall functioning of society.

As discussed in Chapter Seven, restoring human society essentially requires re-engineering it. Whole system thinking facilitates this. It enables us to step back, see the big picture and focus on the endpoint. Whole system thinking helps us to establish the foundational goals and principles for society. The foundational goal is achieving sustainability and real prosperity. With the survival and true prosperity of current and future generations established as the absolute, inviolate objective, we can rationally figure out how to evolve our current unsustainable society into one that is sustainable and truly prosperous.

Intuitive wisdom will be a major part of this process. Many of the details and actions needed to achieve sustainability and real prosperity will not be clear at first. But we do not need the whole path clearly laid out before we begin. We know in our hearts that protecting our children and future generations is the highest priority of human society. This heart-led wisdom will guide us along the path, even if our minds do not clearly see every step. All we need to see are the first steps or the next steps. As we progress along the path to sustainability and real prosperity, more will be revealed. The conscious human mind is not meant to know everything. But we all carry infinite wisdom within. This intuitive wisdom will guide our minds if we humbly ask for guidance.

Many of the early steps on the path to sustainability and real prosperity are obvious when one adopts a whole system perspective. This book has discussed hundreds of sustainability solutions. Sustainability content and process knowledge and expertise are required to achieve sustainability and real prosperity. This whole system book discusses content (i.e. actions needed to achieve sustainability and real prosperity) and process. Sustainable solutions are discussed throughout the book. Overarching economic, political and social systemic solutions are discussed in Chapter Five. Systemic solutions for critical industry sectors and environmental and social issues are discussed in Chapter Six. For example, comprehensive discussions of systemic solutions are provided at the end of the Climate Change, Chemicals, Genetic Engineering, Food Production and Diet, Crime and Education sections.

Chapters Seven and Eight discuss important process issues (i.e. how to effectively implement actions needed to achieve sustainability and real prosperity). These include empowering citizens, establishing democracy, implementing collaborative system change strategies, strengthening communities, and using the TCR model to engage the corporate and financial sectors in system change.

This Restoration section summarizes key higher-level solution areas discussed in this book. These relate to the environment, cohesive society, honest media, good government, public wealth, sustainable economic and financial systems, public online services and global peace.

Environmental Protection

Environmental degradation probably is the best example of human myopia. We collectively seem to take life support for granted. As discussed in the environmental sections, every life support system on this planet is in rapid decline, with some regional exceptions. We are acting like a cancer on this planet. Cancer does not realize that it is about to kill itself by killing its host. In the same way, we as a global society appear to go blithely along our way, largely oblivious to the fact that we are killing ourselves.

Many individuals and organizations work aggressively to reverse environmental degradation. But degradation is accelerating. This indicates that collective awareness currently is inadequate to halt our suicidal actions. Human society is similar to cancer, in that we are killing ourselves, as cancer does. But the mechanism is different. Cancer kills itself by killing its host. But in our case, the host will kill the cancer (humans). Degrading life support systems to the point where human survival is difficult or impossible will be tragic for humans. But it will be just another day at the office for nature. Nature simply will be eliminating another species that was unable to follow the rules (i.e. abide by the laws of nature).

Along with myopia, public deception is a main factor driving environmental degradation. Businesses and their allies use the many deception techniques discussed in this book to block rational consideration of humanity's environmentally destructive actions. This protects shareholder returns. But it is suicidal. Experts have been warning for over 20 years that human induced climate change would cause more severe storms, droughts and disease epidemics. These things are occurring, just as predicted. But the human tendency to not see the big picture and vulnerability to vested interest deceptions is blocking actions needed to protect ourselves and halt environmental degradation.

Businesses, politicians paid by them and other business allies use many deceptions to block environmental restoration, and thereby protect shareholder returns. A common deception is to claim that technology will save us. The implication is that it is okay to pollute the environment and rapidly consume fossil fuels and other nonrenewable resources because technology will be developed to clean the environment and provide new energy sources. But it is not rational to assume that we will be able to clean the land, air, oceans and groundwater.

As discussed in the Externalities section, in many cases, it will not be possible. When it is, remediation costs often will be extremely high. Our lives literally depend on these resources. We should err on the side of caution. The default position should be that it is not acceptable to degrade our life support systems. The vastly superior option is to not pollute them in the first place. We are well beyond this point. But we should rapidly reduce or halt degradation, and do all that we can to restore our life-sustaining environment.

We act as if our generation, and the few generations before and after, have a right to consume all the world's fossil fuels. But we do not have this right. We should not act as if we will be the only people to live on this planet. As discussed in the Climate Change section, we have consumed thousands of times more than our share of fossil fuels. The remaining fossil fuels belong to future generations. If these fuels were necessary for survival, continued consumption might be warranted. But they are not. We are using fossil fuels to run grossly inefficient vehicles, buildings and other technologies.

With natural gas fracking, we are pumping millions of gallons of toxic, often carcinogenic chemicals into the ground to force out ever more difficult to reach fossil fuels. These chemicals obviously often will contaminate groundwater. They already have done so on many occasions. As discussed in the Chemicals section, about 40 percent of the drinking water in the US comes from groundwater. Water is infinitely more important than fossil fuels. We can live without fossil fuels, but not without drinking water. Instead of polluting groundwater so that we can power our grossly energy inefficient economy, we should utilize already developed efficient technologies.

Fracking shows the destructive nature of failing to think from a whole system perspective. Here in the US, many areas are blessed with abundant groundwater. Homeowners sink wells into the ground, and abundant, clean, life-sustaining water often comes out. Energy companies and politicians paid by them have deceived citizens into allowing widespread, inevitable contamination of our precious groundwater. Political puppets often argue that fracking will create necessary jobs. They imply that we only can create jobs by destroying our life-sustaining environment. Obviously, this is incorrect.

As discussed in the Climate Change section, retrofitting homes and businesses with energy efficient technologies and developing energy efficient automobiles and other products will create far more jobs than fracking. It also will benefit society in many other ways, including protecting the environment and preserving fossil fuels for future generations. As discussed in the Externalities section, if we replaced the current reality-ignoring fossil fuel pricing system with a reality-based system that integrates all real, relevant costs into prices, energy efficiency would be vastly less expensive than fracking and other fossil fuel production and use.

As discussed in the Food Production and Diet section, consuming animal products is one of the two largest causes of environmental degradation. (Burning fossil fuels is the other.) It also probably is the largest cause of death in the developed world. Humans did not evolve to eat animal products. We are anatomical herbivores, not carnivores or omnivores. About 75 percent of people in the US die of chronic diseases, such as heart disease and cancer. These diseases are rare among groups of people who eat few or no animal products. Producing animal products is grossly inefficient compared to producing plant products. It uses far more grain and water and causes vastly greater environmental degradation. If the grain currently fed to livestock were fed to humans instead, we could end hunger on this planet, and have a large surplus of grain left over. This would facilitate replacing environmentally destructive, industrial agriculture with sustainable agriculture.

Pain is the great teacher. We are destroying our home by burning fossil fuels, eating animal products, producing synthetic chemicals and engaging in other environmentally destructive activities. Vested interests have deceived many people into believing that these actions are not causing substantial harm. But reality does not care what humans think. If we do not stop our environmentally destructive ways, pain will increase and we will be forced to stop.

It will be truly tragic if we do not wake up and end the degradation of our life support systems. Once we live in a severely degraded environment, we might be angry at the business and political leaders who misled us into believing that we were not destroying our home. But it will be too late. Putting these leaders in jail (if they still are alive) will not restore our once beautiful, vibrant home.

This is why it is essential that we wake up now. Cancer does not have a choice. It keeps killing until it kills itself. But we do have a choice. We do not have to kill ourselves. As discussed extensively, we already have all the technology, know-how and expertise needed to live sustainably on this planet. This book has discussed hundreds of system changes needed to achieve environmental sustainability.

Perhaps the most important change needed is to replace reductionism and myopia with whole system thinking. From a whole system perspective, it becomes obvious that protecting environmental life support systems takes priority over everything else, because everything else is irrelevant if we are dead. Therefore, when evolving our economic, political and social systems, we must establish environmental protection as an absolute, inviolate standard. Then we can figure out how to meet other human needs without violating the standard.

Beyond thinking systemically, two of the most important actions needed to restore our life support systems relate to energy and food. As discussed in the Climate Change section, we already have the renewable energy, energy efficiency and other technologies needed to vastly reduce the use of fossil fuels. These are the actual low-cost technologies in a reality-based pricing environment. As we evolve our systems into sustainable forms, for example by including external costs in prices, environmentally sustainable technologies will be rapidly implemented.

Research of alternate or free energy sources also should be expanded. We are surrounded by energy. Given that we have reached perhaps only one billionth of our potential, it seems highly likely that we could figure out how to extract potentially unlimited, nonpolluting, free or nearly free energy from the energy and forces that surround and pervade us.

One of the most important individual and collective environmental protection actions needed is to greatly reduce or eliminate the consumption of animal products. This would produce vast environmental and human health benefits. It could greatly reduce hunger on this planet. As discussed in the Influenza Pandemic section, it would vastly reduce the risk of an H5N1 or similar pandemic. Also, as discussed in the Animal Welfare section, it would enable us to live up to our name humanity by ending the horrible, inhumane treatment of animals raised for food.

The Environmental Sustainability Principles section discusses principles that would enable humanity to live in an environmentally sustainable manner. The Tragedy of the Commons (i.e. meeting short-term needs in ways that inhibit long-term survival) is optional, not inevitable. It results from myopia. If we wake up, see the big picture and change our environmentally destructive ways, we can survive over the long-term on Earth.

Some people speak of exploring space and colonizing other planets. We might do this someday. But it should not be our strategy for human survival. We evolved with this planet. We are perfectly adapted to it. The chance of finding another planet as perfect for humans as Earth is infinitesimally small. Also, if environmental or other disasters force us to relocate to another planet, it probably would mean that nearly all humans die (perhaps because only a very small percentage of humans could be transported to another planet). This is not the strategy we should be pursuing. We have a perfect home. The optimal, ideal strategy is to restore and sustain it.

Cohesive Society

Developing a cooperative, cohesive society is an essential part of achieving sustainability and real prosperity. Critical aspects of this include emphasizing rational thought, practicing non-judgment, helping others, and requiring honest media and advertising.

This book emphasizes the need for a Second Enlightenment in human society. For much of human history, human consciousness was dominated by superstition, magical thinking and blind faith in frequently irrational dogma. Indigenous groups often considered nature to be divine. From a practical perspective, this was extremely rational. It compelled people to revere and protect life support systems, and thereby enabled long-term survival. However, in addition to this rational and practical foundation of indigenous thinking, there also often were magical or dogmatic aspects.

As we replaced cooperation with domination-based religions and ideas, we cut our tether to rationality and entered the realm of unsustainability. As we lost awareness of our interconnectedness with nature and each other, fear and belief in the need for competition arose. We implemented systems, cultures and lifestyles that degraded life support systems and caused massive pain and suffering among humanity.

In the 1700s, many people left the realm of irrationality during the Age of Reason and Enlightenment. Our country, the United States, is a product of this wiser, enlightened period in human history. This is not to say that the Enlightenment was perfect. Widespread horrors, such as slavery and suppression of women, existed. But people began to reject religious dogma and other irrational, destructive ideas. Instead, they honored and elevated science and rational reasoning.

However, people are highly vulnerable to public deception. Fear and deception largely have suppressed rational thinking again. Blind faith in religious, economic and other irrational, harmful dogma has risen. As discussed in the Misleading the Public section, we have entered a New Dark Age. Blind faith in irrational dogma is rapidly increasing pain, suffering and unsustainability in human society. A Second Enlightenment is needed to reverse these trends. We must emulate our Founders and once again honor rational reasoning.

Instead of being loyal to dogma and political parties, we should be loyal to rational thought and the well-being of our children and future generations. As discussed in the Education sections, replacing forced education with freedom-based education will empower young people and teach them to think for themselves. As part of the Second Enlightenment, we must teach people to emphasize rational thought. This will enable them to see through dogma and deception and understand what actually is happening in reality.

As discussed throughout this book, vested interests are very effective at misleading the public and blocking rational thought. As a result, rational discussion of a particular issue often requires having two conversations. The first conversation involves exposing deception. Emotional manipulation and other deception techniques must be illuminated. Once citizens understand how vested interests are using manipulation and deception to block rational thought, protect shareholder returns and achieve other goals, rational discussions of particular issues become much easier. Helping citizens to see the big picture and understand vested interest deceptions are critical to promoting enlightened, rational thinking and achieving sustainability and real prosperity.

Emulating our Founders also will help to promote a Second Enlightenment. Vested interests often attempt to mislead citizens into believing that our Founders were highly religious and dogmatic. This is incorrect. Our leading Founders (Benjamin Franklin, George Washington, John Adams, Thomas Jefferson, James Madison) were highly moral and rational. As discussed in the US Founders, Religious Dogma and Birth Control section, they were Deists. They did not believe in religious dogma. But as shown in George Washington's Farewell Address, they strongly supported religious, moral principles that obviously benefited society. These principles include treating other people with kindness, love and respect, helping the needy and protecting God's creation (nature and all life).

Religious dogma, such as opposition to same-sex marriage or abortion, often varies among religions. But religious principles, are common to virtually all major religions. They also are laws of nature. The Founders strongly opposed allowing religious dogma to have any influence on government. But they strongly advocated basing human society on religious principles. As discussed in the Misleading the Public section, religious dogma often violates religious principles by pitting humans against each other and suppressing the ability to do God's will or follow one's heart. Dogma frequently compels people to blindly obey religious dogma, rather than act according to their own inner wisdom and guidance. People have a right to live according to their own religious, dogmatic or cultural ideas. But these cultural, often divisive ideas should have no influence on government (as our Founders intended).

Instead, we should do what George Washington encouraged us to do in his Farewell Address. He warned us about divisive political parties. He also wished us brotherly affection and encouraged us to follow religious principles. It is time to abide by these suggestions. It is time to build a culture based on wisdom, cooperation and brotherly affection. It is time to elevate women and wisdom to a place of true equality with men and power.

This will be greatly facilitated by practicing non-judgment. Virtually all people do what they believe is right on some level. The vast majority of harm in society, such as environmental and social degradation, is caused by people who are doing what they believe is right. Criticizing these people, and especially calling them bad or greedy, is ineffective. It builds walls, rather than tears them down. It usually is most effective to assume that all people mean well. Even people who commit crimes often believe, perhaps on an unconscious or delusional level, that their actions are justified.

Striving to see the good in others and understand their perspective facilitates productive engagement. It helps people to understand the unintentionally harmful nature of their actions. This applies to all levels of society, not just in individual relationships. For example, understanding the corporate perspective and assuming that companies are trying to benefit society usually is the most effective way to engage with them and produce beneficial changes.

Another aspect of creating cohesive, cooperative society involves recognizing that all people have different strengths and capabilities. The Bible says, "When someone has been given much, much more will be required." (Luke 12:48) The libertarian, *Atlas Shrugged* mentality of every man for himself – help no one else, is ignorant and suicidal. It produces massive unhappiness in society. In reality, we all are part of one system. We will sink or swim together. When someone with more capability or resources helps a needy person, they help everyone, especially themself.

Having great talent or capability is a blessing that comes with the obligation to give back to society. Helping those who cannot help themselves helps everyone. It elevates all of human society. Rather than being a disincentive for work, showing respect and providing assistance to needy people builds them up psychologically and empowers them to stand on their own. It is ignorant for a talented or wealthy person to see themself as being above or superior to less talented or less wealthy people.

People often rise through their own efforts. But they also frequently have help or innate advantages, such as being born with superior skills or born into a wealthy family. In nature, some creatures or individual lifeforms work harder and contribute more to the success of the overall system. This is how reality works. It is extremely ignorant to say or imply that each person should be industrious and contribute to society. It ignores innate differences and psychological challenges that many people face. Those with more should do more. Those with less should be honored and not insulted for doing less.

The value of each person is absolute, innate and equal. It does not vary based on their contribution to society. This is how people are treated in cohesive, sustainable society. Having the ability to give to someone else or help society is a privilege. It is a gift more to the giver than the receiver. Giving or helping others often produces the greatest joy because we are acting on the reality of our interconnectedness.

People know this when they see it. There are millions of heartwarming examples of more fortunate people helping those in need. For example, the famous singer Taylor Swift visited a six-year-old boy with leukemia, Jordan Nickerson, in a Boston hospital. She brought great joy to the child by singing and dancing for him.[134] In another example, a five-year-old boy who had survived cancer, Ryan Encinas, ran a play with the Cleveland Browns football team. Dressed in a Browns uniform, the child carried the ball across the goal line with his favorite team surrounding him and fans cheering him on.[135] These videos, available on YouTube, are beautiful and moving. A world-famous singer sings for a little boy. Some of the best athletes in the world run with a young fan.

Scenes like this touch our hearts because they show how human society is meant to function. A parent gives love to a child not with the expectation of return, but because this is the natural way of the world. Giving love is the greatest joy. This was Jesus's main message. It is the central theme of virtually all religions. This is the culture we should be promoting and expanding in human society. More than anything else, this is what will enable humanity to reach our fullest potential and create Heaven on Earth.

Honest Media

As discussed in the Advertising, Media and Culture section, media and advertising have a huge impact on culture. As a result, improving media and advertising is a major component of implementing a more cooperative, fulfilling and sustainable culture. The foundational principle of sustainable media and advertising is democracy. In a democracy, the people manage society in ways that maximize their well-being. In other words, the purpose of media is to serve and enhance society. But unfortunately, citizens have been deceived into allowing wealthy citizens to replace democracy with plutocracy. In this environment, the purpose of media is not to serve all of society. It is to serve the small group of wealthy citizens who control media, government and society. Media is a primary vehicle for public deception. Business-controlled media is used to fracture the public into debating factions. This enables wealthy citizens to essentially steal the people's wealth and power.

As citizens wake up from their delusion, we will replace plutocracy with democracy and reassert our control over media. Earning superior shareholder returns in media should be the result of serving society well, not the primary focus of media. Business-controlled government no longer requires media to honestly and fairly present information to citizens. Media companies are allowed to present grossly distorted and deceptive views of reality. As noted, the primary public deception is to split the public into debating factions. Radical media does this in large part by providing a nearly constant, hate-filled invective against the other side. Radical media often appears to implement a simple two-rule system for distorting reality and misleading the public about the opposing party. Rule number one: the other side always is wrong. Rule number two: if the other side is correct, see rule number one.

As discussed in the Misleading the Public section, the Founders' primary concern about democracy was the ease with which non-expert citizens could be misled. Elbridge Gerry, delegate to the Constitutional Convention, said, "The people... are the dupes of pretended patriots. They are daily misled... by the false rumor circulated by designing men... which no one on the spot can refute." We must not allow this situation to exist in media. We must make sure that someone is present to refute the lies of designing, deceptive men and women.

Free speech is not an unrestricted right. Vested interests do not have the right to mislead citizens in ways that enable the theft of the people's wealth and power. Media has great power to mislead citizens and degrade society. Therefore, the people must reassert their power over media and demand that it serves the public. When the US was more focused on serving all citizens, media was not allowed to essentially lie to citizens. The Fairness Doctrine required that media provide fair, balanced coverage of major issues. But being honest with citizens limited the ability of large companies and their wealthy owners and allies to steal public wealth and maximize shareholder returns. As a result, business-influenced government removed the Fairness Doctrine in 1987. This strongly facilitated the development of today's grossly divisive, dishonest and destructive media. Politicians did what they were paid to do. They allowed media to deceive citizens in ways that enabled the theft of the people's wealth and power.

Through media consolidation, a small group of wealthy citizens are gaining control of most major media. Removing the requirement to present issues fairly enables business-controlled media to distort reality in whatever ways are necessary to maximize shareholder returns. Individuals have a right to freely voice their opinions. But media is not an individual speaking freely. Media is a main vehicle for informing citizens about reality. If a biased or dishonest view of reality is presented, citizens have a right to hear the other side of the issue. The highest priority, as stated in our Constitution, is promoting the general welfare (i.e. maximizing the well-being of society). This requires that citizens receive fair, honest, balanced information from media. To ensure that this occurs, intense media consolidation should be prohibited and the Fairness Doctrine should be re-implemented.

In addition, the ability of corporations to mislead the public for the purpose of maximizing shareholder returns should be severely restricted or eliminated. Businesses paid politicians to appoint radical pro-business justices who said that corporations were equal to human citizens and therefore had Bill of Rights protections, such as free speech. This is a gross violation of our Constitution, the Founders' intentions and common sense. Corporations are nonliving tools meant to serve society. They are designed to put shareholder returns before all else. If telling the truth to citizens inhibits shareholder returns, corporations often are forced to lie. For example, companies frequently produce their own biased research which incorrectly claims that their products and activities are safe. Misleading the public into believing that corporate products and activities are safe enables severe environmental and social degradation. Therefore, the well-being of society demands that this corporate deception not be allowed.

Regardless of what business biased or corrupted judges and politicians say, corporations are not citizens. As discussed in the Limited Liability and Corporations section, the Founders severely restricted corporate activities in the early US. These restrictions must be reestablished. Corporations essentially are machines designed to focus on one thing (shareholder returns). We do not give washing machines and other human creations free speech and other rights. We do not need to hear what corporations think. We know in advance what they will say. In the same way that a washing machine always will 'want' to wash clothes, a corporation always will seek to maximize shareholder returns. If addressing climate change reduces shareholder returns, we know that corporations often will 'think' that climate change is not real or it should not be addressed in ways that reduce shareholder returns.

Media is, in a sense, an extension of the human mind. Much of the information in our minds comes from media. If our minds are filled with false or deceptive information, it often will be difficult to act in ways that maximize individual and collective well-being.

To create a cohesive, truly prosperous society, We the People must reassert our control over media. Media should not be a free-for-all where vested interests can lie and deceive without restriction. As we move more into an online world, we must demand that media provides fair, accurate, balanced portrayals of reality. This especially applies to major media sources on TV, the Internet and other mass media. Major media companies are first and foremost public servants. If they do not wish to earn a profit by serving the public fairly and accurately, they should not be allowed to operate in a democracy.

For-profit media companies often will vigorously oppose abiding by the Fairness Doctrine. One of their main arguments will be that compelling them to provide honest, balanced information violates their free speech rights. This is an extremely irrational and destructive argument. Given the strong restrictions placed on corporations in the early US, the Founders obviously did not intend to provide Bill of Rights protections to corporations. As noted, citizens cannot lead effectively in a democracy if they do not have accurate, balanced information. Allowing media companies to provide biased, one-sided information severely degrades democracy and society. As We the People establish democracy in the US, we will require that major media companies abide by the Fairness Doctrine and provide accurate, balanced information.

If media companies want to provide biased, one-sided information, for example by claiming that climate change is not a major threat to humanity, they should not be allowed to call themselves news organizations. Instead, they should be required to clearly present themselves as propaganda or philosophy organizations. They should make clear that they are promoting a particular agenda and intentionally not providing fair, balanced views of reality. Only organizations that provide accurate, balanced information should be allowed to label themselves news organizations.

As discussed in the Privacy section and the Public Internet section below, it probably would be more cost effective and beneficial for society to develop expanded public media options, like the BBC. Public media can be completely focused on maximizing the well-being of society, for example, by providing honest and accurate information. But it often is difficult or impossible for publicly traded media companies to put honesty and the well-being of society ahead of shareholder returns. Under our grossly flawed, suicidal systems, focusing primarily on benefiting society (instead of shareholders) could put for-profit media companies out of business.

As discussed in the Advertising, Media and Culture section, advertising is one of the most destructive influences in society. It often programs people to believe that their value is based on their appearance, possessions or wealth. It produces vast senses of emptiness and inadequacy. The well-being of society demands that we severely restrict the destructive impacts of advertising. Many examples of destructive advertising were provided in the Advertising, Media and Culture section. One example that not only degrades culture but also life support systems is truck advertising. This advertising successfully created the widespread impression that driving a large, fancy truck is an important component of being a man. Driving a large truck facilitates being accepted in certain groups. Many people who drive large trucks do not need a vehicle that large for work or general transportation.

Advertising creates culture by strongly defining the 'successful' life. This degrades society by distracting people from things that actually produce successful and satisfying lives. We should restrict the emotionally manipulative and deceptive aspects of advertising. The priority of society should be maximizing total well-being, not maximizing materialism and shareholder returns. To achieve this, We the People must assert our control over all forms of media, including advertising, and demand that they only serve and do not degrade society.

Honest, society-enhancing media and advertising are extensively discussed in the Advertising, Media and Culture section.

Good Government

This whole system book has extensively discussed the actions needed to implement democracy and good government in the US. This section summarizes several important government changes. The Declaration of Independence implies that the laws of nature govern human society. It also says that all government power comes from the people, and that when government does not serve the people, citizens have a right, even a duty, to overthrow abusive government. The Declaration of Independence states that humans have a right "to assume among the Powers of the Earth, the separate and equal Station to which the Laws of Nature and of Nature's God entitle them…" In other words, the laws of nature grant each person the right to be free and equal.

The Declaration of Independence further states, "WE hold these Truths to be self-evident, that all Men are created equal, that they are endowed by their Creator with certain unalienable Rights, that among these are Life, Liberty, and the Pursuit of Happiness – That to secure these Rights, Governments are instituted among Men, deriving their just Powers from the Consent of the Governed, that whenever any Form of Government becomes destructive of these Ends, it is the Right of the People to alter or to abolish it, and to institute new Government… when a long Train of Abuses and Usurpations, pursuing invariably the same Object, evinces a Design to reduce them under absolute Despotism, it is their Right, it is their Duty, to throw off such Government, and to provide new Guards for their future Security."

Since the 1980s, the people's natural rights to equality, freedom, property and self-government have been violated by corrupt, abusive government. A small group of wealthy citizens essentially has stolen the people's wealth (i.e. property) and right to rule themselves. As our Founders said, we have a right, even an obligation, to put an end to this injustice. While our rights are being violated by abusive government, as they were in the 1700s, the situation is different today. In the 1700s, a distant monarchy abused citizens, and thereby lost its legitimacy and right to rule them.

However today, the abusive government is not distant. It is among us. We do not need to separate ourselves and establish a new government.

Instead, we must reestablish the government established by our Founders. A revolution already has occurred in the US. A small group of wealthy citizens revolted against the Constitution and overthrew the legitimate US government. As discussed in the Libertarianism section and ignorant *Atlas Shrugged*, opposite-of-reality fantasy, wealthy citizens revolted against their obligation to pay their fair share to support the society that made them wealthy. They also revolted against being held responsible for negative impacts that they impose on society. They violated the people's natural and constitutional rights by stealing their wealth, power and freedom.

Unlike the 1700s revolution, this revolution did not occur through military rebellion. It occurred through public deception and government corruption. It was a quiet revolution. To use the language of Thomas Jefferson, it crawled like a worm through our government and poisoned it. Also unlike the 1700s revolution, the revolution occurring since the 1980s has no legitimacy. The 1700s revolution was justified and necessary because the people's natural rights were being violated. The revolution restored the people's rights.

The revolution occurring since the 1980s did the opposite. It has grossly violated the people's rights. A revolution was needed in the 1700s to protect rights. But in this case, we essentially need an anti-revolution. In other words, the goal is not to overthrow government. That already has occurred. The goal is to restore the democratic government established by our Founders. The unjust, abusive revolution over the past few decades overthrew our Constitution. Now we must restore our Constitution. We are not revolting against our country and government. The current so-called government has no legitimacy. It is not the people's government. We are fighting to protect our country and reestablish our true, constitutional government, as Thomas Jefferson said we should in the Declaration of Independence.

We the People are not the revolution. We are the anti-revolution. We are the legitimate force seeking to suppress the unjust revolution. Our Founders gave us a great country, Constitution and government. These gifts are under attack. Our country and legitimate government are severely wounded. We must fight to protect and restore them.

To achieve this, we must end the public deceptions that divide us into liberals and conservatives. These are irrational philosophies that only can be believed through blind faith and the absence of rational thought. Conservatives do not want to destroy life support systems and liberals do not want something for nothing. Virtually all citizens agree that we must abide by our Constitution, require democratic government, and fairly use the public wealth. We must work together on these areas of common interest. If we let a few areas of disagreement prevents us from working together on our massive areas of agreement, such as ending corporate welfare and business control of government, we will remain divided and conquered. We will continue to be the victims of unjust, illegitimate government.

The small group of wealthy citizens who took control of government often wave the flag as if to imply that their actions are patriotic. They steal trillions of dollars from average citizens each year. Then they focus citizens' attention on the tiny percentage of low-income citizens who abuse social welfare programs. In other words, they trick citizens into focusing on the stolen penny and ignoring the stolen thousand dollars. They imply that people who oppose their actions are unpatriotic. This illustrates the disgusting and insidious nature of the big business revolution or insurrection occurring since the 1980s. A small group of wealthy citizens stole the people's wealth and power, and then claimed that they were patriots. But they are traitors. (Or to use the language of *Atlas Shrugged*, they are parasites and takers.) True patriots must stand up to the unjust, unconstitutional, big business-controlled government in the US.

It is time to end the revolution. We were fools to believe the irrational idea that maximizing the wealth of already wealthy citizens is the best way to maximize the well-being of all citizens. The best way to maximize the well-being of all citizens is to focus on maximizing well-being of all citizens. Once We the People, liberals and conservatives, start working together, we can command our political servants to restore our constitutional government by taking the many actions discussed in this book. Several of these critical actions are discussed below.

Congressional Term Limits. As discussed in the Government and Elections section, the Founders obviously did not intend to establish aristocracy in government. Senators and representatives were not meant to serve for decades. We must demand that our congressional servants impose term limits on themselves. More than 60 years ago, Congress initiated a Constitutional amendment that limited the President's term to eight years. Congress believed that the President serving for more than eight years was inappropriate. But apparently Congress believes that it is acceptable for senators and representatives to remain in office for decades, possibly over half a century. Obviously, this is not acceptable. It establishes aristocracy in government and suppresses democracy. The Founders clearly did not intend that senators and representatives would serve for decades.

Electoral College. Also as discussed in the Government and Elections section, our Founders did not intend that the loser of perhaps the most important election in the world sometimes would become President of the United States. They did not intend that the President would give preference to swing states that unfairly have more power when electing the President. The Electoral College gives citizens of small states more power than large state citizens when electing the President. It makes citizens unequal, gives unfair preference to swing states, greatly facilitates election fraud, and sometimes allows losers to win.

The Electoral College was established at the end of the Constitutional convention of 1787 as a compromise largely intended to protect and perpetuate the institution of slavery. More than 100 years ago, we amended the Constitution to allow citizens, rather than state legislatures, to elect US Senators. Changing the Electoral College has been proposed more than any other Constitutional amendment. We should have ended this unfair institution long ago. Citizens should elect the President, not states. The Electoral College must be replaced with popular election of the President. All citizens are equal. This should be reflected in Presidential elections.

Judicial Reform. Some of the most important and necessary government changes are in the Judicial branch. Fortunately, these also are the easiest changes to make. Imposing term limits on Congress and replacing the Electoral College with popular election of the President probably require constitutional amendments. But changes needed in the Judicial branch can be made quickly through legislation. No constitutional amendments are needed.

The revolution that took over the US government since the 1980s is most obvious in the Supreme Court. The Court has made many decisions that greatly benefit the small group of citizens who stole control of government from the people. The Supreme Court is perhaps the greatest enabler of this theft. Several Supreme Court decisions obviously and grossly violate the Constitution. Allowing wealthy citizens and corporations to spend unlimited amounts of money on elections obviously gives them greater control of government than the vast majority of citizens who do not spend large amounts on elections. As discussed in the Influencing Government section, about 90 percent of federal elections are won by the candidate who spends the most money. Winning elections largely has become a matter of money. When those with high wealth are allowed to spend unlimited amounts on elections, they largely control elections and government.

Also, equating corporations to human citizens and giving them Bill of Rights protections obviously violates the intentions of our Founders. From their experience with British corporations, the Founders knew that corporations could enable wealthy citizens to steal the people's wealth and power and degrade society in other ways. As a result, corporations were severely restricted in the early US. They were prohibited from having any influence on elections and government. The ability of corporations to control and abuse society is even greater today than it was in the 1700s. As a result, corporations should be more restricted, not less.

Equating bribery to free speech and corporations to human citizens obviously is incorrect. The Supreme Court essentially is claiming that two plus two equals five. But as discussed in the Judicial Branch section, there are no consequences for a lifetime appointed Supreme Court. Their decisions do not have to be logical or constitutional. The Supreme Court frequently uses illogical arguments to support its grossly business biased decisions.

For example, in overturning campaign finance laws that limited the amount of money that wealthy citizens could spend on elections, the five radicals on the Supreme Court argued that only quid pro quo corruption could be prohibited. In other words, the Supreme Court essentially argued that evidence must show that money was given to politicians in return for specific favors or actions. This is extremely irrational. It is like saying that the naked emperor is wearing clothes. We know that wealthy citizens and corporations directly and indirectly give large amounts of money to politicians. That is a fact. It is obvious to assume that this money is not given freely, as if to a charity. It is overwhelmingly logical to assume that this money is given with the expectation of preferential treatment. It would be irrational to assume that wealthy campaign donors are not asking politicians to protect their interests.

Observing the actions of the US government under both political parties since the 1980s, we see that politicians who received money from wealthy citizens and corporations took many actions that benefited these groups. For example, they cut tax rates, bailed out companies and eliminated regulations that interfered with ever-increasing shareholder returns. These extensive pro-business actions also are an obvious, observable fact. Largely as a result of these actions, wealthy citizens and corporations have experienced rapid wealth and income growth under both political parties, while income and wealth for nearly all other citizens grew far more slowly, remain flat, or declined. This also is a fact.

In other words, we know that wealthy citizens and corporations gave large amounts of money to politicians, who then made many changes that greatly benefited these groups. It is obvious to all rational people that wealthy citizens and corporations asked politicians for preferential treatment and received it. But the five radicals imply that, because we do not have a video or audio recording of these conversations, we cannot prevent this obvious bribery and corruption.

As discussed in the Influencing the Supreme Court section, one of the most important requests made by wealthy campaign donors to politicians almost certainly was to appoint the most strongly biased pro-business justices available. Once again, we know that large amounts of money were given to politicians. We can deduce with virtual certainty that donors requested the appointment of radical pro-business justices. And we see from the actions of these justices that pro-business radicals were appointed.

The Supreme Court radicals require evidence of quid pro quo corruption. All they have to do is look in the mirror. They are the quid pro quo. They are the evidence that businesses paid to appoint justices who would give wealthy citizens and corporations nearly complete control of government. The decisions of the five justices who voided campaign finance laws prove that wealthy citizens requested, paid for and received the appointment of radical pro-business justices who would put the well-being of wealthy citizens before all else, even if it violates the Constitution and rights of all other citizens.

As Thomas Jefferson said, the Supreme Court has become the most dangerous branch of government. The Court unconstitutionally and unilaterally gave itself the power to void acts of the Legislative and Executive branches. They are appointed for life, something that is not specified in the Constitution. Wealthy citizens and corporations succeeded in getting a radical pro-business majority on the Supreme Court. If not for the passing of Justice Antonin Scalia, wealthy citizens could have controlled government for many years. If the people's elected representatives attempted to pass laws that restricted the ability of corporations and wealthy citizens to steal the people's wealth and power, the five radicals could (and regularly did) void these laws.

The pro-business Supreme Court is the most obvious evidence that business controls government and democracy does not exist in the US. An abusive aristocracy has ascended to uncontrollable power. It is perpetuating the ability of wealthy citizens and corporations to steal the people's wealth and power. As discussed in the Judicial Branch section and Chapter Seven, this probably is the easiest major government problem to fix.

The Constitution clearly gives Congress the ability to establish, define and control nearly all aspects of the Judicial branch. The Constitution does not give the Supreme Court the authority to interpret the Constitution or void laws. Instead, as discussed in the Tenth Amendment section, the Constitution gives Congress the near absolute power to implement any law it believes is necessary to promote the general welfare. It makes these laws and the Constitution the supreme law of the land. Congress has strong implied power to determine if laws are constitutional.

As discussed in the Judicial Branch Section, through its strong and obvious power over the Judicial branch, Congress has the authority to interpret Article III and declare that the vague words "shall hold their

Offices during good Behaviour" do not confer lifetime appointments. They only require that judges maintain good behavior to remain in office. Through simple legislation, Congress can impose term limits on the Supreme Court and lower federal courts. Through Article III, Section 2 authority, Congress also can rescind or severely restrict the Supreme Court's unconstitutional, self-imposed power of judicial review. Numerous Congressional efforts to impose judicial term limits and restrict the power of judicial review in the 1800s and early 1900s show that Congress has the power to impose these changes, if it develops the will to do so.

Citizens Divided, *McCutcheon* and several other decisions made by the Supreme Court radicals are Constitutional abominations. They never should have been made. They increase and perpetuate business control of government. They greatly benefit the wealthy citizens and corporations who effectively paid to appoint the five radicals. It is insane that we allow a small group who is not accountable to the people to void laws that protect democracy in the US, such as campaign finance laws. The Supreme Court has no constitutional authority to void laws that limit the ability of corporations and wealthy citizens to control government. We must reverse the plutocracy-supporting decisions of the five radicals.

We must remove the Supreme Court's power to violate the Constitution and democracy. Business control of the Supreme Court (through the appointment of pro-business radicals) greatly benefits wealthy citizens and corporations. As a result, many business puppets in Congress from both political parties probably will vigorously resist reining in the Supreme Court. This is why it is absolutely essential that conservatives and liberals begin to work together. Once we are united on major issues, such as ending business control of the Supreme Court, we can command our supposed political servants to do what we tell them to do.

Congress has clear constitutional authority to impose term limits on federal courts and remove the Supreme Court's ability to void laws. The Founders obviously did not intend that federal judges would serve for decades or that the Judicial branch would be the most powerful branch of government. As Thomas Jefferson, James Wilson, James Madison and other Founders said, it was intended to be the weakest branch of government, in large part because it is unelected, and therefore is farthest from the people. We the People are the highest authority in the US. It is time to stand united and assert this authority over unelected radicals who enable the theft of our wealth and power.

An unjust law is no law. This applies to Supreme Court rulings. Equating corporations to human citizens and allowing the wealthy to spend unlimited amounts on elections is wrong on every level. It violates our Constitution. It severely subverts democracy. And it violates the natural laws and religious principles of fairness, equality and freedom. Citizens Divided and other strongly pro-business decisions made by the five radicals have no legitimacy. They must be voided immediately. Congress can assert its clear constitutional authority over the Supreme Court and rectify these injustices.

As discussed in the Judicial Branch section, Alexander Hamilton said in the Federalist Papers that there is nothing in the Constitution that prevents Congress from reversing judicial decisions, such as Citizens Divided. He also clarifies that the Constitution does not give the Supreme Court the power to void laws and that the Constitution gives Congress the power to restrict and regulate the Supreme Court. In its 1803 *Marbury v. Madison* decision, the Supreme Court had no constitutional authority to unilaterally grant itself the power to void laws. Congress has clear constitutional authority to immediately reverse *Marbury v. Madison* and revoke the Supreme Court's unconstitutional power of judicial review through simple legislation. As noted, no constitutional amendments are needed.

Strengthening Legal Remedies. Another change needed in the US judicial system involves shifting the focus back to protecting citizens and upholding the Constitution. Since the 1980s, business influence of federal, state and other judicial appointments and elections largely has shifted the focus of the judicial system from protecting all citizens to protecting large corporations and wealthy citizens. As discussed in the Chemicals section, business-influenced politicians and media often loudly proclaimed the need to reduce frivolous lawsuits. They implied that many, if not the large majority, of lawsuits against companies were without merit.

Being business puppets, they of course neglected to mention that the need to provide ever-increasing shareholder returns often compels companies to degrade the environment and society. As a result, millions of citizens are being harmed by corporate products and activities. By emphasizing frivolous lawsuits and other deceptions, many legal protections for average citizens, such as the ability to file class-action lawsuits, were restricted or removed. Damages and other remedies also were capped or restricted. These and other actions made it easier for corporations to avoid being held responsible for negative impacts. This in turn facilitated their ability to provide ever-increasing shareholder returns.

Food Libel Laws. One of the most obvious and tragic examples of shifting the emphasis of the judicial system from protecting citizens to protecting business involves food libel laws. As discussed in the Food Production and Diet section, these laws are grossly unfair. They enable food companies to harass and suppress people who expose food risks, and thereby threaten ever-increasing shareholder returns. Food libel laws often place the burden of proof on defendants to prove that they are innocent, rather than on plaintiff food companies to prove guilt. The laws frequently prohibit defendants from collecting punitive damages and attorneys' fees. This enables food companies to initiate unjustified, abusive lawsuits with no fear of consequences. While defendants cannot recover punitive damages and attorneys' fees, food companies often can recover them from defendants. This further increases the power of food companies to suppress critics. Also, food libel laws often require defendants to provide nearly absolute proof that food products and production processes are harmful. This is a nearly impossible standard to achieve, in large part because food companies control most food safety research.

Food probably has a greater impact on human health than any other product class. Citizens have a right to know all risks related to food, even if the risks are small. But business-influenced politicians have severely suppressed the ability to inform citizens about food-related risks. As a result, they have placed citizens at substantially increased risk.

Burden of Proof. A major shift back to protecting citizens and the general welfare is needed in the judicial system. As discussed in the Environmental Sustainability Principles section, business-influenced judges and laws often place the burden of proof on citizens to prove that corporate products and processes are unsafe. This is grossly wrong. The priority, as clarified in the constitutional words promote the general welfare, is to protect the health, lives and well-being of all citizens, not the financial returns of wealthy citizens and corporations. Corporate products and processes should not be allowed until there is overwhelming independent evidence showing that they are safe. But our business-corrupted government often does the opposite of this.

As discussed in the Chemicals, Genetic Engineering and Nanotechnology sections, synthetic chemicals, genetically engineered crops, nano-materials and many other corporate products and processes implicitly are assumed to be safe. This is the wrong perspective. Humans are innocent until proven guilty. But the well-being of humanity demands that anything which threatens humans should be assumed to be guilty or unsafe until proven to be safe with independent research. The burden of proof must be shifted to business in the Judicial branch. The burden must be on businesses to show that their products and processes are safe, not on citizens to show that they are unsafe.

Online Reviews. Another unjust aspect of the business-controlled judicial system involves online reviews. A growing number of online and other businesses require customers to agree to terms that prohibit or limit posting negative reviews online. Companies sometimes fine customers for negative reviews. When citizens do not pay the unjust fines, companies frequently send the fines to collection agencies and harm customers' credit ratings.

Customers must have the freedom to honestly discuss their experiences with companies. This helps citizens to avoid bad businesses. It also strongly compels companies to fix problems and provide good products and services. As with food libel laws, companies silence critics rather than fixing problems and acting responsibly. If citizens fraudulently disparage businesses, the companies can sue with libel laws. But they must not be allowed to suppress honest and accurate negative reviews. (Leading companies often publicly respond to negative reviews and attempt to resolve problems. This reflects good, well-intentioned management. Publicly responding to customers who had bad experiences and attempting to resolve problems enhances the public image of companies. Only cowardly businesses attempt to suppress honest negative reviews. This indicates poor management and inferior companies that probably should be avoided.)

Forced Arbitration. This represents another unfair aspect of the business-controlled judicial system. Recent Supreme Court decisions have upheld forced arbitration agreements. Forced arbitration clauses often are included in employment and product agreements. To get a job or buy a product, employees and customers frequently must give up their constitutional right to a trial by a jury of their peers. Private arbitrators often have financial incentives to rule in favor of corporations. Employees and customers frequently must pay arbitration fees that are higher than court filing fees. In addition, forced arbitration agreements often prevent employees and customers from pooling their resources and engaging in class or collective legal actions.

Many cell phone, credit card and other agreements contain forced arbitration clauses. Citizens frequently do not realize that they have given up their jury trial and other rights.[136] Removing employee and customer rights that interfere with ever-increasing shareholder returns is the expected outcome of business-controlled government. Once We the People regain control of the Supreme Court by implementing the changes discussed in the Judicial Branch section, we can restore our constitutional rights that were removed by business-controlled government.

Full Responsibility. At the general government level, one of the most important changes needed is to hold businesses fully responsible for all negative impacts. This mostly would occur through laws. But it also must be enforced through the judicial system. Since the 1980s, citizens have been deceived into believing and accepting a grossly irrational and unfair position. Individuals are held fully responsible for negative impacts, but corporations often are not. We do not allow individuals to murder a few people or rob a few banks before we hold them responsible. But companies routinely are allowed to impose massive negative impacts on society that are known or highly likely to sicken or kill many people and harm society in other ways. As discussed, failing to hold companies fully responsible for negative impacts through limited liability, bailouts and other mechanisms often compels them to degrade society.

Companies frequently attempt to deceive citizens by arguing that regulations place an unfair burden on business. This would be like saying that the requirement to not murder anyone places an unfair burden on citizens. Regulations are no more a burden on companies that criminal laws are on citizens. Companies massively burden society with negative impacts. Regulations hold companies responsible for the burdens that they place on society. It is absolutely essential that government hold companies responsible for all negative environmental, social and economic impacts. This will compel businesses to use their large creative potential to figure out how to act responsibly and sustainably. It will protect businesses, society and the general welfare.

Campaign Finance. Giving money to politicians directly or indirectly (for example, through spending on political campaigns) should be limited. Allowing wealthy citizens and corporations to give large amounts of money to politicians obviously gives them greater control of government than citizens who do not give money to politicians. This violates democracy and our Constitution. As a result, political campaigns should be publicly funded, as they are in many other countries.

As discussed in the Campaign Finance section, as business influence of government increased, wealthy citizens and corporations compelled the appointment of pro-business judges who gave these groups even greater control of government. Through Citizens Divided and other judicial decisions, business-biased judges allowed wealthy citizens and corporations to spend unlimited amounts of money on political campaigns in secret.

A Wisconsin investigation into political corruption reveals how large, secret donations benefit wealthy donors, but degrade society. The case was brought before the Wisconsin Supreme Court. Justices who received support from the organizations being investigated did not recuse themselves. Instead, they halted the investigation and ordered that all evidence be destroyed. The justices argued that donations were made to independent organizations, and therefore were not illegal.[137]

Under current campaign finance laws, direct donations to candidates must be disclosed. Corporations are not allowed to make direct donations. But wealthy citizens and corporations can make unlimited, secret donations to supposedly independent political organizations that support candidates. Plaintiffs argued that one organization receiving large donations, the Wisconsin Club for Growth (WCG), was not independent because the governor's campaign manager controlled it.

Donors viewed donations to this organization as contributions to the governor's campaign.[138]

The Wisconsin Supreme Court said that WCG was independent because it did not produce advertisements that specifically said "vote for" or "vote against" particular candidates. Instead, the organization produced issue ads that were intended to support certain candidates. For example, a political advertisement might say that supporting a particular issue is important, candidate A supports it and candidate B opposes it. Clearly the campaign commercial is intended to benefit candidate A.

The investigation exposed several instances of corruption. For example, a paint company faced lawsuits for lead poisoning of children. The owner of the company gave $750,000 to the WCG. After the governor was reelected, a law was passed that blocked these types of lawsuits. In another case, a mining company gave $700,000 to the WCG. After the election, the legislature passed a law drafted by the company.

In yet another case, a hardware company had paid millions of dollars of fines for polluting the environment. The CEO of the company gave $1.5 million to the WCG. After the election, the company received $1.8 million in tax credits. In addition, environmental enforcement against the company was reduced.[139] These political decisions benefitted wealthy campaign donors, but degraded society. Campaign contributions were made in secret. As a result, while these issues were being debated in the legislature, citizens were not aware that the politicians deciding the issues had indirectly received large amounts of money that apparently influenced their decisions.

Politicians who benefited from this campaign finance scheme argued that they did not break the law. This illustrates the grossly flawed nature of the US campaign finance system. The types of corruption exposed in Wisconsin almost certainly occur throughout the federal government and other state governments. Business-controlled government passed laws that made corruption legal. Wealthy citizens and corporations are bribing politicians in secret. They receive preferential treatment that degrades society, for example, by allowing pollution and blocking lawsuits that protect children. This is the same type of secret bribery of government officials that occurs in organized crime. These actions are immoral and wrong. They violate democracy and our Constitution. Corrupted politicians made this immorality legal. But an unjust law is no law. We the People must end legalized corruption by demanding public funding of political campaigns.

Lobbying. As discussed in the Influencing Government section, individuals and groups obviously should be allowed to make requests of politicians. They cannot serve the people if they do not know what citizens want. However, individuals and groups do not have a right to lobby for actions that degrade the general welfare, such as weakening environmental and social protections. The primary obligation of government, as stated in our Constitution, is to protect and promote the general welfare. This strongly implies that there are basic standards which should not be violated.

For example, there is no life without environmental life support systems that are clean and stable enough to keep us alive. Also, in a wealthy nation such as the US, there is no need for people to go hungry or not have other basic survival needs met. Protecting the general welfare requires abiding by minimum environmental and social standards. No one has a right to ask politicians to violate these standards. In other words, no one has a right to ask politicians to harm society, for example, by allowing actions that degrade life support systems or cause the basic survival needs of citizens to go unmet. These requests might cause politicians to violate their duty to uphold the Constitution and protect the general welfare.

Once minimum standards are met, individuals and groups can lobby for special requests. However, this should be done fairly. In the same way that allowing wealthy citizens to give large amounts of money to politicians gives them greater influence over government, allowing them to dominate the time of politicians through extensive lobbying efforts also gives them more influence over government than average citizens. This is unfair. It suppresses democracy and violates the intentions of our Founders and Constitution.

Average citizens usually do not have the extensive lobbying resources and representation of wealthy vested interests. To ensure that wealthy citizens and corporations do not gain unfair influence of government, public advocates and other mechanisms should be established to ensure that the requests of average citizens are given equal time and consideration by politicians. Also, lobbying generally should be open and public. Wealthy citizens and corporations should not be allowed to make secret deals behind closed doors that help vested interests, but harm average citizens and society. Politicians are public servants. In the same way that employees should not hide work related activities from their employers, politicians should not hide government related activities from citizens (unless it is truly necessary, for example, to protect privacy or national security).

Limit Direct Democracy. Suppressing direct democracy is another essential aspect of implementing good government that maximizes the well-being of society. As discussed in the Government and Elections section, the US Founders often spoke of the evils of democracy. They knew that democracy was an unworkable form of government for more than small groups. Average citizens usually do not have the time needed to study complex issues and make well-informed decisions that maximize the well-being of current and future generations. This makes citizens highly vulnerable to vested interest deception. The Founders strongly supported democracy in principle – all citizens equally control government. But they established the US as a constitutional republic.

Parents would not diagnose and treat their children's severe medical problems. They wisely delegate their parental authority to doctors. It is the same in republican government. Non-expert citizens delegate their authority to expert politicians who make well-informed decisions that maximize the long-term well-being of society. This is the system established in our Constitution. But it is not the system functioning in the US. As discussed, politicians from both major political parties mainly serve the wealthy citizens and corporations that paid to put them in office. In this system of bad government, citizens often are justifiably angry. They frequently attempt to bypass corrupt politicians through direct democracy mechanisms, such as ballot referendums. But this is extremely dangerous.

The UK decision to leave the EU (i.e. Brexit) perfectly illustrates the danger of direct democracy. As discussed in the Media Deception section below, vested interests whipped up anger at immigrants and EU regulations in the UK. Business-controlled media distracted citizens from much larger problems, such as corporate welfare and business control of government. Largely as a result, a majority of citizens in the UK voted to leave the EU. There is a strong possibility that this will significantly degrade the quality of life of average citizens in the UK over the long-term.

Decisions that could substantially affect the well-being of a nation for generations should not be made by a simple majority vote of uninformed, easily misled citizens. In the same way that parents rely on doctors to treat their children, non-expert citizens must rely on experts to make complex political decisions. Obviously, this requires that politicians be completely focused on equally and fairly serving all citizens, a condition that does not exist in the US, UK and many other countries.

Understanding how citizens could be easily deceived by vested interests, the US Founders made constitutional amendments difficult. Approval by three-fourths of state legislatures or state ratification conventions is required. This high standard ensures that substantial changes to the nation's governance or structure will not be made in a hasty, potentially destructive manner.

Direct democracy is not the solution to plutocracy. The solution is to implement the republican government established in our Constitution. This system never has been fully implemented in the US. It would require weakening political parties and eliminating inappropriate vested interest influence of government. When this occurs, all citizens will equally control government through elected representatives.

Limit Trade Agreements. Another necessary government change is to reestablish the authority of citizens and democratic government over corporations in trade agreements and other areas. As discussed, our flawed systems place the financial well-being of wealthy citizens ahead of all else in the US and many other countries. The ascension of corporations over government shows the suicidal need to push aside anything that interferes with ever-increasing shareholder returns, such as democracy and protecting the well-being of all citizens.

Corporations have grown to represent over half of the world's 100 largest economies. As discussed in the Plutocracy section above, business-influenced trade agreements often place corporations above democratic governments. Trade agreements frequently allow lawsuits that compel governments to weaken or not implement environmental and social protections. To illustrate, a large US tobacco company is suing Uruguay and Australia over their anti-smoking laws. A US energy company is suing Canada for lost revenues due to Québec's fracking moratorium. And a Swedish energy company is suing Germany due to its phase-out of nuclear power.[140]

In a rational world, lawsuits such as these would be seen as ridiculous. They would not be allowed. If people invest in companies that sell potentially harmful products or engage in potentially harmful activities, there is a risk that their companies will be held responsible or harmful products and activities will be prohibited. Investors should do their due diligence. It is fine if they wish to take a calculated risk that their companies will not be held responsible for negative impacts. But they have no right to have their downside covered when companies are held responsible. This would be socialism, not capitalism.

As discussed in the Trade, Scale and Competitive Advantage section, the obvious priority of society should be the well-being of citizens and society overall. Nonliving corporations and financial returns to wealthy people obviously should not be given priority over the health, lives and well-being of citizens. Countries have an absolute right to protect their citizens through environmental and social regulations. It seems insane that companies would be able to force countries and citizens to allow environmental and social degradation. But this is the expected outcome of our suicidally flawed economic and political systems that require never-ending growth of shareholder returns.

Trade agreements that place corporations and shareholder returns above democratic government and the will of the people have no legitimacy. They violate natural laws by allowing companies to harm society. Maximizing the well-being of society requires placing democratic government and the will of the people above corporations. As a result, all aspects of trade agreements that give corporations greater power than government, for example by enabling corporations to force the weakening of environmental and social protections, should be voided or considered to be unenforceable.

Protect Voting Rights. As discussed in the Government and Elections section, another major change needed in government is to greatly increase the percentage of citizens voting. It is impossible to have true democracy when nearly half of adults in the US do not vote. The US has nearly the worst voter turnout in the world. To offset an increasingly nonwhite population, Republicans are implementing voter laws that primarily suppress Democratic votes.

In a 2013 Supreme Court case, *Shelby County v. Holder*, the five Republican-appointed justices, over the bitter dissent of the other four justices, struck down a main part of the Voting Rights Act of 1965. The Act limited the ability of states with a history of voter discrimination (i.e. mostly Southern states) to implement discriminatory voting laws. Shortly after the law was struck down, several states, including Texas and North Carolina, implemented restrictive voter requirements that will substantially reduce the number of minority and Democratic citizens voting.[141]

As noted, both Democratic and Republican politicians primarily are focused on helping wealthy campaign donors. But Republicans usually are more inclined to do what large companies want without hesitation or restriction. Therefore, it generally is a little easier to maximize shareholder returns when Republicans are in office. Striking down a law that protects the ability of mostly Democratic citizens to vote once again shows the radical pro-business bias of the Republican-appointed Supreme Court justices.

It also illuminates the danger of lifetime Supreme Court appointments. As with Citizens Divided and other cases discussed in this book, the five radicals used irrational arguments to support their business-biased decision. The radicals argued that the Voting Rights Act violated the "fundamental principle of equal sovereignty" of the states. But there is no constitutional principle of equal sovereignty. The principal was made up by one of the radicals in a 2009 case that had a minor impact. Then the radicals cited the principal in a major case (*Shelby*) as if it were established constitutional law. Prior to 2009, equal sovereignty applied to the conditions upon which states were admitted to the union. It did not apply to modern treatment of the states by Congress.[142]

The principle of equal sovereignty, as used in *Shelby*, is grossly irrational. The Constitution does not mention the principle. Fairness dictates that the states be treated equally in general. But the priority of the Constitution and government is promoting the general welfare. This obviously will require that the federal government treat the states differently at times. For example, after the Civil War during Reconstruction, the federal government imposed changes on the Southern states to end the legacy of slavery. According to the five radicals' logic, the Southern states could have argued that Reconstruction was unconstitutional because it was not being imposed on Northern states.

The Constitution is the supreme law of the land (along with federal laws). In general, if a state violates the Constitution (for example by suppressing the voting rights of minority citizens), the federal government must force the state to abide by the Constitution. The idea that a state could oppose controls because the federal government is not taking the same actions against states that are not violating the Constitution is ridiculous. This would be like saying that the principal of equality of all citizens means that someone who was incarcerated for murder could argue that their sentence was unconstitutional because they were being treated differently than citizens who did not commit murder.

This is a perfect example of what happens when consequences are removed from the Supreme Court with lifetime appointments. The five radicals can make any argument they want to support the wealthy citizens who paid to appoint them. If enabling the suppression of Democratic votes helps wealthy citizens, the Supreme Court can make it happen, as it did in this case. The consequence-free Supreme Court does not have to abide by the Constitution. Its arguments do not have to be rational. They can be ludicrous, as in this case, Citizens Divided and other cases that benefit wealthy citizens. But the people can do nothing about it.

The five radicals also argued that part of the Voting Rights Act should be voided because it was based on information from the 1960s. If this were true, the other four justices probably would have agreed with them. As noted, shortly after the five radicals voided the Voting Rights Act, several Southern states implemented laws that restrict mostly minority and Democratic votes. This strongly indicates that the Voting Rights Act still is needed. The key issue is not the age of the information upon which the Act is based, but whether the Act still is needed to prevent discrimination against minority voters. By quickly discriminating against minority voters when they once again were allowed to do so, several states proved that the Voting Rights Act still is needed.

Numerous laws have been in place for decades or longer. Using the five radials' illogical arguments, many of these laws could or should be voided because they are based on old information. This of course is ridiculous. The priority is not the age of a law or the information upon which it is based. It is whether the law still is needed to protect society and promote the general welfare. For example, if harmful or unconstitutional actions (such as suppressing minority votes) still occur or would occur without the law, then the law still is needed. One of the dissenting justices said that voiding a law that reduced and continues to reduce voter discrimination because discrimination is low "is like throwing away your umbrella in a rainstorm because you are not getting wet."[143]

As discussed in the Judicial Branch section, the Supreme Court has no constitutional authority to strike down the Voting Rights Act or any other law. Striking down laws that inhibit business control of government is the expected output of business-biased justices. This ongoing desecration of our Constitution and supposedly democratic country must be ended.

We need a paradigm shift in voting in the US. We must work aggressively to increase the approximately 60 percent voter turnout to near 100 percent. This probably means that Democrats would win more elections. But this is irrelevant. The priority is democracy. True democracy only can occur if the people make their will known. Also, Democrats winning more elections is a deception. Democratic politicians still will put wealthy citizens first because that is who paid to put them in office. Environmental and social decline might slow slightly under Democrats. But the decline still will be rapid. The main solution is not to elect more business-controlled Democrats. It is to end business influence of government, in large part by greatly weakening political parties.

Maximize Voting. There are several ways to quickly increase voter turnout. Over 20 countries have compulsory voting laws. Most countries with these laws do not enforce them. Those that do generally provide minor or token penalties if citizens do not vote. Some people say that compulsory voting restricts freedom. But failing to vote, and thereby enabling vested interests to control government, restricts freedom (as well as enables theft of public wealth and power) vastly more.

Alternatively, several suggestions for largely increasing voter turnout are discussed in the Government and Elections section. These include implementing automatic voter registration (i.e. citizens automatically are registered to vote when they turn 18), increasing the number of election days, facilitating online and other voting methods, and ensuring that voting access is easy and fast for all citizens. In white communities in the US, citizens usually can vote quickly, often with little or no wait. But in many African American and other minority communities, citizens frequently must stand in line for hours to vote. Adults with jobs and/or children often cannot spend several hours waiting in line to vote on a weekday. Making voting more difficult in minority communities substantially reduces minority voting. This revolting Jim Crow era behavior must be ended immediately.

Gerrymandering. This represents another technique sometimes used by Republicans to offset an increasingly nonwhite population. Gerrymandering often involves establishing state election districts in ways that give one party an unfair advantage in the House of Representatives. To illustrate possible gerrymandering, the Republican-controlled North Carolina state legislature developed election district maps that produced an unfair outcome in the 2012 congressional elections. Among citizens who voted Democrat or Republican, 49 percent voted Republican. But Republicans won 9 of the State's 13 congressional seats (nearly 70 percent). A statistical analysis by Duke University found that it was highly unlikely that these unfair and unrepresentative results could have resulted from an objective, unbiased districting process.[144] The study strongly indicates that biased drawing of election districts by the Republican-controlled legislature caused the unjust outcome.

The Republican-appointed Supreme Court justices have declined to address partisan gerrymandering cases. The justices argued that neutral principles for drawing election boundaries do not exist. Rules for limiting judicial intervention in gerrymandering cases also do not exist. The lack of standards makes the court unable to determine when gerrymandering has occurred, the justices alleged.[145] This once again potentially reflects the business bias of the Supreme Court. When actions are needed to protect Republicans, such as voiding campaign finance laws, the Republican-appointed justices apparently do not hesitate to act. However, when actions are needed to protect Democrats, the Republican-appointed justices sometimes seem to find excuses for not acting.

Gerrymandering could be greatly reduced across the country by establishing bipartisan, objective, statistically and scientifically valid procedures for drawing election districts. The justices could have encouraged the development of such standards, as well as established trigger points for investigating possible gerrymandering abuses, such as those potentially indicated in the North Carolina example above.

The Judicial branch frequently develops decision rules and standards. It could have facilitated the development of standards that reduce or end the injustice of gerrymandering. But an unaccountable Supreme Court can do whatever it wants. Justices are free to leave an unjust system in place that benefits the party that appointed them. This once again shows the need to make the Supreme Court accountable to the people by imposing term limits and taking other actions discussed in Judicial Branch section.

Proportional Representation. As discussed in the Government and Elections section, in addition to ending gerrymandering abuses, single-seat elections districts often should be changed. Under this system, many citizens essentially are forced to support positions they oppose. A multi-seat, proportional representation system would produce fairer, more democratic results. To illustrate, if 20 percent of citizens in a ten-seat district were liberal or Democratic, their candidates would get two seats. This system would better reflect the will of the people, and thereby enhance democracy.

Another critical change needed in government is to achieve more consensus. As with single-seat election districts, under the current winner-take-all two-party system, large minorities of citizens (often close to 50 percent) frequently feel dissatisfied with election outcomes. They are forced to endure government policies that they strongly oppose. The Government and Elections section discussed several options for increasing consensus in government. Ending the business manufactured civil war between conservatives and liberals and weakening the political party system will greatly reduce dissatisfaction with government, and thereby make the lack of consensus less relevant.

Currently citizens often are deceived into disliking or hating the other party. People from one party often do not want to see or hear leaders from the other party. They oppose the other party largely due to emotional manipulation and deception. If they objectively looked at the actions of the other party, they would see that its actions are similar to their own party's actions in many cases. As we weaken the political party system and end the war between conservatives and liberals, we will focus on objective reality more. We will see that we agree on nearly everything. This will unite and empower us to suppress the unjust business revolution and restore our constitutional government. Ending emotionally manipulated hatred for the other party will reduce dissatisfaction with government among citizens of one party when the other party wins.

Weaken Political Parties. As discussed in the Political Parties section, in his Farewell Address, George Washington called political parties the worst enemy of elected government. He was correct. Political parties severely impede democracy and enable vested interests to control government. The Founders intended that politicians would focus on meeting the needs of their constituents and promoting the general welfare. Widely varying interests and agendas in government would lead to compromise and decisions that maximize the well-being of society.

But the two-party system short-circuits this intended functioning of government. Instead of many diverse goals and agendas, the two-party system reduces the focus of government down to two mega-agendas, both of which are focused on maximizing the financial well-being of the small group of wealthy citizens who control both political parties. The two-party system misleads citizens into giving up their rights, wealth and power to control government, and instead focusing on making rich people richer.

Political parties are not mentioned in our Constitution. They sit above the people's elected representatives and tell them what to do. As George Washington said, political parties are the enemy of the people and democracy. These unconstitutional structures must be severely weakened as quickly as possible. Instead, we must implement the government intended by our Founders and laid out in our Constitution. Politicians should be 100 percent focused on serving the citizens who elected them, promoting the general welfare and abiding by the Constitution. Political parties should have little or no influence on politicians.

Ranked Choice Voting. As discussed in the Government and Elections section, ranked choice voting would greatly alleviate problems caused by the winner-take-all two-party system. The current system inhibits third party candidates by compelling people to vote out of fear. To illustrate, in the 2000 Presidential election, many people voted for Ralph Nader who otherwise would have voted for Al Gore. This split the Democratic vote and enabled George W. Bush to win. Under the winner-take-all two-party system, a vote for a third party candidate often winds up supporting someone's least favorite candidate. Ranked choice voting enables citizens to vote for third party candidates without fear of supporting candidates they oppose. Under this approach, voters rank candidates. If their first choice does not win, their vote goes to their second choice. This system would greatly increase the ability of third party candidates to influence government, better reflect the will of the people, and thereby promote democracy.

Protect Privacy. As We the People assert our constitutional authority over government, we will compel it to fulfill its proper role as the servant of the people. As discussed in the Privacy section, the US government extensively spies on law-abiding citizens. One might ask, why is the servant spying on the master? The obvious answer is that the people are not the master of government, as our Constitution requires. The Traitors Act supposedly was passed to prevent terrorism. But only about one percent of Traitors Act activities involve terrorism prevention. The vast majority of Traitors Act enabled spying is used to suppress citizens and groups, such as Occupy Wall Street, who question the status quo of corporate welfare and business control of government. The Traitors Act also is widely used to monitor and arrest people for drug related crimes.

(As discussed in the Privacy section, the Patriot Act passed after the 9/11 terrorist attacks, and the USA Freedom Act that replaced it in 2015, potentially violate six of the ten Bill of Rights Amendments. Citizens were misled into believing that we must give up our Constitutional rights to prevent terrorism. But this is not true. We are smart enough to figure out how to effectively prevent terrorism while abiding by our

Constitution. Instead of preventing terrorism, the acts empower business-controlled government to spy on and suppress law-abiding citizens who oppose business-controlled government. Like the term Citizens United, the terms Patriot and Freedom Acts are offensive and misleading. Politicians who so grossly violate their obligation to uphold the Constitution by voting for these acts could be called traitors. As a result, to improve clarity and promote honesty, this book colloquially and collectively refers to the Patriot and Freedom Acts as the Traitors Act.)

Require Government Disclosure. Business-controlled government inappropriately uses the national security excuse to hide massive amounts of information from citizens. As discussed in the Privacy section, an employer cannot effectively manage their employees if they are not aware of employees' job related activities. It is the same with Democratic government. The people, the supposed leaders of society, cannot effectively monitor and control their servant government if they do not know what the servant is doing. The US government fails to disclose extensive information about business influence, corruption, mistakes and other information that poses no threat to national security. Citizens have a right to know this information. But exposing it would pose a major threat to ongoing business control of government. As a result, it is kept secret.

Once We the People reassert our legitimate right to control government, it will become our servant. Government no longer will violate the privacy of law-abiding citizens or withhold information that citizen/leaders have a right to know.

Implement True Democracy. As noted, the Constitution gives the federal government nearly absolute power to promote the general welfare. This power is being wielded by a small group of wealthy citizens who steal the wealth and power of nearly all other citizens. Once the people reclaim this power, we can use it to quickly implement the many changes needed to achieve sustainability and real prosperity.

China illustrates the benefits of a powerful government. In China and the US, democracy mostly does not exist. Voting creates the illusion of democracy. But in both countries, a small group of people largely controls government. This enables the Chinese government to quickly implement large-scale changes and programs. The Communist Party does not waste time with democracy. It simply decides what it wants to do and forces citizens to accept it. Fortunately, these actions often benefit the Chinese people.

In the US, it appears that our government is ineffective, divided, unproductive and gridlocked. When it comes to promoting the general welfare, it definitely is all of these things. However, gridlock and lack of productivity is an illusion. The US government is extremely effective at serving those who control it. This is proven by the rapid income and wealth growth of the small group that is controlling government.

Once we end the war between conservatives and liberals, stand together and take back control of government, we can require the US government to be very effective at serving all citizens. We agree on nearly all major issues. Disagreement largely is an illusion and deception. We agree that trillions of dollars of public wealth should not be given to wealthy citizens each year, wealthy citizens and large companies should not be controlling all three branches of government, life support systems should not be destroyed, and a strong, stable economy that provides jobs or business ownership opportunities for all who want or need them should be implemented. When we stand together on these areas of agreement, we can compel our powerful servant government to end corporate welfare and business control of government, as well as implement rigorous environmental, social and economic protections quickly and effectively.

One of the most tragic aspects of right-wing libertarianism and other deceptions that turn citizens against government is that citizens actually are being turned against themselves. Democratic government is an extension of the people. It is the means by which citizens protect and enhance their lives. Through democratic government, the people use their collective wealth and power to protect their rights, freedom, wealth and power.

But this truly democratic government would interfere with achieving ever-increasing shareholder returns. To remove this government 'interference' (i.e. protection of the People's rights, wealth and power), right-wing libertarians and other business allies often turn citizens against government. When this occurs, the people are turned against themselves. Of course citizens should oppose business-controlled government and plutocracy because this is not democracy. But deceiving citizens into blindly opposing government in general is extremely harmful. It implies that all government is bad. This is irrational.

Honest communications with citizens would urge them to oppose bad government (i.e. business-controlled government) and support or demand good government (true democracy). There is no civilization or country without government. Generally opposing government is ignorant and harmful. We must make it clear that we are not against government in general. We are against bad government that steals our wealth, power, freedom and rights. We demand that this be replaced with true democracy. As discussed in the Libertarianism section, the focus on big versus small government is a harmful distraction. It facilitates the theft of the people's wealth and power. The public conversation about government should not focus on size. It should focus on good versus bad government. Good government implicitly is efficient and no larger than necessary to effectively promote the general welfare. The priority is the well-being of society, not the size of government.

The US Constitution requires that the federal government be primarily focused on promoting the general welfare and common good. Our Founders established this country based on the natural laws and religious principles of fairness, equality, freedom and democracy. This system of government mostly worked for nearly 200 years. But our constitutional government has been overthrown since the 1980s. The US is in decline, largely not because other countries are rising, but rather because we no longer abide by our Constitution. We no longer are promoting the general welfare. We concentrate the nation's wealth and power in a small group of people. This drives rapid degradation of the general welfare.

The unjust, unconstitutional business revolution will end one way or the other. Perpetually stealing the people's wealth and power is not sustainable. The only question is, how long will we tolerate this theft? It is time to wake up from our delusion and put an end to the unjust revolution. Our Founders gave us a beautiful, enlightened Constitution, government and country. This is our gift. It is time to reclaim it.

Public Wealth

Public wealth should be used to benefit all citizens equally and fairly. But since the 1980s, extensive public wealth essentially has been stolen from average citizens in the US and many other countries and transferred to the small group of wealthy citizens who largely control government. This section discusses fair use of the public wealth.

In the nearly infinitely more sophisticated economics of nature, resources and wealth are distributed about equally between individuals within species, and between current and future generations. There is no shortage of resources and wealth on Earth. There is, however, grossly unfair and unsustainable resource and wealth distribution. Hunger, poverty and inability to meet basic needs largely are unnecessary in human society. They are caused by myopia, fear and lack of cooperation. Ultimately, they are caused by our flawed ideas and systems. As individuals, we understandably develop ideas and systems from the individual perspective. But as discussed throughout this book, this is not a rational or reality-based perspective for human society. It is unintentionally suicidal. The failure to think from a whole system perspective creates the Tragedy of the Commons.

The first priority, as our wise Founders understood over 200 years ago during the Age of Enlightenment, is the common good or general welfare. Individuals cannot survive or prosper if the larger environmental and social systems that support individuals are not healthy. Vested interests have suppressed rational thought and pushed us back into a New Dark Age. Not only are we largely focusing on the individual rather than whole system perspective. We narrow it down much further and focus on the financial well-being of a small group of already wealthy citizens. Through blind faith in irrational, myopic philosophies, citizens have been deceived into allowing the implementation of systems that place the financial well-being of wealthy citizens ahead of all else, including the survival of our children and humanity overall. Economic growth and investment returns have become the primary focus of measurement and management in society. But the focus should be on the well-being of all citizens, current and future.

Wealthy citizens often act as if they got rich on their own. But they did not. No one could get financially rich on a deserted island. People need resources, services, employees, customers and other support from society to get wealthy. Wealthy citizens frequently seem to act as if they are entitled to receive wealth and support from society without paying a fair price for it. But of course, they are not. They are not entitled to have the downside of business and investing covered through limited liability, bailouts and other mechanisms. They are not entitled to externalize costs and degrade the environment and society without paying for the burdens that they impose on society. They are not entitled to consume clean air, water and land (by polluting it) without paying for it.

They are not entitled to force employees to accept wages that do not meet basic needs when their companies are earning enough to pay living wages. They are not entitled to use publicly funded research, natural resources, broadcast spectrum, infrastructure, the legal system and all other aspects of public wealth without paying fair prices for them. They are not entitled to retain the wealth generated through money creation (fractional reserve lending), shut down small businesses and degrade local economies through unfair competition and government corruption, and pay unfairly low tax rates that force average citizens to make up difference.

Wealthy citizens and corporations are not entitled to take this wealth from society. But they do anyway. As discussed in the Corporate Welfare section, in the US, corporate welfare costs citizens at least several trillion dollars per year. Stealing the public wealth through corporate welfare impoverishes average citizens and severely degrades the economy and society. Stealing the people's wealth suppresses demand for products and services, which is by far the most important factor controlling the economy. Ending corporate welfare would greatly reduce or eliminate the need for income and property taxes on middle-income and low-income citizens. It would hugely stimulate the economy by increasing demand for products and services. Ending corporate welfare also would enable the US to provide a strong social safety net and guaranteed income for all citizens, not just retired citizens.

Some people might argue that providing a guaranteed income for all citizens is unfair wealth redistribution. It steals wealth from wealthy citizens and suppresses the motivation to work. As discussed below, experience with guaranteed income programs shows that they do not promote laziness. The benefits vastly outweigh the costs. Regarding unfair wealth distribution, this already is occurring. Through corporate welfare, we provide trillions of dollars of essentially guaranteed income to wealthy citizens. It would be much fairer and more beneficial to end guaranteed income (corporate welfare) for wealthy citizens and instead use the funds to benefit all citizens. As discussed in the Property Rights section, the public wealth does not belong to government or corporations. It belongs to current and future citizens. Providing a strong social safety net and guaranteed income is fairly distributing the public wealth to the rightful owners.

Through government corruption, wealthy citizens essentially are stealing large amounts of wealth from average citizens. As a result, the vast majority of citizens must divide a greatly reduced share of public wealth. This causes bitterness and division. Taking the public wealth makes life unnecessarily difficult for millions of average citizens. When they are barely able or unable to meet basic needs, people often become unwilling to help others. The solution is not to cut social welfare programs further. It is to end the theft of the public wealth through corporate welfare. Once people have equal access to the full share of public wealth, it will become much easier to meet basic needs and attain a good quality of life. Reducing the financial stress of average citizens through fair use of the public wealth will greatly increase the willingness to help needy citizens.

Currently we essentially take food out of the mouths of hungry children so that we can buy more mansions for wealthy people. Once we end this revolting use of the public wealth, we can make sure that children do not go hungry in this wealthy country as well as ensure that basic needs for nearly all citizens are met. Ending corporate welfare will greatly increase the sense of cooperation and brother/sisterhood in the US and other countries. This section discusses the actions needed to end the theft of the public wealth and utilize it to benefit all citizens equally and fairly.

As discussed in the Corporate Welfare section, there are several types of corporate welfare in the US. To protect the trillions of dollars of corporate welfare received by wealthy citizens and large companies each year, vested interests often attempt to turn citizens' attention away from corporate welfare towards social welfare spending. Social welfare is easier to identify and quantify. For example, the US government spent $3.7 trillion in 2015. About $2.2 trillion represented social welfare spending (Social Security - $888 billion, healthcare including Medicare - $938 billion, safety net programs such as food stamps - $362 billion).[146] Corporate welfare is more difficult to quantify because it usually does not show up as line items in government budgets.

Broadly defined, corporate welfare includes all unfair and inappropriate transfers of wealth from the general public to the small group of wealthy citizens who control government and own most corporate assets. Citizens pay for corporate welfare in many ways, including through higher income and other taxes, higher healthcare and other costs, reduced quality of life, unfairly high prices and unfairly low wages. Corporate welfare flows through the entire economy. While extensive corporate welfare occurs outside of government, essentially all of it is caused by inappropriate government influence. Wealthy citizens and corporations give large amounts of money to politicians, and then receive vastly more wealth in return. Examples of corporate welfare include the following.

Unfairly High Prices. Inappropriate government influence drives extensive corporate welfare in the broader economy in many ways. To illustrate, our flawed systems compel publicly traded companies to provide ever-increasing profits and shareholder returns. Achieving this becomes the primary focus of business-controlled government. Politicians who accept large amounts of money from wealthy business owners help their benefactors to achieve ever-increasing profits, for example by suppressing competition and labor. They often suppress competition by allowing industry consolidating mergers and acquisitions, providing tax and other benefits to large companies that suppress competition from small and medium-sized companies, and passing laws that prohibit competition from the public sector. Suppressing competition enables companies to charge unfairly high prices, and thereby increase profits and shareholder returns. Unfairly high prices, driven by inappropriate government influence, are a major form of corporate welfare.

Unfairly Low Wages. Business-controlled government also helps wealthy campaign donors to increase profits by unfairly suppressing unions and labor in general. Inappropriate government influence is a primary cause of nearly flat wages since the 1980s. Unfairly low wages are another major form of corporate welfare. They help companies to increase profits and shareholder returns.

Declining Customer Value. The financial community requirement to provide ever-increasing shareholder returns drives extensive corporate welfare in the broader economy. This places publicly traded companies under nearly constant pressure to increase prices and/or reduce quantity/quality/costs. The requirement to provide ever-increasing shareholder returns causes citizens to receive frequently declining customer value. They regularly pay higher prices for lower quantities of lower quality products and services. Regularly declining customer value, facilitated by big business control of government, the economy and society, is another major form of corporate welfare.

Helping the wealthy citizens who control government by degrading the rest of society is the expected outcome in a plutocracy. However, if the US were a democracy, as our Constitution demands, the government and economy would be focused on providing ever-increasing value to all citizens. Technology and ingenuity would be used to provide regularly declining prices and increasing quality.

Externalities. Beyond corporate welfare occurring in the broader economy, many specific forms have been discussed in this book. Externalized costs are one of the largest types of corporate welfare. As discussed in the Externalities section, burning fossil fuels, using synthetic chemicals, producing animal products and many other corporate activities cause large environmental and social problems and impose huge real costs on society. Companies frequently are not held responsible for these burdens placed on society. Not holding companies responsible compels them to create problems instead of prevent them. This vastly increases total costs to society because it usually is far more expensive to remediate problems than prevent them.

Ultimately, the value of life support systems degraded by companies is infinite because there is no life without them. In this sense, causing environmental problems is infinitely more expensive than preventing them. Companies must be held fully responsible for negative environmental and social impacts and costs, rather than externalizing them onto society (i.e. forcing citizens to pay for them). This will compel businesses to provide low impact, responsible products and services, because doing so will be the profit-maximizing strategy.

As discussed in the Externalities section, the terminology external costs or externalities is deceptive. External or externalized costs means that companies are not held responsible for real costs and negative impacts imposed on society. External cost implies that it somehow is acceptable for citizens to pay for or suffer from companies' negative impacts. Of course, it is not. To more effectively hold companies responsible for negative impacts imposed on society, we should develop more accurate terminology. Terms could include transferred costs or business costs paid by taxpayers. Regarding corporate welfare, rather than external cost corporate welfare, a more accurate term might be transferred cost corporate welfare.

In addition to being deceptive, the term externalities is reductionistic. It reflects the narrow, irrational, suicidal focus of current economic systems. Externalizing costs often increases profits, but degrades society. Our myopic focus on economic growth and shareholder returns frequently causes us to see the benefits, but ignore the degradation. In the essentially infinitely more sophisticated economics of nature, there are no externalities. Everything implicitly is balanced and taken into account. As we strive to achieve sustainability and real prosperity, in large part by emulating nature, we will discontinue the use of deceptive, reductionistic terms, such as externalities.

Limited Liability. This is another very large form of corporate welfare. As discussed in the Limited Liability and Corporations section, individual citizens and small business owners are held fully responsible for negative impacts on society. If they cause harm, their personal assets can be taken. But corporations and their wealthy owners often are not held fully responsible. For example, a company with $1 million of investment might cause $100 million of harm (i.e. by releasing chemicals into the environment that cause cancer). Investors might lose their investment. But citizens frequently would be required to pay for much of the remaining $99 million through higher taxes and health insurance costs and/or reduced quality of life. Under true capitalism, business owners own the downside and the upside. They assume the risks and get the financial benefits. But with limited liability, taxpayers frequently are compelled to act as the owners of business on the downside, while receiving none of the upside. This is socialism on the downside and capitalism on the upside.

Limited liability is a deceptive term because liability does not magically disappear. It mostly is transferred to government/taxpayers. As a result, the far more accurate term is taxpayer liability or transferred liability. A limited liability corporation is not a private entity because government/taxpayers often are compelled to act as the owners on the downside. Limited liability is a grossly unfair quasi-public organizational structure.

Beyond unfairness, limited liability is highly destructive. It compels businesses to severely degrade the environment and society. Current economic and financial systems require companies to focus mainly on maximizing shareholder returns. The highest risk corporate activities often provide the highest returns. High risk frequently balances high returns and limits engagement in risky activities. But transferring risk and liability to taxpayers greatly improves the risk/return profile. Limited liability often makes engaging in the most risky activities the profit-maximizing strategy. Not holding companies fully responsible for negative impacts greatly reduces the incentive to act responsibly.

Ending limited liability and holding investors and companies fully responsible for negative impacts would substantially change the corporate sector. Many high risk corporate activities, such as using fossil fuels, synthetic chemicals, genetic engineering, nanotechnology and nuclear power, would be done more responsibly or not done at all. These activities usually only are possible because businesses are allowed to transfer downside risks and costs to taxpayers. If companies were required to cover and insure the downside, they often could not afford to engage in these activities. They would be forced to figure out how to provide products and services in a far less environmentally and socially destructive manner. Failing to hold companies fully responsible for negative impacts not only shifts very high costs to citizens. It severely degrades life support systems and society.

Vested interests almost certainly would argue that holding them fully responsible for the externalized costs or negative impacts of burning fossil fuels, producing synthetic chemicals and other destructive corporate activities would substantially raise prices. But this is a gross deception. Not holding companies fully responsible, for example through limited liability, often compels them to cause environmental and social problems, rather than prevent them. Citizens pay for these problems through higher taxes, increased healthcare costs and fees, reduced quality of life and other means. Preventing problems usually is far less expensive than remediating them.

As discussed in the Externalities section, in a reality-based pricing environment that incorporated all real, actual costs, fossil fuels, synthetic chemicals and other high impact products frequently would be prohibitively expensive. But deceptively low prices mislead citizens into thinking that they are not expensive. Switching to renewable energy, energy efficiency and other more responsible products and services would greatly reduce total costs to society, while substantially improving quality of life. Citizens should be encouraged to focus on total costs, rather than deceptively low fossil fuel and other prices.

Underpricing Public Assets. Another large category of corporate welfare includes giving away public resources and assets, or selling them at below market prices. As discussed in Property Rights section, examples include regularly selling fossil fuels and other resources on public lands, taxpayer-funded research and broadband spectrum for far less than market value.

Giving away or selling public land cheaply is another example of this type of corporate welfare. The Founders and early leaders of the US almost certainly did not realize the immense future value and importance of public lands given away or sold cheaply long ago. Had they understood this high value, they probably would have provided long-term leases instead of selling the land. Now vast areas of formerly public land are being utilized for resource extraction and profit maximization. This land often was given away or acquired at unfairly low prices from government. On a total cost/benefit basis, the highest value use to society of this land frequently might be to leave forests standing or keep resources in place for future generations.

The Founders wisely placed the common good/general welfare ahead of all else. As discussed in the Libertarianism section, there is no right to own property stated in the Constitution (except for patents and copyrights). Instead, the Constitution empowers government to take property if necessary to promote the general welfare. Individual property rights obviously are important. But the common good takes priority (because individuals ultimately cannot prosper if the environmental and social systems that support individuals are not stable). At some point, the people might choose to take control of large parcels of formerly public land that are being managed in ways that degrade society, for example, by not protecting life support systems. However, as discussed in the

Property Rights section, resolving this unfair use of the public wealth might be a longer-term issue. In the short term, the most important actions include ending the large and obvious forms of corporate welfare, such as those discussed above and below.

Unfair Taxation. This is one of the largest forms of corporate welfare. The tax system in the US is grossly unfair and inequitable. It shows the great extent to which wealthy citizens and large companies control government. As noted, one study estimated that wealthy citizens avoid as much as $3 trillion of taxes each year. In 2010, federal government revenues were $2.3 trillion. Individual income taxes represent about half of this ($1.2 trillion).[147] If wealthy citizens paid their fair share of taxes, income taxes on middle and low-income citizens probably could be eliminated.

As discussed in the Taxes section, a basic principle of taxation is that citizens pay their fair share. Wealthy citizens require extensive resources, services and support from society to get wealthy. They have an obligation to support the society that made them wealthy. But wealthy citizens and corporations give large amounts of money to politicians and inappropriately influence government in other ways. As a result, political puppets shift the tax burden away from their wealthy benefactors to average citizens. This is extremely counterproductive (as well as extremely unfair). Taking wealth from average citizens suppresses demand for products and services, which degrades the economy and society. During the 1950s, the top marginal federal income tax rate often was over 90 percent. The US was investing in infrastructure, education and other critical aspects of society. We were the most successful economy with the largest middle class in the world.

By not requiring wealthy citizens to pay their fair share and harming average citizens, we are cannibalizing ourselves. Ensuring the well-being of current and future society requires that we compel wealthy citizens and corporations to pay their fair share of taxes. Many actions are needed to achieve this. For example, special deductions, exemptions and loopholes for the wealthy should be eliminated. Currently financial speculation is taxed at a low rate, while working for wages is taxed at a higher rate. This should be reversed. Capital gains for wealthy citizen should be taxed at a higher rate, while labor income tax rates are reduced, possibly to zero.

(Vested interests sometimes argue that taxing stock market gains at regular income tax rates is unfair because this causes double taxation. Corporations pay taxes. Taxing the equity gains of shareholders is double taxation, some allege. But this is deceptive. Equity income often results from stock appreciation, rather than dividend payouts. As discussed in the Finance and Capital Markets section, stock prices are not directly tied to profits or any other hard number. Stock prices are opinions. They sometimes go up when profits go down, and vice versa. Equity gains primarily result from appreciating stock values, not profit distributions. Stock appreciation is not profit distribution. Therefore, taxing these types of equity gains is not double taxation. Even for dividend distributions, as discussed below, corporations often pay very low effective tax rates. As a result, corporate tax rates actually paid combined with capital gains rates on equity investments often are lower than tax rates paid by citizens who work for wages.)

Currently, average citizens usually pay annual property taxes on homes, but wealthy citizens often do not pay annual taxes on many of their financial assets, such as stocks and bonds. As the value of homes increase, average citizens pay higher property taxes. But as the value of equity investments increase, for example, wealthy citizens frequently are not required to pay annual taxes on the principle or appreciation of it. Once they sell assets, they often pay taxes on the capital gain at a lower rate than those who work for a living. Alternatively, wealthy citizens can hide income and assets in tax havens or employ other tax avoidance strategies that frequently are not available to low and middle-income citizens.

Why are the primary assets of average citizens usually taxed annually, but the main assets of wealthy citizens often not taxed? At least part of the answer is obvious. Wealthy citizens give large amounts of money to the politicians who make tax laws. The tax burden should be shifted away from the main assets of average citizens to those of wealthy citizens. Mechanisms should be put in place to ensure that this wealth is partly allocated to communities that currently rely heavily on property taxes from average citizens.

In addition, financial transactions should be taxed. US financial transactions are estimated to be about $3 quadrillion per year. A 0.5 percent transaction tax per dollar (i.e. half cent) could generate about $15 trillion and nearly pay off the national debt in one year. More conservative studies estimate that a financial transaction tax could generate $500 billion per year.[148] This would enable federal individual income taxes to be reduced by nearly 50 percent.

Another important tax solution involves fairly taxing corporations. As discussed in the Taxes section, in the 1940s and 1950s, about one-third of federal government revenues came from corporate taxes. This has fallen to about 10 percent, in spite of record profits.[149] Corporations often mislead the public by arguing that the US has nearly the highest corporate tax rates in the world. But this is deceptive. The more relevant tax rate is not the stated rate. It is the actual rate paid. Corporations depend on many resources and services provided by government and society. But inappropriate influence of government has enabled them to avoid paying the full cost for this wealth taken from society. To rectify this, actual corporate taxes paid should cover services and benefits derived from society. In other words, the tax burden should be shifted away from average citizens back to corporations, where it was when the US had a strong middle class.

One of the most important tax solutions involves job creation in the US. As noted, the current system incentivizes sending jobs overseas. This should be reversed. Companies obviously should pay lower taxes when they keep jobs in the US. In addition, a tax and tariff system should be used to protect US jobs. The priority is having jobs in the US, not cheap products or high shareholder returns. To facilitate national job retention and fair taxation, countries might have to implement global tax rules that restrict the ability to move money around the world for the purpose of avoiding taxes.

In general, if wealthy individuals wish to live in the US and corporations wish to sell products here, they should pay fair taxes. Corrupt government has enabled them to avoid paying trillions of dollars of taxes. This is severely harming our country. Wealthy citizens and companies often wave the flag and claim that they are patriots. But they act like traitors. They want something for nothing. They are not bad people. Flawed systems compel their bad behavior. We must improve these systems, in part by making tax systems fair and equitable.

Some people might say that 'fair tax rate' is a vague, difficult to define term. One person's opinion of what constitutes fair might vary from another person's. However, there are several ways to determine fair tax rates. One is to ensure that people are paying rates that cover the full cost of services and other support received from society. Also, inequality in society strongly indicates tax unfairness. For example, millions of people in the US go hungry and are unable to meet other basic needs. At the same time, a small group of citizens has experienced phenomenal wealth and income growth since the 1980s. This strongly indicates that very wealthy citizens are not paying fair taxes, wages and other fees necessary to support the society that made them wealthy.

While there are many factors that influence tax rates, very generally speaking, one could say that, in a wealthy country, tax rates on wealthy citizens should rise until the minimum basic survival needs of nearly all citizens are met. Obviously, this does not mean the tax rates on wealthy people should rise to a level that causes them to go hungry and become unable to meet other basic needs. This would unfairly transfer hunger and impoverishment from one group to another. However, if wealthy citizens have to sell five of their fifteen mansions to pay higher taxes that cover the full cost of benefits received from society and prevent other citizens from going hungry, in general, this is not unfair.

Another way to estimate fair tax rates for wealthy citizens is to examine other wealthy countries with lower inequality and poverty. As discussed, many countries in Europe have far lower poverty rates than the US. These countries usually provide strong social safety nets and minimum standards of living for nearly all citizens. This strongly indicates that they are fairly taxing wealthy citizens and wisely allocating the public wealth.

Private Sector Money Creation. Allowing banks to create the US money supply through fractional reserve lending is another major form of corporate welfare. As discussed in the Money Creation section, private banks literally create money out of thin air, loan it out and keep the interest as profit. But the interest and profit from money creation largely does not belong to banks. It belongs to citizens.

To illustrate how the private sector uses fractional reserve lending to create the money supply, assume that a person deposits $1,000 in a bank.

At a ten percent reserve requirement, the bank can loan out $900. When it does, it creates $900 of new money out of thin air. The $1,000 deposit has grown to $1,900. The depositor has access to their $1,000, while the borrower has full use of the $900. Obviously, this system only works if not all depositors demand their deposits at the same time (i.e. bank runs occur). The borrower of the $900 might deposit their money in another bank, which could loan out $810. Through this process of depositing and relending, the banking system can grow a $1,000 deposit into $10,000 at a ten percent reserve requirement, and thereby create $9,000 of new money out of thin air. As discussed in the Money Creation section, about ten percent of the US money supply is coins and Federal Reserve notes. The remainder largely is credits or loans issues by banks and other financial institutions.

Allowing the private sector to create the money supply through lending causes many economic and social problems. For example, it potentially increases taxes by over $500 billion per year (i.e. nearly half of federal individual income taxes). When government runs a deficit, banks create money out of thin air, loan it to government and citizens pay interest on it (about $400 billion per year). If We the People reclaimed our right to create the money supply, when government ran a deficit, it would create money instead of banks and citizens often would pay no interest.

In addition, when banks create money, the interest they charge frequently is nearly all profit, because the cost of the money they lend out is very low or zero. They create it out of thin air through fractional reserve lending. If We the People created money, we would loan it to banks at a low interest rate. Banks then would loan it out at a higher rate. Citizens probably lose at least $100 billion per year of interest revenue by allowing banks to create the money supply.

Also, if We the People created the money supply, it would be far more stable. With private sector money creation, money constantly is being created and destroyed as loans are made and repaid. This creates a highly unstable money supply that strongly contributes to economic bubbles and recessions. The Federal Reserve tries to control the money supply through open market operations, quantitative easing and other means that increase or restrict lending. But controlling the lending activities of thousands of financial institutions is like trying to herd cats. If We the People created money, the money supply would be far more stable and easier to control. Money would not disappear as loans were repaid. It would be to vastly easier to stabilize the economy, for example, by expanding the money supply during recessions.

In addition, if citizens/government created money, the goal of the money supply would be to equally and fairly benefit all citizens and society. When banks create money, the systemically mandated goal is to benefit wealthy bankers and other investors. Private banks control how money is used in society by deciding who gets loans. If We the People created the money supply (i.e. democracy existed), money would be channeled into society in ways that create jobs, build infrastructure, expand higher education and benefit society in other ways.

As discussed in the Money Creation section, economic growth is needed in large part to pay interest on public and private debt. If We the People created the money supply, interest rates and the need to pay interest would be much lower. Private financial institutions are required to provide ever-increasing shareholder returns. To achieve this, they often charge very high interest rates and fees. Implementing public sector money creation would greatly alleviate the need to grow the economy, charge high interest rates and concentrate wealth at the top of society.

There is only one public state bank in the US (the Bank of North Dakota). The bank hugely benefits the state's economy. It channels profits back to the state ($82 million in 2012) and supports 80 community banks. The bank funds state infrastructure projects. When it makes loans to businesses, it requires that jobs be created in North Dakota. It makes affordable student loans and does not speculate in financial markets.[150] Establishing public banks in the other 49 states potentially would create over 10 million jobs in the US, reduce interest expenses and benefit society in many other ways.[151]

Republican and Democratic politicians frequently speak about the need to lower the national debt and deficit. But they rarely mention that there would be little or no debt and deficit if fractional reserve lending did not exist (probably because they often receive large amounts of money from the financial community). Ending fractional reserve lending is one of the most important actions needed to lower the national debt and deficit.

Reclaiming citizens' right to create money would greatly benefit society. Public sector money creation would provide a far more stable and vastly lower cost money supply. As discussed in the Money Creation section, switching from private sector to public sector money creation could be done quickly and fairly easily. Important actions include ending fractional reserve lending, requiring 100 percent bank reserves and making the Federal Reserve (Fed) part of the US Treasury. The Fed manages the US money supply. It is completely owned by private banks. Making the Fed part of the US Treasury places We the People in charge of the US money supply.

Citizens have been deceived into allowing banks and other financial institutions to take potentially over $500 billion of public wealth each year. Banks have no right to create money and retain the profits from money creation. Much of this wealth belongs to the people. The Constitution assigns the right to create money to Congress (i.e. We the People). It is time to reclaim our right.

Strengthen Social Safety Net. In spite of being one of the wealthiest nations, the US has nearly the weakest social safety net in the developed world. This is a main reason why we have the highest inequality and near highest poverty among developed countries. The public wealth should be used to benefit all citizens, in large part by implementing a strong social safety net. If we greatly reduce or eliminate corporate welfare, we could provide healthcare for all, secure retirement, low-cost or free higher education, daycare for working parents, and other poverty reduction and social welfare programs. This could be done while greatly reducing income and property taxes on middle and low-income citizens.

In several cases, providing public services would greatly reduce total costs to society while increasing quality of life. Healthcare probably is the best example of this. As discussed in the Healthcare section, other countries prove that the US could vastly lower healthcare costs, possibly by over 50 percent, while providing guaranteed, high-quality healthcare to all citizens if we implement a not-for-profit, government-owned or government-managed healthcare system.

But unfortunately, we are not using the public wealth to strengthen the social safety net. Our flawed systems require that wealthy people get continuously wealthier. After a while, this pushes everything else aside.

Social welfare must be reduced so that corporate welfare and shareholder returns can be increased.

Several deceptive and tragic excuses are used (mainly by Republicans) to justify cutting social welfare programs. To illustrate, North Carolina cut the duration and amount of unemployment benefits in 2013. The rationale for doing so was that cutting benefits would lower unemployment by increasing the motivation to find jobs. But cutting benefits had little impact on unemployment rates.[152] This rationale for cutting benefits shows the ignorant, heartless logic frequently used by politicians who accept money from wealthy citizens. The ignorant rationale implies that unemployed people do not have jobs because they are lazy and unmotivated. But as noted, there are far more people seeking work than there are available jobs. Many people will not find jobs, no matter how hard they look. But ignorant, heartless political puppets make citizens destitute so that they can provide ever-increasing amounts of public wealth to their wealthy masters.

Another ignorant and heartless strategy for cutting social welfare expenditures involves requiring drug testing of social welfare recipients. Tennessee, Florida and Utah, for example, require some social welfare recipients to submit to drug testing. People who fail the tests often are denied benefits. Usually less than one percent of social welfare recipients fail drug tests.[153] Screening all social welfare recipients probably often costs more than is saved by denying benefits to drug users. Beyond financial costs, it also stigmatizes and insults law-abiding citizens who are legitimately using social welfare programs.

Another important aspect of drug testing is denying benefits to needy citizens. This heartless approach often essentially throws drug addicts out in the streets (where the US, unlike other developed countries, frequently makes homelessness illegal). Addiction and other harmful behaviors should not be enabled by social welfare programs. But we should attempt to help troubled or needy citizens, rather than cutting them off. Many wealthy citizens use drugs. But we do not require them to take drug tests before receiving corporate welfare. The abandonment of needy, troubled citizens, while we lavish trillions of dollars of public wealth on wealthy citizens, once again shows the ignorant, heartless and destructive nature of our grossly flawed systems.

Guaranteed Income. In addition to using the public wealth to provide a strong social safety net and other social welfare programs that are taken for granted in most other developed countries, we should provide a guaranteed income to all citizens. Many wealthy citizens, businesses and their media and political allies probably would argue that providing a guaranteed income is unfair wealth redistribution. This is deceptive and inaccurate. It is a good example of the deception strategy, the best defense is a strong offense. As noted, grossly unfair wealth redistribution already is occurring in the US. Trillions of dollars of public wealth are being stolen from average citizens and transferred to wealthy citizens every year. Ending corporate welfare and using the funds to establish a strong social safety net and guaranteed income is appropriately distributing the public wealth to the rightful owners.

But ending corporate welfare would greatly restrict or end ever-increasing shareholder returns. As a result, our flawed systems compel wealthy citizens and their paid political puppets to argue that appropriately distributing the public wealth is inappropriate (i.e. the best defense is a strong offense − to protect corporate welfare, they attack social welfare).

Most parents believe that their children have a right to a portion of the family's wealth. It is the same with nations. Children born in the US are part owners of the public wealth. Instead of using the public wealth to provide essentially guaranteed income to wealthy citizens, we should provide it to all citizens.

Providing a guaranteed minimum income to all citizens would provide numerous large benefits to society. An excellent article by Lynn Stuart Parramore, called *5 Reasons to Consider a No-Strings-Attached, Basic Income for All Americans*, describes these benefits.[154] For example, a guaranteed income would substantially reduce poverty. One study estimated that giving $3,000 per year to each citizen, including children (who would receive the money through parents), potentially could cut poverty in half.[155] (Providing $3,000 per year to each citizen would cost about $1 trillion. However, the net cost would be much lower because several social welfare programs could be reduced. This or higher levels of guaranteed income could be funded through reductions in corporate welfare.)

A guaranteed income also would substantially stimulate the economy. Much of the money would go directly into the economy and thereby increase demand for products and services (as opposed to corporate welfare which frequently is squirreled away in offshore accounts). In addition, it would stabilize society by reducing crime and violence. Inability to meet basic needs often causes desperation and crime. Providing a guaranteed minimum income would greatly improve quality of life for low-income and unemployed citizens, and thereby reduce desperation and crime.

It also would enable people to better themselves by pursuing higher education, starting a business or taking other beneficial actions. In addition, a guaranteed income would compensate citizens who do unpaid, but important work in society, such as volunteering and raising children. It would strengthen families and improve the well-being of children by enabling more parents to stay home and raise children. Furthermore, a guaranteed income often would be a more efficient and effective way to deliver social welfare. It would lower the need for many different programs that frequently overlap or allow people to fall through the cracks.

Guaranteed income also often would increase rather than reduce the motivation to work for at least two reasons. First, social welfare benefits often are reduced as income increases. This discourages work. Providing a constant income to all citizens removes this disincentive. Second, as discussed, the large majority of people in the US dislike or are not engaged in their work. Many people take jobs that they do not like so that they can survive. A guaranteed income would enable people to seek more satisfying, but sometimes lower paying work. Increased work satisfaction would substantially increase the motivation to work. Finally, providing a guaranteed income would enhance the dignity of citizens. Currently, social welfare recipients frequently are stigmatized, especially by radical media. Providing an equal benefit to all citizens removes the stigma.[156]

Experience with guaranteed income programs shows that they greatly benefit society. As noted the poverty rate among elderly citizens would be five times higher without Social Security. A guaranteed income program implemented in the Canadian town of Dauphin in the 1970s further illustrates the benefits of guaranteed income. The program eliminated poverty in the town. It also enabled citizens to take better care of their families, live healthier lifestyles and get an education. Contrary to critics' opinions, the program did not promote laziness. Work hours dropped by one percent for men, three percent for married women, and five percent for unmarried women. People mostly reduced work to raise children, care for family members and pursue education.[157]

All citizens have a right to a decent quality of life with basic needs met. Countries should use the public wealth to ensure a minimum quality of life when they can afford to do so. The US definitely can afford it. As discussed in the Property Rights section, programs similar to guaranteed income already exist in the US. Social Security is the largest. In addition, the Alaska Permanent Fund provides annual dividends to citizens for the use of their fossil fuels and other common property.

Providing dividends from the sale of public resources is only one revenue stream. As discussed above, there are many other, often far larger revenue streams that could be used to provide a guaranteed income to citizens. We can and should use the public wealth to benefit all citizens, in large part by ending poverty, hunger and inability to meet basic needs in this wealthy and prosperous nation.

As discussed in the Inequality section above, the top one percent of society owns about $33 trillion of wealth (excluding wealth hidden in tax havens and the shadow financial market). Much of this wealth was earned fairly. However, as shown with the many corporate welfare examples in this book, a substantial portion of the wealth of the top one percent was not earned fairly. It largely was acquired through inappropriate government influence. Public wealth essentially was stolen from average citizens. With corporate welfare of trillions of dollars per year, possibly over half of the wealth of the top one percent does not belong to them.

About 40 percent of the top one percent's wealth sits idle (i.e. is not invested in ways that create jobs or benefit society in other ways).[158] If the people's wealth was returned, in large part by ending corporate welfare, this wealth could be put to beneficial uses. For example, it would take about 0.5 percent of the top one percent's wealth to end poverty in the US.[159] Some people might say that taking wealth from the top one percent would be unfair wealth redistribution. As noted, this is grossly incorrect. It would be like saying that reclaiming stolen money from a bank robber is unfair wealth redistribution. The essentially stolen wealth of the top one percent probably is at least 100 times greater than the amount needed to end poverty in the US.

Using a more realistic measure of poverty (i.e. inability to meet basic needs), at least 45 percent of children in the US live in poverty.[160] This is unnecessary, and horrible. We are not meeting the basic needs of more than 33 million children so that wealthy people can get continuously wealthier. It is the same situation with elderly citizens. How can we look in the mirror? We should be ashamed of ourselves. We have an obligation to protect those who cannot protect or support themselves, such as children and the elderly. We must put an end to the theft of the public wealth through corporate welfare and business control of government. We must use the public wealth to protect our children and their future society. There is no need for any child (or adult) to be hungry or not have their basic needs met in this wealthy country.

Sustainable Economy

In the same way that the public wealth should be used to benefit all citizens, we should develop an economic system that is focused on effectively maximizing the well-being of all citizens, current and future. To achieve this, we must step back and look at the big picture (i.e. think from a whole system perspective). For example, hundreds of years ago, economic experts probably discussed how to improve feudalism, slavery and other production systems. They probably suggested incremental changes and improvements. They apparently were not looking at the big picture. If they had, they would have realized that these systems grossly violated the laws of nature, including the laws of fairness, equality and freedom. Therefore, they were bound to fail. If experts long ago had been looking at the big picture, they would have realized that the solution was not to improve feudalism and slavery. It was to replace them with systems that abided by the laws of nature, and thereby were sustainable.

The same situation exists today. Economic experts frequently discuss how to solve problems by making incremental adjustments to current systems. We can see from rapidly growing environmental, social and economic problems that this approach is not working. In the same way that improving feudalism or slavery was not the answer long ago, improving the current form of quasi-capitalism also is not the answer. Reality and decades of experience show that this will not work. Environmental, social and economic conditions will continue to worsen if we largely continue to do the same things.

Adopting a whole system perspective enables us to envision sustainable systems and figure out how to implement them. It shows that we are surrounded by an economic system that essentially is infinitely more sophisticated than our own. As discussed, implied operating principles in nature's economic system include seeking balance not growth, producing no waste, achieving equitable resource distribution between individuals and generations, living off of current solar energy, and utilizing local production. As a result, problems in one region frequently do not affect other areas. This is the model and formula for a sustainable human economic system. We do not have to wonder how to become sustainable. The model is all around us and within us.

When re-engineering the human economy, we must focus first on the endpoint (i.e. put the what before the how). The first and most important goal obviously is survival. Environmental protection is the foundation of survival. Achieving it requires abiding by certain principles of nature (i.e. seeking balance not growth, producing zero waste, equally valuing current and future generations, and living off of current solar energy). Achieving economic stability requires abiding by the principle of local production (i.e. economic decentralization).

The economic system also should be focused on helping individuals to reach their fullest potential, in large part by abiding by nature's principle of equitable resource distribution. It should be focused on delivering and supporting activities that provide true life satisfaction, such as doing enjoyable work, spending time with family and friends, participating in a thriving community, being in nature, engaging in spiritual and personal development, fully expressing oneself, and pursuing one's unique interests and passions.

Once goals are identified, metrics can be selected. This helps to ensure that economic measurement and management are focused on the actual goals of the economic system. With goals and metrics identified, a practical plan can be developed for transitioning from current to desired systems. Attaining a sustainable economic system will require major changes to the current economic system. As discussed, the stated goal of the current system might be to maximize the well-being of society. But this is not the measured goal. Measurement largely determines management. As a result, the economic system is not managed in ways that maximize social well-being. Our myopic economic system makes the irrational assumption that maximizing economic growth and shareholder returns will maximize the well-being of society. But focusing on shareholder returns drives price increases, quality and quantity reductions, and environmental and social degradation. In other words, our myopic economic system largely produces the opposite of the intended goal. The system degrades society in many ways.

Sustainable economic systems require far more accurate and sophisticated measurement systems than the current ignorant, unintentionally suicidal system. We must identify, measure and effectively manage all critical environmental and social aspects of the economic system and larger society.

Implementing a sustainable economic system also requires adopting a more accurate, whole system view of trade. The current approach of outsourcing production to regions with competitive advantages is myopic and destructive. It ignores many critical aspects of a sustainable and truly prosperous society. Perhaps most importantly, global trade often drives environmental degradation, and thereby inhibits survival. It also frequently degrades communities by shifting production overseas. As discussed in the Trade, Scale and Competitive Advantage section, when all real environmental, social and economic costs and benefits are considered (i.e. when one stops ignoring reality), local production often will be the lowest cost, most beneficial option. This of course should not be surprising because nature largely operates this way.

Imports and exports are not necessary for a thriving economy and truly prosperous society (again as shown in nature). Foreign trade often helps wealthy citizens to get wealthier. They control government and media. As a result, they can deceive citizens into believing that free trade enhances society and order their political puppets to maximize foreign trade. But blindly believing that free trade is good is irrational and destructive. When social well-being is accurately measured, it becomes clear that free trade often degrades society. As noted, having good jobs is far more important than having a large selection of cheap products.

Demand for products and services is the foundation of the economy in the US. We can meet this demand with far less foreign trade, especially as we refocus our culture away from materialism and onto actions that actually provide satisfying lives.

The degree to which the US engages in importing and exporting should be based on full cost, whole system analyses. The goal is not that the economy grows or that large companies and wealthy citizens get wealthier. It is that the well-being of US society is maximized. This should not be determined by blind faith in the irrational idea that free trade always benefits society. Full cost analysis should be conducted on a case-by-case basis to determine which actions actually maximize social well-being. For example, exporting resources and products might degrade life support systems in the US and cause other problems. Companies should be free to do what they want, provided that they do not harm society. If accurate, full cost analysis shows that exports and imports degrade society in certain cases, they should be restricted or prohibited in these cases.

The current big company-dominated, import-export economy severely degrades local economies. Requiring full cost, whole system analysis will greatly facilitate the expansion and strengthening of local economies. Large companies, exports and imports obviously still will be needed at times. But these options no longer will be pursued without restraint or rational analysis. Objectively focusing on what actually maximizes social well-being frequently will restrict these options and produce a more beneficial balance between small, medium and large companies.

Refocusing the economy on social well-being (instead of economic growth and shareholder returns) will produce huge benefits for citizens. Currently, the focus on shareholder returns drives regular price increases and frequent quantity and quality reductions. To illustrate, several years ago, a well-know privately-held natural personal care products company was bought by a publicly traded corporation. Privately-held companies frequently are not under pressure to provide ever-increasing profits and shareholder returns. But publicly traded companies are. Privately held companies can sell high quality products at a reasonable, but not increasing profit for many years. But this generally would not work for a publicly traded company. The capital markets demand ever-increasing financial returns.

To achieve this, the acquiring company began to gradually change the acquired company's product line. The size of toothpaste tubes, for example, initially was reduced by about 10 percent, but prices of course remained the same or went up. The tube was switched from foil to plastic. Nearly all paste can be extracted from a foil tube because it can be rolled up. But it is much harder to do this with a plastic tube. The original toothpaste only required a small amount of paste to adequately brush teeth. But it appears that the products was reformulated so that more paste was required for each use. All of these changes contributed to increased sales and profits. But they also provided declining value to customers.

These types of ongoing shareholder-enhancing, customer-degrading changes are evident throughout our shareholder-focused economy. For example, decades ago, many types of soap bars seemed to last much longer. To increase profits and sales, soap apparently often was reformulated to provide less lather and be used up more quickly. Some pump bottles have straws that go to the lower corner of bottles and enable nearly full product extraction. But many bottles have shorter straws that leave 5-10 percent of contents in the bottle. As noted, food and other product packages frequently are made smaller, while prices remain the same or increase. Computers and many other products often seem to become obsolete in a few years. These and millions of other customer value degradations are the inevitable outcome of our myopic, shareholder-focused, unintentionally suicidal economic system.

A sustainable economy would be focused on providing continuously increasing value to customers and society. Technology, innovation and know-how would be used to reduce prices and improve quality and value. Technology and automation also would be used to reduce work requirements for citizens and provide other quality of life enhancements.

A sustainable economy would have a different definition of success than the current economy. Currently, success mainly is measured by economic growth and ever-increasing shareholder returns. A sustainable economy would seek to attain ever-increasing social well-being. To achieve this, economic output might decline at times, for example, because production was made more efficient, prices were declining, product longevity was increasing and/or advertising no longer was compelling people to buy things that they did not need. As in nature, the economy might expand or contract at different times. But this mostly would be irrelevant. The emphasis would be on increasing social well-being, not economic growth.

A sustainable economy also would have a different definition of efficiency. Current definitions frequently focus on production measures, such as output per labor hour. But a sustainable economy would be focused on more than profits and production efficiency. The goal is maximizing social well-being. As a result, economic efficiency measures might include achieving full employment, meeting all human needs, and protecting life support systems.

A sustainable economy also would utilize advertising and media differently. Current approaches often encourage citizens to maximize consumption and beat others by having the best appearance and possessions or most wealth. In a sustainable economy, advertising and media would be used to promote cooperation and cohesiveness in society, as well as encourage citizens to engage in activities that actually produce satisfying lives.

In addition, a sustainable economy would have a strong social safety net. This would greatly reduce the need to cover the downside of business. Companies would expand or contract based completely on the value that they provide to society. When companies contract or go out of business, a strong social safety net would ensure that employees who lost their jobs do not become destitute. This would reduce pressure to bailout or protect inefficient companies. It would enable capitalism to function more effectively because inefficient companies regularly would be replaced by more efficient ones.

Fulfilling jobs would be an important component of a sustainable economy. Businesses and the economy would be focused on meeting the needs of all stakeholders, not just shareholders. Education, flextime, family-friendly and other benefits that were widely offered before deregulation would be reestablished. A strong social safety net would relieve companies of the burden and obligation of providing healthcare, retirement security and other benefits to employees. As the fixed cost of employees substantially declines, companies would be able to have more employees working fewer hours. With a strong social safety net, part-time employees would have the same benefits and security as full-time employees. This could enable citizens to improve life satisfaction by working several part-time jobs instead of one full-time job. Citizens might work different jobs at different times of the year or rotate jobs in ways that make life more interesting and enjoyable.

Another critical aspect of a sustainable economy is ensuring fair competition. As noted, large companies often shut down smaller local companies and degrade local economies. In addition to not being held responsible for many negative impacts, large companies unfairly compete by giving large amounts of money to politicians, who then often give tax breaks to large companies. This partly shifts the tax burden to smaller local companies that are trying to compete with new large companies in town.

Another aspect of fair competition involves mergers. In the early 1900s, antitrust regulations were put in place to prevent unfair competition. However, since the 1980s, many of these antitrust regulations have been removed. As a result, substantial merger activity occurs that would have been illegal before 1980.[161] This creates extensive monopoly and oligopoly activity (i.e. domination of markets by one or a few companies). In many US markets, a few large companies have enough market share to control pricing, competition, new entrants and other market activities. This suppresses competition and often causes customers to pay higher prices for lower quality products and services, as occurs in the cable television market. To illustrate, in 1980, there were tens of thousands of grocery stores in the US. Now a few large companies control most of the market.[162]

A record $4.6 trillion of merger and acquisition activity was announced in 2015. For example, Dow and DuPont chemical companies announced that they would merge, and then split into three companies focused on agriculture, material science and specialty products.[163] This probably will reduce competition and increase prices in these areas. But the focus of the business-controlled US government is not on promoting fair competition and low prices. It largely is to ensure that wealthy campaign donors get continuously wealthier. As a result, as shown in the airline and other sectors, extensive M&A activity is allowed that reduces competition, eliminates jobs, harms communities, raises prices and degrades society in other ways.

Right-wing libertarianism and other anti-government public deceptions have facilitated the suppression of capitalism in the US. As discussed in the Libertarianism section, libertarians and other business allies often oppose government, promote so-called free markets, and aggressively support deregulation. But removing regulations intended to ensure fair competition enables monopolies, oligopolies and market concentration. This removes freedom in many ways. Customers often are forced to pay high prices for lower quality goods. Labor and vendors frequently have less freedom because fewer companies are available to buy their products and services. The so-called free (i.e. deregulated) market often is anti-competitive. As large companies control markets, democratic government that is focused on protecting citizens essentially is replaced by private government that is focused on protecting shareholders.[164] To ensure fair competition, regulations that require and protect fair competition must be reestablished.

Another critical aspect of implementing a sustainable economic system is to use rational, fact-based, reality-based, whole system analysis to determine how to best provide products and services. The current economic system mainly utilizes private, for-profit organizations. To protect ever-increasing shareholder returns, businesses and their allies often attack those who suggest that the public sector would be more effective in some cases. As discussed, vested interests frequently attempt to trick citizens into blindly believing that the private sector always is better than the public sector. Analysts who employed this type of blind faith reasoning in business would be quickly fired for being incompetent. In business, rational, fact-based analysis is used to assess various ways to achieve a particular goal. The option that objectively provides the greatest benefits for the least cost generally is selected.

We must use the same rational approach in larger society. Many types of organizations can provide products and services, such as private for-profit, non-governmental nonprofit (NGO), public, employee-owned and cooperative. Organizations can be large, medium or small. To maximize social well-being, we should rationally consider all relevant options, benefits and real costs, and then select the options that objectively provide the greatest benefit for the least total cost.

Large companies and their media and political allies often protect shareholder returns by misleading citizens into blindly believing economic dogma, such as the idea that the private sector always is better than the public sector. To maximize the well-being of society, citizens must be encouraged to think for themselves, rather than blindly believing vested interest positions. They should effectively say "prove it". Citizens should demand that companies and other vested interests provide rational, factual evidence and logic which shows that their positions are the most effective in particular situations. Vested interests routinely and deceptively emphasize points that support their positions, while leaving out those that do not. Citizens must demand that they receive all relevant information, pluses and minuses, about each option. This will enable them to select the approach that truly maximizes the well-being of society.

Wealthy business owners, politicians paid by them and other business allies use many public deceptions to facilitate privatization of public services and provide ever-increasing shareholder returns. For example, business allies often argue that the private sector is more efficient than the public sector. As a result, it can provide higher quality products and services at lower costs. But it is irrational to blindly believe this position. Sometimes it is true. Sometimes it is not. As discussed in the Trade, Scale and Competitive Advantage section, rational analysis reveals that the public sector has several major advantages that often would enable it to provide higher quality, lower cost services. These include economies of scale, lack of the profit motive, and a primary focus on maximizing the well-being of customers or society overall.

There is no inherent reason why a public entity or NGO could not be as efficient and effective as a for-profit company. Virtually every tool used by for-profit companies can be employed by public, NGO, cooperative and other types of organizations. These tools include hiring talented managers and employees, emphasizing high-efficiency, using strong incentives, and establishing good accounting and measurement systems.

The profit motive can be a double-edged sword. It can promote high efficiency. But when coupled with the requirement to provide ever-increasing shareholder returns, it can be a major disadvantage in terms of maximizing social well-being. The requirement to provide ever-increasing shareholder returns creates nearly constant pressure to increase prices and/or reduce costs/quality/quantity. As a result, the suicidal profit motive (i.e. requiring ever-increasing profits) often causes private sector services to be more expensive and lower quality than those provided by the public sector, especially over the mid to longer-term.

Profit essentially represents an extra cost that is not required for nonprofit or public entities. Our flawed systems require that this extra 'cost' (i.e. profit) always increases. As extra 'costs' continually increase, for-profit entities can become less competitive over time compared to organizations that are not hampered by the requirement to provide ever-increasing profits and shareholder returns. (When public or non-profit organizations require financing, they often can use debt or other types of funding that does not require ever-increasing returns to lenders or investors. Equity investments that require ever-increasing financial returns can become extremely expensive and destructive, as discussed in the Sustainable Finance section below.)

The profit motive causes companies to be primarily focused on producing profits and ever-increasing shareholder returns. These goals frequently are in conflict with serving customers and society well. This focus problem means that services that are critical for society, such as military, police, highway and taxation, generally should be provided by public entities. The primary focus of organizations providing these services must be on maximizing the well-being of society. The profit motive often would subvert these goals. As discussed in the Food, Education and Crime sections, human services, such as those related to healthcare, education and incarceration, also should be provided by entities that are primarily focused on maximizing the well-being of service recipients and society overall. The requirement to provide ever-increasing shareholder returns often puts companies in conflict with the well-being of patients, students and inmates.

Rather than blindly believing the business deception that the private sector always is better than the public sector, the private sector should be forced to compete with the public sector. We should require vested interests to back up their words by proving them. But publicly traded companies are structurally required to oppose anything that threatens ever-increasing shareholder returns. Competing with the public sector frequently would threaten shareholder returns because the public sector has several competitive advantages. As shown with the Tennessee

Internet access example discussed above, businesses often will use inappropriate government influence to limit or prohibit competition with the public sector.

As in the Tennessee case, businesses might argue that the public sector has unfair advantages over the private sector. This position of course is ridiculous. If the public sector can provide higher quality, lower cost services, it should provide them. This is not unfair. It is rational. Businesses essentially are arguing that citizens should pay higher prices for lower quality services so that their wealthy owners can get continuously wealthier.

The best example of this probably is the US for-profit healthcare system. US citizens pay 200-300 percent more for healthcare than most other developed countries, while receiving the worst coverage in the developed world, frequently with inferior results. From the perspective of companies, anything that restricts shareholder returns, such as competition, might be seen as unfair. But the true unfairness is forcing citizens to pay higher prices for lower quality healthcare and other services so that wealthy citizens can get continuously wealthier.

Politicians who accept money from business often argue that privatizing public services will lower costs. But this position is myopic and deceptive. Companies often cut costs by reducing wages, firing employees, and making remaining employees work harder. This frequently lowers tax revenues and increases demand for unemployment and other social welfare benefits. In other words, privatizing public services often increases total costs to society, especially over the longer-term. As a result, rigorous, full cost, whole system analysis should be required before privatizing public services. One example of this requirement includes the Pacheco-Menard law in Massachusetts. The law requires that totals costs to society of privatization be analyzed before public services are privatized.[165]

Also, all types of organizations should be allowed to compete to provide services, including NGOs, employee-owned and cooperative businesses. Even with manufacturing, we should not blindly assume that the for-profit private sector always is better. Entities without profit and shareholder return requirements can employ the same efficiency and good management strategies as for-profit companies. Avoiding ever-increasing profit and shareholder return 'costs' often can enable them to provide lower cost, higher quality products and services.

As noted, to protect shareholder returns, businesses and their allies frequently will attempt to deceive citizens. They might suggest that those who say that the public sector should provide certain services are advocating socialism or communism, and are against capitalism. This is highly deceptive. It implies that the US currently is using a capitalist system. This largely is incorrect. Citizens frequently are required to act as the owners of business on the downside, while receiving none of the financial upside. As a result, in the US, we are implementing a grossly unfair form of socialism.

This is why 'ism' words usually should be placed where they belong – in the garbage can. The priority is not supporting a particular philosophy. It is maximizing social well-being. We must use rational thought to determine which options objectively maximize the well-being of society in each situation. Business, government and other organizational structures are tools meant to serve society. Blindly assuming that business always is better than government would be like assuming that a hammer always is better than a screwdriver. But it depends on the job. Sometimes a hammer is the best tool. At other times, a screwdriver is needed. It is the same with business, government and all other types of productive organizations. Each one is best suited for particular applications.

Effectively utilizing government to provide services (and perhaps products when it is more efficient and effective to do so) requires that the US government be converted from bad to good. The US government often does a terrible job of serving average citizens because wealthy citizens control it. Once We the People regain control of government, we can require it to serve all citizens equally and fairly, in part by effectively providing various essential services.

Beyond profit, hierarchy represents another double-edged sword. Private sector organizations often can move quickly due to their hierarchical structure. The need for consensus or wide agreement in more democratic structures, such as cooperatives and democratic governments, can cause organizations to move more slowly. There are many ways to maximize speed and efficiency while still giving stakeholders opportunities to influence organizations. Germany's corporate structure, where labor representatives hold half of board seats, provides a good model. As humanity progresses and uses enlightened rational thinking, we will develop new types of organizations, hybrids perhaps, that combine the most effective features and qualities of several different organizations.

As discussed in Chapters Seven and Eight, another critical aspect of implementing a sustainable economic system involves improving business. Business is a tool meant to serve society. It has no inherent right to exist. In a democracy, citizens define how businesses and the economy operate. Well-informed citizens would require businesses to benefit and not harm society. The primary focus on shareholder returns often degrades labor, the environment, communities and everything else. Therefore, the well-being of society demands that the focus, structure and incentives of businesses be changed. The focus should be on benefiting all stakeholders and not degrading the environment or society. If companies do this well and operate efficiently, they could earn reasonable profits and investor returns.

A sustainability approach called Net Positive Impact (NPI) illustrates myopic business thinking that must be changed. NPI encourages companies to maximize positive impacts and minimize negative ones. This is beneficial in the sense that it encourages companies to identify, quantify and reduce negative impacts. But the approach ultimately is dangerous and flawed. It implies that some negative impacts are acceptable, as long as companies have more positive impacts. This is not true. Doing good does not justify or allow doing bad. We do not allow individuals to murder a few people if they do lots of good in society. Companies must be held to the same standard as individuals – full responsibility. They must not be allowed to degrade the environment or society in any way.

The focus on positive impacts largely is an irrelevant distraction. Companies would not exist if they did not have some positive impacts, such as providing useful products and services. The focus should be on eliminating negative impacts. Instead of net positive impacts, companies should be required to produce zero negative impacts. This is the focus of the TCR model described in Chapter Eight. It emphasizes evolving systems in ways that hold companies fully responsible for negative impacts, and thereby makes acting responsibly the profit-maximizing strategy. At the company level, TCR focuses on helping companies to reduce negative impacts unilaterally and work collaboratively with others on system changes that enable further impact mitigation.

Changing the focus of management and business is an essential component of implementing a sustainable economy. The requirement to put shareholder returns before all else often compels managers to degrade labor, communities, the environment and many other aspects of society. Managers are good people who do not wish to harm employees or anyone else. But they often are compelled to essentially say to employees, "I am sorry. I sincerely do not want to reduce your pay or lay you off. But my hands are tied. I am required to increase shareholder returns. If I do not do this, I will be fired or my company will go out of business."

As we implement a sustainable economy, the requirements and focus of business and management will change. Companies no longer will be allowed to harm the environment, communities, labor or anyone else. They will be required to act in a fully responsible manner. Once this occurs, the above conversation would be different. For example, shareholders might say to managers, we could make more money if we lay off people in the US and send jobs overseas. Then the manager essentially might say to shareholders, "I am sorry. I sincerely would like to help you receive ever-increasing investment returns. But my hands are tied. I am not allowed to harm employees, communities, the environment or anything else. If our company causes harm, by failing to act in a fully responsible manner, it will die. Then you will lose your investment. So unfortunately, I only can provide you with reasonable investment returns. I no longer can provide returns that grow forever, regardless of how much this degrades society."

The statement of sincerity regarding the inability to no longer provide ever-increasing shareholder returns might be inauthentic for some managers. Many managers probably do not like being placed in a position where they often are forced to harm society, for example, by laying off employees, cutting wages, polluting the environment and shutting down local businesses. In a sustainable economic system, structurally mandated conflicts between business and society would be removed because businesses would be held fully responsible for negative impacts.

Many managers will be relieved when they no longer are forced to degrade society. No one wants to head off to work in the morning essentially saying to their spouse, "Honey I'm off to make life more difficult for employees, damage life support systems, make harmful products, degrade our community and harm children. I'll be home in time for dinner." Sustainable businesses operating in a sustainable economy would not degrade the environment or society in any way. They will attain zero negative impacts and total corporate responsibility. By operating in a fully responsible manner, sustainable companies will enhance the lives of employees, customers, shareholders, communities and all other stakeholders.

In summary, a sustainable economy would be primarily focused on delivering constantly increasing value to society. Using technology and innovation, we would focus on enabling citizens to work fewer hours to meet basic needs. We would strive to provide higher quality products and services at continuously declining prices. Current business structures probably would have a limited role in a sustainable economy. The requirement to provide ever-increasing profits and shareholder returns creates ongoing pressure to increase prices and lower quality. Companies sometimes use innovation to deliver higher quality products and services at lower prices. But the requirement to grow forever routinely causes prices to rise while quality declines. This is obvious to many consumers who consistently see prices going up, package sizes getting smaller and products being reformulated in ways that cause them to be used up more quickly.

Sustainable businesses would not labor under suicidal growth requirements. They would be structured to benefit shareholders by acting in a fully responsible manner and delivering continuously increasing value (i.e. declining prices and increasing quality) to individuals and society.

Alternative productive organizations probably would play a much larger role in a sustainable economy and society. As noted, cooperatives, NGOs and government entities often have substantial competitive advantages over for-profit entities. To illustrate, technology might allow the development of a product that lasts 100 years and costs nothing to maintain and operate. A for-profit entity that made a product like this might put itself out of business. In this case, the profit motive could inhibit providing the highest value to society. But the priority in a sustainable economy is not maximizing shareholder value. It is maximizing customer and societal value. Therefore, the economic system would be focused on delivering inexpensive or nearly free high quality products and services that last a very long time. To achieve this, organizations might be developed that are intended to only exist for limited periods, and then go out of existence once they fulfill their objective.

In a sustainable economy, all types of public and private organizations would compete to provide products and services. Those that can provide the highest quality at the lowest cost would dominate the market. This frequently would include NGOs and public organizations. NGOs, cooperatives and public organizations are consistent with a sustainable economy, in part because they produce more equitable resource and wealth distribution, as occurs in nature. The organizations are not focused on providing ever-increasing profits to a small group of wealthy business owners. The wealth produced by these types of organizations is shared among many stakeholders, including customers (through lower prices), employees (through sustainable wages), communities (through responsible operations), and owners or taxpayers (through reasonable profits or surpluses). In a sustainable economy, measurement and management would be focused on providing continuously improving quality of life for current citizens, while maximizing the ability of future generations to prosper.

At the big picture level, large-scale changes are required in the economic area. In the same way that incremental changes to feudalism and slavery were not the answer, incremental changes to current systems also often will not work. We must define a sustainable economic system, and then evolve our current system into this form. Making incremental changes to the current system is not the right overall approach. But there almost certainly will be phased implementation of sustainable economic systems. As a result, incremental improvements might be the first phase of the transition to sustainable economy.

Considering nature can give us a sense of what sustainable human economic systems might look like someday. For example, in the essentially infinitely more sophisticated economics of nature, oak trees do not demand payment from squirrels for providing acorns. The blood

222

system does not demand payment from cells for delivering oxygen and nutrients and removing waste. Long ago, many indigenous societies that were more focused on giving than receiving also did not use money. But the dominant human consciousness of separation and fear inhibits cooperation, trust and sharing. At our current level of consciousness, we probably are not ready to function without money, as nature does. We probably will have to evolve through several levels of consciousness and economic systems before we fully emulate the sophistication of nature's economics.

This section has discussed many changes needed to implement a sustainable economic system, including focusing economic measurement and management on maximizing social well-being instead of economic growth and shareholder returns, emulating nature, and using objective, rational thought to identify optimal means of delivering products and services in each situation. Beyond the changes discussed above, extensive economic and political system changes have been discussed throughout this book that also are needed to implement a sustainable economy. These include implementing reality-based pricing by integrating external costs into prices, holding companies fully responsible for negative impacts, and accurately valuing future generations and resources by reforming myopic time value of money concepts.

Sustainable Finance

Establishing a sustainable financial system is essential for implementing a sustainable economy. In a democracy, the economy is meant to serve all of society. The financial system is intended to serve and support the economy. But plutocracy has reversed this situation in the US and some other countries. Rather than being the servant of the economy and society, the financial sector has become the master in many ways. This section broadly discusses how to evolve our current unfair and destructive financial system into a sustainable form. The Finance and Capital Markets section provides more specific details about implementing a sustainable financial system.

As discussed in the Economic Growth section, growth is limited in the essentially infinitely more sophisticated implied economics of nature. Natural systems focus mainly on maintaining balance and stability, not achieving growth. This also was the case in human society for nearly all of human history. Up to the 1800s, most regions experienced little or no economic growth.[166] Industrialization and population growth have been main drivers of economic growth over the past 200 years.

As discussed in the Population section, one way or the other, human population growth, resource consumption and waste generation will be limited. We either will figure out how to voluntarily live within the limits and laws of nature. Or nature will impose limits on human society involuntarily, probably in a highly disruptive and traumatic manner. The Population section discussed strategies for voluntarily limiting population growth and achieving sustainable population levels. Many other sections discussed how we can greatly improve the efficiency of human society, and thereby substantially reduce resource consumption and waste generation.

Beyond industrialization and population growth, another driver of economic growth has been investor demand for superior financial returns. High investment returns are a main problem in the financial sector. For many years, wealthy investors have come to expect high, often double-digit, financial returns. It will be difficult or impossible to maintain this in a sustainable economic system. High economic growth facilitates high financial returns. But as we transition to sustainable economic balance, high financial returns often will not be available. When society and the economy are focused on maximizing social well-being, instead of economic growth and shareholder returns, the optimal state will be economic shrinkage in many cases.

For example, as we refocus the economy on providing continuously increasing customer and societal value, prices often will decline while product quality and longevity increase. In developed regions with stable populations, this often means that overall consumption will decline. Refocusing society, advertising and media away from materialism to lifestyles that provide true life satisfaction will drive further reductions in consumption. It often will not be possible to provide high returns on debt and equity investments in a zero or negative growth environment.

This begs the question, how will citizens and productive organizations secure necessary financing? Fortunately, there are many ways to address this issue. We know that it is possible to support productive activities without high financial returns because nature has been doing it for billions of years. It also has occurred widely throughout human history.

Decentralization is the key to establishing sustainable economic and financial systems. In nature and human society for nearly all of history, economic activities mainly were decentralized. Largely as a result, high financial returns were not required. The main Founders of the US, including George Washington, Benjamin Franklin, John Adams, Thomas Jefferson and James Madison, believed that the future prosperity of the US depended on the formation of a decentralized economy comprised of free citizens, farmers and small businesses. As discussed in the Political Parties section, Thomas Jefferson and other Founders strongly opposed an economy that was heavily based on financial speculation. But Alexander Hamilton, along with wealthy bankers and merchants, short-circuited this plan by using political parties to divide the people and essentially steal their wealth and power. This facilitated the establishment of a large banking and business class that dominated the economy and concentrated wealth and production.

Centralization is a main driver of high financial returns. Centralized production, as we largely have now, makes society heavily dependent on a relatively small number of large companies. Large companies often require large debt and equity investments to expand. These funds mainly are provided by large financial institutions and a small group of very wealthy citizens.

This situation gives wealthy citizens strong control of the economy and society. They often demand ever-increasing financial returns. Society is held hostage to this irrational, unfair and ultimately suicidal financial requirement. When the primary measured and managed focus of society essentially is ensuring that a small group of wealthy citizens gets continuously wealthier, everything else gets pushed aside. Rising prices, flat wages, and reduced employment and retirement security cause millions of people to suffer and struggle to meet basic needs, while a small group receives vastly more wealth than is needed to live comfortable lives. The centralized, big business economy facilitates the establishment of a leisure class that works little or not at all, while living off of high return investments.

Aside from being unfair, this situation is unsustainable. It will not last. The many public deceptions discussed in this book often mislead citizens into supporting a centralized economy that frequently impoverishes average citizens. As we raise public awareness about vested interest deceptions and economic unfairness, we will replace plutocracy with democracy. We will refocus the economy on doing what is best for all citizens, not just wealthy citizens. We will begin to decentralize the economy and rebuild local economies and communities. As discussed in the Trade, Scale and Competitive Advantage section, full cost, whole system analysis frequently will reveal that local production and economic activities produce the lowest cost, highest benefit outcomes.

Decentralization will reduce the need for 'big' finance (i.e. large transaction, expensive, high return) and loosen the grip of wealthy financiers on society. Centralization obviously still will be beneficial in several sectors. But we do not have to remain hostage to high financial returns. There are several lower cost, fairer and more effective ways to provide debt and equity financing for centralized and decentralized production and other beneficial activities.

One of the most important financial system changes is to convert money creation from plutocracy to democracy. As discussed, banks create about 90 percent of the US money supply through fractional reserve lending. Banks often have most of the money because We the People allow them to create money. When citizens and companies need loans or financing, they frequently go to banks. Through control of the money supply, banks and other lenders set interest rates, decide who gets money, and determine how money is used in the economy. But banks do not own the money supply. We the People do.

As discussed in the Debt and Interest section, for much of human history, charging interest was considered to be a severe crime, often equivalent to murder. Charging interest was seen as abusing or taking advantage of people who need money to survive. Today, people are misled into thinking that banks have a right to create money and retain the profits from money creation. Once we reclaim our right to create and control the money supply, we will use the money supply in ways that benefit all citizens and society.

As discussed in the Finance and Capital Markets section, prior to 1980, charging high interest rates was illegal nearly everywhere in the US. But business-controlled government removed these societal protections (i.e. usury laws). This enabled wealthy citizens to abuse and take advantage of average citizens through high interest charges. Interest rates in general are near historic lows. Low interest rates enable banks and other financial institutions to pay depositors very little for the use of their money. But banks, credit card companies and other lenders often charge high interest, sometimes as high as 30 percent, on money that they create for free through fractional reserve lending or borrow at very low rates.

Low interest rates benefit the small group of citizens who largely control government, media and society. Low returns on debt investments compel many citizens to place retirement savings in equity markets. Like a Ponzi scheme, as long as money is going into equity markets, share prices often go up. Hedge funds, electronic trading and other sophisticated investment strategies, that usually only are available to wealthy investors, enable these investors to receive most equity market growth. In other words, allowing the private sector to control the money supply and interest rates benefits wealthy citizens, but frequently harms most other citizens, by driving equity market growth and enabling lenders to charge very high interest rates.

As citizens take control of the money supply, we can put an end to interest rate abuse. Under a sustainable, more decentralized economy that is focused on maximizing social well-being, economic growth often will be low, zero or negative. The need to charge interest in this environment will be much lower or nonexistent. When citizens control the money supply, we can provide low or no interest loans to support citizens, businesses and other productive, beneficial activities. When interest is charged, We the People will get a return on our investment. The profits or interest from money creation largely will go to the rightful owners (all citizens), not just bank owners and other wealthy investors.

Providing low or no cost debt financing will be relatively easy once the people reclaim their right to create and control the money supply. However, providing affordable equity finance is a much more complex issue. The financial community puts strong pressure on companies to provide very high equity returns. This can make equity financing extremely expensive.

The situation with high equity returns is similar to that with high interest rates. There are upsides and downsides. With high interest rates, people usually focus on the downside. High interest rates make life more difficult for citizens and organizations because debt financing is more expensive. The upside (lenders making more money) does not receive as much attention. The situation with high equity returns largely is reversed. The upside (investors making more money) usually is emphasized. The downside receives much less attention. But in some ways, the downside of high equity returns is worse than the downside of high interest rates. High equity returns often degrade society more than high interest rates.

As discussed in the Finance and Capital Markets section, stock price is a collective opinion. It is not directly tied to any hard number. But profits and stock price usually are strongly correlated. Increasing profits is one of the most effective ways to raise stock prices. When the economy is growing and prosperity is broadly shared, as it was in the 1950s, rising stock prices can benefit society. But since the 1980s, wages largely have been flat, while prices often rose rapidly. Corporate profits and value created by high equity returns largely were concentrated at the top of society. Value was not broadly shared. As discussed in the Stock Market Growth section, rising stock prices often benefited wealthy citizens by degrading the lives of the vast majority of citizens. The demand for ever-increasing profits and shareholder returns frequently compels companies to degrade the environment and society. As noted, 75 percent of S&P 500 profit growth from 2000 to 2007 resulted from cutting employee wages and benefits.

Since the 1980s, stock market growth largely resulted from cannibalizing and degrading society. This is the downside of high equity returns. When true, society-enhancing value is not being created, profits usually are increased by taking value from the rest of society. Speaking favorably of high stock market returns in this environment would be like saying that high interest rates benefit society because wealthy lenders make more money. In the same way that we rightly focus on the downside of high interest rates, we also should focus on the downside of high equity returns much more. Both high cost debt and high cost (i.e. high return) equity frequently severely degrade the lives of the vast majority of citizens, while benefiting a small group of wealthy citizens.

From 2009 to 2014, the S&P 500 grew by an average of about 15 percent per year. Over the same period, the economy and CPI rose by an average of about 1.2 percent and 1.6 percent annually in the US, respectively.[167] During this time, companies often experienced record profit levels, as indicated by high stock market growth. However, this corporate success did not create broad prosperity, as indicated by low economic growth. The benefits of stock market growth were narrowly concentrated among a relatively small group of wealthy investors.

Misleading CPI numbers hide the degradation of society. As noted, the CPI largely no longer measures actual inflation. If inflation were calculated as it were before 1980, it would be nearly 10 percent (as indicated by rising corporate profits and shareholder returns). With flat wages and rising prices, citizens often are forced to reduce consumption. This inhibits economic growth. Stock market growth and misleading inflation statistics hide the declining quality of life of the vast majority of US citizens.

As discussed in the Finance and Capital Markets section, the financial sector in the US and several other countries has grown rapidly since 1980. The sector is not focused on benefiting society. It is focused on benefiting the financial sector and a small group of wealthy citizens. Hedge fund and private equity transactions, mergers and acquisitions, and many other financial sector activities frequently reduce employment, raise prices, concentrate wealth and degrade society in other ways.

As We the People convert our country from plutocracy to democracy, we will rein in the financial sector. There is no divine right to earn high, or especially ever-increasing, returns on equity investments. Financial transactions and structures that degrade society will be restricted or prohibited. For example, financial activities that concentrate wealth by degrading labor, customers, the environment and other aspects of society frequently would be restricted.

Financial institutions compete to provide high financial returns. Strong financial community pressure to provide very high profits and equity returns is one of the most destructive forces in society. Maximizing the well-being of society demands that this pressure be substantially reduced. Many actions discussed in this book will help to alleviate this pressure. For example, shifting the focus of measurement and management from maximizing economic growth to maximizing social well-being will greatly reduce pressure to grow the economy and provide high financial returns.

Holding companies fully responsible for negative environmental and social impacts also will reduce pressure for high financial returns. As discussed, internalizing the real costs of the centralized, big-company economy frequently will make local, smaller company production the lowest cost, highest benefit option. Holding companies responsible will reduce the size and/or number of large companies. This in turn will lower the need for 'big', high return equity finance.

In addition, holding companies fully responsible will reduce their ability to provide high equity returns. Compelling responsible behavior, for example by internalizing real costs, often will reduce profits. Companies no longer will be able to provide high profits and financial returns by degrading customers, employees, the environment and other aspects of society.

Substantially reducing or eliminating corporate welfare will further reduce the ability to provide high profits and financial returns. As discussed, extensive public wealth is transferred to corporations through many forms of corporate welfare. This public wealth often is used to inflate profits and provide high financial returns.

Beyond corporations, extensive corporate welfare also is given to wealthy citizens, for example through tax breaks and loopholes. Ending these forms of corporate welfare will substantially reduce the demand for high financial returns by lowering the volume of investments seeking high returns. Much of the income of the wealthiest citizens is unfairly extracted from society through corporate welfare. They frequently invest this unfairly acquired wealth back into the economy and demand high financial returns. Ending corporate welfare will greatly reduce the wealth concentrated at the top of society, and thereby reduce funds available for big, high return finance.

Providing greater retirement security, for example by substantially expanding Social Security, is an essential component of reducing high financial returns. As discussed in the Finance and Capital Markets section, vested interests have driven changes that often make the retirement security of average citizens dependent on capital market growth (such as converting defined benefit to defined contribution pension plans). The need to protect retirement security frequently compels government to cover the losses of wealthy capital market investors. From the perspective of very wealthy citizens, making the retirement security of average citizens dependent on capital market growth was a stroke of genius. This makes average citizens cheerleaders for a system that often impoverishes average citizens. Rather than giving trillions of dollars of public wealth to wealthy citizens every year, we should use the public wealth to guarantee a secure retirement that at least meets the basic needs of all elderly citizens. Providing retirement security will greatly reduce pressure to provide high equity market returns.

Another critical action needed to reduce high, destructive equity returns is to focus stimulus and economic development efforts on the demand-side, instead of the supply-side. Current efforts are heavily focused on the supply-side. We essentially give large amounts of money to wealthy business owners, for example through tax breaks and other incentives, based on the idea that they will invest this public wealth in the economy and create jobs. But this is not rational.

As noted, the foundational driver of the economy and job creation is demand for products and services, not giving money to rich people. Transferring public wealth from average citizens to wealthy business owners largely will not create jobs or stimulate the economy. Instead, it often will suppress demand, weaken the economy and reduce jobs. Wealthy business owners will not build factories and create jobs in the absence of demand for their products and services. Instead, they frequently will squirrel away their taxpayer subsidies in foreign accounts.

Using the public wealth to ensure that citizens can meet basic and other needs is by far the most effective way to stimulate the economy and create jobs. Public wealth used to support average citizens nearly always will flow straight into the economy, increase demand and create new jobs. Wealthy business owners do not need taxpayer handouts when demand for their products and services is strong because they have attractive value propositions for lenders and investors.

Ending tax unfairness also could reduce high equity returns. As discussed, equity returns frequently are taxed at a low capital gains rate, while working citizens pay substantially higher taxes. In other words, wealthy speculators, who have vastly more wealth than they need to live comfortable lives, often work little and pay relatively low taxes. At the same time, hard-working citizens who frequently struggle to feed their families pay high taxes. This tax unfairness impedes the economy and job creation.

As discussed in the Taxes section, low capital gains and top marginal tax rates encourage financial speculation. This increases inequality and inhibits widespread economic prosperity. Rather than promoting financial speculation, the tax code should be used to promote domestic manufacturing, research and development, and other activities that broadly benefit society. Financial speculators should be taxed at relatively high rates, while citizens who work for a living pay low or no taxes on wages. This would stimulate the economy, create jobs and discourage harmful financial speculation.

Taxing equity returns at a high rate could have a mixed affect. In some cases, companies might feel pressure to provide even higher profits to offset higher tax rates and make equity investments attractive. But actions discussed above and below will limit this effect. In addition, in this case, fairness takes priority over effect. Very wealthy citizens who are sitting at home collecting investment income should be paying higher tax rates than people who are working for wages and struggling to get by.

Vested interests often mislead citizens by arguing that wealthy citizens already pay most of the taxes. But this is highly deceptive. The key issue from a fairness perspective is not absolute taxes paid. It is the tax rate. As discussed, no one gets wealthy on their own. Wealthy citizens have an obligation to pay back more to the society that enabled them to become wealthy. A billionaire should not be paying a five percent tax rate (due to loopholes, government influence and other tax avoidance strategies), while working citizens pay 30 percent or higher.

One of the most important actions needed to reduce high equity returns is to increase competition. Making citizens dependent on large, for-profit companies enables them to provide increasing profits and equity returns by regularly raising prices and reducing quantity/quality/costs. As discussed, companies should be required to compete with all forms of productive enterprises, including NGOs, employee-owned, cooperative and public. The numerous competitive advantages of these types of organizations often will enable them to provide lower prices and higher quality. This competition frequently will greatly reduce the ability of for-profit companies to provide unfairly high profits and financial returns.

Holding companies responsible, increasing competition, and ending corporate welfare, fractional reserve lending and unfair taxation are critical macro-level strategies for reining in the financial community and reducing high, destructive financial returns. But decentralization probably is the most important aspect of sustainable economic and financial systems. Therefore, government and other programs that encourage it can strongly support and accelerate the transition to a sustainable economy and society.

As discussed in the Trade, Scale and Competitive Advantage section, centralization concentrates wealth and power, inhibits democracy, causes economic instability and often increases poverty and unemployment. As discussed in the Population section, the global trend toward urbanization is unsustainable. It is the opposite of what occurs in nature. It produces ghettos and areas of economic stagnation. It also causes unsustainable transportation as citizens commute long distances to work and goods are transported many miles.

We know from observations of reality and nature that decentralized production generates vastly greater economic stability, true prosperity and democracy. Citizens control their destiny. They are not controlled by distant large companies that degrade their environments and communities. Decentralization is far more likely to produce full employment, eliminate poverty, meet basic needs, help citizens to reach their fullest potential and protect local environments (because people living on the land control it).

Decentralization reduces the power of the financial community over society. Debt and equity financing frequently can be provided locally. Locally-owned or cooperative banks can be established that provide low or no interest loans to residents and local businesses, and channel surpluses back to citizens. Decentralization greatly increases opportunities for local equity investing, for example, through local ownership and investment in the local economy. Local debt and equity investing keep wealth in communities and thereby strengthens local economies.

Beyond efforts to specifically decentralize finance, activities that broadly promote decentralization can indirectly support the transition to sustainable finance. These activities include government programs, measurement of success, resource efficiency and cultural awareness. Government can facilitate decentralization by implementing programs that strengthen local economies, support small and medium-size businesses, and promote redesign of communities and society in ways that minimize transportation requirements.

Public and private entities can be established that provide advice, expertise and other services and resources to small businesses, cooperatives, employee-owned enterprises and other organizations. Providing expertise and services that frequently only are available to larger companies will level the playing field and facilitate economic decentralization. Smaller organizations also could be networked together in ways that provide economies of scale and facilitate competition with larger organizations. Small businesses and other groups might pay minimal fees for advisory services. Advisory organizations generally would not receive equity interests because the goal is to promote decentralized, not concentrated, ownership.

Refocusing the measurement and management of government and society on social well-being instead of economic growth will accelerate decentralization and greatly enhance local communities and quality of life. As society refocuses on maximizing the well-being of all citizens, technology and know-how will be used to reduce work hours and make it easier and less expensive to meet basic needs. Far more satisfying and family-friendly jobs will be created.

Improving efficiency is an essential component of reducing the costs of living, and thereby enabling citizens to spend more time doing what they love. Society's use of packaging and many other materials is overwhelmingly wasteful, unnecessary and environmentally destructive. We do not need packaging for many food and other items. We myopically treat the environment as if it can endlessly supply resources and accept our wastes. As discussed in the Waste section, nature produces no waste. But our unsustainable society generates massive amounts of waste that are rapidly degrading our life support systems. We must end this suicidal ignorance. Decentralization and promoting local economies facilitates reduced transportation, packaging and costs of living.

Changing culture is a critical element of decentralization. Our current society essentially is focused on making rich people richer. To achieve this, advertising and media compel citizens to compete on possessions, wealth and appearance. As discussed in the Advertising, Media and Culture section, this produces widespread senses of inadequacy, emptiness and unhappiness in society. People who do not compete well enough, for example by failing to have enough or the right type of possessions, frequently are implicitly or explicitly castigated.

In a sustainable society, we would change the definition of success, and use advertising and media to promote this new definition. As a democratic, wise and compassionate nation, we would use our great ingenuity to meet the basic needs of all citizens. Those with less would not be implicitly seen as less valuable. People would not seek success and happiness by wallowing in material goods. Success largely would result from giving, not receiving. The most admired people would be those who do the most to help others and society in general. The most successful and happy lives would not result from having full bank accounts, but rather from having lives filled with love and appreciation from those one has loved and helped.

Promoting decentralization and ending the pursuit of ever-increasing economic growth and shareholder returns are essential for achieving a sustainable and truly prosperous society. Seeking high financial returns is a main driver of environmental and social degradation. Our myopic focus on growth is killing us. Therefore, we must change our focus, limit our growth and stop pursuing high financial returns.

But limiting financial returns cuts to the heart of our flawed economic and political systems. These systems mandate a primary focus on growth. To protect growth, flawed systems frequently will compel wealthy citizens and large corporations to oppose necessary system changes. For example, vested interests often will strongly oppose ending fractional reserve lending, not only because they potentially could lose up to $500 billion per year in revenue. But perhaps more importantly because it would substantially reduce their ability to control the economy and financial system.

To further protect growth, corporations frequently will use government influence and public deception to oppose being forced to compete with the public sector, NGOs and other types of productive organizations. Competition will severely inhibit their ability to achieve ever-increasing profits and shareholder returns. As a result, they frequently will be compelled to suppress competition.

One deception that probably will be used to oppose competition is to argue that the profit motive is necessary to promote creativity and high productivity. Vested interests might claim that the public and nonprofit sectors are inherently less competitive because they lack this incentive. But this is incorrect. Several other factors can provide equal or stronger motivation than the profit motive. For example, the desire to pioneer, explore and discover and wanting to help others can be more powerful motivators than money.

Culture largely determines the focus of society. In many indigenous societies and US communities prior to omnipresent advertising and media, those who helped others received the greatest honor and respect. The desire to help others and do good in the world compelled people to be creative and productive. In our materialistic culture, people are socialized to believe that they will receive the greatest honor, respect and happiness by making lots of money. As a result, they frequently seek it. But their real underlying goal is life satisfaction, not wealth accumulation. Making lots of money often does not provide true life satisfaction.

As discussed in the Education section, money and other rewards often are good motivators when tasks are boring. But rewards and competition frequently inhibit creativity when tasks are interesting. Humans have a natural desire to be productive and reach our fullest potential. As we shift the focus of society away from making rich people richer to enhancing the lives of all citizens, we will make jobs far more interesting and empowering. The desire to be of service, advance science and technology, and reach one's fullest potential can be more powerful motivators than money. This is especially true when public wealth is used to benefit all citizens, for example, by implementing a strong social safety net that greatly reduces the fear that basic needs will not be met. The public and nonprofit sectors can take advantage of powerful nonfinancial motivators, and thereby achieve equal or better creativity and productivity than the for-profit private sector.

To protect ever-increasing financial returns, wealthy citizens and corporations often will strongly oppose greater government involvement in the financial sector. The structurally mandated focus of private sector finance is on narrowly benefitting lenders and investors. This often degrades other stakeholders and broader society. However, the focus of public sector finance in a democratic government is on broadly benefiting all stakeholders and society.

As we abide by our Constitution, end business control of government and establish true democracy, We the People will direct our servant government to use the public wealth in ways that benefit all citizens. This often will include providing public financing when it is the lowest cost, highest benefit option. As We the People reclaim our right to create and control the money supply, our servant government can provide low or no cost loans to support productive, beneficial activities. We also might use the public wealth to provide equity financing when it is objectively less expensive and more beneficial to society than private sector financing.

Public funding can strongly benefit society. We the People can require that publicly funded activities do not degrade the environment or society in any way, and that benefits are fairly shared with all stakeholders, not just shareholders. Publicly-funded investments often will provide lower financial returns than private sector investing. As a result, vested interests frequently will strongly oppose greater public funding. It substantially lowers their ability to control the economy and earn high financial returns.

As discussed, our flawed systems are not focused on maximizing the well-being of society. They are focused on maximizing the financial wealth of a small group of already wealthy citizens and corporations. These systems often will compel vested interests to oppose greater government involvement in debt and equity financing. They frequently will attempt to retain control of debt financing by maintaining fractional reserve lending. Vested interests also frequently will attempt to retain control of equity financing by protecting trillions of dollars per year of corporate welfare. This ensures that they have the funds available to make high return equity investments. When wealthy citizens and corporations control debt and equity financing, they can ensure that investments are primarily focused on providing ever-increasing shareholder returns, as our suicidal systems require.

Establishing sustainable economic and financial systems requires a whole system approach. This illuminates essential solutions that lie outside the financial area, such as those related to democracy. For example, government probably cannot effectively provide debt and equity financing until it is converted from plutocracy to democracy. The US government largely is controlled by a small group of wealthy citizens and corporations. The puppet US government will continue to do whatever its wealthy masters tell it to do, including maintaining fractional reserve lending, corporate welfare and the primary focus on maximizing shareholder returns.

A whole system focus reveals that converting plutocracy to democracy requires raising public awareness about how vested interests mislead, divide and disempower citizens. We the People have all ultimate power. But we cannot exercise this power when we are divided. We must end the vested interest manufactured war between conservatives and liberals. We must work together on our massive areas of common interest, such as ending corporate welfare, protecting the environment and society, and using the public wealth to equally and fairly benefit all citizens.

A whole system perspective further reveals that we cannot effectively change the financial system by focusing first on the financial system. The financial system is the servant of the economy, which is the servant of society. Establishing a sustainable financial system first requires defining a sustainable society. This sets the parameters for a sustainable economy, which in turn sets the requirements for a sustainable financial system.

A sustainable financial system will seek balance and stability, not suicidal growth. The basis of competition in the financial community will be switched from maximizing shareholder returns to maximizing social well-being. Return on investment expectations will be lower. High ROIs generally will be seen as destructive and unfair, in the same way that high interest rates currently are. High investment returns might occur at times, for example, as new technologies are developed that experience rapid market penetration. But technology development should be managed with a primary focus on maximizing social well-being.

As corporate welfare is ended, more public wealth will be available for science, research and development. Publicly funded technology and research can be placed in the public domain. Then various types of organizations can compete to efficiently provide products and services based on it. As discussed in the Property Rights section, the great US Founder and inventor Benjamin Franklin did not seek a patent on one of his most profitable inventions – the Franklin stove. He put it in the public domain so that many citizens could afford this then leading-edge technology. In other words, one of the greatest US citizens put the well-being of society ahead of his own financial well-being. Thomas Jefferson also invented many useful devices, but never sought patents on them.[168]

We should strive to do the same thing. The primary purpose of human ingenuity and technology should not be to maximize the wealth of a few individuals. It should be to broadly benefit society. By wisely using the public wealth, we can expand publicly funded technology development, and thereby maximize the sustainability and well-being of society.

Dolphins have a larger brain-to-body size ratio than humans. They spend much of their time playing and hanging out with family and friends. We humans can do the same things. Many citizens are forced to work long, boring jobs to survive. When we refocus society on maximizing social well-being, we will use technology and know-how to reduce work requirements and vastly improve quality of life.

US Founders and Finance

Today's unjust, destructive domination of society by the financial community mirrors similar problems in the Founding era. In 1790, Alexander Hamilton, Founder of the Federalist Party and first Secretary of the Treasury, proposed a system for managing the nation's debt and money supply that was very similar to the system functioning today. Alexander Hamilton proposed, and Congress approved, the establishment of a national bank, the Bank of the United States, that would help to manage the national debt and issue money for the United States.[169] Like the Federal Reserve today, the Bank of the United States was owned and controlled by wealthy bankers and investors. The national bank acted on behalf of the federal government. But as Alexander Hamilton said, it was established "under the guidance of individual interest, not of public policy."[170]

The Federalist Party was established by wealthy bankers and merchants. In addition to supporting a privately owned national bank, the Federalists supported the expansion of large companies and a more centralized economy. This facilitated trading and speculation in business ownership shares (equities).

Thomas Jefferson and James Madison strongly condemned and opposed Alexander Hamilton's financial plan for several reasons. The plan allowed a privately owned bank to create money, a power reserved to Congress in the Constitution. It gave a small group of wealthy citizens great control over the economy and society by allowing them to strongly influence the nation's finances. The plan created the ridiculous and grossly unfair situation where government pays interest to use its own money. As discussed, the right to create money belongs the people. The Constitution assigns this right to the people's agent – Congress. When government creates money to pay off debt or fund a deficit, government (and taxpayers) pay no interest. However, when private banks create the money supply, government (and taxpayers) pay interest to use their own money. This causes huge, grossly unfair transfers of public wealth to wealthy bankers and investors (i.e. corporate welfare).

The Federalist financial plan enabled wealthy speculators to profit at the expense of the rest of society. Alexander Hamilton's plan was intended to pay off federal and state Revolutionary War debts by issuing new federal debt. But the plan wound up increasing the national debt. Maintaining high government debt benefits speculators who receive interest on it. When Thomas Jefferson was elected President in 1800, the Federalists were concerned that he would pay off the national debt and thereby reduce interest income to bankers and investors.[171]

During the Revolutionary War, lack of funds compelled the government to issue promissory notes to soldiers and farmers. In anticipation of Alexander Hamilton's plan to pay off existing debt by issuing new federal debt, wealthy speculators were buying up these notes at deep discounts.[172] Soldiers who had risked their lives defending their country and families of soldiers who lost their lives received a fraction of what they were owed, while speculators received full value.

Thomas Jefferson was concerned that the speculation promoted by Alexander Hamilton's plan was severely degrading society. He said, "Ships are lying idle at the wharves, buildings are stopped, capitals withdrawn from commerce, manufactures, arts, and agriculture to be employed in gambling; and the tide of public prosperity almost unparalleled in any country is arrested in its course, and suppressed by the rage of getting rich in a day. No mortal can tell where this will stop, for the spirit of gaming, when once it has seized a subject, is incurable. The tailor who has made thousands in one day, though he has lost them the next, can never again be content with the slow and moderate earnings of his needle."[173]

Thomas Jefferson also criticized the complex and confusing nature of Alexander Hamilton's plan. Complexity made citizens unable to understand how bank-created money and high financial speculation essentially stole the public wealth and degraded society. Thomas Jefferson said that Alexander Hamilton's financial system was designed "as a puzzle, to exclude popular understanding and inquiry." He argued that Alexander Hamilton intentionally made the system complicated so that "neither the President nor Congress should be able to understand it, or… control him."[174]

Referring to Alexander Hamilton, Thomas Jefferson said, "He gave to the debt in the first instance, in funding it, the most artificial and mysterious form he could devise… until the whole system was involved in an impenetrable fog; and while he was giving himself the airs of providing for the payment of the debt, he left himself free to add to it continually, as he did in fact, instead of paying for it."[175]

Following President Jefferson's election in 1800, the Federalist Party declined and then disappeared in the 1820s. The large majority of citizens understood that the Federalists primarily were focused on benefiting the wealthy, not all of society. The Republican and Democratic parties still are in place, largely because they have been much more effective at misleading citizens into believing that they are striving to benefit all of society, instead of just the wealthy citizens who control both parties.

While the business-focused Federalist Party ceased to exist, the financial system that they put in place largely has continued throughout US history. As Alexander Hamilton originally proposed, the private sector continues to create and control the US money supply. The financial community demand for ever-increasing shareholder returns dominates companies and the economy. Nearly everyone in society implicitly is expected to sacrifice so that wealthy speculators can get continuously wealthier.

Allowing a small group of wealthy citizens to largely control debt and equity finance severely degrades society and unjustly concentrates wealth. This grossly unfair financial system is perpetuated by confusion, complexity and public deception. We must pull back the curtain of deception and clearly expose the corrupt, unjust nature of the system.

It is time to finally do what Thomas Jefferson and James Madison, two of the most brilliant men to ever serve this country, strongly advised. We the People must take back control of the monetary system. Profits and other benefits of money creation should be shared equally with all citizens, not given almost completely to a small group of wealthy bankers and investors. We must end the absurd, suicidal financial community demand for ever-increasing shareholder returns. It is ridiculous that we allow financial returns to wealthy people to take priority over everything else, including the lives of our children.

Ending private sector control of the money supply and providing lower-cost, debt financing would be fairly easy. As discussed in the Money Creation section, this could be done by making the Federal Reserve part of the US Treasury and ending fractional reserve lending. This would produce a far simpler, more stable, easier to understand, lower cost and more equitable means of creating money, managing government finances and providing debt finance for productive, beneficial activities.

Increasing the availability of low-cost debt financing will benefit society by reducing the need for equity finance. The current equity finance system degrades society by unfairly concentrating wealth and making financial returns to wealthy citizens more important than anything else.

Decentralization could be promoted and high-cost equity finance reduced by delegating some of the federal government's debt issuing authority to states and local communities. Local communities could provide zero or low interest funding to local businesses and other productive organizations in exchange for long-term commitments to communities and guarantees to treat all stakeholders fairly. This approach would provide long-term economic stability and ensure that business success was shared fairly with employees, customers, communities and business owners. It also would enhance democracy by giving local citizens greater control over the types of businesses operating in their communities.

Substantially reducing the size, role and influence of private sector debt and equity finance would greatly lower the destructive speculation that was so strongly opposed by Presidents Jefferson and Madison. But the wealthy citizens controlling the current financial system often would fight to keep it in place. Many deceptions would be used to confuse the public and maintain the status quo.

For example, vested interests almost certainly would argue that robust debt and equity markets are needed to provide liquidity, facilitate commerce and maximize economic well-being. This liquidity facilitates buying, selling and merging companies. Businesses frequently are churned and turned over in ways that generate huge financial sector fees and concentrate wealth, but degrade society in many ways. 'Robust' capital markets facilitate churning, speculation and concentration of wealth. But these should not be the goals or results of the financial system.

The system should be focused on maximizing the long-term well-being of society. It should promote economic stability by incentivizing long-term, responsible business ownership. Business owners largely would be compensated through reasonable profits, not frequent buying and selling of companies and their stocks. Owners still would be able to sell their companies. Competition would put inefficient companies out of business and promote the development of more efficient ones. But strong financial incentives to churn ownership would be removed. Instead, the financial system would strongly promote long-term, responsible, decentralized business ownership and management. Under this system, robust (i.e. churning, speculative) capital markets would not be needed, or allowed.

As discussed above, nearly all of our main Founders, except Alexander Hamilton, believed that a decentralized, stable, non-speculative economy and financial system would strongly benefit society. They were correct. This is how the essentially infinitely more sophisticated implied economics of nature operate.

The main Founders, again except for Alexander Hamilton, opposed the formation of a large banking and merchant class that would strongly dominate the economy and society. They believed that this was a root cause of the corruption, decadence and tyranny that had destroyed ancient republics and much of Europe.[176] They opposed an economy based on speculation and stock trading. Thomas Jefferson said "wealth acquired by speculation is fugacious [fleeting, tending to disappear]... and fills society with the spirit of gambling".[177]

In a free society, people are free to try to make money by gambling, as long as non-gamblers are not harmed. For example, gambling in a casino is fine because people who choose not to gamble are not hurt. However, gambling or speculating in the economy and capital markets is different than gambling in a casino. Citizens' survival and prosperity are strongly dependent on the economy. Focusing the economy and financial system primarily on earning high investment returns produces excessive churning and speculation in business ownership. It also forces companies to focus mainly on profit maximization. Unlike gambling in a casino where non-gamblers are not hurt, gambling or speculating in the broader economy often harms average citizens. It drives layoffs and extensive environmental and social degradation.

In a democracy, businesses have no right to earn high financial returns by degrading society, for example, by paying wages that do not enable employees to at least meet basic needs. Investors have no right to earn financial returns in ways that degrade the environment and society.

Our economy should be based on activities that produce real value, such as providing useful products and services. It should not be focused primarily on speculation that concentrates wealth and degrades society. Citizens' retirement security should not be based on how well they speculated in the capital markets. Our heroes should not be wealthy speculators who provide little real value and do little real work. As Thomas Jefferson said, the most honored people in society should be those who work hard, produce real value and help other people.

Those who profit from speculation often will attempt to mislead citizens into believing that economic speculation is capitalism and opposing it is socialism or communism. This ignorant position only can be believed through the complete absence of rational thought. Capitalism uses the private sector in ways that produce widespread true value and prosperity. Excessive economic speculation that concentrates wealth, degrades life support systems and makes millions of citizens unable to meet basic needs is not capitalism. It is an insult to the word capitalism to suggest or imply this. Excessive speculation produces the plutocracy and business totalitarianism seen in the US. It definitely is not what the Founders intended.

Control of debt and equity finance by Wall Street and private banks has existed for nearly all of US history. Many people probably see the system as inevitable and unchangeable. Business-controlled advertising and media portray wealthy business owners and investors as our heroes. Many young people aspire to be like them and earn their own fortunes through speculation. Large, familiar systems can seem unchangeable. But they are not.

Our financial system violates the laws of nature and reality. It unfairly concentrates wealth and degrades the lives of the vast majority of citizens. The only thing inevitable about our financial system is that it will change. No amount of public deception or inappropriate government influence will keep this unfair, destructive system in place over the long-term. It is bound to fail.

Given the great injustice and suffering it causes, our financial system probably will change soon. We the People have the natural right to control our destiny, society, economy and financial system. We can demand the implementation of a financial system that ends destructive speculation and concentration of wealth, and instead serves all citizens equally and fairly.

Simplicity and clarity are critical aspects of sustainable finance. Maintaining an extremely complex financial system that largely is incomprehensible to average citizens blocks change and perpetuates concentration of wealth. As Thomas Jefferson implied, debt and equity finance can be far simpler and easier to understand than they are now.

Probably the large majority of citizens do not understand how money is created in the US and many other countries. If they did, they would demand an immediate end to this gross injustice. Non-expert citizens could understand the current complex system if it were clearly explained. To illustrate, citizens should be informed that money can be created by the private or public sector. When wealthy bankers create money through fractional reserve lending, they essentially own the money supply. This enables them to charge interest and keep the profits from money creation. When citizens create money through government, the people own the money supply, as they rightfully should. Under this vastly more fair and beneficial system, the profits from money creation are retained by citizens and used to reduce taxes and benefit society in other ways. The gross injustice of private sector money creation is perpetuated by lack of public understanding.

Millions of people should not be suffering in this wealthy, intelligent, advanced, supposed democracy. We have the ability to greatly improve the quality of life of nearly all citizens. But instead millions of people struggle to survive so that a small group of wealthy citizens can get continuously wealthier. It is time to end this insanity. Implementing a sustainable financial system is a critical aspect of ending this injustice and maximizing the well-being of all citizens and society.

Public Internet and Online Services

The Internet and online services are a critical part of the economy and society. They will become even more important going forward. They increasingly will dominate communications, entertainment, commerce and other important functions. Given the critical importance of the Internet and online services, they should be managed in ways that emphasize maximizing the well-being of society, rather than maximizing shareholder returns. This section discusses the importance and benefits of operating the Internet on a democratic, nonprofit basis and providing public options for major online services.

As discussed in the Privacy section, the Internet in the US is operated mainly by for-profit companies. There are many problems with a for-profit Internet and private online services. When the Internet is operated on a for-profit basis, the primary goal and focus is to provide ever-increasing shareholder returns. To achieve this, Internet companies often attempt to extract ever-increasing amounts of wealth from citizens, for example by segmenting and restricting the Internet. As a result, citizens frequently experience regular price increases, declining service quality and restricted access.

The for-profit focus of the US Internet is a main reason why the US has near the worst Internet performance in the developed world. The average Internet access speed in the US is 9.8 megabits per second (Mbps) and frequently costs \$35 to \$50 per month. In Seoul, South Korea, Hong Kong and Tokyo, citizens can get 1,000 Mbps connection speeds for \$30 to \$40 per month. Residents in New York and Los Angeles can get 500 Mbps connection speeds if they pay \$300 per month.[178] The for-profit focus often compels US citizens to pay more money for lower quality Internet services.

The Chattanooga, Tennessee public utility discussed above provides 1,000 Mbps connection speeds for about \$70 per month.[179] This illustrates the strong competitive advantage that public and nonprofit entities often have over for-profit entities. They do not face ongoing pressure to increase prices and lower costs and service quality so that they can provide ever-increasing shareholder returns. It also illustrates why for-profit entities frequently work aggressively to prevent competition from the public and nonprofit sectors.

In addition to charging users more for faster Internet access, for-profit Internet service providers are aggressively lobbying government to allow them to provide faster Internet delivery for content providers that pay higher fees. As a result, the websites and content of these companies would download faster than other websites. The Internet is based on the principle of net neutrality. This means that all people and organizations have equal access to the Internet. The White House, Congress and the FCC have received millions of comments from citizens who want net neutrality maintained. In 2015, the Democrat controlled FCC voted to maintain net neutrality. But net neutrality could be weakened through legal action or ended by a Republican President. Businesses will continue to pressure their political puppets in both political parties to do what is best for the wealthy citizens and companies who paid to put politicians in office, rather than what citizens want and the Constitution demands (i.e. promote the general welfare).

This is the expected outcome of a for-profit Internet. Internet input and output will be managed in ways that maximize the wealth of Internet companies, rather than maximize the well-being of society. Ending net neutrality not only will help large companies by giving them faster access to citizens and customers. Having different access standards could make it easier to suppress activists and others who threaten the status quo of corporate welfare, business control of government and placing shareholder returns before all else. As the economy moves more online, ending net neutrality will severely inhibit competition. Smaller companies that cannot afford high Internet access fees will be at a major disadvantage compared to larger companies that pay for faster Internet access to customers.

The primary focus of companies that provide online services, such as search, email and social networking, also is to provide ever-increasing shareholder returns. Citizens pay for these supposedly free services by allowing Internet service companies to track and keep massive amounts of personal, private information. Records of virtually everything that citizens do or post online are retained by online service companies. Citizens reveal extensive, often intimate details of their personal lives. Their personal information frequently becomes the permanent property of Internet service companies. These companies use it in many ways to maximize shareholder returns.

Many citizens have become used to paying for Internet access and allowing online service companies to keep their personal information. But this is not necessary. Providing free high-speed Internet access for virtually all citizens, businesses and other organizations as well as providing public online services would massively benefit society. The cost of providing public Internet access and online services would be a tiny fraction of the cost of corporate welfare. Ending corporate welfare would enable the US to provide high quality, free Internet access and public online services, while substantially reducing property and income taxes for low and middle-income citizens.

As discussed in the Privacy section, the Internet is like the public highway and road systems. Public roads greatly benefit society. All citizens and businesses are free to use public roads in ways that maximize individual and collective well-being. The management of public highways and roads must be primarily focused on maximizing social well-being, not shareholder returns. If roads were primarily managed with the goal of maximizing shareholder returns, citizens often would experience price increases and service quality reductions. In addition, access to roads sometimes might be restricted for those who threaten shareholder returns, such as competitors and activists.

It is the same with the Internet. The primary focus of the Internet must be on maximizing the well-being of society. The Internet was developed by government. Turning over operation of it to the private sector and allowing companies to retain profits from the Internet is another large example of transferring public wealth to companies (i.e. corporate welfare). At first, the Internet was a novelty. Now it is a central and increasingly important component of the economy and society. Therefore, like public roads, the Internet must be public, nonprofit, run by citizens through democratic government, primarily focused on maximizing the well-being of society, and based on equal access for all individuals and organizations.

A public Internet would greatly benefit society. As discussed in the Privacy section, high-speed, free Internet access, perhaps through a fiber-optic system, could be provided to nearly all homes, businesses and other organizations. (Heavy users might pay a fee, in the same way that trucks often pay higher taxes and tolls to use roads.) Currently, cable television and other companies that control the Internet often have near monopoly control over pricing, access and sometimes content. A public Internet system would greatly increase competition. Citizens would have access to a greater variety of entertainment, communications and other services online. This would substantially reduce prices and increase service quality. All companies, small, medium and large, would have equal access to the Internet, and through this, equal access to all citizens and society overall.

Currently, for-profit Internet companies keep records of citizens' online use data and use it in various ways to maximize shareholder returns. But they have no right to retain citizens' personal, private information. A public Internet would be operated by the people's agent – government (or an NGO that was controlled by the people/government). The government would not be allowed to track and retain citizens' online use data, unless a court order was issued based on valid evidence of illegal activity.

As discussed throughout this book, a whole system approach is needed to solve all major problems in society. Currently, the US government mainly is controlled by large companies and their wealthy owners. As a result, it is not the agent of the people, as the Constitution requires. Replacing plutocracy with democracy is an essential component of achieving sustainability and real prosperity. Once the government is controlled by the people, we can reestablish the Bill of Rights protections that were removed by the Traitors Act, Supreme Court decisions and other violations of our Constitution.

As discussed in the Advertising, Media and Culture section, business-controlled government takes the position that citizens often give up their right to privacy when they buy something. This opinion helps to maximize shareholder returns. But We the People can decide that our privacy should not be violated. Buying something from one merchant does not give one million other merchants the right to know what someone bought. Once We the People control government and the Internet, we will direct our servant to protect citizens' privacy by not tracking and recording the personal online data of law-abiding citizens. As discussed in the Privacy section, just because we have the technology to track everything citizens do online does not mean we should use it.

Regarding online services, these once were a novelty too. Providing them through for-profit companies spurred innovation and probably caused few problems (except for privacy violations). However, online services, such as search, email, news and social networking, have become critical components of the economy and society. As a result, these services should be managed with a primary focus on maximizing the well-being of society, not shareholder returns.

For example, citizens have access to huge amounts of information through the Internet. Search engines are a primary vehicle for accessing this information. Citizens must be able to trust that search results are accurate and unbiased. For-profit search engine companies have an incentive to slant results in ways that maximize shareholder returns, for example, by highlighting companies that buy advertising and suppressing competitors or activists. In addition, for-profit search companies have no right to keep records of people's online activity. A public search engine would guarantee unbiased results and protect citizens' privacy.

The same applies to email, social networking and free video calls. These online services have become an essential part of the economy and society. They should be primarily focused on maximizing social well-being. For-profit online service companies have no right to track and retain citizens' personal online use data. Public online services would be focused on maximizing the well-being of society and protecting citizens' privacy.

Providing a public news and entertainment service, like the BBC, also would greatly benefit society. As discussed in the Advertising, Media and Culture section, the goal of for-profit media is maximizing shareholder returns. It frequently does this by providing biased, misleading or inaccurate content that divides and disempowers citizens. A public news service would be required to provide honest, balanced, accurate information.

Another critical online service involves sales of conventional books and eBooks (i.e. electronic books). Deregulation has enabled Amazon to dominate this market. Amazon sells 40 percent of all new books. It has even greater control of the rapidly growing eBook market. eBooks represent one-third of new book sales. Amazon sells two-thirds of eBooks.[180] The company routinely forces publishers to sell books at deep discounts and imposes unfair terms. For example, publishers frequently must agree to not sell books for lower prices than Amazon.[181] Amazon dominates the book market by largely controlling pricing and market access. It also is the most powerful reviewer of books. The company played a major role in putting many small bookstores and at least one large chain store out of business.[182] Amazon also has the ability to suppress books that criticize Amazon or its political positions, for example, by delaying delivery, not providing discounts or refusing to publish them. One for-profit entity should not be allowed to control industry-wide pricing and dominate the book writing and publishing industry.

A public platform should be established to sell conventional and eBooks. Universal eBook formats can enable eBooks to be read on many different electronic devices, while protecting the rights of authors and publishers. The online book platform would be a public market that authors and publishers could access. Authors could access the public market directly or through publishers. Authors and publishers would control pricing and terms. The public online book platform would protect citizens' privacy. No records would be kept of citizens' book and other purchases.

Amazon often argues that it is attempting to help customers by keeping prices low. But under current systems, any manager who puts the well-being of customers ahead of the financial well-being of shareholders probably should be fired. As discussed in the Misleading the Public section, publicly traded companies saying that they are primarily focused on helping customers, employees or anything other than shareholders is a deception. Flawed economic and financial systems compel companies to put shareholder returns before all else. If they do not do this, they ultimately will die. By attempting to control prices, authors and publishers, Amazon is building competitive advantage and monopoly power in an effort to protect shareholder returns. But in the process, it often degrades the well-being of authors and publishers, and thereby degrades society.

Literature is essential for maximizing social well-being. For-profit companies with near-monopoly power should not be allowed to suppress prices, harm authors and publishers, and degrade the production of fiction and nonfiction literature for the purpose of achieving ever-increasing shareholder returns. A fair, open public online book market should be established that enables authors and publishers to be fairly compensated for their work.

In addition to a public online book market, a general online public market or platform should be provided for sales of products and services. Amazon has grown to dominate the online merchandise market. It is the largest online marketer in the world. Books represent only seven percent of Amazon sales. Amazon makes over one-third of online sales in the US. It is larger than the nine next largest US online retailers combined.[183]

As in the book area, Amazon often forces vendors to sell products at deep discounts. The company frequently puts competitors out of business by selling products at low prices. This strategy is a main reason why Amazon routinely incurs large losses. Investors usually tolerate losses because they anticipate future profits. Amazon has contributed to the shutting down of many local businesses and weakening of local economies. The company helps to shut down local businesses through a process known as "showrooming". Under this approach, Amazon encourages customers to view products in stores, scan barcodes with their smart phones, and then buy the products for less money on Amazon.com.[184]

As with other large companies, Amazon and other online businesses are not held fully responsible for negative impacts on society. Shutting down local businesses and weakening local economies harms families and communities. Local jobs are lost and wealth is removed from communities (as profits are sent to distant investors and companies).

The expansion of online sales poses a challenge for society. People do not live in the online cyberworld. They live in real, physical communities. It will be difficult for individuals and society to prosper if many local economies and communities are declining. As in all other areas, to maximize well-being of society, we must step back and look at the big picture or whole system. Prosperous communities and local economies are essential to the well-being of individuals and society. Online sales might save customers money through lower prices. But if this replaces good local jobs with distant low-wage jobs and degrades families and communities in other ways, the trade-offs often will not be worth it.

Individuals, communities and society have inherent rights to exist. But businesses do not. Business existence is a privilege contingent on benefiting and not harming society. In a democracy, citizens should use objective, whole system analysis to identify the most effective way to utilize online sales. The goal should be to maximize the well-being of society, in part by protecting communities and local economies. Large online companies have no right to benefit shareholders by degrading society.

One of the most important actions needed to ensure that online sales maximize the well-being of society is to establish a public online platform for selling products and services. As online commerce plays a growing role in society, the emphasis must be on maximizing social well-being, not shareholder returns. Allowing a few large companies to dominate online commerce often will harm vendors, communities and society overall.

A public online general market, perhaps similar to Amazon or eBay, would provide fair, free access to all vendors and customers. (As with a public Internet, heavy users might pay a fee.) Vendors would control pricing and terms. The public online market would promote competition, protect markets and benefit citizens. To protect communities and local economies, advantages or preferences might be given to local vendors. Like the online public book market, citizens' privacy would be protected. No records would be kept of purchases, unless customers opted in to tracking, for example, to facilitate future sales or useful advertising.

To prevent fraud and customer abuse, vendors might be required to meet minimum service, quality, disclosure, verification and customer recourse requirements. Customer feedback systems would help customers to identify high quality, reliable vendors. Many of the best practices of private sector online markets would be utilized in the public platform.

A public online market would be focused on maximizing customer and societal value, not shareholder value. Amazon and other large online retailers potentially have unfair competitive advantages. To illustrate, when customers search for products on Amazon, the company could quickly scan competitive prices online or in frequently updated competitive pricing databases. This would enable Amazon to charge slightly less than the next lowest price offered online, and thereby maximize revenues and profits. This is like an unfair bidding situation where one company is allowed to view competitors' prices and just undercut them. This process could enable Amazon and other large online retailers to unfairly benefit at the expense of customers and other companies.

For-profit online markets also potentially are unfair because they could allow Amazon and other companies to charge customers different prices for the same products. Amazon potentially could acquire data from data brokers, develop customer profiles, and determine customers' personal interests and ability to pay. People with high interest in certain product categories and strong ability to pay might be charged higher prices. This could maximize shareholder value, but reduce customer value.

Unfair gaming of the system like this would be prohibited in an online public market. Prices would be set by vendors, not Amazon. Prices generally would be the same for all customers (except for volume and other reasonable customer-specific discounts). An online public market would strongly facilitate the development of small businesses, prohibit price manipulation and ensure fair competition. By doing so, a public online market would substantially improve customer and societal value.

Widely used software represents another critical electronic service that could be provided by the people through government. Word processing software, for example, is an essential part of the economy and society in today's online world. Microsoft Office has about a 90 percent share of this market. Citizens and businesses buy the software from Microsoft. Then after a brief period, if they have problems or questions about the software, they often must pay Microsoft for assistance. Word processing and a few other widely used types of software have become essential to the well-being of society. As a result, this software should be provided and managed with a primary focus on maximizing social well-being, rather than shareholder returns. Having different types of private software frequently makes it difficult to share documents and inhibits the economy and society in other ways.

Public funds could be used to develop high quality universal versions of word processing and other basic software. This would be provided free to all citizens, businesses and other organizations. Related cloud storage and customer service support also could be free. Universal, standardized word processing and other critical software would facilitate document sharing and other important economic and social functions.

Google and other organizations that provide free word processing and other software often track and retain citizens' personal data. Developing public, universal word processing and other software, along with related public cloud services, would protect citizens' privacy. It also could reduce total costs to society because providing public software often would be less expensive than having individuals and organizations buy it from Microsoft and other private-sector companies.

Obviously, for-profit Internet, online service and software companies often would vigorously oppose public versions of their products (because it might put them out of business). As usual, they probably will employ two primary strategies for protecting shareholder returns – inappropriate government influence and misleading the public. They often will give large amounts of money to politicians and demand that their political puppets prohibit competition from the public sector.

They also frequently will attempt to deceive citizens into believing that government cannot do anything right. This of course is irrational and ignorant. Bad government (i.e. business-controlled government) does a poor job of serving citizens. But good democratic government can employ nearly every tool used by the private sector to provide high efficiency and outstanding customer service. As discussed, the public sector has several inherent advantages that frequently enable it to outperform the private sector. For example, removing the requirement to provide ever-increasing shareholder returns often would enable the public sector to provide lower cost, higher quality services, especially over the longer-term.

To maximize the well-being of society, public Internet, online services and widely used software should be established. Public services could be set up alongside existing for-profit services. By utilizing good management and other traditional private sector approaches, public online services and software could provide equal or better quality service than private companies. Once citizens better understand the great extent to which there privacy is violated by for-profit online service companies, they frequently will switch to public versions that protect privacy, if service quality is similar or better. Citizens also often will switch to public online services because they will be able to trust that the services are run on a democratic basis and focused on maximizing the well-being of society. In addition, citizens frequently will switch to high quality public software because the software, cloud storage and customer service will be free and privacy will be protected.

Many for-profit online service and software companies will have difficulty retaining customers in this environment. They often will not be able to compete with public services. Some for-profit online service and software companies might choose to sell out to government and provide a return for investors. In these cases, government would buy rather than build products and services.

The same is true with the current for-profit Internet infrastructure. Through negotiations with Internet companies, the government could decide whether to buy or build new infrastructure. For-profit Internet companies, such as cable television companies, obviously will not be able to compete with a free, reliable, high-speed public Internet that does not violate citizens' privacy. As a result, for-profit Internet companies probably often would choose to sell out to the government and thereby provide some return for investors. It is highly unlikely that government would have to exercise its power of eminent domain to provide free, high-speed, privacy-protecting Internet access to all citizens and businesses.

In general, rigorous, objective analysis should be conducted to determine if the public or private sector should provide services in a particular situation. However, in some cases, little analysis will be needed because the answer is obvious. Public versus private Internet, online service and possibly software are in this category. Assuming that service quality is similar or better, a free, privacy-protecting public Internet clearly will outcompete an expensive, privacy-violating for-profit Internet. Privacy-protecting public online services will outcompete for-profit services that grossly violate privacy. Free, privacy-protecting public software and cloud storage will outcompete expensive, privacy-violating for-profit software and cloud storage. The key issue will be ensuring that public Internet, online services and software are equal or better quality than private sector services. Inherent public sector competitive advantages cause this to be a highly attainable outcome.

The current, largely for-profit online system is grossly unjust and destructive. As discussed in the Privacy section, citizens are allowing for-profit organizations to gather and own the most intimate details of their private lives, and use this information in nearly any manner they choose to maximize profits. This situation is unfair and totally unnecessary. Why would We the People allow the details of our private lives to become the property of entities that are not focused on maximizing the well-being of society? The answer mainly is that many people do not realize the great extent to which their personal information is being gathered. They also often do not realize that there are far more fair and effective ways to manage the online environment.

Citizens frequently are misled into thinking that government cannot do anything right. Democratic government is the people managing their own lives. When citizens oppose government control of the online environment, they essentially are saying we are too stupid and incompetent to manage our own lives. We must give control of our personal information to large, wealthy companies. Willingness to sacrifice privacy, while resisting self-government, is the fruit of our oppressive, authoritarian education system and society.

Flawed economic and political systems frequently place companies in structurally mandated conflict with society. When there are conflicts between shareholders and citizens, companies often must put shareholders first. It is ridiculous that we allow the online environment to be managed in ways that frequently degrade our lives and violate our privacy. Maximizing the well-being of society requires that We the People take control of the online environment and protect our privacy.

In summary, major portions of the economy and society are moving online. The online environment must be based on democracy, not plutocracy. Citizens must control the Internet, online services and other critical electronic services. In addition, citizens' privacy must be protected. No one has a right to know what someone else is doing online, unless the person is breaking the law. Vendors and citizens must have fair, full, open, equal access to the Internet. The primary purpose of the Internet and essential online and electronic services should not be to siphon off ever-increasing amounts of wealth so that wealthy citizens can get continuously wealthier. The primary purpose and focus should be to maximize the well-being of individuals and society overall.

Global Peace and Human Rights Protection

Ensuring global peace and protecting the natural rights of every human being on this planet is an essential aspect of achieving sustainability and real prosperity. It is one of the most important components after protecting life support systems. Thomas Jefferson spoke of the natural rights of humans in the Declaration of Independence. He did not mean that only people in the United States have natural rights. Every human on this planet has the same innate, natural rights to life, liberty and the pursuit of happiness.

But the natural rights of millions of people are being grossly violated in several parts of the world. In North Korea, for example, if citizens criticize the government, their whole families often are sent to labor camps where they are tortured, starved, worked to death and sometimes forced to dig their own graves.[185] This abuse of people in totalitarian countries in Africa, Asia, the Middle East and other regions is perhaps the greatest disgrace of modern society. How can we allow our fellow human beings to be treated like this? It is like hearing people in the house next door violently abusing their children and doing nothing about it. No human being has a right to take freedom and rights from another human. We all are absolutely equal and worthy of having our basic, natural rights protected. In this sense, the country that a person resides in is completely irrelevant. It has zero impact on each person's innate, natural rights.

In the 1940s, following World War II, there was a strong movement in the US to establish a global government with limited powers for the purpose of ensuring global peace. Over half of state legislatures passed resolutions advocating the establishment of "a limited world federal government able to prevent war."[186] More than 100 US senators and representatives proposed transforming the United Nations into a world Republic. House Concurrent Resolution 64 stated, "it should be a fundamental objective of the foreign policy of the United States to support and strengthen the United Nations and to seek its development into a world federation, open to all nations, with defined and limited powers adequate to preserve peace and prevent aggression through the enactment, interpretation, and enforcement of world law."[187]

An excellent article by Harris Wofford and Tad Daley, called *50 Years Later, JFK's Vision of Enduring World Peace Eclipsed by Focus on Assassination*, describes the global peace movement in the 1940s and President Kennedy's efforts to promote global peace.[188] The article explains that during World War II, there was a growing conviction that anarchy and war could not be permitted on a global level. The rule of law that prevailed within nations also should be enforced among nations. Development of the atomic bomb made the need for global peace even greater because war now put the survival of humanity at risk. Many leaders and prominent citizens in the 1940s and 1950s supported the abolition of war and establishment of a world republic to ensure global peace.

Albert Einstein said, "The world's present system of sovereign nations can lead only to barbarism, war and inhumanity. There is no salvation for civilization, or even the human race, other than the creation of a world government." In 1950, Winston Churchill stated, "Unless some effective world super-Government can be set up and brought quickly into action, the prospects for peace and human progress are dark and doubtful."[189]

General Dwight D. Eisenhower led the Allied D-Day invasion of Normandy in 1944, and later became President of the United States. He visited Normandy 20 years after D-Day. Speaking over the graves of young soldiers who gave their lives at Normandy, former President Eisenhower said, "These boys were cut off in their prime... They never knew the great experiences of going through life... I devoutly hope that we will never again see such things as these. I think, hope and pray that humanity has learned more than we had learned up to that time... We must find some way to... gain an eternal peace for this world."[190]

Having fought in World War II, Representative John F. Kennedy strongly supported the movement to establish a global government to ensure world peace in the 1940s. He continued to strongly advocate and work for global peace when he was elected President of the United States in 1960. President Kennedy said, "Too many of us think... that war is inevitable, that mankind is doomed, that we are gripped by forces we cannot control." But he said that we control our destiny. We are not the victims of uncontrollable forces.

President Kennedy said that world peace could be built "not on a sudden revolution in human nature but on a gradual evolution in human institutions... World peace, like community peace, does not require that each man love his neighbor. It requires only that they live together in mutual tolerance, submitting their disputes to a just and peaceful settlement."

Regarding the UN, President Kennedy said, "We seek to strengthen the United Nations... to develop it into a genuine world security system... This will require a new effort to achieve world law... Our primary long range interest... is general and complete disarmament... to build the new institutions of peace which would take the place of arms."

During his inaugural address, President Kennedy said, "The world is very different now. For man holds in his mortal hands the power to abolish all forms of human poverty and all forms of human life." He said that the goal of the UN should be "To enlarge the area in which its writ may run... and bring the absolute power to destroy other nations under the absolute control of all nations." Our wise President said, "So let us begin anew... [and establish] a new endeavor, not a new balance of power, but a new world of law, where the strong are just and the weak secure and the peace preserved."[191]

Unfortunately, we did not learn the lesson of World War II and heed the advice of President Kennedy and many other wise leaders. As a result, the US and many other countries have suffered the immense cost and tragic lost lives of extensive wars. As President Kennedy said, war is not inevitable. We have the power to end it. We can remove the threat that nuclear and other weapons pose to human society. We also can protect the natural rights of every human being on this planet.

We have the power to do this. No excuse justifies not doing it. We should follow the wise advice given long ago by transforming the UN into an entity with the power to ensure global peace and protect human rights. As President Kennedy said, instead of fighting wars and killing each other, we should submit disputes to fair, impartial negotiation, arbitration and settlement.

We the People of the Earth also should work collectively through the UN to enforce a bill of rights for all humans. Every human has a right to self-government. Democracy should be established in every country. No leader anywhere has a right to suppress democracy and violate human rights. Protecting the natural rights of each human takes massive, essentially infinite priority over national sovereignty. When leaders anywhere on this planet violate citizens' natural rights, they lose their legitimacy and authority to rule. Acting as one global community, we must remove these abusive leaders from power, and then help the people of each region to establish fair, democratic government.

It is an absolute disgrace of humanity that people in North Korea, Sudan, Syria, Myanmar, Somalia, the Democratic Republic of Congo, Afghanistan, and other abusive countries endure such horrible suffering, deprivation and natural rights violations. This outrage should not be allowed to stand for one more day. It is time to exercise the collective power of humanity to protect our brothers and sisters everywhere on this planet. This is the appropriate use of power. It is power guided by wisdom and love for our fellow human beings.

Much of the worst atrocities and human rights abuses occur in developing countries. To illustrate, in January 2015, 17 people were killed in terrorist attacks in France. World leaders and millions of citizens denounced the horror and demonstrated in France and other countries. In the same month, as many as 2,000 people were killed in one terrorist attack in Nigeria. In developed countries, we are justifiably outraged by any terrorist event. But it seems that far more people are killed far more frequently by terrorism in developing countries.

The life of a person in a developing country is worth just as much as the life of a person in a developed country. We as a global community should be working just as hard to stop terrorism and other atrocities in developing countries as we do in developed countries. The UN already seeks to minimize terror and harm in developing countries, for example, by sending peacekeeping forces. But the UN is limited by political and other barriers. A UN empowered by the global community could be far more effective at maintaining peace and ending atrocities around the world.

Some dogmatic Christians oppose the formation of a limited world government because the Biblical books of Revelation and Daniel supposedly oppose it. As discussed in the US Founders, Religious Dogma and Birth Control section, this is a perfect example of why religious dogma should have no impact on national or global governance. The book of Revelation apparently is a dream or vision, possibly by John the Apostle. It implies that Satan will establish a world government during the end times, prior to the second coming of Christ. This fantasy or nightmare has no more validity than a childhood fairy tale.

We must base our actions on rational thought, observations of reality and intuitive wisdom. Allowing religious dogma to interfere with establishing limited global government for the purpose of ensuring global peace and protecting human rights would be irrational and criminally immoral. In this case, religious dogma would be perpetuating the torture, abuse and murder of our fellow human beings. As discussed extensively, religious dogma often is unintentionally harmful. It frequently causes people to violate religious principles and natural laws. The most important commandment of Christianity and virtually all other religions is to love, honor and respect each other. Allowing a religious fairy tale to perpetuate the murder and torture of fellow humans grossly violates the most important commandment of Christianity.

This is why it is absolutely essential that we place rational thought and intuitive wisdom above all else, as our Founders did long ago. As discussed in the Governance section, national boundaries were not developed based on fairness and sustainability principles. They largely evolved from ignorant ideas based on domination and separation. Rational thought should be used to organize human society. As noted, nature mostly is organized into local, largely self-sustaining communities. This strongly indicates that most aspects of human society probably should be decentralized and managed at local or regional levels.

However, rational thought and observations of reality show that some aspects of human society should be centralized and managed globally. These include mediating and ensuring global peace, protecting global environmental life support systems, and enforcing a global bill of rights. The US can and should play a major role in leading the establishment of a limited global government, probably through the UN, for these purposes.

In general, as a leading proponent of democracy (even though we fail to implement democracy in our own country) with the largest economy and military, the US should play a major role in leading and modeling sustainable behavior. Businesses and their allies often block sustainability actions that benefit humanity, but threaten shareholder returns, by arguing that we should not take actions, such as reducing pollution, until other countries do the same. This is a childish and ignorant position. If acting in an environmentally responsible manner threatens US jobs, we should impose tariffs on imports to protect jobs and life support systems.

As discussed in several sections, the US is pursuing an extremely irrational approach to terrorism. From September 11, 2001 to 2013, we spent over $12 trillion on national security. Over this time period, about 300 US citizens worldwide were killed by terrorism. But about 36,000 US citizens were killed by foodborne illnesses. People in the US are 110 times more likely to die from foodborne illness than terrorism. But we spend far more on preventing terrorism than on preventing foodborne illnesses and other environmental and health problems that harm or kill many more people.[192]

As discussed in the Privacy section, most of the so-called terrorism enforcement of the Traitors Act is used to make drug arrests and monitor and suppress activists who oppose the unjust status quo. The US war on terror is focused mainly on the supply-side. We seek to suppress terrorism through military, police, surveillance and other actions. Extensive military actions around the world often increase the demand for terrorism by fomenting anger at the US. In addition, US companies impose extensive negative environmental, social and economic impacts in other countries. This further increases the demand for terrorism and puts US citizens at risk.

The focus on maximizing economic growth and shareholder returns compels the US government to support the expansion of US companies in other countries, in part through the maintenance of extensive overseas military operations. Being a world leader means acting responsibly. Instead of helping US businesses to grow forever, regardless of how much this degrades other countries, we should require that US companies act responsibly at home and abroad. The primary solution to terrorism is to focus on the demand-side. We should end the negative impacts of the US government and businesses around the world. Acting responsibly will build goodwill and probably protect us more than any supply-side action.

The US often has resisted strengthening the UN in part because we do not want anyone questioning our sovereignty. But this is a cowardly and childish position. Business-controlled government does not want to open itself to scrutiny and pressure to act responsibly. But the priority is not national sovereignty. It is doing the right thing for US citizens and all other people around the world. We are part of a global community. We also are a leader in this community. We should act like a mature leader.

If we are doing the right thing for people at home and around the world, we have nothing to fear from a more powerful global government. But we are not doing the right things in many ways. Rather than resisting changes that threaten shareholder returns, but benefit US citizens and people in other countries, we must be willing to change. When we oppose global mechanisms for ensuring peace and protecting human rights, we are perpetuating the abuse, torture and murder of fellow humans in totalitarian countries. Preventing the murder of citizens in North Korea or any other country takes priority over rich people getting richer in the US or anywhere else.

This country was established largely to protect the natural, basic rights of current and future human beings. Our Founders surely would have wanted us to use our great power to further this goal around the world. The most effective and probably only way to ensure global peace and enforce a global Bill of Rights is through some type of limited global government. The most practical and expedient way to achieve this, as President Kennedy and many other US leaders proposed after World War II, is to expand the power of the United Nations.

This might require that the US give up some of our power and autonomy. But we cannot continue to dominate the world with economic and military force. We must become a mature global citizen. In successful, sustainable communities, one member does not dominate the others. All community members are seen as equals. Those with more capabilities are expected to do more to help the community. This helps everyone to prosper and reach their fullest potential. The same is true in the global community. We should act as an equal member of the community. We should contribute our great strength to the community and help it to collectively achieve the goals of global peace and protection of human rights.

Thomas Jefferson said, "I hope that our wisdom will grow with our power, and teach us, that the less we use our power the greater it will be."[193] Attempting to force our will on the world through military and economic power is wrong. It turns millions of people around the world against the US. It greatly increases the demand for terrorism and places US citizens at risk. The US has great power. But we apparently lack the wisdom to use it effectively. Our flawed, suicidal systems compel unwise actions, such as seeking infinite growth in a finite system.

We the People of the United States definitely have the collective wisdom needed to utilize the great power of our country in ways that benefit all people around the world, not just US citizens. To achieve this, we must work together, establish democracy in our country, and then direct our servant government to act as an equal partner (rather than polite tyrant) in the global community.

Regarding empowering the UN to remove abusive leaders by force, one might ask does this apply to the US? US politicians grossly abuse citizens by enabling wealthy campaign donors to essentially steal citizens' wealth and power. These business-controlled political puppets suppress democracy and remove the people's freedom. Should they be removed from power by force if they do not agree to quickly change their ways and implement democracy?

The situation in the US and other plutocracies is different from totalitarian regimes, such as North Korea. In totalitarian countries, people have no choice. They are forced to obey abusive rulers. Citizens frequently are tortured or abused if they fail to obey or worship maniacal dictators. They have no freedom. However in the US and other plutocracies, citizens do have choices and freedom. But they have been misled into voluntarily giving up their freedom. Citizens often have been deceived into thinking that liberals or conservatives are degrading society. Their attention is turned away from those who actually are stealing their wealth and power.

In plutocracies, loss of freedom usually is voluntary. By allowing ourselves to be emotionally manipulated and misled, we voluntarily have given up our wealth, power and freedom. In totalitarian regimes, abusive leaders often would have to be removed by force if they did not quickly allow democracy in their countries. In other words, when citizens' rights and freedom are removed by force, abusive leaders might have to be removed by force. However, when rights and freedom are suppressed through deception (as occurs in the US), removing leaders by force generally would not be appropriate. The solution to deception is awareness raising, not force.

In plutocracies, leaders frequently are elected through deceptive practices. In the US, the two-party system misleads citizens into believing that democracy exists. But both parties are controlled by a small group of wealthy citizens. Therefore, regardless of which party wins, this small group wins. This is not democracy, in part because citizens usually do not have a voting option that promotes the well-being of all citizens. (Third parties focused on promoting the general welfare often have little or no chance of winning.)

In countries where democracy, freedom and natural rights have been suppressed through deception instead of force, force should not be used to remove abusive leaders. Unlike totalitarian regimes, plutocracies such as the US often have constitutions that require democracy. But business-influenced politicians are violating their constitutions. Rather than using force in these situations, it would be more effective to raise public awareness about lack of democracy and vested interest deceptions, and help citizens to understand how true democracy and freedom can be implemented. For example, a global group focused on protecting human rights, such as the UN, might help citizens in plutocracies to organize efforts that compel supposed public servants to abide by their constitutions, end corporate welfare and business control of government, establish true democracy, and use the public wealth to equally and fairly benefit all citizens.

Changing how we define and measure success is an essential component of ensuring peace, protecting human rights and maximizing the well-being of global society. Focusing on economic size and growth strongly drives environmental and social degradation. Instead of focusing on a means to an end (economic growth), we must emphasize the true goal or end point (the well-being of society). Economic growth, productivity, exports and imports ultimately are irrelevant. The success of countries should be judged solely on the extent to which they objectively maximize the long-term well-being of environmental life support systems and society.

National pride or the desire to be more powerful might compel countries to expand military forces or increase exports. As we redefine national and global success, this type of puffery no longer will be needed. National pride and success will be based on how well countries care for current and future citizens and cooperate in the global community of nations.

Guaranteeing true equality for women is one of the most important aspects of implementing a global bill of rights and achieving sustainability and real prosperity. As discussed in the Wisdom of Nature and Women's sections, women innately manifest greater cooperation, empathy, whole system thinking and other aspects of wisdom, in the same way that men innately manifest greater physical strength, aggressiveness, competitiveness and other aspects of power. Rapid environmental and social degradation throughout human society reflect our abundance of power and lack of wisdom. It also reflects the suppression of women. When we suppress those who innately manifest more wisdom, we suppress wisdom, and suffer severe negative consequences.

It probably is no coincidence that countries with the greatest suppression of women also frequently are the largest sources of global terrorism. Blind faith in religious dogma often compels severe suppression of women in countries where radial Islam is widely practiced. It also sometimes drives the killing of those with different spiritual views. Those who kill in the name of God claim to be doing the will of God. But they are completely cut off from God.

Rational thought and intuitive wisdom would reveal that no loving God would compel people to kill those who hold different views of God. Religious dogma that causes killing or abuse of others does not come from God or intuitive wisdom. These are ignorant ideas, created by fearful, myopic men and attributed to God. We all have access to the infinite wisdom of nature through the intuitive function. For those who believe in God, the actual, true word of God is heard within through the intuitive. Blind faith in ignorant, fearful religious dogma cuts people off from God. In other words, those who kill in the name of God are completely cut off from God because God or intuitive wisdom never would direct one human to kill or harm another, except in defense of self or others.

The overwhelming force in nature is cooperation, not competition. The primary commandment of essentially all major religions is to love, honor and respect other people. Those who truly are following the word of God or intuitive wisdom would act on this basis. As discussed in the Women's section, many studies show that women innately cooperate more readily and effectively. Greater empathy better enables women to look beyond their own individual needs and see the importance of cooperation in human society. Greater intuitive capacity better enables them to see through destructive religious dogma and perceive the actual word of God or intuitive wisdom.

Bringing women to a position of true equality with men and implementing a more balanced male-female leadership structure would increase wisdom, cooperation, compassion and sustainability in society. As a result, promoting women's rights in countries that contain large terrorist networks is one of the most important actions needed to end terrorism.

Lack of wisdom is most evident in countries that grossly suppress women and promote terrorism. But wisdom is lacking throughout the world, as shown by rapid environmental and social degradation in developed and developing countries. The most important requirement for achieving sustainability and real prosperity is increasing wisdom in human society. All men and women have access to essentially infinite wisdom through the intuitive. But women innately have greater access to wisdom. Therefore, in this sense, one of the most important actions needed to achieve sustainability real prosperity is to end the suppression of women and bring them to a position of true equality with men. Implementing a global Bill of Rights is a critical component of achieving this equality.

Modern human society is dominated by irrational, fear-based, competitive ideas and systems, as proven by the results we are achieving. A whole system perspective shows the destructive nature of competition and essential need for vastly greater cooperation in human society. Women see the big picture and understand the need for cooperation more readily. Elevating woman to a position of equality with men will increase wisdom in society. Balancing power with wisdom and men with women is essential for achieving global peace.

This book has extensively discussed actions needed to help humanity reach our fullest potential and achieve sustainability and real prosperity. This concluding section discusses additional important actions needed to achieve these goals. These include ensuring true freedom for all citizens, uniting the people, and inspiring citizens by clarifying our destiny – manifesting the nearly infinite wisdom and cooperation of nature in human society, an outcome that could be called creating Heaven on Earth.

Freedom

President Franklin D. Roosevelt said that true freedom requires more than free speech, the right to vote and other aspects of political freedom. High debt levels, low wages and unemployment cause many people to live in fear that they will not be able to meet basic survival needs. Our shareholder-focused economy forces down wages, causes extensive unnecessary unemployment, and compels many people to take on high debt to survive. People essentially are enslaved by fear, economic stress, uncertainty and inability to meet basic needs. True freedom requires more than political freedom. As President Roosevelt said, it also requires economic freedom.

The situation we face today in the US is similar to that faced before and after the 1929 stock market crash. Prior to the crash, financial inequality was high, as it is today. Life was difficult for millions of average citizens during the Great Depression, as it is today. Flawed systems that mainly were focused on maximizing the wealth of already wealthy citizens largely caused the 1929 crash and subsequent depression, in the same way that they caused the 2008 crash.

Franklin D. Roosevelt was elected President in 1932 in large part because he emphasized the need to help average citizens and rebuild the US economy and society. He made many changes during his first term of office that alleviated the economic stress and insecurity of millions of citizens. His success caused him to be nominated to run for President again in 1936. He gave a speech that year at the Democratic national convention which highlighted the major challenges still facing the US. He mainly focused on how a small group of wealthy citizens had extensive control over the US economy and society. He compared this group to 1700s royalists who used their privileges from the British Crown to restrict and abuse the rights and freedom of average citizens. He referred to this new group of overseers as economic royalists. Their strong control of employment, wages, working conditions and many other factors caused unnecessary economic stress for millions of average citizens.

He emphasized that people are not free if they do not have economic freedom. As a result, he said that the US government should work to protect the economic freedom and security of citizens, for example, by providing jobs and social welfare programs that prevent destitution and desperation. President Roosevelt was successful in part because he worked to overcome party differences. With his encouragement, Democrats and Republicans in Congress worked together to pass extensive legislation that improved the lives of average citizens.

In a 1938 message to Congress about curbing monopolies, President Roosevelt further discussed how concentration of wealth and power were causing unnecessary suffering and hardship for millions of citizens. He explained how large companies were unfairly shutting down small companies, reducing competition, and creating widespread unemployment and labor degradation. To provide a decent standard of living for all citizens and a vibrant, competitive economy, he suggested many actions for reducing monopolies and anti-competitive business concentration.

As a result of his success and popularity, President Roosevelt was elected to an unprecedented third, and then fourth term of office. During World War II, in his 1944 State of the Union Address, President Roosevelt further discussed problems caused by a small group of wealthy citizens who were excessively controlling the economy and society. To ensure true freedom for all citizens, he called for the establishment of a second bill of rights – an economic bill of rights.

President Roosevelt's 1936, 1938 and 1944 speeches and messages to Congress nearly perfectly reflect major problems that we currently face. Today, as then, a small group of wealthy citizens essentially are stealing the people's wealth and power. In many ways, this abuse since the 1980s has caused life to become worse for average citizens today that it was in the 1940s and 1950s. As a result, the need to follow President

Roosevelt's recommendation to implement an economic bill of rights is at least as important today as it was then, and probably much more so.

Elements of President Roosevelt's 1936, 1938 and 1944 speeches and messages to Congress that are relevant to modern society are shown below.

A Rendezvous With Destiny
Democratic National Convention
President Franklin D. Roosevelt
June 27, 1936

...we are met at a time of great moment to the future of the nation...

I salute those of other parties, especially those in the Congress of the United States who on so many occasions have put partisanship aside. I thank the governors of the several states, their legislatures, their state and local officials who participated unselfishly and regardless of party in our efforts to achieve recovery and destroy abuses. Above all I thank the millions of Americans who have borne disaster bravely and have dared to smile through the storm.

America will not forget these recent years, will not forget that the rescue was not a mere party task. It was the concern of all of us. In our strength we rose together, rallied our energies together, applied the old rules of common sense, and together survived.

In those days we feared fear. That was why we fought fear. And today, my friends, we have won against the most dangerous of our foes. We have conquered fear.

But I cannot, with candor, tell you that all is well with the world... the rush of modern civilization itself has raised for us new difficulties, new problems which must be solved if we are to preserve to the United States the political and economic freedom for which Washington and Jefferson planned and fought.

Philadelphia... is fitting ground on which to reaffirm the faith of our fathers; to pledge ourselves to restore to the people a wider freedom; to give to 1936 as the founders gave to 1776 – an American way of life.

That very word *freedom*, in itself and of necessity, suggests freedom from some restraining power. In 1776 we sought freedom from the tyranny of a political autocracy – from the eighteenth-century royalists who held special privileges from the crown. It was to perpetuate their privilege that they... put the average man's property and the average man's life in pawn to the mercenaries of dynastic power; that they regimented the people.

And so it was to win freedom from the tyranny of political autocracy that the American Revolution was fought. That victory gave the business of governing into the hands of the average man, who won the right with his neighbors to make and order his own destiny through his own government. Political tyranny was wiped out at Philadelphia on July 4, 1776.

Since that struggle, however, man's inventive genius released new forces in our land which reordered the lives of our people. The age of machinery, of railroads; of steam and electricity; the telegraph and the radio; mass production, mass distribution - all of these combined to bring forward a new civilization and with it a new problem for those who sought to remain free.

For out of this modern civilization economic royalists carved new dynasties. New kingdoms were built upon concentration of control over material things. Through new uses of corporations, banks and securities, new machinery of industry and agriculture, of labor and capital – all undreamed of by the Fathers – the whole structure of modern life was impressed into this royal service.

There was no place among this royalty for our many thousands of small-businessmen and merchants who sought to make a worthy use of the American system of initiative and profit. They were no more free than the worker or the farmer...

It was natural and perhaps human that the privileged princes of these new economic dynasties, thirsting for power, reached out for control over government itself. They created a new despotism and wrapped it in the robes of legal sanction. In its service new mercenaries sought to regiment the people, their labor, and their property. And as a result the average man once more confronts the problem that faced the Minute Man.

The hours men and women worked, the wages they received, the conditions of their labor – these had passed beyond the control of the people, and were imposed by this new industrial dictatorship. The savings of the average family, the capital of the small-businessmen, the investments set aside for old age – other people's money – these were tools which the new economic royalty used to dig itself in.

Those who tilled the soil no longer reaped the rewards which were their right. The small measure of their gains was decreed by men in distant cities.

Throughout the nation, opportunity was limited by monopoly. Individual initiative was crushed in the cogs of a great machine. The field open for free business was more and more restricted. Private enterprise, indeed, became too private. It became privileged enterprise, not free enterprise.

An old English judge once said: "Necessitous men are not free men." Liberty requires opportunity to make a living – a living decent according to the standard of the time, a living which gives man not only enough to live by, but something to live for.

For too many of us the political equality we once had won was meaningless in the face of economic inequality. A small group had concentrated into their own hands an almost complete control over other people's property, other people's money, other people's labor – other people's lives. For too many of us life was no longer free; liberty no longer real; men could no longer follow the pursuit of happiness.

Against economic tyranny such as this, the American citizen could appeal only to the organized power of government. The collapse of 1929 showed up the despotism for what it was. The election of 1932 was the people's mandate to end it. Under that mandate it is being ended.

The royalists of the economic order have conceded that political freedom was the business of the government, but they have maintained that economic slavery was nobody's business. They granted that the government could protect the citizen in his right to vote, but they denied that the government could do anything to protect the citizen in his right to work and his right to live.

Today we stand committed to the proposition that freedom is no half-and-half affair. If the average citizen is guaranteed equal opportunity in the polling place, he must have equal opportunity in the market place.

These economic royalists complain that we seek to overthrow the institutions of America. What they really complain of is that we seek to take away their power. Our allegiance to American institutions requires the overthrow of this kind of power. In vain they seek to hide behind the flag and the Constitution. In their blindness they forget what the flag and the Constitution stand for. Now, as always, they stand for democracy, not tyranny; for freedom, not subjection; and against a dictatorship by mob rule and the over-privileged alike.

The brave and clear platform adopted by this convention, to which I heartily subscribe, sets forth that government in a modern civilization has certain inescapable obligations to its citizens, among which are protection of the family and the home, the establishment of a democracy of opportunity, and aid to those overtaken by disaster.

But the resolute enemy within our gates is ever ready to beat down our words unless in greater courage we will fight for them.

... the only effective guide for the safety of this most worldly of worlds, the greatest guide of all, is moral principle.

We do not see faith, hope, and charity as unattainable ideals, but we use them as stout supports of a nation fighting the fight for freedom in a modern civilization.

Faith – in the soundness of democracy in the midst of dictatorships.

Hope – renewed because we know so well the progress we have made.

Charity – in the true spirit of that grand old word. For charity literally translated from the original means love, the love that understands, that does not merely share the wealth of the giver, but in true sympathy and wisdom helps men to help themselves.

We seek not merely to make government a mechanical implement, but to give it the vibrant personal character that is the very embodiment of human charity.

We are poor indeed if this nation cannot afford to lift from every recess of American life the dread fear of the unemployed that they are not needed in the world...

In the place of the palace of privilege we seek to build a temple out of faith and hope and charity...

In this world of ours in other lands, there are some people, who, in times past, have lived and fought for freedom, and seem to have grown too weary to carry on the fight. They have sold their heritage of freedom for the illusion of a living. They have yielded their democracy.

I believe in my heart that only our success can stir their ancient hope. They begin to know that here in America we are waging a great and successful war. It is not alone a war against want and destitution and economic demoralization. It is more than that; it is a war for the survival of democracy. We are fighting to save a great and precious form of government for ourselves and for the world.

Curbing Monopolies
Message to Congress
President Franklin D. Roosevelt
April 29, 1938

To the Congress:

Unhappy events abroad have retaught us two simple truths about the liberty of a democratic people.

The first truth is that the liberty of a democracy is not safe if the people tolerate the growth of private power to a point where it becomes stronger than their democratic state itself. That, in its essence, is Fascism – ownership of Government by an individual, by a group, or by any other controlling private power.

The second truth is that the liberty of a democracy is not safe if its business system does not provide employment and produce and distribute goods in such a way as to sustain an acceptable standard of living.

Both lessons hit home.

Among us today a concentration of private power without equal in history is growing.

This concentration is seriously impairing the economic effectiveness of private enterprise as a way of providing employment for labor and capital and as a way of assuring a more equitable distribution of income and earnings among the people of the nation as a whole...

Of all corporations reporting from every part of the nation, one-tenth of 1 per cent of them owned 52 per cent of the assets of all of them... Of all the corporations reporting from every part of the country, one-tenth of 1 per cent of them earned 50 per cent of the net income of all of them... the concentration of stock ownership of corporations in the hands of a tiny minority of the population matches the concentration of corporate assets... [In 1929,] three-tenths of 1 per cent of our population received 78 per cent of the dividends reported by individuals...

"the freest government, if it could exist, would not be long acceptable, if the tendency of the laws were to create a rapid accumulation of property in few hands, and to render the great mass of the population dependent and penniless."...

if there is that danger [of loss of the people's freedom] it comes from that concentrated private economic power which is struggling so hard to master our democratic government. It will not come – as some (by no means all) of the possessors of that private power would make the people believe – from our democratic government itself...

Private enterprise is ceasing to be free enterprise and is becoming a cluster of private collectivisms: masking itself as a system of free enterprise after the American model, it is in fact becoming a concealed cartel system after the European model.

We all want efficient industrial growth and the advantages of mass production. No one suggests that we return to the hand loom or hand forge. A series of processes involved in turning out a given manufactured product may well require one or more huge mass production plants. Modern efficiency may call for this. But modern efficient mass production is not furthered by a central control which destroys competition among industrial plants each capable of efficient mass production while operating as separate units. Industrial efficiency does not have to mean industrial empire building...

In output per man or machine, we are the most efficient industrial nation on earth. In the matter of complete mutual employment of capital and labor we are among the least efficient...

Competition, of course, like all other good things, can be carried to excess. Competition should not extend to fields where it has demonstrably bad social and economic consequences. The exploitation of child labor, the chiseling of workers' wages, the stretching of workers' hours, are not necessary, fair or proper methods of competition. I have consistently urged a federal wages and hours bill to take the minimum decencies of life for the working man and woman out of the field of competition...

No people, least of all a democratic people, will be content to go without work or to accept some standard of living which obviously and woefully falls short of their capacity to produce. No people, least of all a people with our traditions of personal liberty, will endure the slow erosion of opportunity for the common man, the oppressive sense of helplessness under the domination of a few, which are overshadowing our whole economic life...

The power of a few to manage the economic life of the nation must be diffused among the many or be transferred to the public and its democratically responsible government...

Government can deal and should deal with blindly selfish men. But that is a comparatively small part – the easier part – of our problem. The larger, more important and more difficult part of our problem is to deal with men who are not selfish and who are good citizens, but who cannot see the social and economic consequences of their actions in a modern economically interdependent community. They fail to grasp the significance of some of our most vital social and economic problems because they see them only in the light of their own' personal experience and not in perspective with the experience of other men and other industries. They, therefore, fail to see these problems for the nation as a whole...

Concentration of economic power in the few and the resulting unemployment of labor and capital are inescapable problems for a modern "private enterprise" democracy...

Once it is realized that business monopoly in America paralyzes the system of free enterprise on which it is grafted, and is as fatal to those who manipulate it as to the people who suffer beneath its impositions, action by the government to eliminate these artificial restraints will be welcomed by industry throughout the nation.

For idle factories and idle workers profit no man.

**State of the Union Address
President Franklin D. Roosevelt
January 11, 1944**

To the Congress:

This Nation in the past two years has become an active partner in the world's greatest war against human slavery.

We have joined with like-minded people in order to defend ourselves in a world that has been gravely threatened with gangster rule.

But I do not think that any of us Americans can be content with mere survival. Sacrifices that we and our allies are making impose upon us all a sacred obligation to see to it that out of this war we and our children will gain something better than mere survival.

We are united in determination that this war shall not be followed by another interim which leads to new disaster – ... that we shall not repeat the excesses of the wild twenties when this Nation went for a joy ride on a roller coaster which ended in a tragic crash...

The best interests of each Nation, large and small, demand that all freedom-loving Nations shall join together in a just and durable system of peace. In the present world situation, evidenced by the actions of Germany, Italy, and Japan, unquestioned military control over disturbers of the peace is as necessary among Nations as it is among citizens in a community. And an equally basic essential to peace is a decent standard of living for all individual men and women and children in all Nations. Freedom from fear is eternally linked with freedom from want...

The overwhelming majority of our people have met the demands of this war with magnificent courage and understanding... However, while the majority goes on about its great work without complaint, a noisy minority maintains an uproar of demands for special favors for special groups. There are pests who swarm through the lobbies of the Congress and the cocktail bars of Washington, representing these special groups as opposed to the basic interests of the Nation as a whole...

In this war, we have been compelled to learn how interdependent upon each other are all groups and sections of the population of America...

I hope you will remember that all of us in this Government represent the fixed income group just as much as we represent business owners, workers, and farmers. This group of fixed income people includes: teachers, clergy, policemen, firemen, widows and minors on fixed incomes, wives and dependents of our soldiers and sailors, and old-age pensioners. They and their families add up to one-quarter of our one hundred and thirty million people. They have few or no high pressure representatives at the Capitol...

It is our duty now to begin to lay the plans and determine the strategy for the winning of a lasting peace and the establishment of an American standard of living higher than ever before known. We cannot be content, no matter how high that general standard of living may be, if some fraction of our people – whether it be one-third or one-fifth or one-tenth – is ill-fed, ill-clothed, ill housed, and insecure.

This Republic had its beginning, and grew to its present strength, under the protection of certain inalienable political rights – among them the right of free speech, free press, free worship, trial by jury, freedom from unreasonable searches and seizures. They were our rights to life and liberty.

As our Nation has grown in size and stature, however – as our industrial economy expanded – these political rights proved inadequate to assure us equality in the pursuit of happiness.

We have come to a clear realization of the fact that true individual freedom cannot exist without economic security and independence. "Necessitous men are not free men." People who are hungry and out of a job are the stuff of which dictatorships are made.

In our day these economic truths have become accepted as self-evident. We have accepted, so to speak, a second bill of rights under which a new basis of security and prosperity can be established for all regardless of station, race, or creed.

Among these are:

The right to a useful and remunerative job in the industries or shops or farms or mines of the Nation;

The right to earn enough to provide adequate food and clothing and recreation;

The right of every farmer to raise and sell his products at a return which will give him and his family a decent living;

The right of every businessman, large and small, to trade in an atmosphere of freedom from unfair competition and domination by monopolies at home or abroad;

The right of every family to a decent home;

The right to adequate medical care and the opportunity to achieve and enjoy good health;

The right to adequate protection from the economic fears of old age, sickness, accident, and unemployment;

The right to a good education.

All of these rights spell security. And after this war is won we must be prepared to move forward, in the implementation of these rights, to new goals of human happiness and well-being.

America's own rightful place in the world depends in large part upon how fully these and similar rights have been carried into practice for our citizens...

if history were to repeat itself and we were to return to the so-called "normalcy" of the 1920s, then it is certain that even though we shall have conquered our enemies on the battlefields abroad, we shall have yielded to the spirit of Fascism here at home.

I ask the Congress to explore the means for implementing this economic bill of rights – for it is definitely the responsibility of the Congress so to do...

Our fighting men abroad – and their families at home – expect such a program and have the right to insist upon it. It is to their demands that this Government should pay heed rather than to the whining demands of selfish pressure groups who seek to feather their nests while young Americans are dying.

The foreign policy that we have been following... is based on the common sense principle which was best expressed by Benjamin Franklin on July 4, 1776: "We must all hang together, or assuredly we shall all hang separately."

...

President Roosevelt was loved by millions of US citizens. As noted, he was the only president to be elected to more than two terms. President Roosevelt was very similar to other great US leaders who put the well-being of citizens before all else. Our country is truly blessed and fortunate to have had such good, devoted, wise and selfless leaders. The greatest concentration of truly outstanding leaders occurred during the founding era. Our great and wise founding Presidents Washington, Adams, Jefferson and Madison could be called gifts from God.

Benjamin Franklin also should be considered an honorary president in this group. If he had been younger, he probably would have been elected President of the United States at some point. During the Founding Era, only George Washington was more highly esteemed by US citizens.[194] In his later years, Benjamin Franklin served as a wise elder statesman. He secured assistance from France that enabled us to win the Revolutionary war. He encouraged compromise during our contentious Constitutional Convention. In general, he devoted himself to the founding of this country and improving the well-being of humanity.

Throughout US history, several of our greatest presidents have strongly warned us about the danger of concentrated business power. Even at the beginning of this country, our great presidents and other leaders knew that a small group of wealthy citizens could and would steal the people's wealth, power and freedom if they were not restrained by the people through democratic government.

Thomas Jefferson saw the growing power of wealthy citizens and corporations early on. He warned, "Our country is now taking so steady a course as to show by what road it will pass to destruction, to wit: by consolidation of power first, and then corruption, its necessary consequence." As corporations were beginning to threaten democratic government, President Jefferson stated, "I hope we shall take warning from the example and crush in its birth the aristocracy of our monied corporations which dare already to challenge our government to a trial of strength and bid defiance to the laws of our country."[195]

As discussed in the Limited Liability and Corporations section, Abraham Lincoln, another one of our greatest presidents, warned that corporations had substantially increased their influence of government during the Civil War. They persuaded legislators to reduce citizen authority over corporations, extend charters and allow limited liability. President Lincoln said, "I see in the near future a crisis approaching that unnerves me and causes me to tremble for the safety of my country. As a result of the war, corporations have been enthroned and an era of corruption in high places will follow, and the money power of the country will endeavor to prolong its reign by working upon the prejudices of the people until all wealth is aggregated in a few hands and the Republic is destroyed. I feel at this moment more anxiety for the safety of my country than ever before, even in the midst of war."

President Lincoln embodied the devotion and wisdom of a truly great leader. He believed that all people, regardless of wealth or race, should be treated equally and fairly. He was deeply concerned about the grave injustice of slavery for many years before being elected president in 1860. In 1855, he said, "I tell you this nation cannot endure permanently half slave and half free."[196]

An event in the same year illustrates his devotion to the freedom and well-being of all people. A free African American man had been arrested in New Orleans. He did not have the papers to prove that he was free. As a result, he was going to be sold into slavery to pay prison expenses. Abraham Lincoln appealed to the governors of Louisiana and Illinois. He asked them to help free the unjustly imprisoned man. Both governors said that they could not intervene. Future President Lincoln stood before the Illinois governor's desk and exclaimed, "By God Governor, you may not have the legal power to secure the release of this poor boy, but I intend to make the ground in this country too hot for the foot of a slave-owner."[197] And he did!

President Roosevelt faced the two largest crises of the 20th century – the Great Depression and World War II. He used his great wisdom and courage to successfully guide our country through these times of suffering and turmoil. His emphasis on justice, equality and opportunity for all citizens brought us into what could be referred to as the Golden Age of the US. Our economy prospered greatly. But as President Roosevelt made clear, this was not enough. It was not acceptable for the economy overall to prosper, while large numbers of citizens struggled to survive. President Roosevelt focused not only on the economy, but more importantly on society. Following his call for an economic bill of rights, the well-being of average citizens grew substantially. We developed the largest and most prosperous middle class in the world.

But our country once again is under assault from the same internal enemy that we faced in the 1930s and 1940s – concentrated business power. Since 1981, a small group of wealthy citizens increasingly has stolen the people's wealth, power and freedom. Our country would greatly benefit from once again having a strong, courageous leader, like President Roosevelt, who would stand up to concentrated business power and all other enemies of the United States. But it would be difficult for a leader who is truly focused on equally and fairly serving and benefiting all citizens to get elected in today's political environment.

The business-influenced Supreme Court has ensured that wealthy citizens and corporations largely control elections. Federal, state and other candidates often could not win without financial and other support from these groups. Essentially forcing candidates to be dependent on wealthy citizens gives the wealthy strong control of government. Even independently wealthy candidates frequently are under the dominion of big business. These people usually became wealthy through business activities and relationships. It is highly unlikely that they would take actions that alienate or hurt the financial interests of their wealthy peers.

This illustrates why it is essential that we change our corrupt, deeply flawed political system. It is unlikely that another great leader like President Washington, Lincoln or Roosevelt would be elected prior to the evolution of our political systems into fair, sustainable forms. Even if another great leader could be elected, we must not place our hopes in one person or a small group of strong, influential people. Instead, We the People must become strong. We are the ultimate, strongest force in human society. We must not wait for someone else to save us. We must save ourselves. The most important action needed to empower and save ourselves is to end the big business manufactured war between conservatives and liberals. When we are divided, we are conquered and easily abused.

As we begin to stand united, we must demand true freedom for all citizens. President Roosevelt explained how to achieve this more than 70 years ago. He correctly and wisely said that true freedom requires political and economic freedom. As a result, he called for the establishment of an economic bill of rights.

Extensive public deception is used to mislead citizens into giving up their freedom and allowing themselves to be enslaved by debt and economic insecurity. We must use rational thought to see through deception and overcome the economic tyranny of a small group of wealthy citizens. As discussed in President Roosevelt's 1938 message to Congress and throughout this book, wealthy business owners are not bad people. They are good citizens who often intend to benefit society. But their narrow perspective frequently makes it difficult to see the negative impacts imposed on society by their companies. Degradation of society mostly is not caused by wealthy citizens and corporations. It ultimately is caused by myopia and flawed systems. These systems force good people to do bad things, such as put shareholder returns before the survival of humanity and all else.

Providing true freedom, including economic freedom, to all citizens would threaten ever-increasing shareholder returns, in part because government and society would be focused on benefiting all citizens, instead of just wealthy citizens. Public wealth would be diverted from corporate welfare to social welfare. Perhaps the greatest threat to shareholder returns posed by an economic bill of rights involves greatly reducing the power of corporations over citizens. Making people dependent on companies and capital market growth for healthcare, retirement security and other survival needs gives businesses great power over citizens. It enables them to force down wages and abuse average people in other ways.

As discussed, companies generally use two primary strategies for opposing actions that benefit society but threaten shareholder returns – inappropriately influencing government and misleading the public. Large companies and wealthy citizens probably would give large amounts of money to politicians and compel their puppets to oppose implementing an economic bill of rights.

Public deception also would be a main strategy for blocking these rights. Several public deceptions used against President Roosevelt in the 1930s and 1940s still are used today. For example, many wealthy business owners and their allies called President Roosevelt and his policies socialist. As discussed in the Misleading the Public section, applying the socialist label is one of the most common public deceptions used in modern times, especially by conservatives.

There are several deceptive aspects related to use of the term socialism. For example, socialist and socialism frequently are used in derogatory ways as insults. They often are employed to turn citizens against government actions that protect citizens or hold businesses responsible for negative impacts. Use of the socialist label implies that government actions to protect labor, for example by requiring minimum wages, represent totalitarianism or abusive, autocratic government. The term also implies that government is against capitalism and that society should be based on capitalism.

These are grossly inaccurate and deceptive positions. For example, capitalism should not dominate society. Capitalism and socialism largely are economic forms. The priority in society is society, not the economy. The economy is the servant of society. Democracy is the primary form of sustainable society. It is based on the natural laws of equality, fairness and freedom. Democracy takes priority over capitalism, socialism or any other economic form.

Large companies and their media and political allies often attempt to deceive citizens into believing that businesses and their owners have a right to dictate business and economic terms to society. But they do not. The servant does not dictate terms to the master. The people are the highest authority in society. We decide how businesses and the economy will function. Through our servant democratic government, We the People dictate the overall terms of business and the economy. Businesses and their owners abide by the people's commands, or they are not allowed to operate in a democracy.

Calling government efforts to protect citizens and society socialism is a tragic and cunning deception. As noted, the approach implies that government is totalitarian. This is another example of the deception strategy, the best defense is a strong offense. As discussed extensively, a small group of wealthy business owners strongly dominates and controls the US government, economy and society. A business dictatorship or totalitarian state has been established in the US since the 1980s. To hide and perpetuate business totalitarianism, businesses often accuse government of being totalitarian or socialist. The best defense is a strong offense.

President Roosevelt said that fascism exists when concentrated business power becomes stronger than the people and their democratic government. This situation also could be referred to as plutocracy or authoritarianism. Destructive concentration of business power and suppression of democracy do not result from greed or harmful intentions. They are caused by flawed ideas and systems. These systems require that a small group of wealthy citizens get continuously wealthier, regardless of how much this degrades society. These business-focused systems inevitably will produce ongoing environmental and social degradation and instability. Large corporations often are highly unstable. They are based on an irrational and suicidal premise – seeking infinite growth in a finite system. If they do not grow, they frequently die. This is an ignorant, suicidal business requirement resulting from myopia.

To achieve this suicidal growth, businesses often are compelled to degrade labor and all other aspects of society. As noted, 75 percent of S&P 500 profit growth from 2000 to 2007 resulted from reducing employee wages and benefits. This essentially was a transfer of wealth from employees to shareholders. It did not create new value. Instead, it cannibalized society by taking wealth from millions of low and middle-income citizens and transferring it to a small group of already wealthy citizens. This illustrates the suicidal nature of our flawed systems.

The requirement to maximize shareholder returns frequently compels companies to oppose government efforts that threaten returns, such as protecting labor and holding companies responsible for negative impacts. To protect shareholder returns, businesses and their allies often characterize these efforts as socialism or autocratic, overreaching government. They frequently argue that markets should be allowed to operate freely and companies should be allowed to self regulate.

When seen from the whole system perspective, these arguments are shown to be irrational and suicidal. The real reason for opposing acting responsibly is protecting shareholder returns, not opposing socialism. But honestly admitting this would not protect shareholder returns. As a result, companies essentially are compelled to mislead the public (i.e. lie). As discussed in several sections, self-regulation of business is a ridiculous, irrational concept. It absolutely cannot work. We do not allow individuals to self-regulate on murder, robbery and other crimes, even though most citizens would voluntarily not commit these crimes if there were no laws against them. It is vastly more illogical to allow companies to self-regulate because flawed systems often force them to degrade society. As noted, beyond a certain point, voluntary corporate responsibility equals voluntary corporate suicide.

Flawed systems make business self-regulation impossible. Without exception, companies cannot voluntarily mitigate all negative impacts without putting themselves out of business. As discussed in the

Libertarianism section, the people through their servant democratic government absolutely must enforce the rule of law against businesses (i.e. prohibit them from harming the environment and society). It is irrational to call this socialism or autocratic government. Holding companies responsible for harming labor and other aspects of society is an essential part of democracy.

We must help citizens to see through irrational deceptions that seek to perpetuate business totalitarianism by calling democracy socialism. Comparisons between socialism and capitalism largely are irrelevant distractions. The absolute priority always is democracy, not capitalism. We must help citizens to see that the absolute allegiance should be to democracy and promoting the general welfare, not to capitalism or any other economic form.

As the people see through the deceptions that divide and disempower us, we will work together to establish democracy and take back control of government. From this united and empowered place, we will define the standards by which businesses must operate. As President Roosevelt said, businesses have no right to compete by reducing wages or taking any other action that degrades society and makes life unnecessarily difficult for citizens.

Business managers and large shareholders often argue that they do have a right to determine wages and other terms of employment. In businesses, managers and large shareholders are above employees (small shareholders usually have little or no management input). But again, democracy takes priority over the economy and business. Citizens are the ultimate leaders in society. In large companies, there generally are far more employees than managers and large shareholders. In a democracy, the majority rules. In this sense, employees are above managers and shareholders. As a result, when managers manage employees, they essentially are bossing their bosses.

A big picture, reality-based perspective shows that business managers and owners often do not have a right to dictate overall terms of employment. They can determine certain specifics of employment. But these should occur within constraints that prohibit degradation of labor, such as the requirement to pay wages that enable employees to at least meet basic needs. Democratic government, controlled by employees and other citizen/leaders, dictates overall economic and business terms to companies.

Some people might argue that the people controlling business and the economy sounds like socialism or communism. This is another largely irrelevant distraction. It is mixing economic and political factors. The priority is democracy (the people ruling themselves). Theoretical socialism and communism are based on democracy. However in practice, communist countries such as China usually are not democratic. They are totalitarian.

In theory, capitalism also is based on democracy. However, in practice, capitalism can become totalitarian, as it is in the US. Capitalism does not mean that capital controls society. Capital (most of which usually is owned by a small group of wealthy citizens) might control the means of production. But in a democracy, the people sit above capital. They control those who are controlling the economy and means of production. However, as so often occurs in bastardized communist and capitalist countries, a small group of powerful citizens push all other citizens aside and take control of society. This is not democracy. In a democracy, the people ultimately control everything, including the economy and means of production.

As discussed in the Misleading the Public section, among average citizens, the terms socialism, communism and capitalism largely should be placed in the garbage can. The absolute focus should be: Are all citizens equally and fairly controlling society, yes or no? Once the people truly are ruling themselves, we will use rational thought to identify the most effective economic forms in each situation. When determining how to provide products and services, no preferences will be given to the public or private sectors. The people will assess which options objectively provide the greatest benefit for the least cost. The same approach will be used to manage trade. Objective, whole system assessments will be used to determine when trade enhances or degrades society. Blind adherence to ignorant dogma, such as free trade always is good or the private sector always is better then the public sector, will have no impact on the management of an enlightened democracy.

In a true democracy, the well-being of society takes essentially infinite priority over the economy. In other words, the well-being of citizens takes massive priority over the well-being of business. Businesses have no right to exist. Business existence is a privilege contingent upon benefiting and not harming society. Citizens not only have a right to exist. They also have a right to a decent quality of life. A major focus of democracy and society should be on ensuring that each citizen has the freedom and opportunity to reach their fullest potential. At a minimum, society should take all actions necessary to ensure that the basic needs of every citizen are met.

To guarantee a decent standard of living for all citizens, we should establish an economic bill of rights. In his 1944 State of the Union address, President Roosevelt laid out such a bill. He correctly said that each citizen has a right to a good job, living wage and fair competition in the marketplace. President Roosevelt also correctly said that each citizen has a right to a decent home, adequate healthcare, good education, retirement security and unemployment protection. Providing social protections such as these, along with protection of environmental life support systems, should be the primary focus of society. Effectively providing long-term environmental and social protection is the hallmark of a high-functioning, sustainable democracy.

Assuming that environmental and social protection will occur if we continue to focus on ensuring that rich people get continuously richer is ignorant in the extreme (as well as suicidal). The primary focus of an enlightened democracy would not be on maximizing business productivity, profits and shareholder returns. Vastly more important metrics would include ensuring environmental protection and full employment.

Some people might argue that requiring environmental and social protections, such as an economic bill of rights, would degrade or destroy the economy. This once again reflects a failure to think systemically. If protecting the environment and society hurts the economy, then our economic system is severely, even suicidally flawed. People often mistakenly think of the economy in large part as businesses growing forever. This is irrational. The economy should not be thought of primarily as businesses. The foundation of the economy is citizens' essential and nonessential needs. As long as people are alive, they will have needs and an economy will exist.

Rational, objective analysis should be used to determine the optimal structure of the economy. Optimal in this case means most effectively meeting all physical and nonphysical needs of citizens and society. A reformulated private sector (i.e. without the suicidal requirement to grow forever) probably would play a major role in a sustainable economy. But this should not be assumed beforehand. Biases and philosophies such as these interfere with rational, objective assessment of which options maximize the well-being of society in each situation.

Some people argue that capitalism and competition are essential for maximizing efficiency and the well-being of society. Again, this reflects a failure to think systemically. The economics of nature essentially are infinitely more sophisticated than human economics. The model for a sustainable economic system is all around us in nature. In nature, individuals sometimes compete. But the vast coordination, symmetry and sophistication of nature show that competition is limited in ways that humans do not fully understand.

In nature, limited competition at the individual level combines to form nearly infinite cooperation and beauty at the whole system level. One animal might compete with another for food. But plants and animals do not take 100 or 1,000 times more than they need from nature. As a result, there often are enough resources for nearly all individuals. As humans evolve more intellectually and intuitively, we will begin to match the wisdom, cooperation and limited competition seen in nature.

At our current low level of intellectual development (compared to nature), we often irrationally and suicidally emphasize the individual perspective. This frequently leads to competition without restraint. This ignorant and suicidal mode of thinking and acting often compels a small group of citizens to take far more resources and wealth than they need, while millions of people are unable to meet basic needs. It is not surprising that we frequently honor and even give prizes for ideas and theories that promote this destructive behavior. If enough of us recognized that it was wrong, we would stop doing it, and certainly not give prizes for it.

To protect shareholder returns, businesses and their allies often emphasize and promote capitalism. This usually is an intentional or unintentional deception. When citizens hear capitalism being promoted, they should assume that people are misled or trying to mislead. The priority is democracy, not capitalism. Under true democracy, the people would use rational, objective analysis to determine the optimal economic forms. Citizens and their leaders would not ignorantly and blindly implement philosophies such as the many different forms of socialism or capitalism. The people will rationally determine the optimal mix of private and public sector services that objectively provide the greatest benefits to society for the lowest cost, while imposing no negative environmental and social impacts.

Those who promote capitalism often are unintentionally seeking to place business above society or capitalism above democracy. They are implying that a small group of wealthy citizens should control much of society. Probably without realizing it, they essentially are saying that democracy should be replaced with plutocracy. Promoting capitalism instead of democracy perpetuates the business totalitarianism that dominates US society.

This is not to suggest that capitalism is not important or might not be useful. Rather it is to say that capitalism is not the highest state of society. All capitalism conversations should be grounded in the context that democracy and promoting the general well-being are the absolute, highest priorities of society. Capitalism simply is a tool. The extent to which this tool is used depends on what objectively maximizes democracy and the well-being of society.

Use of the terms capitalism and socialism also is deceptive because it implies that society would or should do one or the other. But again, the priority is democracy and society, not the economy. A totalitarian regime might implement pure socialism or capitalism. For example, the totalitarian business regime controlling the US since the 1980s apparently is attempting to implement nearly pure capitalism by taking over a growing number of public sector services.

In a democracy, rational thought would be used to determine how to best provide products and services. A rational, enlightened democracy would use a mix of public and private sector activities to most efficiently and effectively meet the needs of society. Using the term socialism or capitalism often is irrational. It implies that people should blindly support either philosophy. Instead, citizens should be encouraged and political leaders required to use rational, objective analysis to determine the optimal mix of public and private sector activities.

During the presidential election season of 2016, candidate Senator Bernie Sanders frequently used the term socialism. It probably would have been more effective to emphasize the term democracy. Many people assume that socialism means greatly reducing or eliminating the private sector. Of course, this is not what Senator Sanders meant. He discussed returning control of government to the people and using the public wealth to benefit all citizens, not just wealthy citizens. Regarding socialism, he almost certainly meant that when the public sector can objectively provide high quality services for lower costs, maximizing the well-being of society demands that we use the public sector.

To summarize about the socialism deception, democratic government is an expression and extension of the people. It is the vehicle through which the people protect their wealth, rights, power and freedom. Only government can hold businesses fully responsible for negative impacts on society, and thereby eliminate conflicts between business and society. But flawed systems often compel companies to oppose government efforts to hold them responsible. Labeling these efforts socialist is a common deception. People essentially are encouraged to blindly believe that government efforts to hold business responsible are bad. This is similar to misleading people into thinking that murder laws and other laws that prevent individuals from harming society are bad.

Through public awareness and other efforts, we must help citizens to see through the ignorant socialist deception. Prohibiting companies from degrading society, for example by requiring them to pay living wages if they wish to operate in the US, is an essential part of democracy and promoting the general welfare. It is not socialism.

Christian dogma represents another public deception related to an economic bill of rights. As discussed in the Population section, some dogmatic Christians argue that the US was established as a Christian nation. This is exactly incorrect. The Founders strongly supported religious freedom and enshrined it in our Constitution. However, George Washington, Benjamin Franklin, Abraham Lincoln, Franklin D. Roosevelt and many other great US leaders strongly supported the idea that the US should be based on religious principles. George Washington discussed the importance of this in his Farewell Address. Religious principles include treating other people with kindness, love and respect, helping the needy, and protecting God's creation (i.e. the environment and all species).

Public deception results from the frequent conflict between religious dogma and religious principles. As discussed in the Education section, religious principles are common to virtually all religions. They also are laws of nature. Religious dogma, on the other hand, often varies from religion to religion. It involves cultural ideas, such as those related to same-sex marriage and abortion. Religious dogma that attempts to control which adults are allowed to marry or how women use their bodies violates the most important commandment and principal of Christianity (and all other religions) – treating people with kindness, love and respect.

Dogmatic religious leaders and politicians often criticize people on social welfare programs. They frequently say or imply that social welfare recipients are lazy. Their benefits should be cut off. They should be forced to work for a living. This is not Christian. It is anti-Christian. It violates another foundational religious principle – help the needy.

The economic bill of rights proposed by President Roosevelt largely defines a truly Christian nation. Actions count far more than words in this physical world. A truly Christian nation would be based on principle led actions, not principle violating dogmatic ideas. In a truly Christian nation, we would use the public wealth to provide an economic bill of rights and a decent standard of living for all citizens. People would be free to live according to their own religious and moral beliefs, rather than be forced to abide by religious dogma. Instead of destroying the environment and other species, we would protect them. Rudeness, disrespect and deception would not dominate media in a truly Christian nation. Instead, media would model kindness, respect and honesty to our children and all other people. A truly Christian nation would not castigate social welfare recipients and other needy citizens. They would be honored, respected and empowered. Democracy would not be suppressed in a truly Christian nation. Instead, we would protect all citizens' freedom, wealth and right to rule themselves.

Our Founders were well aware of the immense destruction and suffering caused by religious oppression in Europe. As a result, they strongly opposed allowing religious dogma to have any influence on government. This would oppress citizens by forcing them to follow someone else's religious ideas, rather than leaving them free to live according to their own religious and moral views. While the Founders opposed forcing people to abide by religious dogma, they encouraged us to abide by religious principles. Implementing an economic bill of rights and other social and environmental protections are major components of establishing the society envisioned and advocated by our Founders – a nation based on religious principles and natural laws.

We should not do this out of moral obligation. Instead, we should do it because treating others with kindness, love and respect, helping the needy, and protecting the environment are laws of nature. If we do not abide by them, there inevitably will be negative consequences. Our society will decline, and perhaps disappear. We also should do it because helping others and ensuring that each person has a decent standard of living usually produces the greatest true success and satisfaction in life. Our society cannot prosper when many people suffer. Doing all that we can to help each person prosper enables us (humanity) to reach our fullest potential, individually and collectively.

Economic insecurity often makes people desperate and afraid. This makes it easier to mislead, manipulate and abuse citizens, for example, by stealing their wealth and power. As President Roosevelt said, the people have given up their freedom and democracy in exchange for an income. This trade-off should not be necessary. As noted, in 1929, the top one percent of society had 23 percent of income in the US. Largely as a result of President Roosevelt's policies to protect average citizens and strengthen the middle class, this fell to 9 percent in the 1960s. But wealthy citizens have reestablished their dominance of society since the 1980s. The top one percent once again is receiving over 23 percent of income. If technology and economic policies had been focused on benefiting all citizens, quality of life would be vastly better in the US. But technology and the economy mainly were focused on benefiting wealthy citizens. This made life more difficult for millions of average citizens.

As noted, the wealthiest US citizens potentially avoid nearly $3 trillion in taxes each year. This makes life difficult for average citizens because they often must pay extra taxes to make up for the unfairly low taxes paid by wealthy citizens. Social welfare programs that benefit average citizens frequently are underfunded when wealthy citizens do not pay their fair share for benefits received from society. Allowing banks to create and control the money supply further increases the economic stress of average citizens. It causes debt levels and interest rates to be much higher than they would be if the people controlled the money supply.

None of this stress and suffering is necessary. In this wealthy nation, we can afford to ensure that the basic needs of all citizens are met. Every person has a right to economic security and freedom. They should be free from the fear of unemployment and inability to meet basic needs. Alleviating the fear and economic insecurity of citizens would empower them to exercise their authority as the true, rightful leaders of society. They would demand democracy and put an end to corporate welfare and business control of government. This illustrates why many wealthy business owners and their media and political allies probably would strongly oppose ending the economic insecurity of average citizens, for example by implementing an economic bill of rights. Keeping the people afraid, desperate and economically insecure makes it easier to steal their wealth, power and freedom.

But the one percent are not stronger than the 99 percent. The only reason that many people remain afraid, disempowered and insecure is that we voluntarily allow ourselves to be divided, misled and conquered. Once we wake up from our deception, we can stand united and require that the public wealth be used to ensure a decent standard of living, free from economic fear and insecurity, for all citizens. We can expand the work of our Founders by adding an economic bill of rights to the political Bill of Rights provided in our Constitution. This can be done through legislation once we establish democracy and compel politicians to do their jobs – serve all citizens equally and fairly.

Many actions can be taken to fund an economic bill of rights and provide economic freedom for citizens. The main overall strategy is to end welfare for wealthy citizens. Key actions include implementing fair taxation, reclaiming the people's right to create the money supply, and holding companies fully responsible for all negative environmental and social impacts.

Providing economic freedom and security to all citizens will provide vast benefits to society. For example, it will greatly reduce crime and terrorism threats. Desperate, economically insecure people often resort to crime. They also are highly vulnerable to radicals who promote terrorism and hatred in society. Ending economic insecurity will vastly reduce the number of people who are vulnerable to recruitment by terrorist, racist and other radical organizations. Overall, ending economic insecurity will strongly promote the truly Christian nation that many citizens say they want. It will greatly expand the brotherly affection that George Washington strongly wished for us in his Farewell Address.

As discussed in the Judicial Branch section, James Madison and other leading Founders understood that the US government must be empowered to take any action necessary to promote the general welfare. Article I, Section 8 of the Constitution gives our government nearly unlimited power to do this. President Roosevelt, along with Congress, effectively used the great power of the federal government to substantially improve the lives of millions of citizens. He believed, as many Founders did, that the federal government should be an active force in society, seeking to resolve major problems. It should not passively allow problems to linger or worsen.

The federal government is the people. It is the collective expression of our wealth and power. It is the vehicle through which we protect our rights, freedom and well-being. Vested interests often successfully turn citizens against government. When this occurs, we are turned against ourselves. The vehicle intended to protect us is weakened. As a result, we become vulnerable to the theft of our wealth and power.

Again, this is not necessary. Deception is voluntary. We can do what President Roosevelt did, and more. President Roosevelt used the public wealth to create jobs, build infrastructure and benefit society in many other ways. Working with Congress, he established extensive protections for workers and other citizens. Many of these protections have been dismantled or weakened by business-controlled government. It is time to turn this around. It is time to do what President Roosevelt did, and then go beyond it.

In 1936, President Roosevelt said that we should base our country on faith, hope and charity. Vested interests have deceived many citizens into believing that helping needy people is providing handouts and promoting laziness. This position reflects profound ignorance and heartlessness. Currently we are 'handing out' trillions of dollars of corporate welfare to already wealthy citizens. The fools who argue against helping needy citizens imply that it is acceptable to use the public wealth to essentially buy mansions for billionaires, but not to feed hungry children. We must rise above this truly tragic deception.

It is not acceptable to provide vast amounts of welfare to wealthy people who do not need it. Instead, we should use our wealth and power to help everyone equally and fairly. It is foolish, unchristian and just plain stupid to assume that needy citizens are lazy. Many people diligently search for jobs, but cannot find them. Many other people work more than one job, but still cannot meet basic needs. Still others are incapacitated by physical or mental problems. How is it Christian to deny these people dignity, economic security and a decent quality of life?

Even for the small percentage of people who abuse social welfare programs or are lazy, this is an extremely minor problem compared to corporate welfare. Giving food to lazy people might be questionable in a society that speaks about Christian values, but does not implement them. However, giving trillions of dollars of public wealth to already wealthy people definitely is wrong. Regarding laziness, our disempowering culture and shareholder-focused economy make people feel inadequate and create millions of boring and difficult jobs. This discourages work. Refocusing the economy and society on benefiting all citizens will empower citizens and create far more satisfying jobs. This will greatly increase the desire to work and be productive.

Our apparent unwillingness to help needy citizens while giving trillions of dollars to wealthy citizens makes it seem that we have gone over the edge – that we have descended into division, hatred and madness. But we can pull ourselves back from the abyss. We have nearly infinite potential to produce goodness, love, charity and sister/brotherhood in society.

To protect shareholder returns, businesses and their allies often argue that we should go slow. We might make a mistake. But the priority is not avoiding mistakes. It is ending hunger, fear and desperation in society.

As President Roosevelt did, we must begin. Take action. Do something. Refocus the wealth of society away from buying mansions for billionaires to ending hunger and suffering among the people. If we make a mistake, so be it. It is better to try to end hunger and suffering, and fail in the process. Allowing desperation to continue in society because we are afraid of making a mistake is perpetuating ignorance and heartlessness.

President Roosevelt encouraged Republicans and Democrats in Congress to work together. As a result, many highly beneficial changes were made during his first term in office. However, a small group of wealthy citizens has even greater control of government today than in the 1930s. They tightly control their Republican and Democratic puppets in Congress. These puppets probably will continue to grossly violate their constitutional duty to promote the general welfare. They will serve their wealthy masters, in large part by continuing to steal the people's wealth, power and freedom.

As a result, We the People largely are on our own. We can continue to fight each other, and thereby remain divided and conquered. Or we can wake up, see our overwhelming common interests and begin to work together. As we stand united, we will end the theft of our wealth, power and freedom. We will compel our constitutional government to protect all citizens, especially our children and future generations. Uniting and empowering the people are discussed in the following section.

Uniting Citizens

We the People are the sleeping giant of society. Hundreds of system changes needed to achieve sustainability and real prosperity have been discussed in this book. Most of the changes are so far-reaching that only the people can implement them. We the People are by far the most powerful force in society. Our life support systems and society are rapidly declining. If we work together, we quickly could end environmental and social degradation. We could begin to restore and protect the society and world that our children and future generations will inhabit.

But we are divided. We are not working together on our common interests. Vested interests have fractured us and turned us against each other. This is not what the Founders intended. They intended to establish a society where citizens equally control government and their destiny. They intended that We the People be free from religious, political and economic oppression. They intended that we all be free to exercise our natural right to the pursuit of happiness. Most importantly, the Founders intended that we love and protect our children and future generations. As discussed in the Time Value of Money section, the Founders often used the word posterity. In his inaugural address, Thomas Jefferson spoke of preserving the Union for the ten thousandth generation.

Exploitation and oppression drove the formation of this country. Our Founders rebelled against this injustice. Thomas Jefferson said in the Declaration of Independence that we had a duty to do so. The Founders intended to establish a country where the people would be free from exploitation and oppression. But right from the beginning of this country, the same forces that oppressed us before the revolution began to divide, conquer and oppress us again. Wise President Washington warned us about this in his Farewell Address. He correctly predicted that vested interests would use political parties to divide the people and steal their wealth and power.

British corporations abused the people before the Revolution. Concentrated business power took over that role after the Revolution. Throughout US history, concentrated business interests have been abusing citizens to varying degrees. In the late 1800s and early 1900s, business trusts shut down small businesses and abused labor. When the abuse became intolerable, the people rose up and directed their servant democratic government to rein in big business abuses of the people. This produced greater equality, fairness and democracy, which led to several decades of great prosperity in the US.

While concentrated business power has suppressed democracy throughout US history, this is not a black and white issue. In spite of this injustice, we lived up to many of the Founders' expectations. As the US displayed greater democracy, equality and fairness at home from the 1930s to 1970s, we became a model of success and democracy for many other countries. As we treated our people at home more fairly, our status as a world leader increased. We became the most prosperous nation with the largest middle class in the world.

But democracy has ebbed and flowed in the US. Since the 1980s, concentrated business power has been rising. As a result, democracy, fairness and equality have been declining. A big business revolution has occurred in the US since the 1980s. Democracy has been replaced with plutocracy. A totalitarian business state has been established. As vested interests abused citizens at home, our reputation around the world often became tarnished. Many people believe that we are hypocritical. We speak of democracy, but do not implement it at home. Through economic and military power, we frequently attempt to force our will on other countries. Our country is run by a small group of wealthy citizens who impose their will on US citizens and other people around the world.

As discussed extensively throughout this book, this has virtually nothing to do with greed, immorality or poor intentions. The small group of wealthy citizens who steal our wealth and power are no better or worse than anyone else. They largely are good people who intend to benefit society. The real enemy is not this group. It is the flawed ideas and systems that compel their bad behavior.

Probably the greatest enemy of humanity is myopia. The individual perspective dominates human society. We largely do not see reality. We are not thinking clearly. Our flawed ideas produce flawed systems that are driving us to destruction. In reality, we are not separate. Just like cells in the human body, we must cooperate and work together to survive and prosper. Focusing on what is best for individuals literally is killing us. We must focus first on what is best for all of us, as the Founders did through their primary focus on promoting the general welfare.

Our flawed ideas and systems are causing us to massively violate the laws of nature and reality. Our myopic systems are in the process of collapsing in the US and around the world. The rising inequality and injustice we see at home and abroad violate the laws of nature. This absolutely will end. Reality and nature will not allow a small group of wealthy citizens to essentially steal far more than they need from society, while billions of people suffer around the world. Reality will not allow this for very much longer. The small group who steals our wealth and power are harming themselves and their children. Current unsustainable systems do not work for anyone. They might appear to work for some people. But oppression and injustice harms everyone, victims and abusers alike.

There are many good people in the world who are following their hearts and living satisfying, productive lives. But this is occurring within a larger context of degradation. There are healthy cells in a body with terminal cancer. But this does not mean that the cancer ultimately will not kill all cells in the body. On a deeper, often unconscious level, suffering and injustice in the world affects us all. We the People (all the people of the world) cannot truly prosper unless we begin to act as the one people, the one system that we are in reality.

Here in the US, We the People allow vested interests to divide us and fail to see our common interests. We essentially are asleep. The unassailable power of a united people is not being used. It is time to wake the sleeping giant. As we see our common interests, we will work together to protect our children and ourselves.

The founding of this country provides a good example of how to do this. Our Constitution begins with the words "We the People". The people of the early US empowered their elected representatives to improve government during the Constitutional Convention of 1787. This did not mean that We the People agreed on everything in the early US. There were deep divisions on slavery and other issues. But this did not prevent us from seeing our broad common interests. Like mature adults, we essentially agreed to work together in our areas of common interest. The existence of divergent issues did not prevent us from uniting. As they say, the rest is history. The fruits of our working together are evident in the immense success of the US.

Exploitation and oppression by concentrated business power have created the need for another great uniting of the people. We do not need a revolution. That already has occurred. An unjust business revolution essentially has ended democracy in the US since the 1980s. We the People are the anti-revolution. We seek to restore the democratic government enshrined by our Founders in the Constitution.

We know that our unjust systems will change. Not changing is not an option. Our only options are voluntary or involuntary change. Voluntary change of overarching economic and political systems has been difficult or impossible throughout human history. Given the interconnected nature of modern society, involuntary change (i.e. collapse) of current systems

303

will bring unprecedented pain and suffering to humanity. It might even destroy us.

Voluntary system change is the obvious, vastly superior option. There probably only is one way to achieve voluntary high-level system change. Vested interests are extremely powerful. They control government. They will use it to suppress citizens and block changes that threaten their unjust concentrated wealth and power. The only force in society powerful enough to overcome vested interests and drive voluntary high-level system change is We the People.

The power of vested interests essentially is an illusion. It only can be exercised when the people are asleep. All forms of civilization require cooperation from the people. Civilization means that most people voluntarily agreed to act responsibly and abide by common rules and systems. If a large percentage of the people stop cooperating with authorities, prevailing systems would collapse. Even the most abusive totalitarian states, such as North Korea or Nazi Germany, could not stand against a united people. Any broad human system requires the cooperation of most people to function. If the people withdraw their support of the system, it will collapse very quickly.

To restore democracy and protect our children and ourselves, We the People – the sleeping giant of society – must awaken. To achieve this, we need a massive movement to unite and empower the people – a We the People movement.

This section broadly discusses how such a movement could be established and operated. Critical aspects of this work, such as empowering citizens and establishing democracy, were discussed in Chapter Seven. This section builds on these ideas. It discusses various aspects of building a We the People movement, including the structure of the movement, raising public awareness, exposing media deceptions, providing a political party or voting option that truly is focused on benefiting all citizens (as opposed to the Democratic and Republican parties that are almost completely focused on benefiting wealthy campaign donors), and engaging in peaceful, cooperative activism.

We the People Movement

Several liberal, progressive and Democratic leaders and experts have said that the conservatives are doing a better job of organizing citizens and winning elections. As a result, they suggest that liberals implement more effective strategies for organizing citizens and defeating conservatives. But this probably will have little impact on the lives of average citizens. Two main political parties have been fighting each other since the beginning of this country. One party routinely beats the other and takes over control of government. But little usually changes for average citizens. This occurs mainly because both parties largely are controlled by a small group of wealthy citizens and corporations. Especially since the 1980s, regardless of which party wins, this small group wins, while nearly everyone else in society loses.

The solution largely is not to develop more effective strategies for beating conservatives. This will perpetuate the division in society that enables a small group of wealthy citizens to steal the people's wealth and power. Rather than trying to fight conservatives (or liberals) more effectively, the solution is to unite conservatives and liberals and encourage the people to work together in their areas of common interest.

As discussed in the Political Parties section, aside from Alexander Hamilton, most of the main Founders of the US were strongly against the formation of political parties. They feared that it would destroy the republic. George Washington, John Adams, Thomas Jefferson, James Madison and other early leaders knew that vested interests would use political parties to divide the people and steal their wealth and power.

As discussed in the Judicial Branch section, Alexander Hamilton greatly admired the aristocracy and monarchy of the British government. He did not believe that the people could rule themselves effectively. Instead, he believed that society should be controlled by a small group of elite, powerful citizens, as it was in England. During the Constitutional Convention, he proposed that the President, Senators and federal judges serve for life once elected or appointed. He also proposed that Congress appoint state governors and have veto power of state legislation. His proposals were ignored during the Convention because they established aristocracy and took too much power from the states. James Madison referred to him as a monarchist.

305

However, Alexander Hamilton ultimately was successful in securing the US aristocracy that he strongly advocated. He largely is responsible for three of the most important factors that enable a small group of wealthy citizens to control society – a lifetime appointed, unelected Supreme Court that has absolute authority over the elected branches, private sector control of money creation and the US money supply, and political parties.

In the Federalist Papers, Alexander Hamilton advocated lifetime appointment of Supreme Court justices and empowering the Supreme Court to void laws, neither of which are established in the Constitution. His influence led to the current aristocratic, unconstitutional structure of the Supreme Court. Through influence of judicial appointments, wealthy citizens gain long-term control of the most powerful branch of government. Alexander Hamilton also established the first national bank of the US. This privately owned and controlled bank gave wealthy citizens strong control of the US economy, monetary system and government finances.

In addition, Alexander Hamilton, along with wealthy bankers and merchants, formed the first political party, the Federalist Party. In response, Thomas Jefferson and James Madison were compelled to form the Democratic-Republican Party to fight the concentration of wealth and power promoted by the Federalists. But this was a suboptimal solution. The preferred solution was to allow our government to function as it was designed. As discussed in the Political Parties section, political parties are not mentioned in our Constitution. But they nevertheless sit above politicians and largely tell them how to vote. These unconstitutional structures have stolen the people's ability to control government and rule themselves.

The ultimate solution being proposed here is not to develop a third political party. It is to weaken the political party system and unite the people under a movement that uses the name given to us by our Founders – We the People. However, the transition to the political party-free system established under our Constitution probably requires working within the current system. As a result, this section discusses establishing a We the People political party that has the ability to defeat the Republican or Democratic parties. As We the People gain control of society, we can greatly reduce or eliminate vested interest-controlled political parties that facilitate the theft of the people's wealth, power and freedom.

Uniting the people under a We the People movement can be facilitated by helping conservatives and liberals to see that they agree on nearly all major issues in society. As discussed, virtually all citizens want a strong economy, good jobs, low crime, good education and healthcare, a clean environment, efficient and effective government, and good international relations. Some people argue that liberals and conservatives agree on major goals, but disagree on how to achieve them. But this largely is a deception. Disagreement about how to operate the government, economy and society results almost completely from the suppression of rational thought. People are encouraged to blindly believe in philosophies and dogma, such as those related to small government, free markets and free trade. Vested interests whip people up into an emotional frenzy. People who question economic and political dogma often are insulted and ostracized.

This is why we need a Second Enlightenment. We must emulate our Founders by using our gifts of rational thought and intuitive wisdom more effectively. Rather than blindly believing in dogma, we must rationally analyze each situation and determine which strategy objectively provides the greatest benefit for the least cost. Once we use rational, objective, reality-based, fact-based analysis to identify optimal strategies for dealing with specific economic, social, political and environmental issues, liberals and conservatives will realize that they largely agree on how to operate society and resolve major problems.

In reality, there is little division between conservatives and liberals. Division largely is an illusion manufactured by vested interests. These deceptions enable vested interests to divide and conquer the people. The small group of wealthy citizens who steal the people's wealth and power are metaphorically using sleeping gas on the people. By using emotional manipulation to compel people to blindly believe dogma, vested interests essentially have put many citizens into a unthinking stupor. By falsely dividing the people, vested interests have put the giant to sleep.

Fighting between conservatives and liberals is essential for establishing and maintaining plutocracy in a country that is not overtly totalitarian. (The US is a constitutional republic. But we operate as a business totalitarian state.) The civil war between conservatives and liberals probably is the most important factor blocking democracy and degrading the general welfare in the US and many other countries. To establish republican government and maximize the well-being of all citizens, we must end the business-manufactured war between conservatives and liberals. Instead of wasting our energy on fighting false enemies (i.e. each other), we must unite and prevail against our real enemies (ultimately myopia). Once a large majority of citizens are united and focused on our massive areas common interest, we will be an unstoppable force.

A primary motto of the US since our founding has been E pluribus unum (out of many, one). We united long ago and reaped great benefits for doing so. But we have not been nearly as successful at promoting the general welfare (i.e. the well-being of all citizens) as we could have been because a small group of wealthy citizens essentially has implemented a different motto in the US – out of many, two.

As discussed in the Political Parties section, James Madison argued at the Constitutional Convention that a wide variety of special interests in a large republic would prevent large interest groups from forming and abusing citizens. But political parties overcame this intended diversified protection of society. The people mostly have been fractured into two major political parties, neither of which is focused on serving average citizens. Examining results shows that both the Republican and Democratic parties are focused primarily on benefiting wealthy campaign donors, usually at the expense of average citizens.

The US was born from the revolutionary spirit. We rose to fight injustice. Once again, injustice dominates the people of the US. It is time to awaken the spirit from which we came – the spirit of uniting and fighting injustice. This is revolutionary in the sense that we are throwing off injustice and oppression. But it is anti-revolutionary in the sense that we simply are standing up for our Constitution. We are throwing off the business revolution – the usurpers who suppressed our constitutional government and stole the public wealth.

Pain is a great teacher, motivator and often uniter. President Roosevelt harnessed the pain of the Great Depression to unite the people and political parties. Republican and Democratic citizens and politicians worked together for several years and made huge progress. The prosperous middle class that emerged in the US in the 1940s and 1950s largely was birthed in the 1930s. It primarily resulted from Democrats and Republicans working together to implement programs that maximized the well-being of average citizens, such as fair taxation, union protection and Social Security. We the People must unite and once again compel our supposed servant government to do what is best for all citizens, not just wealthy campaign donors.

Division and hatred in society create fear. They make people afraid to change. Citizens often cling to current systems and focus on helping themselves (because others are unlikely to help them in a divided, angry society). But this fear-induced selfishness and unwillingness to help others is not our natural state. Nearly all sane people want what is best for everyone, not just themselves. We know on an intuitive level that widespread prosperity produces the greatest life satisfaction, individually and collectively. When those around us are happy and prosperous, we each are more likely to be happy and prosperous.

The conservative-liberal war poisons US prosperity and happiness. Hatred and division often produce apathy. We violate Christian principles by losing concern for our fellow human beings. But as President Roosevelt said, we must fight apathy. We each should take responsibility for the degraded and declining state of society. We are not powerless. Collectively, We the People are the most powerful force in human society.

Addressing the immense economic, social, environmental and political problems in the US and other countries can seem overwhelming. Even for experts, it often is difficult to envision how these problems might be fully resolved. Inability to see how we could change overarching systems and resolve major problems also frequently produces apathy. But We the People do not need to know all the details of system change and problem resolution. We are the leaders of society. Like CEOs leading companies, we set the higher goals, and then direct our servant politicians and experts to work out the details. The higher goals are clear. Our Founders established them for us long ago – implement republican government and promote the general welfare. Once we establish republican government and take our rightful place as the leaders of society, we will direct our political servants to effectively promote the general welfare (i.e. equally and fairly protect and benefit all current and future citizens).

Some liberal leaders and experts suggest that liberals should focus more on local organizing efforts. This could be useful. But the US is controlled in large part at the federal level. Therefore, a We the People movement should address all levels of society – local, state and federal.

Many high-level system changes are needed to achieve sustainability and real prosperity. But as discussed in Chapter Seven, nearly all of these changes only can be made by a united and empowered people. A We the People movement is the heart of achieving high-level system change, sustainability and real prosperity. Without a united people, improving overarching economic, political and social systems and resolving major problems largely will be impossible. A divided public will not be able to act on our common interests. Vested interests will continue to play the people like fools. We will continue to irrationally blame each other (i.e. conservatives or liberals) for our problems, while vested interests continue to steal our wealth and power, laughing all the way to the bank with our money.

However, if we wake up from our vested interest-manufactured delusion and begin to work together, virtually everything is possible. We have the power to implement a truly prosperous, equitable and sustainable democracy, but only if we work together.

A We the People movement obviously would be based on widespread collaboration. The movement could be initiated or expanded by one or more organizations that currently are focused on using collaboration to promote the general welfare, or have an interest in engaging in this work. An initial step might involve assembling NGOs, foundations and other organizations and individuals who are interested in launching a We the People movement or expanding existing movements that have similar goals. Through brainstorming, the group could develop an initial action plan.

An effective We the People movement would include many different actions at all levels of society. As in nature, thousands of actions combine to form effective whole system solutions. This book is intended to facilitate a We the People movement. It can be used to develop a blueprint or roadmap for the movement. The book provides detailed discussions of nearly all major high-level system changes needed to resolve the major economic, social, political and environmental challenges facing humanity, especially here in the US. The book also extensively discusses and exposes the many vested interest deceptions that are used to perpetuate the war between conservatives and liberals. As discussed below, raising public awareness by exposing vested interest deceptions is a critical aspect of uniting and empowering citizens.

In developing a We the People action plan, whole system thinking is essential. As discussed extensively, achieving sustainability and real prosperity requires high-level system change. But major system changes cannot be done in isolation because, in the real world, everything is connected. Attempting to resolve environmental, economic, social and political problems in isolation will produce what we have now – unintended negative consequences. Success requires an integrated whole system change strategy.

Key areas of focus in this integrated strategy include implementing democracy, promoting the general welfare and holding businesses fully responsible for negative impacts. These three areas include nearly all of the hundreds of system changes discussed in this book. For example, implementing democracy requires imposing term limits on Congress and the Judicial branch, limiting judicial review, implementing popular election of the President, and weakening political parties.

Promoting the general welfare requires actually measuring and managing the general welfare, instead of myopically focusing on economic growth and shareholder returns. It also requires ending corporate welfare and using the public wealth to equally and fairly benefit all citizens, in large part by establishing a strong social safety net. Promoting the general welfare further requires increasing freedom in society by implementing freedom-based education, guaranteeing economic freedom for all citizens, and reversing the constitutional rights violations of the Traitors Act. Holding businesses responsible requires ending limited liability, incorporating external costs into prices, and prohibiting time value of money related undervaluing of future generations and resources. Holding companies fully responsible for negative impacts will drive major change in virtually all sectors, especially including energy, agriculture, chemicals, genetic engineering and manufacturing.

The first priority of a We the People whole system change plan probably should be establishing democracy. Once this occurs, the united people can implement nearly all other changes through their servant democratic government. Another high priority should be implementing economic changes that create widespread high-quality jobs and small business ownership opportunities. This will stabilize families and society, and thereby facilitate social welfare improvements and other system changes.

Regarding principles, we should emulate our Founders by basing a We the People movement on natural laws and religious principles, including love, honor and respect other people, help the needy, and protect the environment and all life. A primary focus of a We the People movement should be to unite conservatives, liberals and other groups in society by emphasizing our common ground. The tagline of a We the People movement could be – "Uniting on our massive common ground, building bridges on the rest".

Non-judgment should be an essential principle and priority of a We the People movement. Everyone makes mistakes. We all have negative impacts on society. The focus of a We the People movement should not be on blaming others and assigning responsibility. The focus should be on uniting to solve common problems. This often would require businesses and other groups to take responsibility for their negative impacts. But this should be encouraged and facilitated through a spirit of collaboration and non-judgment, rather than condemnation.

Funding mechanisms for a We the People movement should be established that limit the ability of funders to alter the We the People movement mission and activities. Foundations with similar missions could provide valuable guidance and support. But there is a danger that business funding could be used to modify We the People activities in ways that protect shareholder returns, but allow ongoing degradation of society. A We the People movement obviously would not be opposed to investors earning reasonable returns. This is essential for the private sector. But as discussed extensively, businesses have no right to prosper by degrading society. Seeking ever-increasing shareholder returns, regardless of negative impacts on society, is an irrational, suicidal business requirement. Myopic shareholder return requirements must not be allowed to inhibit a We the People movement in any way. Extensive grassroots, social media and other efforts can be used to engage volunteers, and thereby minimize funding requirements.

A We the People movement should focus extensively on building community and meeting the emotional and other needs of citizens. Raising awareness about systemic problems and solutions is important. But we must do far more than link people through intellectual means and ideas. Humans are innately gregarious. We have foundational needs for community and emotional support. To be successful, a We the People movement must strive to meet these needs.

This book discusses hundreds of potential focus areas for a We the People movement. However, to summarize a few, critical focus areas include replacing plutocracy with democracy, guaranteeing economic and political freedom for all citizens, protecting life support systems, establishing a strong social safety net, using the public wealth to equally and fairly benefit all citizens, requiring honest media and advertising, implementing freedom-based education, and developing mechanisms that compel politicians to vote for democracy and promoting the general welfare. Expanding the labor movement should be another main focus of a We the People movement. As discussed, the majority of citizens are employees or dependents of employees. Vested interests have deceived many average citizens into opposing the labor movement. When this occurs, many citizens essentially are arguing for making their lives worse.

Another major focus of a We the People movement should be on economic reform. While current economic systems are being evolved into sustainable forms, a transitional parallel economy could be expanded. The primary focus of the parallel economy would be on maximizing the well-being of customers and society overall, instead of shareholder returns. Reasonable investment returns would result from serving society well. The parallel economy probably would have extensive nonprofit and cooperative organizations and activities. As discussed, organizations that are not burdened by the requirement to provide ever-increasing shareholder returns often could provide lower cost, higher quality products and services. For example, a national network of locally owned, cooperative grocery stores could be established or expanded. This group could integrate backwards into the supply chain, and thereby support the expansion of sustainable agriculture, food production and manufacturing.

Four other critical action areas of a We the People movement include raising public awareness, exposing media and religious deceptions, giving citizens a voting option that is truly focused on benefiting all citizens, and facilitating peaceful, cooperative activism. These are discussed in the following subsections.

Raising Public Awareness

Raising public awareness should be a central focus of a We the People movement, especially in the early stages. Public deception is the primary factor enabling the existence of corporate welfare, business control of government and nearly all other major problems and injustices in society. As discussed, the primary deception is to divide the people into conservatives and liberals, and then get them to dislike or hate each other. This dilutes and disempowers people. They focus on false enemies (each other) and frequently ignore the actual causes of their increasingly difficult lives. The theme of a We the People public awareness effort could be "darkness cannot survive in the light".

Using emotional manipulation to divide people and compel them to blindly believe economic, political and religious dogma keeps them in the dark. People are not objectively observing reality, thinking rationally and utilizing intuitive wisdom. The Second Enlightenment involves using the shining light of objective, rational, reality-based thinking to illuminate the darkness of public deception. Rational whole system thinking reveals that liberals or conservatives are not the cause of major economic, social, political and environmental problems. The ultimate cause often is blind faith in ignorant, myopic dogma, such as the idea that putting economic growth and shareholder returns before all else will maximize the well-being of society.

Many actions are needed to raise public awareness about the actual causes and most effective solutions to major problems in society. Critical awareness raising components include content and delivery. In other words, what ideas should be emphasized to the public and how can they be communicated most effectively. This book synthesizes thousands of articles and other information sources about major problems and solutions in society. Information is written in ways that non-expert citizens can easily understand. As a result, this book and similar resources can provide content for public awareness raising efforts. In today's online world, the Internet and social media would be critical content delivery vehicles.

The primary or initial focus of public awareness raising efforts should be on the positive, not the negative. Rather than emphasizing problems, focus on a positive vision for humanity and society. Emphasize our potential to reach our fullest potential and achieve sustainability and real prosperity. Comparing the level of human sophistication to that of nature shows that we probably have not reached one billionth of our potential. We can display nearly infinitely greater cooperation, wisdom, technical sophistication and beauty. Poverty and hunger largely are unnecessary in human society. These and other problems ultimately are caused by our flawed, myopic thinking, and the systems and actions that result from it.

To get a sense of our potential, all one has to do is look at the wonder and beauty of nature. Imagine what human society would look like when we display the same level of wisdom, cooperation and sophistication seen in nature. This would be Heaven on Earth. Humanity would be reaching our fullest potential, individually and collectively.

Another important part of the positive vision involves emphasizing doing the right thing. Nothing is more right than protecting our children and future generations. Love for children is one of the strongest forces in humanity. We evolved to love children. It enables the perpetuation of the human race. Protecting our children takes priority over everything else, except our own survival (because children will not survive if we do not). As the US Founders did, we must be willing to make any sacrifice necessary to protect our children and future generations.

If protecting children requires questioning dogma and being more open-minded and rational, we absolutely must do it. Dogmatic, myopic thinking literally is killing us. We absolutely must find the courage to question our limited, unintentionally harmful economic, political and religious ideas. Being open-minded and thinking rationally, instead of blindly believing in dogma, is a small price to pay to protect our children. As people courageously replace blind faith with rational consideration of new ideas, they will discover that they are not paying a price. Instead, they will attain far more successful and satisfying lives.

Humility is another critical aspect of the positive vision. If we divided all we (humans) know by all there is to know and rounded it off to the nearest thousand decimal places, it still probably would round down to zero. We know a lot compared to past generations. But the essentially infinitely greater sophistication of nature shows that we still know nearly nothing, compared to all there is to know. Therefore, humility is highly rational. Acknowledging that we know little will open our minds to unlimited new ideas and possibilities for humanity.

This leads to another critical aspect of the positive vision in public awareness raising efforts – confidence. While we know nearly nothing compared to nature, we are part of nature. Therefore, we have the innate ability and potential to display the same level of cooperation, sophistication and beauty seen in nature. We know nearly nothing in our minds. But in our hearts, we know everything. Through the intuitive function, we have access to all possible knowledge on all possible levels of reality. As we learn to make our minds the servants of our hearts, we will manifest an indescribable level of joy, love and beauty in human society. As discussed in the final section, this is our destiny.

Promoting the positive vision described above will empower people. It will build confidence that we can solve all major problems facing humanity. It will help us to realize that each one of us is a leader, not only of our own lives, but also society. Each person has an equal, natural right to say how society should function. No person's opinions or views are more important than another's. Every person on this planet should have an equal vote in determining the destiny of humanity.

In addition, as discussed in the Environmental Sustainability Principles section, all creatures have implied rights. All life is precious. In reality, human lives are not more important than the lives of other creatures. The myopic, self-serving human perspective says that we are more important and have more rights. But this is a suicidal, human-created fantasy. In reality, according to nature, we are no more important than other lifeforms. We could not survive without the web of life.

Other creatures cannot consciously vote to determine the destiny of life on Earth. But their implied vote already is cast. All creatures have the same rights as humans to live in a life-sustaining environment. Destroying our life support systems is grossly unfair to future generations and all life. Human life is part of a larger web of life. We do not have a right to determine which parts of this web live or die. Humans and all other life forms have an implied vote in determining the destiny of life on this planet. The implied vote of all other lifeforms is life, not death. Fairness and our own well-being requires that we honor the rights and implied decision to live of all creatures on this planet.

Authoritarian society suppresses people. It often makes them doubt their minds and hearts. Dogmatic, authoritarian leaders imply that they know the answers for people better than the people themselves. But as long as someone is not harming anyone, no one knows what is best for another person better than that person. The Second Enlightenment involves empowering people to think for themselves.

One of the most important aspects of thinking for oneself is learning to think from a whole system or big picture perspective. This book illustrates how to apply whole system thinking to nearly all major issues in human society. Whole system thinking involves seeing how everything in human society is connected. It illuminates root causes and most effective solutions.

For example, whole system thinking can help citizens to understand the democracy deception in the US. Politicians and other leaders often speak reverently about democracy and doing the will of the people. Citizens vote on Election Day, believing that they are helping their democracy to function. But whole system thinking reveals that democracy largely does not exist in the US. Voting often has little impact because a small group of wealthy citizens largely control both major political parties.

Whole system thinking reveals that democracy largely was ended in the US in 1803. In that year, the unelected, lifetime appointed Judicial branch violated our Constitution by unilaterally giving itself absolute, irrevocable authority over the two elected branches of government. Since 1803, the highest effective authority in the US has not been the people. It has been a majority of aristocratic Supreme Court justices who are not accountable to the people. The Founders obviously did not intend that five lifetime appointed, unaccountable Supreme Court justices would have absolute, irrevocable authority over all other people in the US and their elected leaders. This obviously violates the Republican government clearly established in our Constitution.

The first step to establishing democracy in the US is to understand that democracy largely does not exist. Once We the People realize that our right to rule ourselves has been stolen, we can say enough is enough. We can demand that democracy be reestablished. Once we are united, we can do this and everything else necessary to protect our children.

Whole system thinking also can be utilized to illuminate the crime deception. Vested interests often castigate criminals and deceive citizens into thinking that harsh punishment is the best way to deal with crime. But as discussed in the Crime section, incarceration and policing are end-of-the-pipe solutions. They do not address the root causes of crime. As a result, they are grossly inefficient and counterproductive ways to address crime. Crime largely is a symptom of economic, political and social problems in society. Our business-focused economic and political systems create vast and unnecessary unemployment and destitution among the people. This strongly promotes crime.

Radical conservative media often foments anger at African Americans who commit crimes. They frequently argue that African Americans should do a better job of solving crime and other problems in African American communities. Whole system thinking reveals the ignorance of these positions. As discussed in the Crime section, white people largely control the US economy and society. We (whites) largely are responsible for many of the problems in African American communities, including lack of jobs, excessive incarceration, poor education and inadequate policing. These factors strongly contribute to crime, family instability and many other problems.

Whole system thinking reveals that white people often are saying African Americans should take responsibility for problems largely caused by whites. This clarity will help us to stop blaming others for problems that we caused. It will help white people to take responsibility for our actions. As whole system thinking reveals root causes, we can implement effective solutions to discrimination, crime and lower prosperity in African American communities.

Another major benefit of whole system thinking is illuminating economic problems. As discussed in the Freedom section, many citizens are encouraged or compelled to blindly believe in the philosophy of capitalism. This enables a small group of wealthy citizens to replace democracy with plutocracy. Whole system thinking reveals that the measured and managed focus of our economic system is not to maximize the well-being of all citizens, as the Constitution requires. It largely is to maximize the financial well-being of already wealthy citizens. Whole system thinking shows that placing shareholder returns and economic growth before all else inevitably will severely degrade, and possibly destroy, society.

The US airline industry provides a good example of this. When the sector was deregulated in 1978, companies argued that increased competition would lower prices and improve service quality. This often occurred early on. But the requirement to provide ever-increasing shareholder returns frequently causes increased prices and reduced quality, especially over the mid to longer-term. Business-controlled government has allowed reduced competition and increased airline mergers. As a result, there only are four major airlines in the US, the lowest number since 1978. To maximize shareholder returns airlines often are raising fares, cutting free services, charging extra fees, and crowding more people onto planes by reducing the number of flights and moving seats closer together.[198]

The requirement to always increase shareholder returns frequently causes airlines to reduce service quality. For example, instead of providing adequate legroom in the economy or main section of airplanes, airlines sometimes create more legroom in the front of planes by squeezing seats closer together in the back. In this way, if passengers want adequate legroom, they must pay extra for it. This helps airlines to increase revenues. But it severely degrades service quality for many passengers. With included meals and adequate legroom in economy class, air travel often used to be a pleasant experience. Now, as airline seats are moved closer together, if someone in front of a passenger reclines their seat back, people frequently cannot work on their computers, eat a meal, read a book or even cross their legs. They often must endure someone's head intruding into their personal space for several hours.

The situation for airline passengers inevitably will get worse under current shareholder-focused systems. Government is supposed to protect citizens, for example, by ensuring a minimum level of comfort on airplanes. But when politicians are allowed to accept large amounts of money and other inappropriate influence from businesses, the primary focus of government becomes protecting shareholder returns, instead of protecting the rights, health and comfort of citizens.

Fuel usually is the largest airline cost. When fuel prices rose in 2013, airlines raised prices substantially. However, in 2014, as fuel prices fell, airlines often did not lower prices.[199] They frequently are charging based on demand, not cost. By reducing flights, airlines can increase demand per flight and charge higher prices. Higher airfares often would attract new airlines, increase competition and reduce prices. But business-controlled government has reduced competition. This enables a small number of large airlines to fulfill their primary objective – maximizing shareholder returns, regardless of negative impacts on passengers and society.

In general, our shareholder-focused systems often compel companies to charge far more than cost. If companies can get away with charging 100 times cost, they frequently are compelled to do it. This action helps shareholders, but obviously harms citizens and society. Charging 100 times cost to help shareholders has nothing to do with morality. Morality does not apply to nonliving human creations. Saying that it is immoral for a company to charge 100 times cost is like saying that it is immoral for a washing machine to only 'want' to wash clothes. Our ignorant economic system primarily is focused on benefiting shareholders, not customers or society. Expensive, unpleasant, low quality air travel and millions of other quality of life degradations are the inevitable result of our myopic, unintentionally suicidal economic and political systems.

One of the most important public awareness raising activities needed to unite conservatives and liberals is to help each group understand how they are misled by vested interests. This is a difficult issue. Success requires that it be handled very carefully. Many people would not want to hear that they are being misled and abused by those they trust. Some people simply will refuse to believe it. But ending the war between conservatives and liberals requires that many, if not most, people become aware of how they are being deceived. If most people continue to believe vested interest deceptions, deep divisions will remain in society and voluntary high-level system change probably will be impossible.

One way to maximize the number of people who open their minds and rationally consider how they might be deceived is to emphasize good intentions. Virtually everyone does what they believe is right on some level. The small group of wealthy citizens who mislead conservatives and liberals are good people who mean well. They usually are saying and doing what they believe is best for society. Many leaders and citizens subscribe to the idea that maximizing economic growth and shareholder returns is the best way to promote the well-being of society. The people who deceive mean well. The harm they cause is unintentional. If conservatives and liberals feel that those they trust and admire are not being attacked, they will be more likely to consider how these people might be mistaken or providing misleading information.

As discussed in the Public Deception section above, different strategies are used to mislead conservatives and liberals. Liberal politicians often focus on important issues, such as the environment and labor. (As noted, a whole system perspective shows that the environment is the most important issue in human society because everything else is irrelevant without an environment that is clean and stable enough to support human life. Labor metrics also are important because they directly measure the well-being of a far greater number of people than economic growth.) The liberal deception involves misleading citizens into believing that liberal or Democratic politicians will protect the environment, labor, children and other critical components of society. But they are not paid by wealthy campaign donors to do this. Liberals often are deceived because they think Democratic politicians will protect society. But Democratic politicians, like conservatives, mostly do it they are paid to do – protect wealthy campaign donors.

The conservative deception often involves ignoring or discounting important issues, such as the environment and labor. Instead, as discussed, conservative citizens often are distracted with religious, racist, entitlement and other deceptions. A primary conservative deception involves distracting citizens from major issues, such as corporate welfare and business control of government. Instead, they are misled into focusing on less expensive issues, such as how some low-income people abuse social welfare programs. In other words, citizens essentially are manipulated into being incensed about the mosquito biting their arm and ignoring the tiger biting off their leg. Both the liberal and conservative deception strategies enable a small group of wealthy citizens to continue essentially stealing the people's wealth and power.

Another way to differentiate the conservative and liberal deception strategies involves differentiating leadership styles. The conservative or Republican mode of leading society often involves a patriarchal, strict father model, whereas the liberal mode frequently is based on an egalitarian, nurturing parent model.[200] The liberal model often involves espousing a caring society that strives to meet the needs of all citizens equally and fairly. While liberal politicians often espouse this view, they frequently duplicitously subvert it by weakening environmental and social protections and helping wealthy citizens who gave large campaign contributions.

The strict father model of society implicitly espoused by many Republican politicians is extremely beneficial to the small group of wealthy citizens who control society. As discussed in the Education section, conservative ideas and philosophies often emphasize not questioning authorities. Citizens are encouraged and expected to obey authorities, as they obeyed their fathers when they were children. This emphasis on not questioning authority enables and supports authoritarianism, totalitarianism and fascism.

Citizens frequently are emotionally manipulated into not thinking for themselves. Those who question prevailing conservative ideas and philosophies often are criticized and ostracized. Dealing harshly with citizens who attempt to think for themselves, as a strict father might deal with a disobedient child, keeps the flock in line. It enables vested interests to essentially control the thinking of citizens. Through this Republican strict father mode of leadership, many conservative citizens are compelled to focus on social welfare instead of corporate welfare. This enables the wealthy citizens who control the Republican Party to continue stealing the people's wealth and power.

A main part of the solution to conservative and liberal deceptions is to encourage citizens to think for themselves, rather than blindly believe liberal or conservative leaders. By rationally analyzing reality, citizens can see that most liberal and conservative politicians are in office because they accepted money and other support from wealthy citizens and corporations. As a result, regardless of what liberal or conservative politicians say, their primary focus often will be on supporting those who paid to put them in office.

A critical aspect of thinking for oneself is not buying into liberal or conservative labels and philosophies. Instead of blindly believing ignorant philosophies, such as those related to small government or free markets, think about each situation. Rationally consider options and pick the one that objectively provides the best results.

One of the most important actions needed to end the civil war between conservatives and liberals is to help citizens see their massive areas of common interest. Illuminating the numerous common goals of liberals and conservatives will help people to see that they mostly want the same things and fighting each other is counterproductive and irrational.

Media Deception

Another critical action needed to raise public awareness and end the conservative-liberal war is to expose media deception. Liberal and conservative media deceive citizens in many ways. A main deception involves not adequately discussing major problems in society, such as corporate welfare and business control of government. These issues probably are not fully addressed because both types of media largely are controlled by a small group of wealthy citizens and large corporations.

While liberal and conservative media both deceive citizens, the greater problem usually lies with conservative media. As noted, liberal media outlets often discuss some major issues in society, such as those related to the environment and labor. This can put pressure on companies to act more responsibly, which could reduce shareholder returns. Liberal and conservative politicians are primarily focused on helping wealthy campaign donors. But conservative politicians often are more inclined to do whatever large companies and wealthy citizens want without hesitation or restriction. That is the main reason why these groups usually prefer the Republican Party. The same generally is true with conservative media. It frequently is less likely than liberal media to report on issues that threaten ever-increasing shareholder returns. As a result, greater public deception frequently occurs with conservative media.

Among major media and news networks, conservative media is more concentrated in the US. The largest conservative media network was established in 1996. It grew to become the largest cable TV news network. Nearly half of conservative citizens get their news mainly from this network.[201] Networks considered to be liberal are more diversified. There is no equally dominant network on the liberal side.

While the leading conservative network is the most watched, it also is the most deceptive and inaccurate. An organization called Politifact analyzes the accuracy of media claims. It found that 60 percent of the claims made on the leading conservative news network were mostly or completely false. Inaccuracy among major liberal media networks ranged from 20-44 percent.[202]

(As discussed, the purpose of this book is not to criticize individual leaders or companies. Flawed systems compel well-intentioned leaders to degrade society. The purpose of this book is to help improve these systems. Therefore, when negative actions are attributed to particular individuals or organizations, such as the conservative media network noted above, names are not discussed, unless it is necessary to promote system change.)

A critical aspect of understanding media deception is questioning the source. The major conservative media network discussed above was established by a foreign billionaire. The primary goal of this person probably was not to accurately inform US citizens and help to improve their lives. Instead, it is more likely that the primary goal was to help himself, his company, and other individuals like him by providing society-dividing, big business-enhancing content.

The main conservative media network and conservative media in general mislead citizens in many ways. A foundational theme is that liberals are the main evil in society. Conservative media frequently provides a nearly nonstop invective against liberals. They often are portrayed as fools who will destroy society. The implied solution is to beat the liberals. Conservatives must take over society and force liberals to do what conservatives believe is right (because liberals are too stupid or deluded to know the right thing to do). The frequently implied goal is not to find common ground, work together and help all citizens.

The strongly implied goal is to do whatever is necessary to beat the liberals. If public deception and dishonesty are necessary to achieve this paramount goal, so be it. The end justifies the means. The well-being, even survival of society, demands that liberals not be allowed to control society. In other words, the implied strategy and goal of conservative media often seems to be war with liberals. This media-perpetuated war and division in society enables a small group of wealthy citizens to continue stealing the people's wealth, power and freedom.

To perpetuate the conservative-liberal war, conservative media frequently delivers information in a sarcastic, condescending, moralistic manner. Emotional manipulation is used to keep the conservative flock in line. Those who dare to question conservative dogma often are viciously attacked.

Conservative media also often misleads citizens by speaking in broad, meaningless generalizations. For example, one frequently hears conservative media figures bemoaning widespread irresponsibility or a great wave of entitlement sweeping across society. The implication is that nearly all people using social welfare programs are lazy degenerates who want to be supported by hard-working conservatives. This ignorant portrayal of society facilitates cutting social welfare and increasing corporate welfare.

Of course, conservative media usually neglects to mention that the large majority of social welfare recipients are legitimately using the programs, our shareholder-focused economy produces vast, unnecessary unemployment, there are far more people seeking jobs than there are available jobs, and much more public wealth is inappropriately used for corporate welfare than social welfare. This honesty would threaten the shareholder returns of conservative media and their corporate advertisers.

Another conservative media deception involves implying that nearly everything is an opinion. Society often is portrayed as a battle between conservative and liberal ideas and philosophies. Conservative commentators sometimes dismiss dissenting views with comments like, "Of course you'd say that, you're a liberal." Or "That's just your liberal opinion, I have a different view." These types of comments block rational thought. Conservative citizens are encouraged to ignore ideas that conflict with conservative philosophy, without rationally considering their merit.

Of course, many issues are a matter of opinion. But many others are matters of fact and objective reality. For example, it is not debatable (within the realm of logic) that a small group of wealthy citizens should not be unconstitutionally controlling government and essentially stealing trillions of dollars of public wealth from average citizens every year. Acknowledging this obvious point would threaten the owners of conservative media. As a result, it rarely, if ever, is done. As discussed in the Misleading the Public section, dismissing facts, logic and objective reality as opinion is a common public deception technique.

As shown by the Politifact study, conservative media frequently misleads citizens by providing partly or completely false information. But the largest public deception usually involves lying by omission – failing to disclose major problems and solutions. (This applies to liberal media as well.)

Media driven public deceptions about many different issues have been discussed in detail throughout this book. However, to illustrate critical conservative media deceptions, several are summarized below. Important deceptions relate to meritocracy, freedom, democracy, government, military, national debt, taxes, trade, environment, education, elitism, family values, healthcare, unions, being a man and honoring the flag.

Meritocracy

Conservative media often hammers away at the idea that the US is a meritocracy. The idea is that people are successful because they worked hard. They deserve their rewards. The flipside is that, if people are struggling, it is their own fault. They are not working hard enough. Of course, it is true that people who work hard deserve the fruits of their success. But the meritocracy argument is extremely myopic and ignorant. It largely ignores reality.

The reality is that our shareholder-focused economic and political systems create vast and unnecessary unemployment and suffering for millions of hard-working average citizens. The meritocracy deception misleads many citizens into believing that their inability to find jobs or meet basic needs is their own fault. They simply are not smart enough, good enough or diligent enough. They should not complain because their difficult life is no one's fault but their own. Those who complain often are portrayed as whiners who want something for nothing. This castigation conditions many conservatives to silently accept their systemically-induced declining quality of life.

326

Of course, the reality is that there are millions of smart, hard-working citizens who are struggling, and often failing, to make ends meet. Our systems are not focused on helping average citizens. If they were, we would adequately protect labor and other aspects of society. But honestly disclosing how our flawed systems create widespread suffering among average citizens would threaten conservative media owners and other wealthy citizens. As a result, this information generally is not disclosed by conservative media.

Another deceptive aspect of the ignorant meritocracy deception is the idea that wealthy people earned and deserve all of their wealth. But as discussed extensively, trillions of dollars of public wealth essentially are stolen from average citizens and transferred to a small group of wealthy citizens through many forms of corporate welfare every year. As discussed, no one gets wealthy on their own. People usually require employees, customers, infrastructure and many other services and resources from society to get wealthy.

When wealthy citizens control government, they often implement systems that do not require them to pay fair prices for the services and resources that enabled them to become wealthy. Business-controlled government also frequently does not require wealthy citizens to pay for negative impacts and burdens that they impose on society. As a result, in a plutocracy such as the US, much of the wealth of those controlling society is not fairly earned. These citizens do not deserve it.

But again, disclosing this would threaten the wealthy citizens who control conservative (and liberal) media. Therefore, it generally is not disclosed that the US largely is a plutocracy, not a meritocracy. Wealthy citizens often did not fairly earn much of their wealth. And hard-working average citizens frequently are not being fairly compensated for their meritorious efforts to support themselves and their families.

Freedom

The issue of freedom also is commonly used by conservative media to mislead citizens. Conservative media figures often argue that government regulations take away citizens' freedom. They also frequently claim that forcing wealthy citizens to pay for social welfare programs that they do not use takes away freedom. As discussed in the Libertarianism section, these are extremely irrational and harmful arguments. Regulations primarily are intended to prevent harm by protecting individuals, life support systems and society overall. There is no right or freedom to harm others in a civilized society. Therefore, regulations that prohibit causing harm do not restrict rights or freedom.

Also, the greater wealth of wealthy citizens does not magically materialize out of thin air (except in the case of fractional reserve lending). As noted, they usually require employees, customers, government services and other resources from society to become wealthy. They have an obligation to pay fair prices for these resources. This enables healthy, fair and productive society to continue. Wealthy citizens do not have a right to unfairly extract wealth from society, for example, by not paying for services received or negative impacts imposed. Therefore, taxing wealthy citizens to pay for social welfare programs does not restrict rights or freedom because there is no right to receive vast benefits from society without paying for them. (In a civilized society, all citizens have a right to have basic needs met, even if they do not pay taxes, in part because we all collectively own the public wealth. But citizens do not have a right to receive opulent, massive and disproportional benefits from society without paying for them.)

Government is supposed to be the agent of all citizens, not just wealthy citizens. It is supposed to protect people, in part by compelling wealthy citizens to pay fair prices for the massive benefits they receive from society. Government also is supposed to protect the freedom of citizens. But business-controlled government mainly protects wealthy people, not all citizens. It allows large corporations that give substantial amounts of money to politicians to unfairly shut down small companies and pay wages that do not enable employees to meet basic needs. Business-controlled government also often does not ensure affordable higher education or protect life support systems.

Citizens are not free without these protections. People are not free to start small businesses if large companies are allowed to unfairly compete. Citizens are not free to support their families if society does not provide jobs that pay living wages. Young people frequently are not free to pursue higher education if they must take on large, burdensome debt. Citizens are not even free to remain alive if life support systems are not clean and stable enough to support human life.

Conservative media often misleads citizens into believing that government restricts freedom and harms citizens. This shows the danger of blind faith in ignorant conservative and other dogma. Rational thought reveals the flawed nature of this argument. Business-controlled government frequently harms citizens because the focus is not on helping average citizens. It is on helping wealthy campaign donors. Wealthy citizens and their conservative media allies often argue that the solution is to shrink government. But this frequently will allow wealthy citizens to take even more wealth from society. Saying that reducing government will increase freedom is like saying that reducing police will reduce bank robberies. Weakening and reducing the entity that is supposed to protect citizens' freedom and other rights will lower freedom, not increase it.

Another major aspect of the freedom deception relates to terrorism. The terrorism excuse is used to substantially reduce the constitutional rights and freedom of people in the US. Conservative media extensively emphasizes terrorism risk. It frequently discusses the atrocities of radical Muslims, without acknowledging that these radicals only are a tiny percentage of the global Muslim population (in the same way that irrational, dogmatic Christians only are a small part of the global Christian population). Conservative media often creates an omnipresent sense of terrorism danger. This increases fear in society. It conditions citizens to accept the loss of their constitutional rights and freedom.

The main deception about terrorism and freedom relates to the demand-side. As discussed, the US government and companies do much good around the world. But we also impose extensive negative impacts in other countries. If there are conflicts between ever-increasing shareholder returns and imposing negative impacts (as there often are), US companies usually are compelled to degrade the culture, environment, labor and/or environment of other countries. US negative impacts create legitimate grievances against the US. These impacts are the primary cause of terrorism. But conservative media generally is silent about the actual causes of terrorism. Instead, it often vaguely implies that jealousy of the US and similar ignorant factors are the primary cause of terrorism.

The most important, least expensive and most effective action the US can take to reduce terrorism is to reduce our negative impacts in other countries. But instead of focusing on reducing the demand for terrorism (i.e. the factors that cause others to want to harm the US), we focus on the supply-side (i.e. reducing terrorism through military and police action). Not only are we not reducing demand for terrorism, we are increasing it because the requirement to provide ever-increasing shareholder returns and economic growth compels companies to cause negative impacts in other countries. In other words, we fan the flames of terrorism, and then try to put the fire out more effectively. The obviously superior strategy is to not start the fire in the first place.

But highlighting this obviously superior solution often would threaten ever-increasing shareholder returns and the wealthy citizens who control conservative media. As a result, conservative media usually focuses on the supply-side. It states or implies that we must sacrifice some freedom to prevent terrorism. It rarely, if ever, discusses the main cause and most important solution to terrorism.

Overall, conservative media often promotes a highly hypocritical position on freedom. It frequently trumpets the importance of freedom. But then it strongly espouses conservative philosophies and positions that enable corporate welfare, business control of government, authoritarianism and gross loss of citizens' freedom. In other words, conservative media often hypocritically advocates freedom, and then supports actions and philosophies that hugely restrict freedom.

Democracy

Democracy represents another major deception frequently promoted by conservative media. As discussed above, one aspect of this deception involves not disclosing that democracy largely does not exist in the US. However, a less common but more odious deception involves claiming that the US has too much democracy. Conservative media outlets sometimes promote the views of libertarian politicians and other people who claim that the US has too much democracy. These anti-democracy advocates frequently suggest that civil rights laws and union, labor and environmental protections violate the rights and freedom of businesses. They sometimes argue that the Supreme Court should play a more dominant role in society, for example, by voiding environmental and social protections that interfere with business freedom. These and other libertarians often argue that the primary purpose of the US Constitution is to protect individual liberties.[203]

Advocacy of views such as these is the expected outcome of our flawed systems. These suicidal, myopic systems require that shareholder returns take priority over the survival of humanity and all other factors. Right-wing libertarians and other business puppets recognize that, under current constitutional interpretations, the Supreme Court has the power to void laws that protect the environment and society because it is not controlled by the people. It is aristocratic and autocratic.

The fact that some average citizens consider these anti-democracy views to be valid and rational is a testament to the ease with which citizens can be misled. They are emotionally manipulated into believing irrational, harmful ideas. Rational thought reveals the flaws of the above arguments. As discussed in the Libertarianism section, the primary purpose of the US Constitution is not to protect individual liberties. The primary purpose can be identified by reading the preamble. The preamble states, "We the People of the United States, in Order to form a more perfect Union, establish Justice, insure domestic Tranquility, provide for the common defence, promote the general Welfare, and secure the Blessings of Liberty to ourselves and our Posterity, do ordain and establish this Constitution for the United States of America."

Every purpose stated relates to the common good and well-being of all citizens. Promoting the general welfare is the primary purpose stated in the Constitution. It encapsulates all other stated purposes. There is no mention of individual liberties or rights in the preamble. Instead, it seeks to secure the blessings of liberty for all current and future citizens collectively.

The Founders were rational, enlightened thinkers. They understood that the first priority should be promoting the general well-being of society, because individuals cannot prosper if the overarching systems that support individuals are not stable. The original Constitution did not contain a bill of rights. As discussed in the Second Amendment section, James Madison and other main Founders did not think that one was necessary because the Constitution did not take rights from citizens. The Founders were primarily focused on protecting the collective well-being of society, not individual rights. Protecting individual rights obviously is a component of promoting the general welfare. But it is not the only or even most important component. For example, individual rights mean little if the environment and society cannot protect and sustain individuals. While many Founders did not think that a bill of rights was necessary, the states' concerns about the stronger federal government established in the Constitution compelled the Founders to add the Bill of Rights.

To protect shareholder returns, libertarians and other business allies often attempt to mislead citizens into believing that businesses have a right to force citizens to endure difficult, unsafe jobs that do not pay enough to meet basic needs. Citizens frequently are vulnerable to business abuse. If the choice is no job or a poverty-level job, parents trying to feed their children often will be compelled to take the poverty-level job. Businesses might have a right to abuse and take advantage of desperate parents and other citizens in a plutocracy. But they do not have the right to do this in a democracy. As discussed in the Freedom section, in a democracy, We the People set the standards by which businesses operate. For example, we can require that businesses operating in the US pay wages that enable employees to have a decent standard of living. We also can protect businesses and jobs (but not ever-increasing shareholder returns) with import tariffs and other mechanisms.

The ability of the Supreme Court to void environmental and social protection laws shows the dangerous nature of the Supreme Court. As discussed in the Limited Liability and Corporations section, President Lincoln warned that businesses had gained greater influence of government during the Civil War. After the war, several pro-business justices were appointed to the Supreme Court. These justices restricted the ability of government to reign in harmful business practices and tax wealthy citizens.[204]

The essentially business-controlled Supreme Court is moving in the same direction. It already protects wealthy citizens and corporations, for example, by voiding campaign finance laws. But our suicidal systems say that wealthy citizens never can make enough money. Therefore, the pro-business radicals on the Supreme Court probably will continue to void environmental and social protections that interfere with ever-increasing shareholder returns. Supreme Court driven degradation of society is inevitable. Radical justices will continue to protect those who paid to appoint them, until We the People put an end to this injustice by implementing the changes discussed in the Judicial Branch section.

Rational thought reveals the pure ignorance of the idea that the US has too much democracy. Democracy is the only sustainable form of government. It is based on the innate equality of all people. The alternative is that some people have more power to control society than others. Of course, plutocrats will attempt to deceive citizens into giving up their natural rights to equality, freedom and self-government. But one might ask, why would average conservative citizens buy into the idea that the US should have less democracy? In large part, the answer probably is that they have been emotionally manipulated. Radical conservative media protects shareholder returns by turning citizens attention away from corporate welfare and business control of government to social welfare.

White citizens often are misled into believing that low-income minority citizens who use social welfare programs are responsible for high taxes and their declining quality of life. Taking away the ability of low-income minority citizens to influence government by suppressing democracy might be appealing to some angry, misled white citizens. They might be willing to accept less democracy if it means that those they have been manipulated into disliking lose their ability to influence government. They also might accept less democracy because the authoritarian, strict father conservative mindset compels them to trust conservative leaders. Of course, this naïve trust usually is misplaced. Conservative leaders mainly are not focused on protecting middle-income white conservative citizens or any other average citizens. They are paid to protect wealthy campaign donors.

Promoting the general welfare requires that citizens be encouraged to think for themselves, rather than blindly believe conservative media deceptions. Arguing that the US has too much democracy is a perfect example of the deception strategy, the best defense is a strong offense. As discussed in the Judicial Branch section, establishing democracy (i.e. control of government by the people) was one of the two primary goals of the Founders, along with promoting the general welfare. But democracy largely does not exist in the US. Honestly disclosing this would increase pressure to return control of government to the people. But our flawed systems require that financial returns to the small group of wealthy citizens who control government always must increase.

Democratic government protects the people by prohibiting the theft of their wealth, power and freedom. These protections inhibit ever-increasing shareholder returns and economic growth, the primary measured and managed focus of government and society. To protect shareholder returns, democracy and many other protections for average citizens have been removed. But our insane, suicidal systems never will be satisfied. Any interference with ever-increasing shareholder returns must be eliminated. Therefore, conservative media and other business allies must mislead citizens into accepting the loss of their few remaining democratic protections. Admitting that democracy largely does not exist would not achieve this goal. Therefore, vested interests deceptively argue that we have too much democracy. In other words, instead of honestly admitting that we have far too little democracy in the US, business puppets argue that we have too much. The best defense is a strong offense.

Government

The democracy deception is related to the small government deception. Both involve limiting government actions that protect society, but threaten ever-increasing shareholder returns. Small government is one of the most common positions promoted in conservative media. As discussed in the Libertarianism section, advocating small government is extremely irrational and harmful. The focus, as shown in our Constitution, should be on maximizing the well-being of society, not minimizing the size of government. Government is essential to protect citizens and society. There would be no country or civilized society without government.

Conservative media misleads people into blindly believing that reducing government would enhance society. But the slightest amount of rational thought shows this position to be illogical. Citizens should rationally consider each situation to determine what level of government effort maximizes the well-being of society. The ignorant small government philosophy implies that nearly all government activities are bad. This irrational position is necessary to protect shareholder returns. Rational thought would show that environmental and social protections are essential for maximizing well-being of society. But this rational thought often would inhibit shareholder returns. Therefore, it must be suppressed with the ignorant small government deception.

Citizens understand that murder laws should not be eliminated, even though this would make government smaller. But they often are misled into believing that eliminating other environmental and social protections enhances society. In other words, citizens essentially are misled into thinking that government can prevent murder. But it should not prevent children from starving or prohibit companies from harming employees, customers and life support systems.

The small government deception is tragic. It imposes great harm on society. Democratic government is structurally required to protect society, in large part by imposing the rule of law on citizens and businesses. As discussed in the Libertarianism section, libertarian philosophy strongly supports the rule of law, but then often hypocritically opposes applying it to business. The rule of law says that people and businesses should be free to do what they want, provided that they do not harm others.

Prohibiting companies from harming or degrading life support systems and society frequently would restrict ever-increasing shareholder returns. Companies cannot admit that the reason they oppose acting responsibly (i.e. abiding by the rule of law) is to protect financial returns. Citizens would say that the lives of their children and well-being of society take priority over financial returns to wealthy investors. In other words, honesty would not achieve the primary goal of maximizing shareholder returns. Therefore, dishonesty or deception is required. Through the small government deception, conservative media and other business allies protect shareholder returns by misleading people into blindly opposing government and regulations.

This is tragic because citizens are manipulated into attacking the entity that is structurally required to protect them, and implicitly supporting entities that often are structurally compelled to harm them. As discussed in Chapter Eight, publicly traded companies frequently are required by flawed systems to put shareholder returns before the environment, customers, employees and all other aspects of society.

In the absence of regulations that hold businesses fully responsible for negative impacts, companies cannot voluntarily act in a fully responsible manner and remain in business. Citizens can and usually do voluntarily act responsibly. As a result, it is far more important to apply the rule of law to businesses than to individual citizens. Honest media would make people aware of the essential need for effective government and regulations that hold companies fully responsible for negative impacts.

Military

Military issues represent another major area of public deception in conservative (and liberal) media. Conservative media frequently discusses honoring and supporting our troops. They often provide heartwarming vignettes of soldiers returning home to their families. Troops are honored at major sporting events and many other venues. But as discussed in the Supporting Our Troops subsection of the Misleading the Public section, this support of our troops often is hypocritical and deceptive.

The US has been in a nearly constant state of war since 2001. Overall, we have initiated an open-ended global war on terrorism that is primarily focused on Islamic terrorists.[205] A large percentage of US military services are provided by private sector companies. These companies are structurally required to provide ever-increasing shareholder returns. They have huge financial incentives to initiate, expand and sustain wars and other military activities. There is little incentive to end or minimize wars.

In 1961, President Eisenhower warned us about the large, growing and dangerous influence of business on the military. Business influence of government has strongly contributed to the US military being the largest in the world by far. In many ways, we have taken on the role of the world's policeman.

Flawed systems that place economic growth and shareholder returns before all else perpetuate war directly and indirectly. The systems directly promote war through government influence. Politicians who initiate and sustain wars often receive large amounts of money and other inappropriate influence from defense companies that substantially benefit from war. The focus on ever-increasing shareholder returns indirectly promotes war by compelling US companies to cause negative impacts in other countries. As noted, this increases demand for terrorism, which drives increased military spending. Reducing negative impacts often would threaten ever-increasing shareholder returns. A large military protects the ability of US companies to increase shareholder returns, continue negative impacts in other countries, and force our will on the world.

Maintaining a constant state of war requires extensive public deception. If the public strongly opposed war, as occurred during the Vietnam War, it would be difficult to maintain ongoing wars. Citizens often would say that we should work as part of a true global coalition to suppress terrorism and ensure world peace. We should not engage in extensive unilateral military action, often through deceptive coalitions of small countries cobbled together with incentives and coercion.

Several deceptions are used to mislead the public into supporting ongoing wars and a large military. For example, conservative media and other business allies often wave the flag and imply that war is noble, patriotic and somehow consistent with US values. But as discussed in the Supporting Our Troops section, President Washington, President Jefferson and many other US Founders and great leaders were adamantly opposed to war and maintaining a large military. Invading other countries and imposing our will on the world through military force is absolutely against the values and principles upon which the US was founded.

Maintaining a large military is not noble or patriotic, especially when it diverts resources from promoting the general welfare at home. Instead, it is imperialistic and ignorant. The US military is vastly larger than is necessary for national defense. Our extensive foreign military operations largely are not necessary to protect the US and our citizens. Every other country protects itself with a far smaller military. Rather than national defense, it appears that the massive US military is intended in large part to protect the growth and shareholder returns of companies that give large amounts of money to politicians and inappropriately influence government in other ways.

Wise countries largely protect themselves by minimizing negative impacts in other countries, acting as mature global citizens and working with allies. Using military force or the threat of force to get one's way is ignorant. It begets more force and violence. This obviously does not mean that we should naïvely ignore threats and fail to protect ourselves. But we almost certainly can enhance our national security by acting more responsibly around the world, reducing impacts in other countries, not trying to force our will on other countries through economic and military force, reducing military spending and using these funds to meet needs at home.

As discussed in the Governance section, national security is multifaceted. Military security only is one component. National and global environmental protection is a more important aspect of national security because everything else is irrelevant without an environment that is clean and stable enough to support human life. Making economic growth and shareholder returns the number one priority is increasing environmental and social problems around the world. This will increase social disruption, regional conflicts and the need for military action. Using our technology and know how to maximize the well-being of national and global society (instead of maximizing shareholder returns and economic growth) will minimize environmental and social problems, and thereby reduce the need for military action.

As noted above, another conservative media tactic used to mislead the public into supporting war and a large military is to frequently raise the alarm about terrorism risk. This increases fear in society and misleads citizens into supporting war and sacrificing their constitutional rights.

Another conservative media deception used to support ongoing wars involves not disclosing relevant and important information. Military mistakes and the horrors of war often are hidden from citizens. Whistleblowers who attempt to inform citizens about what actually is happening frequently are severely suppressed. Iraqis and other people often are deceptively portrayed as savages, rather than honestly acknowledging that the vast majority of them are peaceful citizens attempting to live good lives, just like US citizens. This media deception strategy used to mislead people into supporting ongoing wars and a large military could be described as treating citizens like mushrooms – keep them in the dark and feed them dung.

The most tragic media deception used to support ongoing wars and high military spending involves misuse of the concept of supporting our troops. Conservative media and other business allies often wave the flag and show our troops. They create the impression that supporting our troops is the same as supporting war. Those who oppose war often are explicitly or implicitly attacked for not supporting our troops. This is a vile and hideous deception. Soldiers risk their lives and health for their country. They deserve the highest level of honor, respect and support.

Conservative media and other war supporters often attempt to mislead the public by creating the impression that there is a group of people in society who do not support our troops. True Americans must stand up and fight these evil Americans who do not support our troops, conservative media implies. This is an irrational characterization. All sane people support our troops. It goes without saying. It is the same as supporting our children. There is no group of people in society who do not support our troops. This is a false division created to deceive citizens into supporting war and a large military.

The most tragic aspect of the support our troops deception is that we often support our troops in word, but not in deed. The primary focus on shareholder returns means that our country frequently supports wealthy citizens and large companies, but not average citizens. The same happens in the military. Military expenditures that help shareholder returns, such as defense contracts, often are promoted. But like the suppression of social welfare programs, military expenses that potentially increase taxes and reduce shareholder returns frequently are discouraged.

As discussed in the Supporting Our Troops section, veterans seeking healthcare from the Veterans Administration often must wait six months before services are approved. If a sick veteran is denied services, their appeal can take up to four years. Also as discussed, at least half of veterans do not get adequate treatment for psychological problems developed during military service. This contributes to high suicides in the military. In addition, the US military denied the existence of Gulf War Illness (GWI) for nearly 20 years. Many veterans with severe medical problems were denied services, until the military finally acknowledge the existence of GWI. A large percentage of homeless people are veterans who are not being supported by their country.

Also as noted, until recently, veterans seeking education benefits under the G.I. Bill had to pay a $1,200 fee. Apparently putting their lives on the line for their country was not a high enough price to get education benefits. Charging high fees reduces the number of veterans who take advantage of the G.I. Bill, and thereby increases funds available for defense contracts and corporate welfare. Difficulty getting benefits and denied medical services are the expected outcome of our flawed systems. As in broader society, our suicidal systems require that defense company shareholder returns always grow. Anything that interferes with this, such as actually supporting our troops, often is suppressed.

Not providing services to worthy soldiers and veterans is tragic. But the worst form of failing to support our troops is putting them in harm's way inappropriately. The most important way to support our troops, probably more important than all other forms of support combined, is to never place them in harm's way unless it is absolutely necessary. Every possible action should be taken to achieve peace and avoid military conflicts. Failing to do so is a gross violation of our duty to support our troops. In particular, troops never should be placed in harm's way to protect the shareholder returns of defense and other companies.

But this is exactly what many experts and other people believe is happening. As discussed in the Privacy section, US citizens were misled about the Vietnam and second Iraq Wars. Citizens were told that we had evidence of weapons of mass destruction in Iraq and involvement in the September 11th attacks. But our government knew that this information was false. This deception misled many citizens into supporting the second Iraq War. A main reason for the war appeared to be securing access to Iraq's vast oil reserves. In cases like this, our troops are risking their lives more to protect shareholder returns than national defense. This is a heinous, hideous violation of our obligations to support our troops.

Conservative media often essentially uses our troops as pawns to manipulate citizens into supporting war and extensive military activities. We honor troops on television at sporting events. Then we frequently put them in harm's way unnecessarily and do not provide the support that they earned through their brave service. In effect, we honor our troops when the cameras are rolling, and then slap them in the face or stab them in the back when no one is looking.

Probably many soldiers and veterans would say do not pretend to honor us, and then fail to do so. Rather than being hypocritical, it often would be better and more honest to say nothing about supporting our troops. (It should be noted that the failure to support soldiers and veterans is unintentional. Virtually everyone believes that we should support them in word and deed. But our flawed systems require that shareholder returns take priority over all else, including supporting soldiers, veterans and other average citizens. As a result, we often fail to support our troops.)

War is not noble, patriotic or consistent with US values. We were not established to be a warmongering, imperialistic nation. War and military action sometimes are necessary. But they always should be the last resort. To truly support our troops, we never should put them in harm's way unless it is absolutely necessary. We also should provide them with adequate healthcare, education and other benefits. But minimizing war and military spending, combined with using public wealth to adequately support soldiers and veterans, often would limit the shareholder returns of defense and other companies. As a result, conservative media and other business allies often fail to disclose that we frequently do not support our troops in the US.

One might ask, why are troops honored at sporting and other events, but police officers, firemen and other citizens who place their lives at risk to protect society appear to be honored much less frequently? The lives of nearly all police and firemen are at risk every day. But many military personnel never or rarely face combat and risk their lives. What about paramedics and emergency room doctors and nurses who regularly save lives? What about teachers in dangerous inner city neighborhoods who risk their safety to teach the most needy children? There are many heroes in society. Why are military personnel singled out, allowed to board planes first, and frequently honored more than other heroes who face greater risks?

The answer at least in part appears to be that honoring our troops is not the goal. The goal often appears to be manipulating citizens into supporting war and a large military. Soldiers and the military are portrayed as our last line of defense against a dangerous world. Creating fear of attack manipulates citizens into supporting high and unnecessary military spending. Troops put a face to this deception. To support these heroes, we must support high military expenditures, conservative media falsely implies.

These positions are deceptive. As discussed, threats to the US largely result from our own actions. Countries do not randomly say, I think I'll harm the US. Their desire to harm us nearly always results from negative impacts that we caused in their countries. The best defense against a dangerous world is not to build walls and expand our already too large military. It is to stop taking the actions that create threats to the US (i.e. increase the demand for terrorism).

The most important way to support our troops is not to increase military spending. As noted, it is to never put them at risk, unless it is absolutely necessary. Therefore, opposing war is the highest level of support that we can provide to our troops.

National Debt

High national debt is another deceptive issue frequently discussed by conservative media. Commentators in conservative media often emphasize the danger of the high US national debt. They state or imply that the well-being of the economy and country require that we quickly pay down the debt and reduce deficit spending. Our flawed systems require that anything which interferes with ever-increasing shareholder returns, such as maintaining a social safety net, must be reduced or removed. The need to reduce national debt is a primary justification given for reducing spending on Social Security, Medicare and other social welfare programs. There are several deceptive and illogical components to this argument.

For example, reducing government spending during a weak economy to pay off debt often will further weaken the economy. It frequently will inhibit job creation and consumer spending. Reducing social welfare spending when citizens are suffering the most during a recession is ignorant and heartless. Germany and many other countries do the opposite. Social welfare spending is increased when life becomes more difficult for average citizens. This maintains consumer spending, minimizes economic decline and hastens recovery. As shown in the US during the 1930s and 1940s, and in other countries around the world, increased stimulus and other spending frequently is the most effective way to improve the economy and quality of life for average citizens.

Another major deception related to national debt involves fractional reserve lending. As discussed in the Money Creation section, there would be little or no national debt and deficit spending if We the People reclaimed our right to create the money supply. Currently, when the US government runs a deficit, banks create money out of thin air and loan it to government. Then citizens pay interest on it (about $400 billion per year). In addition, citizens probably lose over $100 billion per year in interest revenue by allowing banks to create the money supply. Fractional reserve lending potentially costs US citizens over $500 billion per year. If We the People created the money supply, when government ran a deficit, we often would create money out of thin air (instead of allowing banks to do it) and pay no interest on the money. In addition, We the People would retain much of the profit from money creation, and thereby further lower taxes. We also would ensure that the money supply was used to benefit all citizens, instead of being used primarily to enrich wealthy bank owners.

Another deceptive aspect of the national debt issue relates to corporate welfare in general. Fractional reserve lending only is one form of corporate welfare. As discussed in the Corporate Welfare section, larger forms include limited liability, tax loopholes and externalized costs. Corporate welfare probably costs citizens at least several trillion dollars per year. It is unfair and unjustified. Social Security, Medicare and other social welfare programs benefit many average citizens. They enable a prosperous middle class and society to exist. Providing a strong social safety net is an appropriate and logical use of public wealth. Providing trillions of dollars of public wealth to wealthy citizens is wrong.

Maintaining or increasing government spending during a weak economy, ending fractional reserve lending and greatly reducing or eliminating corporate welfare would hugely benefit the economy and society, while also greatly reducing or eliminating the national debt. But discussing these fair and effective solutions to the national debt issue would threaten the owners of conservative media and other wealthy citizens. As a result, conservative media frequently fails to mention them. Instead, it misleads the public by promoting unfair and destructive ways to reduce national debt, such as cutting social welfare programs.

Taxes

Taxation is another deceptive issue frequently discussed in conservative media. As noted, wealthy citizens in the US avoid as much as $3 trillion per year in taxes. Politicians who receive large amounts of money from wealthy citizens and corporations often do not require their benefactors to pay their fair share for the massive benefits received from society. When this occurs, low and middle-income citizens frequently must pay higher taxes. In addition, society declines due to lack of investment in infrastructure, public education and other critical areas. This unfair and destructive situation is the expected outcome of our flawed systems. Anything that interferes with ever-increasing shareholder returns, such as requiring wealthy citizens to pay fair taxes, must be removed.

Honestly discussing underpayment of taxes by wealthy citizens and corporations would threaten ever-increasing shareholder returns. As a result, conservative media and other business puppets rarely discuss it. To protect shareholder returns, the deception strategy, the best defense is a strong offense, often is employed. Conservative media generally would not admit that their owners and other wealthy citizens and corporations are underpaying taxes. Instead, they often deceptively argue the opposite – that taxes on wealthy citizens and corporations are too high. For example, conservative media commentators often criticize the high US corporate tax rate. They imply that US companies are paying unfairly high taxes. But this is dishonest. The stated corporate tax rate (up to 35 percent) generally is not the relevant rate. It is the one that corporations actually pay. As noted above, from 2008 to 2012, large US companies paid an average tax rate of about 10 percent, in spite of record profits.

In addition, the top marginal tax rate for wealthy citizens is less than half of what it was in the 1950s. And the primary income of many wealthy citizens (investment income) is taxed at substantially lower rates than the primary income (wages) of many middle-class citizens. To hide the unfairly low taxes paid by wealthy citizens and corporations, conservative media frequently discusses studies which say that wealthy citizens pay the majority of taxes. The implication is that wealthy citizens are paying unfairly high taxes. But these studies usually are biased and deceptive. For example, they often do not disclose the assets and income of wealthy citizens that are hidden through tax havens and other means.

Also, the focus on absolute taxes paid is deceptive. Of course, wealthy citizens will pay more taxes. But from a fairness perspective, the key issue is the tax rate, not the absolute amount paid. Many citizens who are struggling to get by pay relatively high tax rates on wages, while wealthy citizens and profitable corporations pay much lower tax rates, sometimes as low as zero. This is grossly unfair.

Observations of reality show the true tax situation in the US. If wealthy citizens and corporations were paying fair taxes, wealth and income inequality would not be rising rapidly. Wealthy citizens have experienced phenomenal wealth and income growth since the 1980s, while quality of life for nearly all other citizens has declined. Infrastructure, public education and other aspects of society are declining in large part because wealthy citizens and corporations are not paying their fair share for benefits received from society. But disclosing this would threaten the owners of conservative media and ever-increasing shareholder returns. Instead of honestly disclosing tax underpayments, conservative media frequently misleads the public by arguing that wealthy citizens and corporations are paying too much tax. The best defense is a strong offense.

Another deceptive aspect of taxes frequently promoted by conservative media relates to inequality. Extremely high inequality is such a large and obvious issue in the US that it no longer can be ignored. During the 2016 elections, conservative media and other Republicans often discussed the need to reduce inequality. These positions frequently are extremely deceptive. Conservative media is a major proponent of the main causes of inequality, such as cutting spending on public education and social welfare programs as well as maintaining low taxes on wealthy citizens. Conservative policies and deceptions strongly facilitate corporate welfare and business control of government, probably the two main drivers of high inequality.

Conservative media criticizing inequality and saying it should be reduced, while simultaneously deceiving citizens into supporting the main causes of it, is hypocritical. But unfortunately, once again, this is the expected outcome of our flawed systems. Conservative media and other business puppets often are compelled to do whatever is necessary to protect ever-increasing shareholder returns, including deceptively using the inequality issue to help win the 2016 Presidential and Congressional elections.

The situation in Kansas well illustrates Republican policies that promote inequality. Republicans have been cutting taxes based on the idea that this will increase tax revenues, for example, by helping the economy. When tax revenues did not increase as anticipated, a substantial budget deficit resulted. To close the deficit, Republicans are cutting spending on public education and infrastructure, taking money from the state's pension fund, and imposing new sales taxes that will disproportionally affect low-income citizens. At the same time, tax cuts for corporations and wealthy citizens are being implemented.[206] Cutting programs that help low and middle-income citizens, while reducing taxes on the wealthy, will reduce consumer spending, hurt the economy, make life more difficult for average citizens and increase inequality. This perfectly illustrates the big business focus of the Republican Party. Politicians take actions that help the wealthy citizens who paid to put them in office, but harm average citizens. It also illustrates how conservatives are misled into voting for politicians who hurt average conservative citizens.

Trade

Promoting free trade represents another way that conservative media protects shareholder returns, but degrades society. Conservative media commentators often argue that free trade will improve the US economy and create high-quality jobs. But the opposite often is true. Protecting domestic manufacturing and limiting imports usually is one of the most effective ways to build a strong manufacturing sector and large middle class. As discussed above, Alexander Hamilton introduced a program to protect US manufacturing at the beginning of this country. We maintained this protection for nearly 200 years. Average tariffs on imports throughout most of the 1800s and 1900s were about 40 percent.[207]

Protection of US manufacturing enabled the US to become the global manufacturing leader prior to 1980. Other manufacturing leaders, including South Korea, Japan, Germany and China, used similar approaches. For example, South Korea began supporting, subsidizing and protecting domestic manufacturing in the 1960s. Imports largely were limited until the country could compete. This protection enabled South Korea to become a global manufacturing leader.[208] Japan also heavily subsidized and protected domestic manufacturing. For example, the country subsidized Toyota losses for about 20 years and limited foreign automobile imports. This enabled Toyota to become a leading automobile manufacturer.[209] Germany and China also protected and continue to protect domestic manufacturing. Largely as a result, they also are global manufacturing leaders.

Saying that allowing cheap imports will protect domestic manufacturing is not rational. Conservative media often uses emotional manipulation to mislead citizens into believing that free trade benefits the economy and society. Those who question the dogma of free trade often are criticized and insulted. As noted, in the 1980s, the US became increasingly focused on maximizing the financial well-being of the small group of citizens who were controlling government. Sending jobs overseas through free trade agreements often increases shareholder returns. Business-controlled government facilitated sending US manufacturing jobs overseas through tax, trade and other policies. As a result, average US tariffs have fallen to about two percent.[210]

Sending jobs overseas severely degrades US manufacturing and the middle class. High-quality manufacturing jobs often are replaced with lower quality service jobs. But promoting the general welfare is not the focus of business-controlled government. Rational thought shows that rebuilding the US economy, manufacturing sector and middle class requires protecting domestic industries, as we did for nearly all of US history up to the 1980s. But limiting free trade and rebuilding US manufacturing would threaten ever-increasing short-term shareholder returns. As a result, conservative media and other business puppets often mislead average citizens into blindly believing that free trade is good for average citizens and the US in general.

As noted, having the abundant cheap products sometimes provided by free trade is beneficial in some ways. But having a decent job or small business ownership opportunity that enables people to buy these products and support their families in other ways is more important. Having good jobs generally is more important than the availability of cheap products. Product costs can be minimized by efficiently operating domestic manufacturing and other productive activities. In addition, ending the ignorant, suicidal requirement to provide ever-increasing shareholder returns will yield substantially lower prices, especially over the mid to longer-term.

As discussed in Trade, Scale and Competitive Advantage section, if imports were limited to protect US manufacturing, the focus on shareholder returns often would compel US companies to use this protection to increase shareholder returns, instead of enhance jobs and product quality. When Japan, South Korea and other manufacturing leaders limited imports, domestic companies largely used this protection to enhance product quality, not shareholder returns. Corporate or national pride probably at least partly motivated this behavior. But the systemic focus on shareholder returns frequently would push corporate pride, national pride and everything else aside. US companies probably often would be compelled to use import protection to reduce quality, increase prices and thereby maximize shareholder returns. But the purpose of import restrictions should be to protect jobs, domestic manufacturing and society overall, not shareholder returns. Therefore, a whole system approach to restoring US manufacturing and the middle class must ensure that the benefits of import restrictions flow mainly to employees, customers and society, not shareholders.

Environment

The environment represents one of the most important areas of public deception in conservative media. As discussed in the environmental sections, all major life support systems are in rapid decline, with some regional exceptions. By degrading that which sustains life, we literally are killing ourselves. This perfectly illustrates the suicidal nature of our economic and political systems. These systems require that shareholder returns and economic growth take priority over all else, including the survival of humanity. Of course, no one intended that our economic theories and systems would wipe out humanity. The destruction of our life support systems is the unintended consequence of our boneheaded, uber-myopic systems.

It is truly tragic that millions of citizens, primarily conservatives, are misled into believing that climate change and other environmental degradations are not major problems that require massive, immediate attention. But once again, this is the expected outcome of our suicidally-flawed systems. Conservative media and other business allies essentially are compelled to mislead the public about environmental issues and anything else that threatens ever-increasing shareholder returns.

Conservative media employs many of the deception techniques discussed throughout this book to mislead the public about environmental and other issues. Two of the most frequently used deception techniques include Wrong Reference Point and My Team Versus Your Team. As discussed in the Misleading the Public section, the Wrong Reference Point deception technique involves claiming that we should be nearly certain that environmental and other problems are occurring before taking action to protect our children and society. But near certainty is the wrong reference point. The priority is protecting citizens and society, not shareholder returns or the economy.

Parents would not wait until they were 90 percent certain that their children were at risk before acting to protect them. In the same way, we should not wait for high levels of certainty that climate change or other problems are occurring before taking action to protect society. The appropriate trigger point for action perhaps is in that 10-20 percent certainty range. We reached 20 percent certainty that substantial negative impacts were occurring from burning fossil fuels, using synthetic chemicals, planting genetically altered crops and other environmentally destructive activities long ago.

More than 20 years ago, many independent scientists said that climate change would cause increasing droughts, more frequent and severe storms, rising sea levels and many other negative impacts. These impacts are occurring and causing the predicted disruption and destruction. But our suicidal systems never will be satisfied. To protect shareholder returns, conservative media misleads citizens into believing that business activities are not causing major environmental degradation. As a result, no changes that might threaten ever-increasing shareholder returns are needed.

My Team Versus Your Team probably is the most important deception technique used to mislead conservative citizens into allowing environmental degradation. It is the central strategy of the war between conservatives and liberals. The approach involves building great disdain for the other team/party. In this divided and angry environment, emotions often trump logic. Conservative media and other business puppets often slap the liberal label on climate change and other environmental problems. This frequently compels conservative citizens to dismiss environmental concerns without rationally considering them.

Conservative media often creates the sense that anyone who considers climate change and other environmental problems to be real is a traitor to the conservative team. Conservatives who attempt to rationally discuss environmental problems frequently are insulted and attacked. This helps to suppress rational, independent thinking and corral wayward conservatives back into the flock. People who attempt to think for themselves, consider the grave risks to our life support systems and protect their children often are mocked or belittled by conservative media and other business allies.

It will be truly tragic if we do not wake up, work together and end the degradation of our life support systems. If some people survive, they probably will look back to our once beautiful and abundant home. They will wish that vested interests had not been so effective at misleading us into not protecting our life support systems. But it will be too late. We must not allow this to happen. We must courageously use rational thought to see through conservative media deceptions about environmental and other problems.

Education

Education represents another important area of media deception. Conservative media often strongly promotes privatization of public schools, expansion of charter schools, suppression of teachers unions, increased standardized testing, expansion of online education and other aspects of US education reform. These changes greatly benefit for-profit education and related companies. However, as discussed extensively in the Education section, US business-style education reform has failed to improve academic performance or close performance gaps between minority and white students and students from low-income and wealthier families. Instead, education reform has substantially degraded public education and education quality in general.

World leaders in education are not using the education reform strategies being employed in the US. Instead, they largely are doing what the US did when we were a world leader in education in the 1960s – maintaining strong teachers unions and well-funded public education. Promoting education reform once again illustrates conservative media supporting actions that help shareholder returns, but harm children, average citizens and society overall.

Education follows society. If the focus of society were on promoting the general welfare, as the Constitution requires, US education would be very different. The current structure of US education reflects our primary focus on maximizing economic growth and shareholder returns. The US education system is a legacy of the Protestant Reformation and Industrial Age. The goals mainly were and still are indoctrination and obedience training.

As discussed in the Freedom-Based Education section, standardized curriculums force many students to study subjects in which they have no interest. Competitive grading constantly ranks students against peers and teaches them that they are inadequate when they receive average or below average grades. Young people are constantly monitored and strictly disciplined. Much of the so-called necessary information that they learn in forced K-12 education is quickly forgotten and not needed for life success. Children and teenagers sit in sterile rooms for many hours each day listening to adults talk to them. Humans did not evolve to learn this way. This unnatural approach produces extensive boredom, inattention, hyperactivity, anxiety and stress. This strongly contributes to drug abuse, rebellion, delinquency and other behavioral problems.

Finland has nearly the best education performance in the world. Students in Finland spend much less time in school, do far less homework and take nearly no standardized tests. The country achieves far better results, while spending about 40 percent less per student than the US. If the purpose of US education were to maximize the long-term well-being of young people and society, we would emulate Finland's more effective, less expensive approach. But the US education system reflects broader society. The focus is on helping a small group of wealthy citizens get continuously wealthier. The boring, strict US education system facilitates this by training young people to tolerate boring jobs and control by authorities for the rest of their lives.

Finland's approach honors and respects young people. They are encouraged to enjoy their early lives. This produces empowered young people who grow up to be empowered adults. They do not tolerate abuse by authorities or employers. This type of education system would greatly benefit young people and society overall. But it would severely inhibit unfair wealth accumulation by the small group that controls government, the economy and society.

The US education system also strongly suppresses rational, critical thinking. Students are rewarded for learning prevailing economic and other ideas. They generally are not taught to analyze the flaws of current economic and political systems and consider more effective alternatives. The strict, boring US education system conditions young people to not question major injustices in society, such as corporate welfare, business control of government and degradation of life support systems. This obedience and blind faith in economic and other dogma facilitates ever-increasing economic growth and shareholder returns.

Conservative (and liberal) media rarely honestly discuss these major problems in US education, or highlight the more effective, less expensive approaches being employed in countries that outperform the US on education. Instead, the deceptive term 'reform' is applied to the privatization of US education. Reform implies improvement. But young people and education overall are being degraded so that the wealthy citizens who control media, government and (to a growing degree) education can get continuously wealthier.

As discussed in the Education section, as the level of education increases, people tend to increasingly vote Democrat or liberal. A main reason for this is that higher education generally teaches people to think for themselves and question ideas, rather than blindly accept them. Conservative philosophies often emphasize not questioning authorities and dogma. Linking higher education to increased Democratic voting certainly is not meant to imply that liberals are more intelligent than conservatives. There are millions of brilliant conservatives and millions of less than brilliant liberals. The key issue is not intelligence. It is tendency to not question authority and prevailing ideas as well as vulnerability to emotional manipulation, such as that used in the My Team Versus Your Team deception technique.

US education 'reform' has been reducing funding for public higher education for many years. This lowers the number of young people who go to college and learn to think for themselves. It also often compels those who do go to take on high debt. Financial stress caused by high student debt frequently inhibits the tendency to question the unjust status quo. Suppressing public education and rational thought compels people to blindly believe conservative media deceptions, such as the idea that social welfare spending is the primary cause of high taxes and the declining quality of life experienced by most citizens. Emotionally manipulating people into not thinking for themselves prevents them from seeing through media deception and understanding the actual causes (mainly corporate welfare and business control of government).

Suppressing public education and rational thought benefits wealthy shareholders, business-controlled government and conservative media owners. As a result, conservative media often does not discuss the failure of education reform and the need to reestablish strong public K-12 and higher education in the US.

Elitism

Elitism represents another conservative media deception. In their attempts to beat liberals, conservative media commentators frequently portray liberals as intellectuals or elitists who are out of touch with average citizens and reality. They often state or imply that liberals promote impractical policies that do not work in the real world. This is a good example of the old saying, the pot calling the kettle black.

The real elites in society are the small group of wealthy citizens who largely control government and essentially steal the people's wealth and power. Liberal and conservative politicians mainly are focused on supporting this small group of elites. But as noted, conservatives generally do so more aggressively without hesitation or restriction. It is the same with conservative media. It generally is more likely to protect the true elites in society by not disclosing information that threatens ever-increasing shareholder returns. It often misleads conservative citizens into supporting policies that help wealthy citizens and corporations, but hurt average citizens. Conservative media deceptions facilitate corporate welfare, business control of government and many other policies that severely degrade the lives of average conservative and liberal citizens.

Deceptively discussing elitism misleads many conservative citizens into acting like they have Stockholm syndrome. Conservative media deceives average citizens into supporting the wealthy business owners and corporations who steal their wealth, power and freedom. At the same time, conservative citizens frequently are misled into attacking or ignoring those who truly are trying to help average citizens.

Family Values

Family values represent one of the most odious deceptions used in conservative media. Conservative media commentators often trumpet the importance of family and family values. They frequently state or imply that liberals promote ideas and actions that severely degrade families, such as abortion and same-sex marriage. The conservative media and general conservative position on family is extremely hypocritical. The most important family value is survival because there are no families without it. To survive, families require food, shelter, healthcare and other basic supports. Good education also is critical for family success.

Conservative media often essentially is a mouthpiece for wealthy citizens and corporations. It frequently deceives citizens into opposing programs that are essential for family well-being, but threaten ever-increasing shareholder returns. Social welfare programs that provide healthcare, education, food, shelter and other basic needs often are critical for maintaining the well-being of struggling low and middle-income families. Conservative media frequently apparently attempts to hide its opposition to programs that actually support families by making general religious or moral arguments. It attempts to impose its moral and religious ideas on others. The ignorant implication seems to be that same-sex marriage and abortion are the main threats to families, rather than inability to find jobs, feed hungry children or meet other basic needs.

Maternity leave provides a good example of the hypocritical conservative position on families. Women having children is the central aspect of many families. It often is what creates or expands families. As noted, out of 188 countries only eight do not provide some type of paid maternity leave, the US and seven small developing countries. The US Family and Medical Leave Act requires companies with 50 or more employees to provide 12 weeks of *unpaid* leave to full-time female employees who have been with the company for over one year. Part-time, temporary and small company employees are not covered. Only about 12 percent of women in the US get paid maternity leave.[211]

Our suicidal systems place shareholder returns before all else, including supporting families. Providing paid maternity leave threatens ever-increasing shareholder returns. As a result, conservative media and other business allies use various deceptions to mislead citizens into opposing it. For example, business allies often argue that having children is a personal choice. Taxpayers and businesses should not be forced to support women having children. But nearly every other developed and developing country believes that society has an obligation to help raise the next generation.

Business allies also frequently argue that mandatory maternity leave is anti-business. In a country that gives higher priority to economic growth and shareholder returns than to supporting families, maternity leave could be seen as anti-business. But business is supposed to be the servant of society, not the master. Essentially every other country believes that families should not have to suffer so that wealthy citizens can make more money. Here in the US, we easily could afford to provide generous paid maternity and paternity leave to new parents, along with free childcare, if we eliminate or substantially reduce corporate welfare. This would massively benefit US families. But it also would threaten the financial returns of conservative media owners and other wealthy citizens. As a result, conservative media rarely discusses how we fail to provide maternity leave and other essential services and support to millions of US families.

The family values deception is truly tragic and heartbreaking. It shows how our suicidal systems compel conservative media to mislead citizens in ways that harm families. The family values deception is like other conservative media deceptions. Conservative media often loudly promotes ideas such as freedom, democracy, responsibility and supporting our troops. But the primary focus on maximizing shareholder returns frequently compels it to advocate programs and policies that severely degrade freedom, democracy and our troops. Conservative media often says people should act responsibly. But then it usually vehemently opposes regulations that hold large companies responsible for negative impacts on society.

The family values deception is one of the most tragic because family values are used (probably unintentionally) to attack families. Morality arguments apparently are used to hide the fact that conservative media often supports policies that cause destitution, suffering or degraded quality of life for millions of US families.

Healthcare

Healthcare represents another harmful conservative media deception. Conservative media and other business allies frequently criticize the Affordable Care Act (ACA). The act provides health insurance to millions of previously uninsured citizens. But conservative media nevertheless frequently portrays the act as horrible for our country. Opponents of the ACA rarely suggest alternatives that would cover the millions of uninsured citizens in the US and substantially reduce healthcare costs. In particular, conservative media and other business allies rarely discuss the vastly less expensive, higher coverage healthcare systems of all other developed countries, except to criticize them. This is extremely deceptive.

As discussed in the Healthcare section, every other developed country and many developing countries provide guaranteed healthcare to all citizens, usually at one-third to one-half the cost of US healthcare. Healthcare is seen as a basic right, like education, in all other developed countries. But our suicidal systems suppress anything that interferes with ever-increasing shareholder returns, such as public education and healthcare.

Conservative media uses several deception techniques to turn citizens against public healthcare. For example, utilizing the My Team Versus Your Team deception, public healthcare often is labeled as a liberal issue. This frequently manipulates conservative citizens into feeling that if they support public healthcare, they are betraying their conservative team. Conservative media and other business allies also often deceptively imply that government cannot do anything right and public healthcare in other countries is terrible compared to the US. To mislead citizens into thinking that the US for-profit healthcare system is better than the not-for-profit healthcare systems in all other developed countries, conservative media and other business allies frequently emphasize minor factors while ignoring major ones, as well as use anecdotal evidence inappropriately.

For example, business allies often argue that citizens must wait longer for noncritical care or specialized services in other countries. But this factor is less important than many other healthcare metrics. When comparing healthcare or other complex systems, one must identify critical measurement factors and then take them into account. Business allies often irrationally draw conclusions based only on a few, less relevant factors. When comparing healthcare systems, key metrics include cost, coverage and outcomes. Wait time for noncritical care is important, but not as important as these other factors. In terms of cost and coverage, the US is by far the worst in the developed world. In terms of results, we are mediocre. Business allies discuss waiting longer for noncritical care, but usually neglect to mention that virtually no one dies or goes bankrupt in other developed countries due to lack of health insurance. Waiting longer for noncritical care could be inconvenient. But it would be more inconvenient to be dead or have to use up life savings, sell homes or file for bankruptcy due to not having adequate or any health insurance.

Conservative media and business allies frequently show people from Canada and other countries who criticize their public healthcare systems. But as discussed in the Healthcare section, they neglect to mention that usually over 90 percent of people in Canada and other developed countries strongly support keeping these systems. Highlighting a few people from Canada who oppose public healthcare, and not mentioning the 90 percent of citizens who strongly support the system, is a deceptive use of anecdotal evidence. A few anecdotal examples from a large population usually are irrelevant, unless they illustrate larger trends. Honest use of anecdotal information would involve publicizing opinions from the vast majority of people who support public healthcare in Canada and other developed countries.

Vested interests often argue that US healthcare is more expensive than other developed countries because we provide higher quality service. But this is extremely misleading. The main reason that US healthcare is far more expensive than all other developed countries is that our for-profit healthcare system is focused on maximizing shareholder returns, instead of the health and lives of citizens. Unnecessary, wasteful treatments and procedures often are done because this enhances profitability and shareholder returns. Massive amounts of wealth are removed from the system and transferred to shareholders. Other developed countries frequently are able to provide superior healthcare quality/quantity/coverage at much lower costs because healthcare funds are used almost completely to provide healthcare services, rather than to enrich shareholders.

Beyond superior cost and coverage, people in other developed countries do not have to fight with for-profit healthcare companies about coverage for their loved ones or themselves. As noted, the for-profit US healthcare system demands that shareholder returns take priority over the health and lives of citizens. This suicidal system literally ends or degrades the lives of many people.

The healthcare situation in the US is tragic. In other developed countries, citizens do not have to worry about receiving adequate healthcare. But millions of people in the US have inadequate or no health insurance. People often start online fundraising efforts to pay the healthcare bills of friends and family members. For example, a GoFundMe page was established for a paralyzed five-year-old girl.[212] GoFundMe efforts also were established for victims of the 2012 Aurora, Colorado theater shooting.

But this should not be necessary. Money often can be raised online to help pay the medical bills of children and victims of tragedy. But what about the millions of other US citizens who cannot afford healthcare and do not have heartbreaking stories? Should they suffer because they cannot raise healthcare donations online? The fact that people in the US have to seek charity to pay medical bills is insane and barbaric. This does not happen anywhere else in the developed world. Healthcare is a basic human right. It should be provided to all citizens, not just financially stable people and those with tragic, poignant stories.

A study of 11 developed countries found that the US had the worst healthcare system in the developed world. The UK's National Health Service was found to be the best, even though healthcare costs per person are about 60 percent less in the UK than in the US. The study also found that many developed countries, including Germany, Netherlands and the UK, provide timely access to specialized services.[213]

This illustrates the inevitable result of our flawed systems. Putting shareholder returns before all else often means that citizens will pay higher costs for lower quality services. Within the realm of logic, it is not debatable that the US should emulate the proven more effective, lower cost healthcare systems of other developed countries. No one should die or go bankrupt due to lack of healthcare. We should not be paying two to three times more for the worst healthcare coverage in the developed world. Switching to a government-owned or government-managed healthcare system probably is the only way to match the low cost, high coverage and frequently superior results of other developed countries. Every other developed country proves that, in the healthcare area, the private sector cannot compete with the public sector, especially over the mid to long-term.

The US for-profit healthcare system gives business great power over citizens. The ability to get healthcare should not depend on whether someone has a job or can afford health insurance. Public healthcare is more important than public education. People can live without education, but often not without healthcare. The existence of the worst in the developed world US healthcare system (based on cost, coverage and other key metrics) is a testament to the ease with which non-expert citizens can be misled. Debates about the ACA are deceptive distractions. The ACA provides insurance to millions of previously uninsured citizens. But as discussed in the Healthcare section, it is a huge giveaway to the for-profit healthcare sector. True healthcare reform requires emulating the proven more effective systems of other developed countries. But this would threaten ever-increasing shareholder returns. As a result, conservative media and other business allies rarely discuss this obviously superior option.

Converting from a for-profit to a not-for-profit healthcare system illustrates the complexity of system change. Many healthcare companies would shrink, or possibly go out of business. They would fight aggressively to maintain the current shareholder-focused healthcare system. But as noted, businesses have no right to exist. The priority is maximizing the well-being of citizens and society. If the private sector cannot compete with the public sector in the healthcare area, it should be reduced.

As we make the transition from for-profit to not-for-profit public healthcare, businesses have no right to have their downside covered by taxpayers. Business is risky. That is why average citizens often should not put their life savings in risky equity investments. But converting from defined benefit to defined contribution pension funds caused millions of average citizens to invest in the capital markets. As a result, taxpayers often are forced to cover the downside of business investing so that the retirement savings of average citizens are protected. This illustrates the need for a whole system approach. Changing healthcare and other systems cannot be done in isolation. Economic and political systems must be changed through a coordinated whole system approach.

Unions

Unions represent another major and tragic area of public deception in conservative media. The requirement to provide ever-increasing shareholder returns often compels companies to force down employee wages and benefits. Only unions and government can protect employees from business abuse. Unions strongly promote a large middle class by ensuring that employees fairly share in the success of companies.

In the early US, small family farmers were the closest we had to a middle class.[214] But industrialization, railroads and agricultural monopolies nearly wiped out the farming middle class. By 1890, the average income of the bottom 92 percent of society was $380 per year (equivalent to $7,900 today). The large majority of citizens lived in deep poverty. From the late 1800s to the early 1900s, unions were strongly suppressed. Union leaders often were jailed. Protesters frequently were beaten by police, and sometimes murdered.[215]

As discussed in the Labor section, in 1935, the National Labor Relations Act guaranteed employees' right to unionize. This combined with raising tax rates on wealthy citizens led to the emergence of a true middle class in the 1940s. About 35 percent of workers were unionized. Unions forced up nonunion wages. As a result, about 70 percent of citizens could raise a family, meet basic needs and save for retirement on a single salary.

In 1947, Republicans passed the anti-union Taft-Hartley Act. As a result, unions slowly declined to about 25 percent of workers by 1980. But about 50 percent of workers still could afford a middle class life. However, in the 1980s, degradation of the middle class accelerated rapidly. As noted, free trade increased, taxes on wealthy citizens were substantially reduced, and unions were severely suppressed. As a result, only about seven percent of workers are unionized and the middle class has been severely degraded.[216]

Maintaining a large middle class often threatens ever-increasing shareholder returns because businesses are not able to continuously force down wages and benefits. To protect ever-increasing shareholder returns and the ability to force down wages, conservative media and other business allies misled citizens into opposing unions. Irrational arguments were used, such as equating unions to communism or calling them un-American. But unions simply are structures that limit business abuse of labor, and thereby protect the middle class. The union deception is tragic because the middle class essentially is misled into attacking the middle class. Average citizens (primarily conservatives) are misled into supporting policies that impoverish average citizens.

As discussed in the Labor section, one of the most destructive union deceptions involves right-to-work laws. Republican politicians and conservative media frequently strongly support these laws. Right-to-work is an extremely misleading term. It protects shareholder returns by misleading citizens into supporting laws that severely degrade labor and unions. Anti-union laws, such as right-to-work laws, limit the ability of unions to compel employees to join unions or pay union dues. This creates an unfair free-rider problem. Employees get the benefit of union membership (i.e. higher wages and benefits, better working conditions) without paying to support the unions that provided these benefits. If employees want to avoid paying union dues, they should receive the reduced wages and benefits that would exist if no unions were present. Once employees realize that the benefits of union membership usually vastly outweigh the costs, they will be glad to pay union dues.

The term right-to-work is meant to deceive citizens into supporting actions that harm average citizens. So-called right-to-work laws enable management to abuse labor by forcing down wages and benefits. Therefore, a more accurate term is right-to-abuse laws. Unions do not prevent people from working, as the ignorant right-to-work term implies. Unions protect the middle class and ensure that people have fair, decent jobs. But honestly discussing unions and right-to-abuse laws would limit ever-increasing shareholder returns. Therefore conservative media rarely discusses these issues honestly.

Being a Man

The percentage of citizens who identify as conservative has increased from 18 percent in 2004 to 27 percent in 2014.[217] An interesting question is, why are so many low and middle-income, hard-working people switching from the Democratic to Republican Party? The Democratic Party usually more strongly supports programs that enable average citizens and families to meet basic needs and prosper. Republicans more often oppose unions, healthcare for all citizens, public K-12 and higher education, Social Security expansion, environmental protection and other programs that enable average citizens to have a good quality of life.

Several possible explanations have been provided for this apparently illogical behavior. For example, conservative media often promotes party switching by misleading people into focusing on relatively small problems, such as abuse of social welfare programs, and ignoring much larger ones, including corporate welfare, business control of government and degradation of life support systems.

In addition, the overemphasis on economic growth and shareholder returns gives business high status in society. Businesses usually more strongly support and identify with the Republican party. The desire to enhance status or success could cause party switching.

Another possible explanation involves taking advantage of men's desire to appear manly and tough. Conservative media and other business allies often implicitly portray Democrats as weak, bleeding heart liberals who do not think people should have to work for a living. Conservatives, on the other hand, implicitly frequently are portrayed as tough men who work hard and do the right thing.

As discussed in the Men's section, our competitive society strongly conditions boys to never appear weak. Media and broader society often convey grossly inaccurate ideas about what it means to be a man. Media commentators frequently model aggressive and rude behavior. Advertising and media often mislead men into thinking that growing a beard, riding a motorcycle or owning a large truck are important components of being a man. There is nothing wrong with these things if people like them. However, having a beard, truck or motorcycle has nothing to do with being a man. These are childish portrayals of men. As discussed in the Inner Activism section below, being a man largely involves protecting loved ones and broader society. It involves thinking for oneself and rationally considering problems and solutions.

To illustrate, flawed systems often compel conservative media and other business allies to attack anything that threatens ever-increasing shareholder returns, such as science and rational reasoning. Climate change provides a good example. As discussed in the Climate Change section, about 97 percent of climate scientists agree that human activities are substantially contributing to global warming. But 66 percent of Republican citizens do not believe this.[218] Instead, they frequently ignore science and buy into irrational ideas, such as climate change is a liberal conspiracy to destroy the economy. Men often apparently are emotionally manipulated into believing that they are weak or liberal if they acknowledge the science and logic of climate change and other major problems.

Growing overt racism in society indicates that conservative men frequently are being deceived into criticizing the small percentage of minority citizens who abuse social welfare programs and ignoring much larger problems. Allowing oneself to be manipulated and deceived like this is not manly or tough. Vested interests are taking advantage of men and misleading them into believing that being irrational and rude is manly and tough. But it is not.

A group of motorcyclists in DeKalb, Indiana recently demonstrated what it means to be a man. An 11-year-old boy, Phil Mick, was considering suicide after being bullied at school. The boy's mother asked a family friend for help. He and 50 other motorcyclists accompanied Phil to school to show support and oppose bullying. The boy was beaming.[219] These men understood what it means to be a man.

In our often angry and divided society, being a real man frequently requires courage. It sometimes involves questioning those one trusts and admires. It includes thinking for oneself and making decisions based on sound scientific or rational information, rather than vested interest deceptions. A main part of being a man involves doing what is objectively best for society, regardless of whether these actions are supported by Republicans, Democrats or anyone else.

Deceptions such as those noted above mislead many working class men and women into leaving the party that historically supported the working class and joining the one that suppresses it. This position is not intended to support the Democratic Party. Democrats only are slightly better at helping average citizens. Like Republicans, they primarily are focused on benefiting wealthy campaign donors.

Reduced quality of life under a Democratic administration almost certainly is another reason why people switch to the Republican Party. This is deceptive and tragic because it will accelerate quality of life degradation. Refocusing government on serving all citizens through a We the People movement is the best and perhaps only way to improve quality of life for all current and future citizens.

Honoring the Flag

Conservative media and other conservative groups and citizens often display the US flag in ways which imply that they are the true Americans because their views are the most aligned with the Constitution and Founders' intentions. Those holding differing views implicitly are seen as not being true Americans, or even as traitors to their country. This misuse of the US flag is one of the most tragic and harmful public deceptions. Good, well-meaning conservative citizens are misled into supporting policies that grossly violate the Constitution and Founders' intentions.

The stated goals of conservative media and philosophies might be to abide by the Constitution and promote the well-being of all citizens. But they often hypocritically support policies that grossly subvert these goals. To protect corporate welfare, average conservative citizens are emotionally manipulated into attacking low income, often minority citizens who use social welfare programs. In other words, they are tricked into attacking the needy and supporting those who abuse the needy.

Since the 1980s, conservative (and liberal) business-first policies have concentrated wealth at the top of society, severely degraded life support systems and made life more difficult for the large majority of citizens. When displaying the flag, many conservatives seem to believe that they are supporting their country by opposing those who would harm it (i.e. liberals and low income citizens using social welfare programs). But in reality, they are being deceived into supporting the small group of wealthy citizens who steal their wealth, power and freedom.

As discussed in the Well-Being of Society section, the Founders were strongly focused on maximizing the long-term well-being of all citizens and society. George Washington, Benjamin Franklin and other main Founders encouraged us to work together and promote the common welfare. The Founders would have adamantly opposed the wealth concentrating, environment and society-degrading policies that were implemented over the past 40 years. Using the flag in ways that mislead citizens into supporting these policies is an abomination. It is a greater disgrace than burning the flag. Our flag stands for unity, brotherhood and promoting the general welfare. The flag means that we help those in need, protect those who cannot protect themselves (especially future generations), and require those who benefit the most from society to pay their fair share to support it.

The wealthy citizens who steal the public wealth, power and freedom are not the enemy. Flawed systems compel their bad behavior. Liberals or conservatives also are not the enemy. There is no human enemy. We are all each other's brothers and sisters. The true enemy of humanity is our flawed, myopic thinking. This produces flawed systems and the public deceptions needed to maintain them.

The Founders established a country where people would be free to live according to their own moral, religious and philosophical beliefs. They enshrined this in our Constitution. Implying that the flag stands for one set of beliefs or dogma, such as conservative or Christian, and that those holding differing beliefs are not true Americans is a gross misuse of the flag. Our flag stands for unity, not division. The flag means that we are all free to hold our own views and live according to our own ideals. Saying or implying that the flag stands only for conservative beliefs also is a greater disgrace than burning the flag, especially when these so-called conservative beliefs and policies grossly violate the Constitution and degrade society.

(As discussed in the Libertarianism section, the word conservative implies minimizing risks. But business-first, so-called conservative policies are severely degrading life support systems and society. These policies often would be more accurately described as radical risk taking.

It is an insult to the word conservative to suggest that concentrating wealth, degrading life support systems and making life more difficult for the vast majority of citizens is conservative.)

Being a true American means emulating our Founders. They did not blindly believe British rulers or economic and political dogma. They thought for themselves. We must do the same. Being a true American means that we do not allow children to go hungry in this wealthy country. We do not allow individuals and families to become destitute. And we do not allow a small group of wealthy people to cause this destitution by unfairly controlling government, misleading the public and taking the public wealth. We dishonor the flag when we allow ourselves to be manipulated into attacking fellow citizens. We honor the flag, Founders and Constitution by standing united and ensuring that every current and future citizen has a secure, satisfying life.

Beyond flag waving and other specific deceptions discussed above, some of the most dangerous media deceptions occur in conservative media. Several deceptive and dishonest approaches are used to mislead the public. For example, conservative media often denies reality, ignores facts, promotes false information, and, if these do not work, uses belligerence to shout down opponents.[220]

In terms of ignoring reality and facts, one of the greatest public deceptions involves climate change. As discussed, virtually all scientists who are not paid or influenced by energy and other companies say that humans are substantially contributing to global warming. But about two-thirds of Republicans do not believe this. This is a perfect example of how easy it is to mislead citizens into protecting the shareholder returns of energy and other companies, but harming their children and themselves.

To illustrate public deception regarding climate change, when a Republican became governor of Florida in 2011, he prohibited the Department of Environmental Protection from publicly using the terms climate change, global warming or sustainability.[221] Florida is highly vulnerable to climate change impacts, including rising sea levels, increased droughts, and more frequent and severe hurricanes. But business-influenced politicians regularly put the interests of wealthy campaign donors ahead of the safety and well-being of citizens and society. Several Republican candidates for president in 2016 believed that humans are not causing climate change. Future generations will view this willful ignoring of reality as criminal. But millions of conservative citizens are misled into not seeing climate change denial by politicians for what it is – a crime against humanity.

To illustrate promoting false information, conservative media and politicians often support trickle-down economics and the universal benefits of tax reductions. This helps wealthy media owners and campaign donors, but severely degrades society. As discussed, trickle-down economics essentially is the idea that focusing on making rich people richer is the best way to benefit all citizens. The idiocy of this approach is shown by the vast inequality and destitution it caused since the 1980s. Regarding tax reductions, conservatives often cite a study which found that tax increases ultimately could reduce tax revenues. This is used to support the irrational, destructive idea that all tax increases are bad.[222] Further illustrating promoting false information, conservative media and politicians have opposed job creation and anti-outsourcing bills. They ignorantly imply that creating and protecting US jobs somehow will harm the US.[223]

When facts reveal that conservative media has misled the public, the response frequently is to belligerently shout down opponents. To illustrate, an announcer at a more liberal news organization was suspended for six months for providing misleading information about his activities in a war zone. Extensive evidence and witness testimony indicated that an announcer from a conservative news network provided misleading or false information in his stories about war zones and other issues. But the announcer was not reprimanded. Instead, he belligerently and publicly threatened his accusers and said the accusations were the result of a liberal conspiracy. Many conservative citizens simply accepted this explanation, rather than considering the facts, because they have been manipulated into hating liberals.[224]

Conservative media deceptions frequently are working. As noted, the percentage of citizens who identify as conservative is increasing. Many conservative citizens have been misled into believing that minorities and other people who use social welfare programs are the primary cause of high taxes and declining quality of life. This degrades society by replacing empathy with hatred and division.

Deceptive media has severely degraded society. Conservative media rarely discusses two of the most important problems in society – business control of government and corporate welfare. Instead, they focus on smaller problems, such as abuse of social welfare programs. Conservative media fosters bitter division, hatred and rivalry in the US. A generation ago, elected officials regularly worked across party lines to do what was best for the country. But the division promoted by radical, deceptive media has seeped into government. Little work occurs across party lines. Government becomes gridlocked. Wealthy campaign donors get wealthier, while life gets more difficult for average citizens.

Prior to the radical, divisive media that has evolved since the mid-1990s, people often could have rational political conversations. Citizens frequently said, for example, I'm generally conservative, but I agree with the liberals on certain issues. However, in today's childish, divisive media environment, this type of statement often would be severely criticized. Our authoritarian education system indoctrinates young people to blindly believe authorities and prevailing ideas, rather than think for themselves. Conservative media sends the strong implied message that people are expected to blindly believe and obey. Any divergence from conservative dogma, for example by saying that liberals might be right on a few issues, usually is severely attacked and suppressed.

As discussed in the Advertising, Media and Culture section, angry, rude commentators in radical and mainstream media make horrible role models for children and society. People often look up to media commentators. Role models like these strongly influence how people behave in society. A generation ago, media personalities usually were rational and respectful of others, even those with differing opinions. These leaders modeled and promoted civilized, productive behavior, and thereby greatly benefitted society.

But today, commentators in radical, often conservative media frequently act like rude, aggressive children. They tolerate no questioning of their often ignorant, irrational positions. They cowardly cut off those who are about to expose their irrational thinking and prove them wrong. These ignorant fools teach children and adults that it is acceptable, even admirable, to be rude and disrespectful to others, especially those with different opinions or positions. It is no coincidence that rude, aggressive, irrational behavior is growing in government, communities and even families in the US and some other developed countries with extensive radical media. This type of media builds hatred and division in society. This enables the small group of wealthy citizens who control government and media to continue stealing the people's wealth, power and freedom. But it severely degrades individual and societal well-being.

In the late 1800s and early 1900s, concentrated business power abused labor, small businesses and citizens in many ways. These industrialists frequently were referred to as robber barons. The people rose up and put an end to this injustice. However, if the deceptive media environment functioning today were present then, many average citizens would have been deceived into supporting the robber barons. As a result, injustice and degradation of society would have continued. Like the robber barons a century ago, the small group of wealthy citizens and corporations that control government, media and society today are abusing labor, small businesses and average citizens. Media deception perpetuates this abuse and degradation of society by keeping the people divided and conquered.

Deceptive media has fostered intense anger, hatred and racism in society, especially among middle-aged and older white men. A recent study of US citizens found that whites and Republicans are the angriest people in society. Regarding income, low-income citizens were the angriest, while wealthy citizens were the least angry.[225] This is the expected result of divisive, radical media. Nearly all major media outlets, conservative and liberal, are owned by wealthy citizens. As a result, private sector media rarely discusses problems caused by the wealthy, such as corporate welfare and business control of government. Rather than focusing on the main causes of the increasingly difficult lives of average citizens, conservative citizens are misled into focusing on lesser problems. The nonstop radical conservative media invective against minorities, liberals and low-income citizens is a main cause of anger among white, low and middle-income citizens.

Radical, divisive conservative media appears to have created an angry force in society that the wealthy no longer can control. Establishment Republican candidates in the 2016 presidential primary lost to someone who overtly expressed racist ideas. Angry Republicans largely supported a candidate who expresses the anger, hatred and racism that many people feel, but do not say in public. The rise of a racist candidate, who was opposed by many Republican Party leaders, largely is an unintended consequence of radical conservative media.

Across the ocean, radical conservative media also played a large role in the UK decision to leave the EU (Brexit). Like the US, business influence of government has been growing in the UK since the 1980s. As the wealthy gained greater influence over the UK government, inequality rose over the past 30 years, like it did in nearly all other developed countries. As the rich got richer, the quality of life of average UK citizens often declined. As in the US, privatization of public healthcare and education is raising costs and reducing service quality.[226]

Also like the US, business-controlled media in the UK largely does not tell citizens about major problems, such as corporate welfare and business control of government. Instead, citizens are misled into focusing on immigrants and low-income citizens on social welfare programs. This media deception increases anger and hatred of immigrants. This in turn was a main cause of the Brexit vote. The tragedy of Brexit is that leaving the EU almost certainly will reduce quality of life for average UK citizens. Reduced EU regulations often will facilitate greater theft of the public wealth through corporate welfare and reduced protections for the environment and society.

Back in the US, one of the greatest tragedies of radical conservative media is the promotion of mass shootings and gun violence. As discussed in the Crime section, radical conservative media greatly increases anger, hatred and racism among conservative citizens. This sometimes pushes mentally unstable people over the edge. Several mass shooters in the US self-identified as conservative. They sometimes openly expressed hatred for minorities and liberals. Conservative media usually refers to these shooters as lone wolves. But the anger and hatred of so-called lone wolves does not evolve in a vacuum. These people often were poisoned by divisive media. The rise of racist presidential candidates, Brexit and mass shooters inflamed by hate-filled media are some of the truly tragic consequences of media deception.

The government discussed by Thomas Jefferson in the Declaration of Independence (i.e. formed by and with the consent of the governed) was revolutionary. At that time, many people thought that the church or monarchy/aristocracy should be in charge. This type of government was based on fear and force. Many of the Founders believed that the strength of republican government, the people, was also its weakness. Free people are vulnerable to corruption, selfishness, division and deception. The main Founders believed that a successful republic required promotion among the people of self-control, moral integrity, industriousness and abiding by religious principles, such as treating others with kindness, love and respect. Benjamin Franklin said, "Only a virtuous people are capable of freedom... As nations become more corrupt and vicious, they have more need of masters."[227]

Advertising and deceptive media strongly inhibit freedom, democracy and the successful republic that our Founders wished for us. Advertising strongly promotes inadequacy, selfishness and materialism. Deceptive media strongly drives anger, division and hatred in society. Angry, divided, selfish people are more vulnerable to authoritarianism. They are more inclined to blindly believe the vested interest promoting, society degrading deceptions of conservative media.

Exposing conservative media deception is critical for promoting the general welfare. As noted, liberal media generally is more honest about discussing environmental and other major problems in society. Conservative media often is a mouthpiece or public deception tool of wealthy citizens. It regularly uses emotional manipulation to mislead the public into believing that environmental and other major problems are not real. Emotional manipulation blocks rational assessment of major problems and solutions. As noted, the main deception or emotional manipulation is getting conservatives to dislike or hate liberals.

Our flawed political system usually only provides two options that have a chance of winning – Democrat/liberal or Republican/conservative. By creating disdain for liberals, many conservatives would not vote liberal, even if they disagree with several conservative approaches. In other words, emotional manipulation frequently enables conservative politicians to do whatever they want. Regardless of how bad theses politicians are, many conservative citizens will not vote Democrat/liberal, because they have been manipulated into disliking or hating liberals.

This successful vested interest deception and division of society frequently is shown through bumper stickers that say things like "Not a

Liberal". People often take pride in their conservative team, as they do in their favorite sports team. This irrational, emotional division enables a small group of wealthy citizens and corporations to continue stealing the people's wealth, power and freedom.

A major public awareness raising action needed to overcome conservative media deception involves encouraging citizens to rationally consider the endpoint of the conservative philosophy. As noted, conservative media frequently reverently discusses families, freedom and democracy. But this is not the measured and managed focus of conservative (and liberal) philosophies. Conservative media and other business allies often strongly advocate suppressing unions, weakening environmental regulations, reducing social welfare programs that benefit low and middle income families, and weakening privacy and other constitutional rights through the Traitors Act.

The slightest amount of rational thought shows the inevitable conclusion of these conservative policies. Removing labor, environmental, social and constitutional protections will not enhance average citizens and society. This conclusion only can be reached through the complete absence of rational thought. We do not have to speculate or theorize about the inevitable result of conservative policies. Reality provides the obvious answer. Conservatives and liberals have been implementing essentially the same big business-first philosophy since the 1980s. This has achieved the measured and managed focus. Wealthy citizens and large corporations did phenomenally well, while most average citizens and society overall were degraded in many ways.

Donald Trump said he would like to return the US to post-World War II prosperity levels. But he apparently is continuing the same business-first policies of the past 35 years. In the 1950s, the US had the largest middle class in the world. Most families could own a home and raise their children on a single income. Top marginal tax rates were over 90 percent. Those who benefited the most paid their fair share to support the society that enabled them to become wealthy. But Mr. Trump proposes to lower taxes on wealthy citizens and is staffing many cabinet positions with wealthy business and financial leaders. Emulating or expanding the big business-first policies of the past 35 years will not restore the middle class. The wealthy citizens who control government will continue to get wealthier, while life becomes more difficult for nearly everyone else.

This is perhaps most tragic for young people. Focusing the government, economy and society on maximizing the wealth of the already wealthy has severely degraded society. As discussed in the Poverty section, 25 to 34 year-olds are doing substantially worse than the same age group in 1989. Their median income and net worth have fallen by 20 percent and 56 percent, respectively. Millions of young adults are living with parents, saddled with high student debt, and delaying marriage and home buying. We have an obligation to help the young prosper. But by focusing on the financial returns of wealthy citizens, instead of the well-being of all citizens, we are grossly violating this obligation.

It is not rational to conclude that suppressing unions will help average citizens, reducing constitutional rights will increase freedom, or weakening environmental regulations will protect life support systems. But emotional manipulation is used to mislead conservative citizens into believing these irrational positions. This is why it is essential that citizens be encouraged to think for themselves, rather than blindly believe conservative shareholder-enhancing, society-degrading philosophies.

Republicans winning the Presidency and both houses of Congress in 2016, and probably gaining stronger control of the Judicial branch, will pose a difficult challenge for conservative media. For many years, radical conservative media has been blaming liberals for problems in society. Republicans taking over government will not solve these problems. The greater big business focus of the Republican Party almost certainly will accelerate the decline of the environment and society, and make life more difficult for average conservative and liberal citizens.

As society gets worse, it will be difficult for conservative media to continue blaming liberals for the problems in society because conservatives will control all three branches of government. With their traditional enemy weakened and society continuing to decline, conservative citizens might begin to focus on the actual causes of their increasingly difficult lives, mainly corporate welfare and business control of government. This could pose a serious challenge to the unjust status quo.

To protect their wealthy owners and other wealthy citizens, conservative media must distract attention from real problems and solutions, and focus on false enemies. As a result, conservative media almost certainly will be compelled to find ways to continue blaming liberals. With liberals out of power, it will be difficult to do this rationally. They will be compelled to use irrational arguments. As long as conservatives are manipulated into disliking liberals, emotions often will trump logic. Irrational arguments frequently will work. And society will continue to decline.

Reversing the decline of society only can be achieved by ending the war between conservatives and liberals. To facilitate this, conservatives should be encouraged to ask keys questions, such as the following. Do we want to continue fighting and hating liberals? Or do we want to implement true democracy, end corporate welfare and refocus society on doing what is best for all citizens, not just wealthy citizens? We cannot have both. The only two broad options are continuing to hate liberals and thereby remain divided and conquered, or work together to achieve the prosperous, democratic vision of our Founders.

If we want to end corporate welfare and resolve major problems, conservatives must work with liberals. There is no other option. Conservatives beating liberals will not enhance society. It will enhance the small group of wealthy citizens who control the Republican and Democratic parties. When conservative politicians win, average conservative citizens lose, in the same way that average liberal citizens lose when liberal politicians win. Average liberal and conservative citizens cannot win unless they work together.

A major way to work together is to stop using the liberal and conservative labels. These philosophies are used to block rational thought. We agree on nearly all major issues. We must stop using ignorant labels that divide us when there is little division in reality. As discussed below, the conservative and liberal labels and philosophies have so much baggage and deception attached to them that neither can be used to unite the people and resolve major problems. We must give citizens a third voting option that has a good chance of winning elections – an option that truly is focused on benefiting all citizens – a We the People option.

Stepping back and looking at the big picture (i.e. using whole system thinking) is essential for seeing beyond media deception. Being immersed in society often makes it difficult for citizens to see problems in their own country. It frequently is easier to understand problems in other countries because citizens are detached and naturally have a higher perspective.

To illustrate, it often is easier for US citizens to understand problems in China than in their own country. For example, the Chinese government sometimes temporarily moves citizens out of cities or shuts down polluting industries to improve appearances for visiting dignitaries. It is clear to people outside China that the totalitarian Chinese government frequently does whatever it wants, regardless of citizens' needs and comfort. If China actually were a People's Republic (i.e. democracy), foreign dignitaries would not be seen as more important than Chinese citizens. Citizens would be the dignitaries. Cities would be cleaned up all the time, not just when outsiders arrive. Many Chinese citizens probably accept this government disruption as a normal part of life. They perhaps do not understand that they should be at least as high a priority as foreign dignitaries, if not higher.

However, citizens in China probably often have an easier time seeing problems in the US than US citizens. As discussed in the Public Deception section, several studies have shown that Republican and Democratic politicians focus almost exclusively on meeting the needs of wealthy campaign donors. The needs and requests of average citizens have virtually no impact on politicians' voting. Business-controlled government essentially steals trillions of dollars of public wealth from average citizens every year and transfers it to the small group of wealthy citizens who control government. Vested interests divide people into debating factions. Citizens largely are focused on beating the other team/party. They are distracted from focusing on the most important problems in society, such as corporate welfare and business control of government.

Due to their broader, outside perspective, Chinese citizens probably often can more easily see that the US government largely does not serve US citizens. Stepping back and adopting a higher, whole system perspective makes it easier for citizens to see through media deception and understand problems in their own countries.

Regarding media deception, two critical actions needed to achieve honest media are reestablishing the Fairness Doctrine and expanding public media. Conservative media frequently vehemently opposes the Fairness

Doctrine. But it simply requires media to provide citizens with honest, balanced information. By opposing the Fairness Doctrine, conservative media clearly signals that it wants to continue deceiving citizens in ways that help conservative media owners and other wealthy citizens.

Regarding public media, as discussed in the Advertising, Media and Culture section, the systemically mandated goal of for-profit media companies is maximizing the wealth of media owners, not honestly informing citizens. A primary goal of public media is to benefit the public by providing honest, balanced information. As a result, expanding public media will greatly help to maximize the well-being of society and end the civil war between conservatives and liberals.

Media deception frequently manipulates citizens into supporting actions that harm them and opposing actions that help them. One would expect that politicians seeking to get elected would take actions that benefit many citizen/voters. But politicians from both major parties routinely act in ways that benefit the small group of wealthy citizens who control government, while harming nearly everyone else. Public deception enables them to get away with this harmful, unconstitutional behavior.

To protect shareholder returns, for-profit media manipulates many citizens into opposing social welfare programs that enable millions of low and middle-income citizens to meet basic needs, while implicitly supporting corporate welfare programs that transfer trillions of dollars of public wealth to wealthy citizens every year. People are misled into opposing protection of environmental systems that are essential for the survival and prosperity of humanity so that wealthy media owners can earn higher financial returns. Effective democracy cannot be achieved unless media deception is ended and citizens receive accurate information.

Religious Deception

Religious deceptions are among the most harmful in society. Like conservative media deceptions, religious deceptions perpetuate the civil war between conservatives and liberals by strongly suppressing rational thought. Religious deceptions frequently mislead good, well-meaning religious people into supporting ideas and actions that harm average citizens and society overall, but benefit the small group of wealthy citizens who are stealing the people's wealth, power and freedom. These deceptions often strongly support authoritarianism and conservative philosophies.

Religious deceptions mostly involve encouraging blind faith in religious dogma and not questioning authorities. Tragically and ironically, this dogma often is in strong opposition to religious principles and actual religious teachings. For example, in some Muslim countries, dogmatic ideas distort the peaceful religion of Islam in ways that compel believers to harm innocent citizens and nonbelievers. Similar types of deception occur with Christianity in the US. In Christianity, the primary commandment, the commandment that takes priority over all other commandments, is to love, honor and respect other people. (As discussed in the Misleading the Public section, some people argue that loving God is the number one commandment. But this is an interior commandment. In this physical world, actions count more than anything else. The physical manifestation of loving God is loving God's creation and other people. The actions of someone who claims they love God but treats other people poorly say they do not love God.)

Jesus lived a humble, modest lifestyle. Towards the end of his life, he spent nearly all of his time teaching and helping average citizens, especially needy citizens. Through his actions and words, he taught us that helping needy citizens also is a primary commandment of Christianity. And yet like the peaceful religion of Islam, the beautiful, peaceful, loving religion of Christianity often is turned into the opposite of what it was meant to be – the opposite of what Jesus taught and modeled with his life.

As noted, in the 1990s, the Democrats adopted essentially the same policies as the Republicans. They deregulated the capital markets, cut social welfare programs, expanded free trade, increased incarceration and suppressed unions. In effect, the Democrats stole the Republicans' thunder. This compelled the Republican Party to attempt to differentiate itself from Democrats on social issues, often referred to as God, guns and gays.[228]

Over the past at least 25 years, conservative/Republican leaders increasingly have aligned themselves with dogmatic Christian sects. Dogmatic Christianity essentially is the perfect partner for conservative philosophy. The stated goal of conservative philosophy might be to maximize the well-being of citizens and society. But as shown since the 1980s, the measured and managed goal of Republican (and Democratic) politicians mainly is to maximize the financial wealth of wealthy campaign donors, usually at the expense of average citizens and society. Conservatives (and to only a slightly lesser extent liberals) have substantially cut programs that benefit low and middle-income citizens, while hugely increasing corporate welfare.

Jesus displayed the greatest love to children and needy citizens. In the few cases where he got angry, it usually was at leaders who misled and abused citizens. Tragically, many dogmatic Christians have been misled into doing the opposite of what Jesus did (i.e. the opposite of Christianity). As strong supporters of the conservative/Republican party, they have facilitated policies that severely degrade the lives of millions of low and middle-income citizens (usually including themselves), while at the same time lavishing trillions of dollars of public wealth on those who abuse average citizens. In other words, they are misled into hurting the needy and supporting those who abuse the needy.

Reflecting similar anti-Christian behavior, the pomp and lavish lifestyles of some former Catholic Church leaders was the opposite of how Jesus lived. But Pope Francis is moving the church back to true Christianity by living a modest lifestyle and focusing on helping the needy.

As discussed in the Misleading the Public section, the deception of dogmatic Christians is tragic. They are among the best, most well-intentioned people in society. But their blind adherence to dogmatic ideas frequently causes them to unintentionally insult others and harm society. As noted, religious dogma, such as that related to same-sex marriage and sex outside of marriage, often conflicts with religious principles. When well-meaning dogmatic Christians attempt to force their views about sex, marriage and birth control on other citizens, they unintentionally violate the primary Christian commandment – treating others with love, honor and respect. They disrespect the privacy and rights of other citizens to make their own decisions about their lives.

Probably the vast majority of Christians are rational people who strive to live good lives and treat other people well. Being rational, they see that many biblical dogmatic ideas, such as supporting slavery and suppressing women, obviously are incorrect. As a result, they often are guided by the word of God heard in their own hearts, rather than by dogmatic religious ideas. But as in broader society, average religious citizens frequently are highly vulnerable to deception. Religious leaders often pressure followers into blindly believing dogma. Those who question it sometimes are threatened with eternal damnation. Those who do not question dogma frequently are promised eternal bliss with God in heaven.

Blind faith adherence to religious dogma strongly facilitates and perpetuates the authoritarian society functioning in the US. An excellent article by Valerie Tarico, called *6 Ways Religion Does More Bad Than Good*, summarizes problems with religious blind faith.[229] For example, dogmatic religion promotes tribalism. Believers frequently are taught that their version of God is the only true, correct version. Those with different spiritual or religious views often are seen as outsiders, treated with suspicion and sometimes considered to be the enemies of God. This dogma-induced tribalism divides and disempowers the people. It makes it easier for vested interests to steal the people's wealth, power and freedom.

One of the most harmful aspects of religious dogma is that it makes ignorance a virtue. Thinking for oneself and questioning whether dogmatic ideas help or harm society frequently is seen as sinful. People are encouraged to blindly believe in dogma and commended for this blind faith. In other words, ignorance is seen as a virtue. Not questioning religious leaders and politicians supported by these leaders is extremely beneficial to the small group of citizens who control government and society. Dogmatic Christians can be manipulated into opposing actions that benefit average citizens and society, but threaten ever-increasing shareholder returns.

As discussed in the Education section, the Christian-conservative alliance has deceived many Christian and conservative citizens into thinking that protecting the environment, for example by reducing greenhouse gas emissions, is ungodly. This is the fruit of blind faith. Saying that protecting God's creation (i.e. the environment) is unchristian is the height of idiocy. But blind faith in dogmatic religious ideas and leaders enables businesses and their allies to frequently manipulate conservative and Christian citizens into opposing protection of the life support systems that their children will need to survive.

The idea that addressing climate change and other environmental problems is ungodly mostly occurs in radical or extreme Christian sects. They are encouraged to blindly believe dogma and their frequently misguided leaders. However, most mainstream Christians understand the importance of protecting life support systems and other aspects of God's creation. The Catholic Church, for example, strongly supports environmental protection.

Religious dogma also misleads citizens and degrades society by diverting good intentions.[230] Many good, well-intentioned Christians truly want to make the world a better place. As discussed throughout this book, there are massive environmental and social problems in the US and many other countries. People literally are dying due to lack of food, healthcare, shelter and other basic necessities. The decline of our life support and social systems are the true threats to humanity. We should be focusing much of our good intentions and energy on resolving these major problems.

But instead, dogmatic Christians often focus much of their time and energy on attempting to convert people to their religious views. While done with good intentions, other people often perceive this proselytizing as offensive. It implies that Christian spiritual views are absolutely right, while other views are wrong. As discussed in Well-Being of Society section, it is impossible for the human mind to fully understand God or infinity. All interpretations of God are attempts to explain something that ultimately is incomprehensible to the human mind. Therefore, all versions of God logically should be seen only as symbolic. Debating which unprovable version of God is correct distracts energy, resources and good intentions from resolving the major issues that will determine whether humanity survives and prospers.

Another major problem with religious dogma is that it can promote helplessness.[231] Dogma often misleads Christians into believing that poverty, hunger, suffering, environmental degradation and other problems are inevitable or the 'Will of God'. But in reality, as discussed in Chapter One, nearly every major problem in society results from human ideas and actions. We created the problems and have the ability to solve them. But this empowered, reality-based view would threaten ever-increasing shareholder returns, for example, as companies were held responsible for negative impacts. Misleading Christians into believing that major problems are the will of God or inevitable parts of life on Earth enables vested interests to continue degrading the environment and society and stealing the people's wealth, power and freedom.

Dogma frequently misleads citizens into believing that all they have to do is obey dogma and accept the so-called will of God (i.e. doing what religious authorities say is the will of God, rather than listening to the word of God or intuitive wisdom in their own hearts). If they obey dogma, they will wind up in Heaven. This often misleads good, well-meaning people into accepting environmental and social problems, rather than doing something about them. We are all responsible for problems in society (either directly or indirectly through inaction). We all have a responsibility to do all we can to resolve major problems (again, directly and/or by requiring leader/servants to do so).

Dogma frequently misleads citizens into believing that suffering and problems are inevitable in this world. The good life will come after we die and go to Heaven, dogma often says or implies. Misleading Christians into thinking that problems are inevitable enables businesses to continue maximizing shareholder returns by degrading the environment and society. But most problems in society are not inevitable. We have the (perhaps) God-given gifts of rational thought and intuitive wisdom. We can use these gifts to resolve our problems, reach our fullest potential and create Heaven on Earth here and now.

Misleading citizens into thinking that the good life begins when we die is like a cruel practical joke. People are manipulated into enduring a degraded society and unnecessary suffering for their entire lives. We have an obligation to our children, future generations and ourselves to set dogma aside and use our powers of rational thought and intuitive wisdom. As discussed in the Time Value of Money section, virtually all religions say that the quality of the afterlife depends on the quality of this life. If we create hell on Earth by allowing the degradation of environmental and social systems, why should we expect Heaven in the afterlife? If we want Heaven after we die, we must create it here and now.

Religious dogma further degrades society by frequently stating or implying that life is difficult and humans are inherently flawed. In an authoritarian society, such as the US, many people must be compelled to do things they do not want to do so that a small group of wealthy citizens can get continuously wealthier. Convincing people that life is inherently difficult (the good life comes after you die) often encourages people to take boring, difficult jobs, endure boring education and do other things they do not want to do. Convincing people that they are inherently flawed also facilitates authoritarianism. It encourages citizens to not expect much from life. They should gladly accept the boring, low paying jobs and other crumbs thrown to them by authorities because this is all they deserve.

Another harmful and deceptive aspect of religious dogma relates to the frequent conflict between religious principles and religious dogma. As discussed, religious principles are absolute truths and laws of nature. They include treating others with kindness, love and respect, helping the needy, and protecting the environment and all life. These principles essentially are the same for all religions. However, dogmatic religious ideas are not absolute truths. They frequently vary between religions. The deception and harm occurs when religions portray their dogmatic ideas as if they were absolute spiritual truths or laws.

Sex provides a good example of this. Christian dogma often says that sex only should occur among married people. Sex outside of marriage frequently is said to be sinful and harmful. This dogmatic idea is not based on reality. Promoting it often violates absolute spiritual truths, such as treating others with kindness, love and respect. The dogmatic opposition to sex outside of marriage results from good intentions. The goal probably is to protect people from harmful sex. But the premise is not rational. The implication is that, because some sex outside of marriage is harmful, it all is. This of course is incorrect.

As discussed in the Population section, many people's lives are greatly enhanced by sex outside of marriage. Sex is powerful and could be harmful, in the same way that eating can be harmful if it is done excessively. But sex is a biological imperative. It is not innately harmful. Labeling sex outside of marriage as universally sinful or harmful is arbitrary, irrational and incorrect. People should discern what is right for them. Saying or implying that someone else's nonharmful sex ideas and activities are wrong violates the supreme commandment to treat others with kindness and respect.

Reflecting cultural and religious differences, for thousands of years, in many parts of Asia, sex outside of marriage was seen as beautiful and sacred, not sinful. Among Hindus, sex often was seen as a way to reach a high spiritual state or Divine connection. Tantra combines elements of Buddhism and Hinduism. It provides a way to reach spiritual enlightenment through sex. In several cultures, homosexual behavior was accepted and respected, rather than stigmatized.[232]

The dogmatic Christian idea that sex outside of marriage is sinful unintentionally degrades society. It often makes people feel ashamed or guilty about natural desires and activities. This dogmatically-induced shame and guilt about natural feelings produces many harmful outcomes in society. As discussed in the Men's section, it contributes to increased sex crimes, problems in relationships, and sex and pornography addiction.

Blindly believing dogma is intellectually easy. But it often degrades life by cutting people off from the actual word of God (or intuitive wisdom) heard within. As discussed in Chapter Four, discerning inner wisdom can be difficult. At first, people might mistake their fears and flawed ideas for true intuitive wisdom. But seeking intuitive wisdom is worth the effort. It ultimately is the only way to live a truly successful, satisfying, authentic and meaningful life. Raising public awareness about religious deception includes encouraging people to have the courage to go beyond dogma, find their own truth within and live authentic lives.

One of the most harmful religious deceptions involves misleading citizens into thinking that anti-Christian ideas are Christian. For example, many conservative Christians have been misled into believing that free market capitalism and the ideas in the book *Atlas Shrugged* are consistent with Christianity. But they strongly violate fundamental Christian principles. Free market capitalism largely involves removing regulations that protect average citizens, the environment and society, but interfere with ever-increasing shareholder returns. This frequently harms the needy and God's creation, while strongly benefiting the wealthy. This is the opposite of what Jesus taught. As discussed in the Education section, *Atlas Shrugged* promotes helping oneself and not helping others. This selfish neglect of the needy also obviously is not what Jesus taught.

As Christians are misled into believing that anti-Christian ideas are Christian, life often becomes more difficult for low and middle-income citizens (including Christians). This increases fear in society and makes people more vulnerable to deception by vested interests. They frequently are told that the main problems in society result from lack of morality and godliness. The solution in large part is to force moral ideas, such as those related to sex, marriage and birth control, on society. But this makes society less godly because it violates the highest Christian commandment. Instead of focusing on the actual causes of their increasingly difficult lives (i.e. corporate welfare and business control of government), citizens are misled into trying to control how women use their bodies or which adults are allowed to marry.

Several studies have shown that the most peaceful, prosperous and equitable countries are the least religious.[233] In countries with strong fundamentalist, dogmatic religion, citizens often seem to be conditioned to accept the declining state of society as inevitable or God's will. The emphasized solution often is to impose religious dogma on all citizens and make the country more 'godly'. This acceptance of degradation and avoiding real problems enables a small group of wealthy citizens to continue stealing the people's wealth, power and freedom.

But in more equitable and truly prosperous countries, such as in Western Europe, people do not accept inequality and degradation. They do not blindly trust authorities who steal their wealth and power. They use rational, reality-based thinking to focus on problems and develop effective solutions, such as implementing a strong social safety net that guarantees a decent standard of living for all citizens.

Our Founders also used rational, reality-based thinking. This country was formed during the Age of Enlightenment and Reason. The Founders strongly opposed blind faith in Christian and other dogma, while strongly supporting rational, enlightened problem solving. They used rational thought to develop a new, better form of government that guaranteed citizens the freedom to live according to their own religious and moral ideas.

From the 1940s to the 1970s, Christian fundamentalism was not a strong political force in the US. It remains a weak political force in Western Europe, Canada, Australia and other equitable democracies.[234] But in the

1980s, as the focus of the US switched from helping all citizens to helping wealthy citizens, life became more difficult for average citizens. When people are afraid and desperate, they are more vulnerable to deception. They are more likely to believe authorities who say that radical, fundamentalist solutions are needed, as occurred in Germany before World War II.

As life became more difficult for average citizens since the 1980s, fundamentalist, dogmatic Christianity became a more powerful political force in the US. The growing fundamentalist Christian dominance of the Republican Party facilitates ever-increasing shareholder returns. It misleads citizens into focusing on imposing dogma on others (i.e. related to same-sex marriage and abortion) instead of focusing on major problems (corporate welfare and business control of government).

Perhaps most tragically, as fundamentalist Christians gained greater control of the US government, our society became less Christian. In a truly Christian society, we would not allow children to go hungry, while essentially using the public wealth to buy mansions for billionaires.

Establishing a truly Christian nation requires doing what our Founders said and did. We should base our society on fundamental Christian principles, such as helping the needy and protecting the environment. We also should abide by our Constitution and guarantee religious freedom for all. We should not violate the primary Christian commandment by trying to impose religious dogma related to sex, marriage, birth control and other issues on citizens. Attempting to impose religious dogma on people violates our Constitution. It makes the US like Muslim countries that suppress religious freedom by making Sharia law the law of the land.

The hypocrisy and deception of the conservative-fundamentalist Christian coalition is shown by anti-Sharia laws in the US. Several Republican politicians have promoted anti-Sharia bills that prohibit the establishment of Sharia law in the US. This is hypocritical in the sense that the same politicians often violate our Constitution by attempting to make Christian dogma the law of the land. However, the greater problem with anti-Sharia laws is public deception. Less than one percent of US citizens are Muslim. Probably the vast majority of Muslims in the US would strongly oppose replacing the Constitution and US laws with

Sharia laws. The 99 percent of non-Muslims in the US also obviously would strongly oppose it.

In other words, there is virtually no chance that Sharia law could be established in the US. In the extremely unlikely event that a community with a large Muslim population attempted to implement Sharia law, it would be struck down for violating the First Amendment. It is absolutely ridiculous that politicians waste taxpayer money by debating and passing anti-Sharia laws. It is similar to passing laws that say elephants are not allowed to sprout wings and fly. Anti-Sharia laws well illustrate how business-controlled politicians use religious deceptions to mislead the public and protect their wealthy benefactors. Citizens are emotionally manipulated into focusing on religious issues, such as imposing religious dogma on others (i.e. violating true Christianity and the US Constitution), instead of focusing on how a small group of wealthy citizens are stealing the people's wealth, power and freedom.

Another example of religious deception involves so-called religious freedom laws. Republican politicians in several states are aggressively promoting laws that allow businesses to discriminate against lesbian and gay people. Proponents of the laws argue that forcing business owners to serve customers who are living a lifestyle with which they disagree violates religious freedom. This is a perfect example of abusing the Christian name by labeling anti-Christian activities as Christian. It is another example of how our country is becoming less Christian as dogmatic Christians gain greater political influence.

As discussed, the primary commandment of Christianity is to love, honor and respect others. Christians are not supposed to judge anyone. Instead, they are supposed to treat everyone with kindness and respect. Opposition to same-sex activities largely is a Christian issue. Enshrining this dogmatic religious idea into law violates the First Amendment by establishing Christian dogma in the legal code. The First Amendment prohibits passing laws that establish religion. Prohibiting discrimination does not interfere with business owners' ability to freely exercise their religion. It is ridiculous to suggest that treating people kindly and fairly violates Christianity. The opposite is true. Discrimination violates Christianity. Deceptively named religious freedom laws violate the primary commandment of Christianity and nearly all other religions.

These laws would be more accurately named anti-Christianity laws or pro-discrimination laws.

But the key issue with anti-Christianity laws such as these is not discrimination. It is public deception. Pro-discrimination laws are like anti-Sharia laws because they distract public attention from more important issues, such as corporate welfare and business control of government. Hateful, anti-Christian laws masquerading as Christianity divide the people. This keeps citizens deluded and perpetuates the unjust status quo. So-called religious freedom laws usually are promoted by Republicans. This further reflects the big business focus of the Republican Party. Religious deceptions are used to divide the people and protect shareholder returns.

In summary, raising public awareness is one of the most important actions needed to end the civil war between conservatives and liberals, unite the people and establish true democracy in the US. Citizens must be made aware of conservative, liberal, Christian and other deceptions that are used to divide and disempower the people, and thereby protect the status quo of corporate welfare and business control of government.

We the People Political Party

Establishing a We the People political party will greatly benefit the US and help to align our political system with the intentions of our Founders. Some people have said that the Founders were wealthy white men who, in writing the Constitution, were mainly focused on protecting their personal interests. This is incorrect. James Madison, Benjamin Franklin, George Washington, John Adams, Thomas Jefferson, James Wilson and other leading Founders had a sense of destiny. They knew that there were few examples of true democracy in the history of civilization. They were trying to alter the course of human history by developing a new and better form of government, a true democracy that would be a model for the rest of the world.[235]

The Founders were not trying to protect their interests by establishing plutocracy. In many ways, they went against their financial interests. James Madison's notes from the Constitutional Convention were not released until 1840, after the last delegate passed away. Part of the reason for this probably was that he did not want to reveal that wealthy delegates were betraying their economic class by establishing democracy instead of plutocracy.[236]

The Founders began our Constitution with the words, "We the People". They did not write, we the wealthy people. As shown by the Preamble words "promote the general Welfare", the Founders' primary focus and purpose was to maximize the well-being of all current and especially future citizens. In discussing the Constitutional Convention, George Washington said, "In all our deliberations on this subject we kept steadily in our view, that which appears to us the greatest interest of every true American, the consolidation of our Union, in which is involved our prosperity, felicity, safety, perhaps our national existence." His "most ardent wish" was that the Constitution "may promote the lasting welfare of that country so dear to us all, and secure her freedom and happiness..."[237] The US government was intended to be the trustee and protector of the people's common wealth, property and destiny. It was intended to protect our natural rights and vast areas of common interest.

The Founders well understood the extreme threat that concentrated wealth posed to democracy. Thomas Jefferson said, "an enormous proportion of property vested in a few individuals is dangerous to the rights, and destructive of the common happiness of mankind, and, therefore, every free state hath a right by its laws to discourage the possession of such property."[238] Thomas Jefferson did not mean that there should be no wealthy people. Rather he probably meant that, in a democracy, the people have a right to establish controls which ensure that society's wealth is used fairly. This essentially means that as people take or receive more wealth from society (i.e. become wealthier), they have an obligation to give more back. The people have a right to establish labor and other protections which ensure that wealthy citizens do not extract unfair amounts of wealth from society.

Our Constitution was intended in part to prevent vested interest abuse of the people by giving all eligible voters an equal say in government. Beyond our Constitution, the Founders and early US leaders took several other steps to protect citizens from abuses by concentrated wealth, including severely restricting the power of corporations.

But as discussed in the Political Parties section, vested interests used political parties to overcome democracy protections established by our Founders. In his Farewell Address, George Washington strongly warned us about political parties. He called them the worst enemy of elected government. Political parties have done what George Washington warned they might do. They have divided the people and fostered a spirit of division, hatred and revenge in society. This division disempowers the people. It enables wealthy citizens to replace democracy with plutocracy. Political parties and other factors essentially have ended democracy in the US. If political parties truly represented the people, they might have facilitated democracy. But as discussed extensively, both major political parties largely are controlled by a small group of wealthy citizens. They control the agendas of both parties. They ensure that both parties are primarily focused on benefiting wealthy citizens, not all citizens, as our Constitution requires.

The battle between the two major political parties is a sham that has existed since the founding of the US. We the People agree on nearly all major issues. But we have been turned against each other by vested interests who play us like finely tuned instruments. We have been deceived into not working together on our massive common interests, most importantly protecting our children and future generations.

Probably the large majority of citizens have been deceived into thinking that the most important action needed to achieve a prosperous society is to beat the other party (Republicans or Democrats). A whole system perspective shows the pure idiocy of this position. Putting conservatives or liberals in power will not solve our major problems. It will maintain the status quo. Conservatives and liberals will continue to transfer trillions of dollars of public wealth to the small group that controls the Republican and Democratic parties. As discussed above, several studies have shown that Republican and Democratic politicians focus almost completely on serving wealthy campaign donors. The requests and needs of average citizens have virtually no impact on politicians' voting.

As part of a We the People movement and party, politicians' voting records should be tracked and publicized. Several organizations already track voting on environmental and other issues. But many citizens are not aware of this information. Voting in ways that help wealthy campaign donors but harm average citizens only can be sustained through lack of public awareness. This darkness cannot survive in the light.

Media often focuses on and rewards politicians for party line voting. Instead, the emphasis should be on how voting impacts average citizens. For example, average conservative citizens often vote for Republican politicians who reduce taxes on wealthy citizens. Not requiring these citizens to support the society that enabled them to become wealthy harms average citizens. It often raises their taxes and causes underfunding of education, infrastructure and other critical areas. Publicizing the extent to which politicians vote to support wealthy campaign donors versus average citizens will compel them to do their jobs – serve all citizens equally and fairly.

Nearly all Republican and Democratic politicians are mainly focused on helping large companies and wealthy campaign donors. But this focus usually is even stronger among Republicans. This is well illustrated by the Tennessee public utility example noted above. Mainly Republicans passed laws that limit the ability of public utilities to compete with private sector companies in 20 states. When the FCC ruled in favor of public broadband utilities in Tennessee and North Carolina, Republicans attempted to remove the FCC's authority on this issue.[239] As noted, public utilities in Tennessee and other states frequently provide faster Internet access at lower prices. As a result, many municipalities are seeking to adopt similar strategies.

Republican efforts to block this shows the true focus of the Republican Party. If Republicans truly were focused on maximizing the well-being of citizens and society, they would support whatever option provides citizens with the highest quality service at the lowest cost, regardless of whether the service is provided by the public or private sector. But the focus of Republicans (and Democrats) who accept large amounts of money from wealthy citizens and companies is not to maximize the well-being of all citizens. It is to maximize the wealth of wealthy campaign donors.

To hide this focus, Republicans used several deceptive arguments. For example, some Republican politicians argued that municipal broadband utilities have failed and cost taxpayers money. Some have. But the vast majority have been successful. Also, the argument ignores the fact that many largely ratepayer-funded private telecommunications companies failed.

The most irrational and even ridiculous argument made by Republicans is that public utilities have an unfair advantage over the private sector. Therefore, the public sector should not be allowed to compete with the private sector. This is ridiculous. These business puppets essentially are arguing that citizens should pay higher prices for lower quality services. If the public sector has a competitive advantage, citizens should take advantage of it and get services from the public sector.

Republican puppets imply that the shareholder returns of telecommunication companies should take priority over the well-being of citizens (i.e. they are violating the Constitution). As discussed, public utilities and other public entities are not hindered by the requirement to provide ever-increasing shareholder returns. Private telecommunications companies secured billions of dollars of rate increases and promised to deliver high quality Internet services. But as shown by poor performance relative to other developed countries, this performance often did not materialize. Ratepayer funds frequently were used to increase shareholder returns instead of investing in infrastructure. Public utilities do not have to siphon off ratepayer funds to increase shareholder returns. As a result, they frequently can provide higher quality at lower costs.

Privatizing Medicare also shows the true focus of the Republican Party. Many Republican politicians promote privatizing parts of Medicare. As discussed in the Healthcare section, this inevitably will increase costs, lower coverage and reduce quality, as occurred in the broader US healthcare sector when it largely shifted to a for-profit approach in the 1970s. Every other developed country proves that the public sector can provide far lower cost, far better coverage and frequently superior results. As noted above, a recent study found that the US had the worst healthcare system in the developed world, while the UK had the best. If Republican politicians truly were focused on providing citizens with the highest quality healthcare at the lowest cost, they would promote what every other developed country proves is the most effective approach. But the true focus of Republican (and Democratic) politicians is not on maximizing the well-being of all citizens. It is on maximizing the financial returns of wealthy campaign donors.

Right-to-work laws also illustrate the true focus of the Republican Party. As discussed, these laws mainly are promoted by Republican politicians. They greatly weaken unions, and thereby enable businesses to force down wages and abuse labor in other ways. As noted, the term right-to-work law is deceptive and dishonest. More accurate and honest names for these laws include right-to-abuse, labor abuse or union dismantling laws.

Attempts to sell public lands further illustrate the big business focus of the Republican Party. Many Republican politicians strongly advocate selling off public lands or transferring control to states (which would allow Republican-controlled states to sell of the lands).[240] Public lands represent a major component of the common wealth. The federal government is supposed to hold these lands and other assets in trust for future generations. But the requirement to maximize shareholder returns takes priority over all else in our myopic, suicidal systems. Therefore, business-controlled political puppets violate their oath to uphold the Constitution and protect future generations. Instead of closing budget deficits by requiring wealthy campaign donors to pay fair taxes, they sell off the people's property to wealthy corporations and citizens, often for far less than full, fair value.

Opposing the expansion of low-cost public utilities, supporting labor abuse laws, selling off public lands, and thousands of other examples show that the primary focus of the Republican Party is on helping wealthy campaign donors. As noted, the Democrats are only slightly less focused on this. Only Republicans and Democrats usually have a chance of winning elections. This system provides average citizens with two options – horrible or slightly less horrible.

A main reason why the Democrats are slightly better than the Republicans (from the perspective of average citizens) relates to the Supreme Court. As discussed in the Judicial Branch section, Republican politicians appointed radical pro-business justices. These justices violated the Constitution in ways that support those who paid to appoint them. They ignored the preamble to the Second Amendment, violated the First Amendment and Founders' intentions by allowing public funding of religious education, and voided campaign finance laws that prevented wealthy citizens and corporations from controlling elections and government. Regarding the Supreme Court, average citizens are better off voting Democrat. But overall, Democratic politicians, like Republicans, mainly will continue to focus primarily on benefiting wealthy campaign donors.

Perpetuating the conservative-liberal war inevitably will degrade society. Greater division and deception will be needed to extract ever-increasing amounts of wealth from a continuously declining middle class and society. Illustrating this growing division, 47 Republican senators wrote a letter to the Iranian government that sought to undermine President Obama's negotiations on nuclear power and weapons. This unprecedented Congressional action violated the President's constitutional authority to conduct foreign policy.[241] This type of fracturing and ineffectiveness of the US government inevitably will get worse under the current two-party system.

As discussed, since the 1990s, the Democrats essentially have been implementing the pro-big business conservative philosophy. Attempting to beat the Republicans or Democrats is a deception because both parties largely are implementing the same approach. The inevitable result of the Republican or Democratic strategy will be ongoing decline and possible collapse of society. The economy and stock market might be going up. But essentially all benefits of this growth are going to a small group of wealthy citizens. Good jobs often are being replaced with poor jobs. Wages frequently are nearly flat while living expenses rise rapidly. The middle class continues to decline.

If we want to halt the degradation of society, we must change our systems. The first priority is to unite. We the People must work together. Republicans or Democrats acting alone cannot reverse the decline of society. Under current campaign finance and other systems, the two parties cannot shift their focus from benefiting wealthy citizens to benefiting all citizens. Both parties have too much baggage. Division and hatred are too strong between the parties. The people cannot be united under either party. Many Republicans never will work with Democrats, and vice versa.

To reverse the decline of the US middle class and overall society, we must give citizens a voting option that truly is focused on maximizing the well-being of all citizens. The ultimate solution is to heed President Washington's advice and weaken the political party system. But this could take some time. Millions of US citizens and families are suffering unnecessarily. Immediate action is needed to end this suffering and destitution. Probably the fastest way to do this is to establish a third political party that unites the people and has the ability to win elections.

As noted, the tagline of this party could be – Uniting on our massive common ground, building bridges on the rest. The party could be called "We the People". Parties called the "People's Party" existed in the US in the 1890s and 1970s. Both were defeated by Republicans and Democrats. The term "We the People" is more inclusive and personal. It says to every person (Republican, Democrat, African American, white, rich, poor), "I" am a member of this party.

The party could be referred to as a Second Enlightenment party. Democratic and especially Republican politicians often appear to suppress rational thought and mislead the public by promoting blind faith adherence to irrational philosophies. The We the People party and movement would strongly promote rational, objective, critical freethinking. Major problems and solutions would be rationally and objectively analyzed and addressed.

As President Washington encouraged, the We the People party could be based on natural laws and religious principles. Differing views would be respected and welcomed. The party would be largely focused on treating others with kindness, love and respect, helping the needy, and protecting the environment and all life.

There are many small political parties in the US. Some are established or supported by wealthy citizens. These parties often appear to be focused on perpetuating divisions in society and ever-increasing shareholder returns. However, other smaller political parties are focused on protecting the environment and/or all citizens. A We the People party possibly could be formed from a combination of these types of parties. Or it could be established as a new political party.

In terms of funding, the ultimate solution is to prohibit giving money to politicians (i.e. bribery) by implementing full public funding of political campaigns and elections. But prior to this system change, all contributions to the We the People party should go into a blind fund that makes it impossible for We the People politicians to know who contributed and how much they gave. Some wealthy citizens in the US understand that current shareholder-focused systems unfairly concentrate wealth and should be changed. A truly blind contribution system would enable wealthy citizens to support the We the People party without giving them unfair influence.

Unlike the Republican and Democratic parties, governance of the We the People party would be Democratic. As discussed in the Political Parties section, average citizens have nearly no influence on the agendas and other activities of the Republican and Democratic parties. Both are nearly completely controlled by wealthy campaign donors. Democratic governance mechanisms would be established in the We the People party to ensure that citizens who join the party have equal ability to influence its agenda and activities.

If the people approved, an optimal initial agenda of the We the People party would be to focus on the primary goals of our Founders – establishing democracy and promoting the general welfare. As noted, establishing democracy is critical because this enables all other necessary system changes. Without democracy, a small group of wealthy citizens and large corporations will continue to steal the people's wealth, power and freedom.

Establishing democracy requires implementing the many political system changes discussed in this book. As discussed in the Judicial Branch section, one of the most important and fastest possible changes (because no constitutional amendments are needed) is to impose term limits on the Judicial branch and remove its unconstitutional power of judicial review. The Founders did not intend to give an unelected, lifetime-appointed branch absolute, irrevocable authority over the two elected branches and all citizens of the US. The people are the absolute highest authority in the US, not Supreme Court justices.

Once the government is converted from plutocracy to democracy, we can systematically, efficiently and quickly refocus the US government, economy and society on promoting the general welfare. We the People will end the unfair theft of our wealth through corporate welfare. Instead, we will use the public wealth to equally and fairly benefit all citizens, in large part by establishing a strong social safety net and an economy that is focused on providing excellent jobs, abundant small business ownership opportunities and high-quality, low-cost products and services.

As discussed, the first political party, the Federalist Party, was established by bankers and businessmen in the early 1790s. The political party system has been used ever since to divide the people and steal their wealth and power. The Founders absolutely did not intend this. This is not the government established in our Constitution. We the People are the ultimate authority established in the Constitution. The Founders clearly intended to establish democracy (through republican government) in the US.

Democracy was greatly weakened in the 1790s when political parties were established. As discussed in the Judicial Branch section, democracy essentially was ended in 1803 by the Supreme Court case *Marbury v. Madison*. The US essentially never has been a democracy. We the People have allowed ourselves to be deceived into giving up our power to rule ourselves for virtually all of US history.

Now, it is time to change history. Our Founders intended to make history by establishing true democracy. But concentrated wealth quickly subverted their goals. It is time to put an end to this suppression of democracy. It is time to wake the sleeping giant – We the People. United, we can have the beautiful democracy that our Founders envisioned, intended and attempted to establish. It is all there in our Constitution. All we have to do is stand up, work together and demand what our Founders intended – democracy.

Activism

Activism is a critical component of a We the People movement and political party. Activism is the opposite of inertia. If We the People continue to think, say and do the same things (i.e. perpetuate the conservative-liberal civil war), we will get the same results – ongoing degradation of society. Activism involves fighting inertia. It is the opposite of taking the easy way out. Activism often requires courage and hard work. But doing what one believes is right and trying to make a difference in the world is worth the effort. It frequently produces a truly successful and satisfying life. As one nears the end of their life, having engaged in activism often produces the sense of a life well lived.

Activism can include nearly any activity that one believes will improve the lives of others, their community, their country or the world. People can engage in activism by taking certain types of jobs, working with NGOs, participating in demonstrations and protests, buying environmentally and socially responsible products and services, or working at home by making calls, sending e-mails or engaging in online activities. Broadly defined, activism can include revolutions and other large-scale efforts to improve the human condition. Throughout history, activism has hugely benefited humanity. Our country, the United States, is the fruit of activism.

While activism often is hugely beneficial, it also can be ineffective, or even destructive. The civil war between conservatives and liberals is one of the best examples of destructive activism. Many conservatives and liberals passionately spend their time and energy trying to beat the other party. But as discussed extensively, this makes society worse. It perpetuates the status quo of corporate welfare and business control of government. Vested interests are manipulating millions of people into wasting their time on activism that has the opposite result of what they intend. Their goal is to improve society by beating the liberals or conservatives. But they make society worse.

Massive amounts of good intentions, time, energy and money are being wasted on beating the other side. Reversing the degradation of society requires that we reverse the focus of activism in the US and many other countries. The huge focus on dividing society (by beating the other side) must be shifted to uniting society. That is the purpose of the We the People movement – to unite the people and empower them to promote the general welfare.

We cannot expect Republican and Democratic politicians to work together because this often would hurt the wealthy citizens and corporations who give them large amounts of money. Keeping the people divided enables the ongoing theft of their wealth, power and freedom. Therefore, it is highly likely that many Republican and Democratic politicians will continue to fight each other, rather than working together to promote the general welfare. They frequently will be forced to make irrational, destructive arguments when necessary to protect shareholder returns. Their focus often is not on being rational and protecting society.

It is on protecting the financial wealth of those who paid to put them in office.

However, average citizens are not under the direct control of wealthy campaign donors. They are free to think for themselves and do what they believe is right. Therefore, the early focus of the We the People movement should be on raising awareness among citizens and uniting them, instead of uniting politicians. Once We the People are united, we can compel business-controlled politicians to abide by the Constitution by serving all citizens equally and fairly.

To raise awareness and unite citizens, many types of activism are needed within the We the People movement. A major focus must be on forming alliances with traditional opponents, such as conservatives and liberals. Uniting the people probably is the most important type of activism because it makes nearly everything else possible. As discussed, when a large enough percentage of the population demands change, it will happen. Vested interests and their puppet government will not be able to stop We the People. Our government will be forced to do its duty and abide by the Constitution.

We the People activism should include exposing how vested interests manipulate, divide and disempower citizens. Darkness cannot survive in the light. Business-controlled media pulls the wool over citizens' eyes. We must counter this with honest media and other information sources that pull the curtains back on public deception.

People often work together during times of crisis. But this propensity to unite is being thwarted by public deception. Exposing the lies (i.e. poor people mainly are responsible for high taxes and the decline of the middle class) will help citizens to see the true causes and ultimate solutions to major problems in society. We must help people to see our massive common ground. We should find ways to build a community of citizens at all levels of society. We should respect and listen to each other. We also should help people to understand that, although they might disagree on abortion and a few other issues, they agree and can work together on many other issues, such as protecting life support systems, establishing democracy and ending corporate welfare.

We must find ways to overcome the forces that divide us. Vested interests are masters at manipulation and division. For example, business-controlled media frequently divides the people by turning those trying to protect the environment against those trying to protect labor. They might argue that blocking a pipeline to protect the environment, for example, would inhibit job creation. We must model and help citizens to use rational thought much more extensively. The flaws of vested interest arguments usually become obvious when people think for themselves, rather than blindly believe the deceptions. To illustrate, the idea that protecting the environment will inhibit job creation is ridiculous. The implication is that we only can have jobs if we destroy our life support systems. But as discussed in the Climate Change section, protecting the environment will create far more high-quality jobs than destroying it.

Effectively uniting the people under a We the People movement requires a major shift in focus. The enemies of society must be redefined. The enemies are not liberal or conservative leaders and citizens. The true enemies are flawed ideas and systems that compel good, well-intentioned people to take actions that degrade society. The focus of the We the People movement and political party is not to defeat the conservatives or liberals. It is to unite the people, protect their common interests, and defeat the true enemies of society.

However, it is not necessary to unite all the people. Many conservatives and liberals are so emotionally invested in their views that they will not be able to think rationally and see through vested interest deceptions. But this is irrelevant. Once enough people unite and begin to change society, those with rigid views often will go along. They will see the goals that conservatives and liberals discussed but never achieved finally coming to fruition.

The primary goals of We the People activism probably should be establishing democracy and promoting the general welfare. The second goal broadly includes all of the systemic and other changes discussed in this book. As part of promoting the general welfare, critical We the People activism objectives should include protecting life support systems, enhancing unions and labor, guaranteeing economic and political freedom for all citizens, and empowering the UN to enforce a global Bill of Rights.

Activism can take many forms. These include protests, one-on-one activism and inner activism. These are discussed in the following sections.

Protests

Demonstrations and protests frequently are an important and necessary component of activism. This type of activism probably would be used periodically by a We the People movement. Protests could help to unite the people, in part by raising public awareness about the destructive, vested interest-manufactured war between conservatives and liberals.

The First Amendment guarantees citizens' right to peacefully assemble and petition the government for a redress of grievances (i.e. peacefully protest). Protests have been a main factor driving large-scale positive change throughout US and world history. They have played a pivotal role in hugely beneficial changes in the US, including ending slavery, allowing women to vote, providing safe working conditions and fair wages, reducing discrimination, guaranteeing civil rights, protecting the environment and ending the Vietnam War.

However, as discussed in the Privacy section, protests often appear to be less effective since the 1980s than they were before then. This mainly is because large companies and their wealthy owners and allies have become masters at misleading the public and suppressing anything that threatens ever-increasing shareholder returns, including protests. The main public deception strategy is to divide the public into debating, acrimonious factions. When this occurs, conservatives often will not care what liberals protest about, and vice versa. This division inhibits the formation of large majorities that have the power to change the unjust status quo.

Conservative media frequently denigrates liberal or progressive protest movements, such as Occupy Wall Street (OWS). As conservatives were manipulated into disliking or hating liberals, brutal police suppression of OWS and other more liberal citizens often was tolerated, and sometimes even commended by conservatives.

The difference in police treatment of OWS and Tea Party protests mainly results from the different focus of the two movements. As discussed in the Privacy section, OWS protesters often were brutally suppressed with extensive police force. Tea Party and other conservative protesters sometimes carried guns, attacked immigrant buses and took other threatening actions. But they rarely, if ever, were treated harshly by police. News footage sometimes showed police pleasantly speaking with armed protesters, as if they were brothers in arms.

This essentially is what they were. That is why Tea Party and other conservative protesters generally are not suppressed by police. As noted, liberals and conservatives are misled in different ways. Liberal politicians often discuss important issues, but then do little about them. Conservative politicians, on the other hand, frequently ignore major issues, such as corporate welfare and environmental and social degradation. Instead, they mislead citizens into focusing on less expensive issues, such as abuse of social welfare programs. In other words, conservative citizens frequently are misled into focusing their anger and protests on low-income citizens, minorities and immigrants, instead of on the small group of wealthy citizens and corporations who are stealing their wealth, power and freedom.

They also are manipulated into attacking 'big government'. These deceptions facilitate removing regulations and programs that protect low and middle-income citizens, but threaten ever-increasing shareholder returns. Good, well-meaning, middle class conservative citizens are manipulated into attacking and opposing programs that protect the middle class and society overall.

As a result, the Tea Party and other conservative protest movements, not only often represent no threat to the unjust status quo of corporate welfare and business control of government. They protect it. Police are controlled by politicians, who are controlled by wealthy campaign donors. The job of police mainly is to protect the wealthy citizens who control police. Tea Party and other conservative protesters also protect wealthy citizens because they have been deceived into opposing protections for average citizens, while largely ignoring corporate welfare and business control of government. In effect, police and conservative protesters are brothers in arms. They are forced or manipulated into serving the same master – the small group of wealthy citizens who steal their wealth, power and freedom.

OWS and other more progressive protest movements challenge corporate welfare and business control of government. They represent a substantial threat to the status quo and ever-increasing shareholder returns. As a result, business-controlled government often directs police to brutally suppress them. If Tea Party and other conservative protesters begin to challenge the main factors degrading average citizens and society, they probably will get the same brutal police oppression as OWS.

Conservative and liberal protests often seem to have little impact. As noted, conservative protesters usually are misled into not focusing on major issues. Liberal protesters often focus on major issues. But business-controlled government directs police to brutally suppress them, and conservatives frequently do not seem to mind. To have effective protests in the US, protests that change the unjust status quo, We the People must unite. Liberals and conservatives working together on their massive common interests will be an unstoppable force.

As discussed above, uniting the people requires exposing public deception, especially among conservatives. They often are misled into thinking that prohibiting abortion and same-sex marriage and reducing government regulations are main actions needed to create a prosperous society. But these conclusions are not rational. They result from emotional manipulation and suppressing rational thought. We must encourage all citizens to rationally think for themselves and see through vested interest deceptions.

To illustrate seeing through deception, a recent study ranked the happiest, most prosperous countries in the world. The study analyzed factors including life expectancy, GDP per person, social support, generosity, freedom to make life choices and lower perceptions of corruption. The top ten countries in descending order were Denmark, Norway, Switzerland, Netherlands, Sweden, Canada, Finland, Austria, Iceland and Australia.[242] These countries did not have the happiest, most prosperous citizens because they prohibited abortion and same sex marriage and limited government regulations. They were the happiest and most prosperous largely because they used the public wealth to equally and fairly benefit all citizens.

In addition, equitable and prosperous countries seem to more effectively implement the religious principles of treating others with kindness, love and respect and caring for the needy. As noted above, more successful countries usually are less religious. Blind faith in religious dogma can compel citizens to accept problems and injustices in society, rather than resolve them. People in countries that are not hobbled by blind faith in religious dogma use their gifts of rational thought and intuitive wisdom to maximize the well-being of citizens and society.

Conservative politicians often discuss the importance of family and children. But it is very difficult for millions of low and middle-income families to raise children in the US. And the situation is rapidly getting worse. Conservative citizens are misled into thinking that the main assaults on US families include abortion, same-sex marriage and government regulations. But rational thought shows this to be false. The main factors making it difficult to raise children in the US include the high cost of childcare, lack of paid maternity leave, declining public education, stagnant wages, declining unions, the high cost of healthcare and college, and sending high-quality jobs overseas.[243]

To reverse the decline of the middle class and restore true prosperity in the US, liberals and conservatives must begin to work together on these and other major problems and solutions. We must not let disagreement in some areas prevent us from working together on our many common interests.

As conservatives and liberals begin to work together and protest against corporate welfare and other major problems, business-controlled politicians almost certainly will direct police to severely suppress protesters, in the same way OWS was suppressed. To protect themselves and maximize their effectiveness, protesters should understand how business-controlled government suppresses protests. This will enable them to act in ways that minimize the ability of vested interests to defeat them.

As discussed in the Privacy section, one of the most effective ways to suppress protests is to turn public attention away from the message or issue being protested. Dividing the people into vengeful, hateful factions facilitates this distraction. When vested interests divide society, one group (i.e. conservatives or liberals) often blindly believes any negative things said about the other group. As a result, their attention can be easily diverted from the issues being protested.

One of the most common ways to turn public attention away from the protest message is to label protesters as lawbreakers or violent. If one or a few people in a large group break the law or act violently, business-controlled media can (and frequently does) call the whole group violent lawbreakers. This often is a very effective way to suppress important messages about corporate welfare and other injustices in society. In addition, if someone breaks the law or acts violently, business-controlled police can use this as an excuse to brutally suppress protesters.

Awareness of this business-controlled government approach illuminates the most important protest strategy – nonviolence. It is essential that protesters remain nonviolent and obey the law. When this occurs, it is much more difficult to turn public attention away from the protest message and justify brutal police action. (There might be times when protesters consider breaking unjust laws, such as ones that unconstitutionally restrict the right to protest. But this should be done with the advice of legal experts and always nonviolently. In addition, filming police and notifying media of the protest rationale and planned actions will help to minimize police abuse.)

However, even acting nonviolently and obeying the law sometimes will not be enough to protect protesters and their message. As discussed, flawed systems often compel wealthy business owners and their allies to oppose any action that threatens shareholder returns. Protesting against corporate welfare and business control of government could severely threaten these injustices in society. As a result, it is virtually guaranteed that business-controlled media and police will attempt to suppress these protests in many cases.

As discussed in the Privacy section, a common strategy for defeating protests that challenge the unjust status quo is to put police, government or corporate spies in protest groups. In several cases, government spies have been caught fomenting and encouraging violence and lawbreaking. This distracts attention from the protest message and justifies brutal police action. For every government spy caught in a protest group, there almost certainly were many more who were not caught. It is logical to assume that there are government spies in nearly any large protest movement that threatens corporate welfare, business control of government and ever-increasing shareholder returns. This once again shows the essential need for nonviolence and obeying the law. When this occurs, spies will have little to report to their business-controlled superiors. All they can say is that the group is focusing on its message, obeying the law and emphasizing the need to remain nonviolent.

Protest leaders and members should be careful to not let awareness of possible spies in their midst weaken the group's resolve, focus, cohesiveness and camaraderie. Working with like-minded individuals to improve society can be exhilarating and empowering. This sense of purpose, friendship and unity is essential for the group's success. Fear of spies could build distrust and weaken the group, if it is not handled carefully. People are free to share their views with others. As long as they are not espousing violence or lawbreaking, they have nothing to fear.

To weaken the divisive effect of possible spies in a group, protest leaders might say something like the following to the group. "We understand that our message threatens vested interests. It is possible that they will try to defeat us by placing spies in our group. We must not allow this to weaken our resolve and unity. We have nothing to hide. If there are spies among us, we welcome you. We are all in this together. We are trying to make this country a better place for everyone, including you."

As discussed in the Privacy section, government spies who attempt to incite passionate, impressionable young people to violence and lawbreaking are a substantial threat to protest movements. Protest groups can weaken this threat through effective communications with participants, media and police. For example, they might post messages online and hand out flyers to members that say something like the following.

"Thomas Jefferson said that we have a duty to protect our country by opposing injustice and abuse of power. We have a constitutional right to protest this injustice. It is absolutely essential to our cause that we all remain nonviolent and obey the law. If any one of us breaks the law or acts violently, police could use this as an excuse to beat, taser, pepper spray, arrest, incarcerate or conduct body cavity searches (i.e. government-sanctioned rape) on us. In addition, violence or illegal activity by any of our members will enable business-controlled media to turn public attention away from our cause and cast us as violent lawbreakers. We must protect ourselves and our cause. That is why every one of us must be peaceful and law-abiding. Obey police officers. It is better to live to fight another day, than to allow police abuse. Business-controlled police may attempt to make an example of us. By severely abusing us, they could create fear and dissuade others from protesting injustices in society. Therefore, please protect yourselves. Do not allow yourself to be abused by police. Protecting yourself protects our whole movement."

"It is possible that government spies have been placed among us. They may try to thwart our efforts by fomenting violence and illegal activities within our group. Therefore, please be aware of anyone who encourages violence or lawbreaking. Film and record them. They are intentional or unintentional enemies of our cause. Some people might believe that violence is effective. If you believe this, please leave our group. It absolutely is not part of our agenda. Also, those advocating violence and lawbreaking might be spies intentionally trying to harm us. By recording and exposing them, we will weaken the ability of business-controlled government to sabotage our efforts by placing spies among us. If you see anyone in our group acting violently or illegally, or promoting such activities, please point them out to police, provide videos and other evidence if you have any, and ask that they be removed. They are the enemies of our group."

After communicating this information to protest members, protest leaders also might communicate with media. They could provide research, facts and logical arguments that support their positions and goals. They also could explain their proposed strategy and protest activities. Protest leaders might say something like the following to media.

"Our efforts to promote (fair use of public wealth, democracy, etc.) probably will threaten some vested interests who have substantial government influence. We know from many examples across the country that government spies regularly are placed in protest groups. These spies sometimes attempt to thwart the group's purpose by fomenting violence and lawbreaking. This distracts public attention from the protest message and can be used to justify brutal police suppression of protesters. As shown in the attached note to our members, we have made it clear that we are adamantly opposed to violence and lawbreaking. Therefore, if anyone engages in or promotes these activities, it is highly likely that they are government spies trying to thwart our efforts. As you can see, we have instructed protest members to record anyone who engages in or promotes violence and lawbreaking, and provide this evidence to police. We also will provide videos and other evidence of people promoting or engaging in violence and lawbreaking to media. This will enable you to expose government spies who are attempting to sabotage our group. By exposing these activities, we hope to minimize the use of this unfair business-controlled government tactic to suppress our just cause."

Protest leaders could communicate similar information to police. They might say something like the following. "We provided the attached information to our members. As you can see, we are adamantly opposed to violence in our group. We have instructed all members to obey police and the law. We also have asked them to report anyone who engages in or promotes violence and lawbreaking to the police. We want to emphasize that anyone who breaks the law or acts violently is the enemy of our cause. Therefore, we ask you, the police, to remove them from our group and take whatever action you feel is necessary against them."

Proactively communicating this type of information before protests will not prevent business-controlled government from placing spies in protest groups. But it will substantially reduce the ability to use those spies to foment violence and lawbreaking. It will make such efforts counterproductive. It will create the widespread public perception and presumption that violence or illegal activities in protest groups are being fomented by government spies. This will backfire on the wealthy citizens and corporations who control government and police. It will expose their use of dishonest and dishonorable means to protect their theft of the people's wealth, power and freedom.

Media always is looking for interesting stories. Videos and other evidence of government spies infiltrating and thwarting protest movements would be widely reported in many media outlets. Even business-controlled conservative media generally could not avoid the story. Although they might try to put a positive spin on government spying and cast those who protest against corporate welfare and business control of government as terrorists.

Some people might argue that attempting to control the behavior of protest group members (by strongly discouraging violent or illegal activities) violates the democratic spirit that should pervade protests. But democracy requires ground rules. For example, there could be no effective democracy without the rule of law. Civilized society cannot exist if citizens are allowed to harm others. Protesting against injustice by engaging in it (i.e. violence, lawbreaking) would be ineffective. To be effective, protests must be peaceful and law-abiding. (This conversation applies to countries with constitutions that require democracy and protect individual rights, such as the US. Protests in oppressive, totalitarian countries sometimes might require violating unjust laws. But even in these countries, peaceful protests often would be more effective. It will provide more protection from brutal government suppression.)

Some people might believe that violence is necessary for change. They might form their own violent protest movements. But these groups have virtually no chance of succeeding in a country such as the US. Our military takes over whole countries in a few days. Violent action against police or the US government will be met with swift, harsh, overwhelming suppression. The only thing that violence will guarantee is failure.

The need for peaceful, law-abiding protests will be even stronger going forward. As our flawed systems compel a small group of wealthy citizens and corporations to steal ever more wealth and power from society, life will continue to get worse for millions of low and middle-income citizens. This will not stop. Our myopic systems will pursue ever-increasing shareholder returns until society collapses or we voluntarily change them. As life continues to get more difficult for average citizens, our real enemies will become obvious and protests will increase. To protect shareholder returns, wealthy citizens and corporations will direct their Republican and Democrat political puppets to use ever more severe police action to suppress citizens. As discussed in the Privacy section, police departments across the country have been militarizing. They increasingly use military weapons and strategies against peaceful protesters, such as OWS.

Acting peacefully and obeying the law and police officers is the best protection against inevitably increasing police brutality. Protesters should strive to be polite and friendly to police. Some might carry signs that say things like, "Police, we're all in this together. We're standing up for you too!"

In our increasingly divisive and repressive society, some people are being attracted to police forces who have psychological problems, such as the need to dominate or control others. This is the expected outcome of plutocracy. Police who lack empathy and want to dominate others are good partners for business-controlled government. But as We the People establish democracy in the US, we will demand different policing. Police will be community allies rather than suppressors of the people. Extensive psychological evaluations will be conducted to ensure that no one with the need to dominate or control others becomes a police officer. Any officer who abuses their power over the citizens they are supposed to protect will be quickly removed from their job.

One of the most reprehensible means of suppressing protests is to label protesters and protest groups as terrorists. This is unconscionable. But it also is the expected outcome of our flawed systems. To the British government, the Founders of the US were traitors and terrorists. But as Thomas Jefferson said, the Founders were exercising their natural right to throw off oppressive, unjust government.

Business-controlled government is unjust and unconstitutional. Citizens have a duty to oppose it. From the perspective of business-controlled government, those who oppose it are traitors, as the Founders were traitors to the British government. Calling someone a terrorist is like calling them a traitor. Domestic terrorists often seek to cause large-scale harm in their countries. In this sense, they are traitors. But citizens protesting to protect life support systems, end theft of the public wealth through corporate welfare and establish democracy are not traitors or terrorists. It is extremely irrational to even suggest this. These people are patriots, like our Founders. They often courageously protest, while risking reprisal from business-controlled police, in an effort to protect and improve their country.

Business-controlled media and government frequently will attempt to portray those who protest against corporate welfare and other injustices in society as terrorists. Rational thought shows that the opposite is true. These people are patriots. Future generations will see them as courageous heroes and heroines.

The effectiveness of peaceful protests is shown by some of the greatest figures to ever live on this planet, including Jesus, Gandhi and Martin

Luther King. We should follow their example. Conservatives and liberals protesting alone often will have little impact because millions of citizens have been manipulated into disliking or ignoring the other side. But when We the People begin to work together, we will overcome injustice. We will attain the prosperous democracy that our Founders intended.

One-on-One Activism

Two of the most important aspects of working together and ending the conservative-liberal civil war involve relating better to others and thinking for oneself. These could be referred to as one-on-one activism and inner activism. The business and media manufactured civil war between conservatives and liberals has caused great division and animosity in society. Even among family and friends, political ideas and philosophies often cause division, distance and ill will. These divisions at all levels of society mainly result from blind faith in deceptive, frequently irrational philosophies. If people thought rationally and saw the big picture, they would realize that they often are being manipulated into attacking and disliking the other side. They also would realize that they actually agree on most major issues. Healing divisions and finding common ground at the one-on-one relationship level is essential for ending the conservative-liberal civil war.

It also is essential for life success and happiness. Many studies have shown that the quality of one's relationships is the most important determinant of happiness.[244] Many other studies have shown that kindness is the most important determinant of good relationships. Marriages last the longest when couples treat each other kindly, focus on the positive, and sincerely and regularly complement and support each other. Marriages and other relationships that are filled with criticism, contempt and hostility rarely last.[245]

There are many techniques and strategies for effectively discussing political issues and finding common ground. One of the most important is to honor and respect other people and their opinions. Everyone has a right to their own opinions, even if those opinions and ideas cause harm to themselves and others. Validating and respecting someone else's opinion is not the same as condoning or accepting it. The maintenance of civilized society requires that harmful actions and sometimes harmful speech be prohibited. People are more likely to change harmful or irrational ideas if they are treated with honor and respect, rather than being criticized and ostracized.

Humility also is critical for successfully discussing political issues. People sometimes feel superior when they see the logic or factual flaws in other people's opinions and arguments. But this is not rational or effective. We all have blind spots and weaknesses. None of us is perfect. People sometimes criticize other people's behavior and arguments, but fail to see the irrational or harmful actions in their own lives. Humbly treating other people as equals will be far more effective at helping them to understand flawed, harmful ideas. Displaying superiority or condescension often will push people away and cause them to defend their flawed positions more strongly.

Humility also involves truly listening to another person and trying to understand their viewpoint. Many people arrogantly believe that their views are correct and logical. But if they open their minds and rationally consider the other person's position, they sometimes realize that the other person has a more logical and beneficial viewpoint.

Non-judgment is another essential component of effectively discussing political issues and finding common ground. As discussed throughout this book, the primary, foundational cause of virtually all major problems facing humanity is flawed ideas and systems, not individuals. In other words, the main enemies are ideas or myopia, not people. Probably nearly everyone says and does what they believe is right on some level. They might realize later that they made a mistake in a misguided or passionate moment. But overall people usually do what they feel is right.

That is why it is essential and highly effective to try to understand other people's motivations and viewpoints. For example, someone might be espousing an irrational, harmful political philosophy. But as one digs deeper, they find that the person truly believes that the philosophy will benefit society. Their motivations are pure and honorable. But their reasoning is flawed. Validating someone's good intentions is a far more effective way to begin a discussion than criticizing their reasoning. In general, it is highly effective to assume that all people mean well, even if they are espousing obviously harmful viewpoints. This validation fosters respect and productive dialogue.

For example, white supremacists believe (irrationally) that inequality somehow will enhance society. Calling them racist fools will not help white supremacists to see the flaws in their reasoning. Giving them the honor and dignity that every human being deserves can encourage them to be more open-minded and realize that every person on this planet is absolutely equal, regardless of the color of their skin.

As discussed in the Advertising, Media and Culture section, people are not born hating others. The natural tendency is to cooperate and treat other people kindly. Probably over 99 percent of human interactions are kind or at least civilized. Racism must be taught. Hateful, racist parents might teach their children to be like themselves. Treating racists with the disrespect and hatred that caused them to become racists will not help. Giving them the respect that they perhaps never received will encourage them to respect others. Again, this does not mean condoning hateful, racist speech and action. Treating all people with respect will reduce hatred and racism in society.

Another useful technique when discussing political issues is to politely ask questions instead of pointing out flawed reasoning. Help people to discover logic flaws on their own. To illustrate, someone might be espousing the importance of small government. Rather than using the logic discussed in the Libertarianism section to show why this position is irrational, someone might ask a series of questions. For example, they might ask, why is small government important? At some point, the person probably will say, because it will make society better. This reveals that the ultimate goal is making society better. Small government is a supposed means to this end.

Then one could ask, when seeking to maximize the well-being of society, should we rationally consider all valid options, and then select the one that objectively provides the greatest benefit for the least cost? Or should we apply a particular philosophy, such as minimizing government, and assume that it always will produce the optimal outcome? In cases where government clearly and objectively can provide higher-quality services at a lower cost, shouldn't we utilize the public sector? This sequence of ideas and questions could help people to rationally and objectively think for themselves, rather than blindly believe vested interest deceptions and philosophies.

Another important one-on-one strategy is to honor people's enthusiasm, rather than try to dampen it. Business-controlled media has built great division, anger and hatred in society. People often are emotionally manipulated into blindly defending their team and attacking the other side. Emotions frequently suppress logic. When someone on the other team/side/party says something political, there frequently is a tendency to lash out, say that is wrong, and then try to explain why the person's position is incorrect. Not surprisingly, this usually does not work. It frequently makes the situation worse. Emotionally manipulated people who are defending their team/party often hear "you're wrong" as "you're stupid". This frequently causes them to more strongly defend their position, creates distance and harms relationships. Telling someone that they are wrong or being illogical builds resistance. Rather than trying to dampen someone's enthusiasm for their political views, it generally is more effective to honor it.

For example, in response to a passionately stated, though myopic and harmful, political view, one might say, clearly this is an important issue for you. I see your passion. I agree that this is an important issue for society. We obviously have major problems in this area. In addition to the problems you've pointed out, I believe there are other factors that should be considered. For example, have you considered (critical issue missed due to myopia or vested interest deception)? Honoring someone's passion and position, and then suggesting additional issues for consideration, usually will be a more effective approach than saying or implying you're wrong.

Another extremely important aspect of effectively discussing political issues is to focus first on the relationship. Whenever possible, try to build a foundation of friendship, trust and respect before questioning someone's political views. A good way to build this foundation is to practice focusing on the positive and sincerely complementing others. This is discussed in an excellent article by Dr. Raj Raghunathan, called *The Art of Complimenting and Criticizing.*[246]

Obviously, people prefer to receive sincere compliments rather than criticism. Sincere compliments have no hidden agenda. People are not trying to get something in return. Learning to see the positive in others and providing sincere compliments provides many benefits. It enhances the self-esteem of the giver and the receiver because the giver sees themself as a bighearted, generous person. It attracts people who are generous and positive. People who frequently criticize others usually attract other negative, critical people into their lives. And perhaps most importantly from the perspective of political discussions, sincerely complimenting others builds trust. It encourages others to be more open-minded, authentic and forgiving. This can greatly facilitate successful political conversations.

Another important aspect of productive political discussions involves effectively dealing with negative people. Some people will not change their political or worldviews, even in the face of overwhelming evidence that their positions are irrational and harmful. People have identified a particular enemy, such as conservatives, liberals, big government or social welfare programs. Their reason to exist in large part is to defeat this enemy. Taking away their enemy (through logical analysis which reveals that liberals, conservatives, social welfare programs or big government are not the real enemies of society) could take away their main reason to exist. This would be too traumatic for some people. Their worldviews are their security blankets. They will not let them go. This is fine. We do not need everyone to think rationally and focus on defeating the true enemies of humanity. A substantial majority as all that is needed to drive necessary system changes.

Having negative, irrational people in one's life can be difficult and draining. Dr. Raghunathan wrote another excellent article about this, called *How to Deal with Highly Negative People*.[247] He points out that people often are negative because they fear bad things will happen or they will not be loved and respected by others. Feeling that their lives are out of control, they frequently try to control others. They tend to blame their negativity on external factors, rather than on their own attitudes or beliefs about themselves and life.

In his article, Dr. Raghunathan describes a method for dealing with negative people. He suggests first having compassion. These people are suffering. But it usually is not a good idea to try to help them understand the source of their suffering (their attitudes and beliefs). Negative people generally cannot take criticism. It often will make the situation worse. Dr. Raghunathan also suggests setting boundaries. Negative people's demands for love and attention could become never-ending. He further suggests taking responsibility for one's own happiness and positive beliefs. In this way, negative people cannot erode one's happiness.

Finally, Dr. Raghunathan suggests acting maturely by modeling positive ideas and behavior. It might take a while. But people are drawn to positive people. Modeling a positive, happy, successful life often will influence negative people to move in this direction over time. In terms of political discussions, it frequently would not be productive to discuss political issues with a negative person who has rigid political ideas and worldviews.

Another important aspect of dealing with negative people involves Internet trolls. These people spend much of their time rudely and irrationally attacking other people's positions in online forums and other online environments. This generally is cowardly because they are hiding behind anonymity. In addition to Internet trolls, corporations often hire companies and individuals to monitor and participate in online discussions. Flawed systems often compel publicly traded companies to oppose any information, position or action that threatens ever-increasing shareholder returns.

Online forums frequently discuss research and other evidence of corporate negative environmental and social impacts. If the research and evidence is logical and valid, companies often will not be able to honestly and rationally challenge it, without revealing their self-interest. As a result, dishonest and deceptive means frequently are used to disrupt or neutralize online forums that threaten ever-increasing shareholder returns. For example, corporate online agents might act like Internet trolls and rudely attack those providing information that threatens shareholder returns. Of course, corporate online agents virtually never disclose that they are acting on behalf of corporations. Instead, they might pose as concerned citizens. One could identify potential corporate online agents by their arguments. If they are irrationally challenging valid evidence of negative environmental and social impacts, it is possible that they are working on behalf of corporations.

One of the most effective ways to deal with Internet trolls and online corporate agents who post rude and/or irrational information is to ignore them. Do not respond. Act as if they are not part of the discussion. Internet trolls are attempting to share their self-loathing by upsetting others. Corporate online agents often use irrational attacks to shift online discussions away from evidence that threatens shareholder returns. The strategy of trolls and corporate agents frequently is to insult others and trigger emotional responses. It is important to not let one's ego be affected by online postings. Trolls and corporate agents seek emotional responses. If they are ignored, they often will change their strategy. Trolls frequently will seek greener pastures with more vulnerable egos.

But corporate agents will not give up. If rudeness does not protect shareholder returns by disrupting or diverting online discussions, they will use other approaches. For example, they might pose as a concerned parent whose child was saved by the supposedly dangerous product being discussed. This is why rational thought is so important. It would reveal that the fake parent is suggesting continued use of a product, when extensive valid evidence shows that it is harmful. Exposing or ignoring irrational arguments can help to marginalize online corporate agents and prevent them from disrupting online discussions.

Another critical aspect of effective political discussions involves not taking things personally. As discussed in the Education section, our deeply flawed competitive education system often makes people feel inadequate and stupid. This inadequacy frequently causes people to be overly sensitive about criticism of their ideas. They often irrationally view criticism of their ideas as criticism of themself. Taking things personally is a main reason why political discussions often become emotional, angry and counterproductive. Another reason is that these discussions frequently involve blindly defending irrational philosophies, rather than thinking rationally and seeking common ground.

When people emotionally defend their political views, they often unconsciously are defending their egos and political parties. Questioning their views can feel like a personal attack. As a result, they frequently respond in a rude or irrational manner. When this occurs, it sometimes makes sense to end the conversation or change the subject. However, if someone cares about the other person, they might hang in there. They might remain calm, realizing that the rude response resulted from feeling attacked. One could assure the other person that they only are seeking to understand their viewpoint, find common ground and rationally do whatever is best for society, without having any predetermined ideas about what is best. In other words, logic is king. They are willing to consider any viewpoint or idea that is logically supported and objectively enhances society. This type of open-mindedness and friendly response can greatly facilitate productive discussions about political, economic and other issues.

Inner Activism

Inner activism ultimately is the most important form of activism. If We the People do not think for ourselves, we will remain vulnerable to vested interest deceptions and false divisions in society. We will be unable to work together in our massive areas of common interest. Inner activism involves finding the courage to open one's mind, rationally and objectively examine current beliefs, and, if irrational, harmful ones are found, replace them with rational, beneficial ideas.

As discussed in the Life Satisfaction, Twelve Step Programs and other sections, this courageous inner journey usually is the most important work that people do in their lives. The outer reflects the inner. When one's inner life is peaceful, productive, focused and rational, the outer life usually will be the same.

Changing one's beliefs and worldviews can be difficult. As discussed in the Advertising, Media and Culture section, our divided, myopic society produces widespread senses of fear and inadequacy. When people are afraid or doubt themselves, it can be even more difficult to change beliefs. Worldviews, such as political philosophies, become their security blankets. Changing them could seem traumatic. That is why inner activism requires courage.

As discussed in the Well-Being of Society section, Joseph Campbell explains how people can go on an inner journey, a courageous hero's journey. Along the way, they encounter demons (fear, doubt, inadequacy). But as they press on, following their hearts, seeking truth, demons and inner obstacles are overcome. Doing what one believes is right, especially if it is difficult, enhances one's sense of self-worth and purpose in the world. As people are true to themselves, their minds become clearer and stronger. They are better able to understand the big picture forces manipulating society and see through vested interest deceptions. This greater allegiance to truth and rational thought is essential for ending the civil war between conservatives and liberals.

Dealing with anger is a critical part of inner activism. Anger is perhaps the defining characteristic of the conservative-liberal civil war. Radical conservative media extensively foments anger and hatred of liberals, minorities, immigrants and those on social welfare programs. It manipulates citizens into being angry at government, instead of at the puppet masters who are pulling the strings of government. Anger often suppresses rational thought. Angry emotions trump logic. Thinking rationally, seeing through vested interest deceptions and being effective in life requires mastering anger.

Understanding anger facilitates mastering it. Beyond initial responses to disruptive events, anger essentially is a choice, usually an unconscious one. Anger virtually never is caused by what someone else says or does. It essentially always is caused by perceptions of events, rather than the events themselves.

In his book *The Seven Habits of Highly Effective People*, Dr. Stephen Covey provides a perfect example of this.[248] A father boarded a train and sat quietly while his children ran around making noise and disturbing passengers. A man sitting nearby became increasingly annoyed that the father was not controlling his children. Finally, the man asked the father if he would quiet his children. The father looked up and said, I'm sorry. We just came from the hospital. Their mother died this morning. I do not know what to do, and I don't think they do either. The man's anger immediately was transformed to compassion.

Radical media announcers often provoke anger among those who agree and disagree with their positions. If the announcer discusses poor people abusing social welfare programs, those who are misled into believing that this is the main cause of high taxes might get angry at poor people. Those who disagree might get angry that the announcer is not discussing the vastly larger problem of corporate welfare. Both of these angry responses are choices. One results from blindly believing the announcer. The other frequently results from feeling powerless to address injustices in society.

In general, anger and violence often result from feeling powerless. In the case of violence, people frequently are trying to compensate for a belief that they lack power. They are trying to get power by taking it from someone else. Acting violently toward others can make someone feel more powerful. If they did not feel powerless to begin with, the violence would not be necessary.

Anger frequently results from feeling powerless to change another person, something that just happened or injustices in society, such as wealthy people stealing public wealth through corporate welfare. A solution to anger and violence is to recognize that we all have power to change our lives and respond to circumstances. One does not need to take power from someone else, for example by oppressing them or beating them in an argument, to have power.

Another solution to anger is to recognize that it is a choice. In Buddhism, anger is considered to be an unproductive defilement of the mind. It blocks rational, productive action. Anger can be eliminated by choosing to view circumstances differently. For example, instead of getting angry at a radical media announcer who castigates poor parents trying to feed their children while ignoring wealthy citizens stealing trillions of dollars of corporate welfare, one could recognize that the media announcer probably sincerely believes that their words will benefit society. In addition, one could recognize that they are not powerless to address injustices in society. One person cannot end corporate welfare and business control of government. But they can work with others to end these and other injustices in society.

Assuming that everyone means well is an important way to alleviate anger and replace it with more productive attitudes and actions. We all are trying to do the best we can. Granting people the benefit of the doubt will facilitate ending the civil war between conservatives and liberals. It will expand the brotherly affection that President Washington wished for us in his Farewell Address.

Another critical aspect of inner activism involves understanding what it means to be a man. As discussed in the Men's section, in our male-dominated society, men often lead through intimidation. They frequently model and establish false standards for what it means to be a man. As discussed in the Education section, radical media announcers often treat those with different opinions in a rude, condescending manner. They model and glorify bullying. An excellent article by Thomas Fiffer from The Good Man Project, called *6 Ways 'Tough Guys' Are Actually Weak*, discusses poor male role models and effective leadership.[249]

In many religious, political and other groups, leaders use Rule of Dumb techniques to coerce people into blindly following irrational dogma. Like radical media, these groups often criticize and make fun of those who are different. Male leaders of these groups frequently act like tough guys and pressure others to conform. Men who disagree with dogma and show compassion for those being criticized often are called wimps, made fun of or expelled from the group. Leaders of these types of dogmatic groups often want followers' approval, loyalty and servitude. They dominate others with a culture of fear, stifle people's freedom and independence, and provide horrible role models for what it means to be a man.

Weakening the influence of these poor leaders on society is facilitated by exposing that they are not strong or manly. They are cowards who are threatened by other people's free thinking and action. Truly strong men and leaders respect others and encourage them to be who they truly are. They do not need other people's approval or agreement. They encourage challenge and develop other leaders. They earn respect, rather than demand it. They respect others' free will and right to disagree and depart. Truly strong men and leaders do not suppress their emotions. They express compassion and other authentic emotions, and encourage others to do the same.

As discussed in the Women's section, the greater physical strength and aggressiveness of men enabled them to best fulfill their evolutionary role as protectors of women and children. The greater physical nurturing characteristics and empathy of women enabled them to best fulfill their evolutionary role of raising children. Everyone is different. We all have protective and nurturing capabilities. Women protect their children and others they love. Men often nurture their children and others they care about. But the primary instinctual drive of men is to protect. This frequently takes priority over the survival instinct. Men have been drawn to stories about heroes throughout human history. We (men) often aspire to see justice done in the world. We frequently want good to triumph over evil, and are willing to take a stand to make sure it happens.

The male drive to protect and see justice done in the world is reflected in the fascination with video games. As discussed in the Men's section, boys, teenage boys and young men often spend thousands of hours playing video games, far more time that is spent by girls and women. In the fantasy cyberworld, boys and men frequently are fighting evil forces and ensuring that justice prevails. But this fighting for justice provides no benefit in the real world. It represents no threat to actual injustice, such as the flawed systems that steal the people's wealth, power and freedom. The protective instinct is wasted in the cyberworld, when it could be usefully applied in the real world. Fighting injustice in the cyberworld is easy. But fighting it in the real world often is difficult. The losses and setbacks are real. But the satisfaction of success is far greater. People actually fought injustice and made a difference.

The protective instinct of men is being partly wasted in the cyberworld. But the far greater squandering of this precious resource occurs in the real world. Pressure to blindly believe and conform to dogmatic cultural, religious, political and other ideas inhibits the protective instinct. When men blindly focus their anger and attention on poor people abusing social welfare programs, they are being made into patsies by those who are stealing their wealth, power and freedom.

When we men allow ourselves to be deceived by vested interests, it not only hurts us. It hurts those we are supposed to protect. As discussed extensively, there is a vast absence of wisdom in the world (as shown by the rapid destruction of our life support systems and widespread inequality and suffering). Women innately manifest more wisdom than men, in the same way that men innately manifest more power. Power and wisdom both are necessary for achieving sustainability and real prosperity. Women can model and enhance wisdom in society.

But men must do a better job with power. We are not exercising it wisely. It is our job, our evolutionary role, to stand up for those who cannot protect themselves, especially future generations. It is our job to make society safe for everyone. We must not allow vested interests to treat us like fools any longer. We must find the courage to think for ourselves. We must not blindly buy into religious, political and other ideas that unintentionally create division and suffering in the world. We men must not allow ourselves to be manipulated by the Republican and Democratic parties. The slightest amount of rational thought shows that both parties mainly are focused on benefiting wealthy campaign donors, not all citizens.

Our Founders were men. Let's start acting like men, as they did, and do the right thing for society. Let's put the interests of everyone above our individual interests, as they did and our Constitution requires. When it comes to producing children, women do the hard work. They must endure pregnancy, giving birth and nursing infants. Men's hard, risky work is in other areas. It mainly involves protecting. It takes courage to be a man, stand up to vested interests, endure cowardly, irrational criticism, and do the right thing for society. But this is what we were meant to do. This is what will produce the deep sense that life has meaning and we made a difference. As individual men, we cannot correct the major injustices in society. But working together, we can drive the systemic and other changes needed to achieve sustainability and real prosperity.

This discussion of course is not meant to exclude the critical role that women's wisdom and power will play in changing society. We are all one community. We must work together. But men largely lead society. Therefore, we have the greatest ability to drive rapid, beneficial change. It is time to fulfill our evolutionary role by protecting society.

In summary, all men and women have a responsibility to improve society and think for themselves. When we think for ourselves and see the big picture, instead of blindly believing vested interests, the inevitable result of current systems becomes obvious. If we continue to put economic growth and shareholder returns before all else, the environment and society will continue to decline at an accelerating rate. The civil war between conservatives and liberals is the glue that holds our unsustainable house of cards together.

As long as we remain divided, We the People remain conquered. Flawed systems will compel a small group of wealthy citizens and corporations to continue stealing our wealth, power and freedom. This group largely controls government, the economy and society. They seem powerful. But this is an illusion. All their power comes from our deception and inaction. All ultimate power resides with We the People, as our Founders intended and Constitution stipulates. Once we rouse ourselves from our vested interest-induced slumber, we can reclaim our power. We the People are the sleeping giant of society. It is time to wake up, work together and reclaim our power to rule ourselves and control our destiny.

When we set aside blind faith in dogma, philosophies and deceptions, and think for ourselves, it becomes clear that the Republican or

Democratic parties are focused on serving wealthy citizens. The fighting between the parties is a sham. They both serve the same master. That master is not We the People. That is why We the People need our own party and movement. We the People working together make all other changes possible. Many actions are needed to unite the people. Several were discussed in this section, including raising public awareness, exposing media deceptions, forming a We the People political party, and engaging in various types of activism. Extensive collaboration between many organizations, experts and citizens will be needed to effectively implement these and other critical actions.

Probably the most important action needed to unite the people is to encourage citizens to think for themselves. We all have free will. We all control the focus of our minds. Blind faith in economic, political and religious dogma is a choice. In these cases, we choose to not think for ourselves. Blind faith often is easier than thinking for oneself. But blind faith literally is killing us. We have a responsibility, not only to ourselves, but to everyone else in our interconnected society to think for ourselves.

The need to think for oneself will be absolutely essential in the early stages of a We the People movement. Flawed systems compel a small group of wealthy citizens and their media and political puppets to oppose anything that threatens ever-increasing shareholder returns. The two-party system is a main factor, if not the main factor, perpetuating corporate welfare and business control of government. Uniting the people probably is the only way to take control of government away from a small group of wealthy citizens and give it to all citizens.

Massive public deception will be used to oppose a We the People movement and anything else that severely threatens ever-increasing shareholder returns. A wall of angry lies and deception will slam down on the people. When people think for themselves and consider the forces and systems discussed in this book, they will know that massive public deception is coming. This will empower them to see through inevitable public deception.

One of the most effective ways to see through deception is to focus on the well-being of society. Our flawed systems focus on the well-being of the economy and assume that this will maximize the well-being of society. Focusing on the economy makes it the master of society. We put economic growth and shareholder returns before all else, and then ignorantly and irrationally assume that this will maximize social well-being.

But the economy is the servant of society, not the master. We should demand that our leaders focus on society, not the economy. As discussed in the Economic Growth and Well-Being of Society sections, this requires that we refocus measurement and management on the well-being of society. Instead of measuring economic growth (which mostly measures rich people getting richer), directly measure the well-being of citizens, families, communities and life support systems. We must hold our leaders primarily accountable for these metrics. Holding leaders accountable for actually maximizing the well-being of society makes it easier to see through deceptive communications that are intended to protect shareholder returns. For example, when leaders discuss the economy, we should require them to explain how these actions will benefit society. Ask what metrics they will use to prove that economic actions actually benefit society. We must focus accountability on these direct measures of social well-being, not on indirect measures, such as economic growth.

Overall, we owe it to our children and ourselves to think for ourselves. We know that ever-greater public deception will come our way once We the People begin to take back control of government and end theft of the public wealth. If we think for ourselves, we will find trustworthy information sources and make ourselves immune to vested interest deceptions.

Vested interests often fight to keep unjust systems in place. That is a main reason why major system change usually happens through collapse, as occurred in the former Soviet Union and during the US and French revolutions. To avoid this great disruption, we must demand a peaceful transition to democracy and fair use of the public wealth. Vested interests will attempt to overwhelm us with lies. They will appear strong and perhaps undefeatable. But this is an illusion.

If the US were a true democracy, the wealthiest one percent of society would have one percent of the power. But we have allowed ourselves to be put to sleep. A small group of wealthy citizens and their media puppets have lulled many citizens into a deep slumber. They have been misled into blindly believing irrational political ideas and other dogma. Through blind faith, many people have voluntarily stopped thinking for themselves. As a result, many citizens have given away their power. They have allowed a small group of wealthy citizens to exercise near absolute power over government, the economy and society. Once we take back our power by beginning to think for ourselves, the bottom 99 percent of society will exercise 99 percent of the power. But we only can exercise this power to rule ourselves if we work together.

The great work needed to unite the people is well worth the effort. Our grossly flawed economic and political systems massively violate reality and the laws of nature. They absolutely will change, probably very soon. If We the People remain divided and conquered (i.e. by continuing to focus on beating the liberals or conservatives), our systems inevitably will collapse and cause great suffering.

Voluntary system change is the vastly better option. There only is one way to achieve it – working together. The 1800s Civil War showed what happens when we violate the laws of nature. All people are innately equal. Therefore, reality and nature would not allow slavery to exist indefinitely. The collapse of slavery was inevitable. But the means of ending slavery was not. We did not have to endure the immense death and suffering of the Civil War. But we were not able to work together and end the injustice of slavery. As a result, we paid the price through traumatic system change.

Now we are on the precipice of another great decision. We are engaged in another great civil war. Millions of families and citizens already are suffering. But it could get much worse. Our brothers and sisters 150 years ago were not able to find a way to work together. (Perhaps if our sisters had equal power in society, we might have found a way to wisely work together and avoid the Civil War.)

We must learn from our mistakes. It is time to end the current civil war peacefully. We have massive common ground. We all mostly want the same things. We all want a prosperous, sustainable society. In the first Civil War, there were real differences between those who wanted to maintain slavery and those who opposed it. But now the differences mostly are illusions. There is no need to continue fighting each other when we agree on nearly everything. Virtually everyone (except vested interests) agrees that we should have democracy instead of plutocracy and that we should not be giving trillions of dollars of public wealth to already wealthy people. As we begin to work together, let us focus first on these and other critical issues, such as protecting our life support systems and guaranteeing economic and political freedom for all citizens.

Large-scale changes, like the kind needed to avoid collapse, can seem difficult. But as said at the beginning of this book, many changes that once seemed impossible are taken for granted today. Change is coming. That is certain. We have the power to manage this change in a positive way, if we work together. When we wake the sleeping giant, We the People will achieve our destiny – reaching our fullest potential and creating Heaven on Earth. This is discussed in the final section.

Our Destiny

What is the destiny of humanity? As discussed at the beginning of this book, it is whatever we make it. We have free will. Virtually all of the problems and injustices in human society result from flawed human ideas and actions. Therefore, virtually all problems can be solved and all injustices ended. Poverty, hunger, inequality and suffering are not inevitable in human society. If we observe the trajectory of life on Earth, it is far more likely that the opposite of these conditions is inevitable. Life on Earth has progressed from disorder to ever-higher levels of order and sophistication. The ability to self-reflect appears to be unique among humans. Other animals obviously 'think' in some ways and solve problems. But animal consciousness appears to be focused on what is happening in the present moment.

Humans, on the other hand, have the intellectual freedom to think about the past, future, ourselves, other people and broader society. Why did this ability evolve among humans? One could speculate that human consciousness is part of some broader, transcendent consciousness becoming aware of itself. Reality on Earth is seen from seven billion different human perspectives. Why? What is the purpose of this? In the realm of infinity, where all things are possible, perhaps transcendent consciousness explores different options simply because they are available.

426

However, understanding whether transcendent consciousness exists and what its purpose might be are not necessary for considering and perhaps deducing the purpose or destiny of humanity. We can speculate about this purpose by observing reality and deducing expected outcomes based on the trajectory of humanity and life on this planet.

As discussed extensively throughout the whole system book, the overwhelming force in nature is cooperation, not competition. Limited competition exists at the individual level. But at the whole system level, nature displays nearly infinite cooperation, sophistication, coordination and symmetry. All creatures in nature, except humans, implicitly are guided and coordinated in ways that produce nearly infinite cooperation and sophistication. This guidance occurs through instinct, DNA and/or other mechanisms that we do not fully understand.

The implied guidance of nature compels it to act as one unified, coordinated whole system. This level of consciousness, the implied consciousness of nature, could be thought of as unconscious unity. Plants and animals do not reflect on what they do. They simply do it. In the process, they produce no waste, take only what they need for nature and produce essentially infinite cooperation, coordination and sophistication. This strongly indicates the presence of some coordinating mechanism, as many of our Founders and other Deists believed.

When human self-reflective consciousness (i.e. the ability to think about oneself) began to emerge from the unconscious unity of nature, we apparently brought some of this implied awareness of unity with us into consciousness. As discussed, indigenous religions often saw the Divine in nature and believed that humans were part of nature. This compelled humans to respect nature as the source and sustenance of all life. This logical and accurate understanding of reality enabled humans to survive on Earth for thousands of years.

Early humans often appeared to act upon intuition more than modern humans. They seemed to implicitly and intuitively understand their oneness with nature. But as human consciousness evolved, we seemed to place greater reliance on the intellect, while the intuitive seemed to fade into the background. Through the intellect, we observed reality, thought logically, and developed the wheel and other inventions. As we shifted from the intuitive that implicitly guides nature to the intellect, our perspective changed. As noted, in the early phase of human consciousness, we apparently retained the intuitive understanding that we were interconnected parts of a larger system. But as the intellect ascended over the intuitive, we seemed to lose this perspective. Instead, we largely focused on ourselves as separate individuals. As human consciousness changed from integration to separation, greater fear and the belief in the need for competition arose.

This consciousness of separation has been the dominant force driving humanity since the agricultural revolution. We have consciously explored our separation from each other. In reality, we always have been interconnected parts of one whole system. But as consciousness lost sight of this reality, we moved into the illusion or fantasy of separation. This false and illusory perspective produced many painful outcomes, including racism, discrimination, widespread poverty and hunger, coercion and genocide.

Our flawed, myopic ideas and systems are compelling us to rapidly degrade our life support systems and destroy life on this planet. As discussed in the Biodiversity section, since 1970, we have wiped out over half of the vertebrate populations on Earth, including mammals, birds and fish. As discussed in the Education section, we fondly discuss freedom, but teach our children the opposite of it. Young people's personalities and psyches often are formed in freedom-restricting education and other environments. They are taught to obey authorities, tolerate boredom and do things they do not want to do. They might be theoretically free as adults. But they were not taught to live freely. As a result, they frequently have difficulty exercising their freedom, or even knowing what it looks and feels like.

Poverty, environmental destruction and the freedom-restricting education of young people produce great pain and suffering in society. Reality and pain are great teachers. When we live in the fantasy and illusion of separation, we suffer the consequences. Pain and ignoring reality are bringing us very close to the next evolution in human consciousness.

Why did we explore the illusion of separation for thousands of years, and suffer immense negative consequences? Who knows? Perhaps because it was an option. If we had not explored separation, and the vast suffering it caused, we could not have experienced the immense joy and prosperity that will result from reintegration and awakening to the reality of our oneness. Prior to humanity, nature abided in a state of unconscious integration and unity. As we gained the ability to observe and think about ourselves, we often lost the awareness of unity. To be aware of ourselves individually, we apparently needed to dwell in the illusion of separation for a while. Now as reality and nature teach us that we are not separate, we are returning to conscious awareness that we are one. We are interconnected. But there is a major difference between the unconscious awareness of unity that implicitly pervaded nature prior to humanity. We now are, or very soon will be, conscious of our unity.

This broader consciousness evolution of humanity perfectly matches the evolution of individual consciousness discussed in the Woman's section. Infants do not know that they are separate from their mothers. They feel or know on a deep level that they are one with their environment. The mother's love for her child also causes her to feel a deep connection or unity with her child. But as the child grows, they gain the ability to self-reflect. As they become conscious of themself, they perceive that they are a separate individual. As discussed in the Women's section, psychology refers to this process as individuation. The person becomes aware of themself as a separate, autonomous, individual being. Psychology often stops at this point. It frequently refers to individuation or conscious awareness of separation as the highest or healthiest state of human consciousness.

But this is a limited perspective. It does not go far enough. The evolution of human consciousness does not stop at individuation or conscious separation. Individuation is a step along the path to full evolution of human consciousness. Full evolution, the highest state, could be referred to as conscious unity. At this point, the mind consciously recognizes that the individual is an interconnected part of a larger system, like a cell in the human body.

This strongly indicates the purpose of humanity and consciousness. A child moves from a state of unconscious unity sensing or knowing on a deep or unconscious level that they are one with their surroundings, as nature implicitly operates. Then they gain conscious awareness of themself as a separate individual. Finally, as their consciousness evolves further, they realize or remember that they are not separate. They are one. But now, in the highest state, they are able to consciously reflect on their unity. To move from the unconscious unity state of infancy and nature, they apparently had to move through a consciousness of separation, before achieving conscious awareness of unity. In other words, the three stages of individual consciousness evolution discussed in the Women's section (unconscious unity, conscious separation, conscious unity) perfectly match the three stages of evolution of collective human consciousness.

This indicates what we (humans) have been doing collectively on this planet. We left the unconscious unity of nature, and traveled through a consciousness of separation. Now we are on the verge of reaching the highest collective state of human consciousness – conscious unity. Throughout human history, individuals such as the Buddha and Jesus, lived in a state of conscious unity. Many people have achieved it in modern times through meditation and other practices. Conscious unity is spreading rapidly in human society. It is like the hundredth monkey syndrome. Once enough humans abide in the reality of conscious unity, we collectively will flip into this state.

But the birth of higher collective consciousness can be painful. The flaws of modern society resulting from the consciousness of separation include authoritarianism, totalitarianism, plutocracy and widespread inequality. Those who benefit from these systems can live in fear that their unjust dominion of society and theft of public wealth will end. This fear of system change, fear of equality and fairness, can produce strong resistance to change.

The old saying, it is darkest before the dawn, applies here. Vested interests often will not let go of their stolen wealth and power easily. They might fight to the death to retain their unjust dominion of society. This is tragic because they fight against achieving true happiness and prosperity for their children and themselves. Society often has conditioned them to believe that their value in society is based on their wealth, power and possessions. Compelling them to stop unfairly taking the people's wealth, power and freedom can feel like death. But it is not.

The goal is not to harm anyone. It is to help everyone. True democracy would not allow individuals to unfairly take the people's wealth and power. True happiness does not result from amassing it. This often produces fear among those who have it (i.e. that they will lose their unfairly accumulated wealth and power) and great suffering among those whose wealth and power was stolen.

The evolution of human consciousness can be painful. It is like we (humanity) are at an awkward stage of development. We are trying to figure out how to survive and prosper on this planet. In doing so, we make mistakes. We are conditioned to think that the best, most successful people amass great wealth and power. We implicitly are told that we will be happiest if we win this game of wealth and power accumulation. We will be protected from the scarcity of a dangerous and divisive world. But this massive concentration of wealth and power, not seen in the essentially infinitely more sophisticated and intelligent realm of nature, produces immense pain and suffering among billions of people, and often little or no happiness among those who have it.

Perhaps we had to go through this awkward, painful phase of separation consciousness to reach our fullest potential. But whether we did or not is irrelevant. We already have gone through it. This phase, the awkward, painful phase, the phase of separation consciousness, is about to end. We are on the verge of elevating our consciousness from separation to interconnectedness and creating Heaven on Earth.

What is Heaven on Earth? As said at the beginning of this book, Heaven on Earth does not refer to religion, dogma or a theoretical afterlife. It also does not refer to an ideological, utopian or unattainable society. The term Heaven is used because many people think of it as an optimal state. But we do not have to wait for a supposed afterlife to attain this state. It is available to us here and now.

Heaven on Earth, as used in this book, refers to reality and the logical, ongoing progression of humanity. It is humanity reaching our fullest potential. Heaven on Earth involves manifesting the wisdom of nature in human society and producing the highest possible levels of sustainability, prosperity and happiness amongst humanity. Heaven on Earth is based on the inevitable trajectory of humanity. Living massively at odds with reality and nature, as we are doing now, is utopian in the sense that it absolutely will not last. It is an irrational fantasy to think that we can continue to destroy our life support systems and maintain widespread poverty and suffering amongst humanity.

However, it not only is logical and rational to assume that we will reach our fullest potential and produce Heaven on Earth. It is the expected outcome. We all want to live peaceful, satisfying, truly prosperous lives. All sane people want this for others too. In other words, the deepest desire of humanity is to create Heaven on Earth, to reach our fullest potential, to achieve sustainability and real prosperity.

What does this look like? How can we achieve it? Many great people throughout human history have described a state that could be called Heaven on Earth. One of the best descriptions is contained in John Lennon's beautiful song *Imagine*. He describes what human society might look like when we manifest the nearly infinitely greater cooperation, sophistication, sustainability and prosperity seen in nature. John Lennon encourages us to imagine a world where all people live in peace, where there is no greed or hunger, where we are a brotherhood of man, living for today and sharing all the world. He describes a world with no heaven or hell, no religions, no countries, no possessions, and nothing to kill or die for.

This is a very advanced view of humanity, perhaps the most advanced. From the current human perspective and level of development, it might be difficult to understand how such a world could be achieved. Our consciousness probably would have to evolve substantially before we manifested a society with this level of sophistication and cooperation – the same level seen in nature.

For example, someone might ask, why would we want a world with no religion, where people focus on living in the present, instead of yearning for an afterlife in Heaven, or fearing an afterlife in hell? Answering this question requires understanding the difference between religion and spirituality. As discussed in the Life Satisfaction and Twelve Step Programs sections, spirituality could be thought of as acting on the reality of our oneness and interconnectedness by treating other people with kindness, love and respect.

Perhaps the simplest and most practical definition of spirituality is love. From this perspective, spirituality has little to do with God or religion. Rather than thinking about God or an afterlife, spirituality involves being the best person that one can be in the present moment, in large part by treating others with kindness, love and respect. Spirituality often involves going on an inner journey, realizing that we all are interconnected parts of one system, and helping others based on the understanding that this ultimately is the same as helping oneself. In other words, spirituality involves living in the reality of our oneness.

Regarding religion, as human consciousness moved from the unconscious unity and coordination of nature to the consciousness of separation, it appears that we began to wonder how humans were connected to the cosmos and where we came from. Early humans often apparently retained their intuitive understanding of their connection to nature and all else. But the conscious human mind is not capable of fully understanding infinity or everything. As we moved from the unconscious unity of nature to conscious awareness or self-reflective consciousness, the focus of consciousness had to narrow tremendously. As discussed in Chapter Four, at the intuitive level, we know everything. But the conscious human mind only can ponder an infinitesimally small amount of all knowledge at one time. Individual focus would be impossible if we did not hugely narrow our awareness. This narrowing of awareness means that our conscious minds cannot fully understand everything and our connection to it.

But the mind still frequently yearns to know this connection. To address the questioning mind, simplified stories, myths and religions were created. Early religions or creation myths frequently saw humans as interconnected parts of nature. These highly logical, reality-based views of humanity worked well for thousands of years. But as humans began to violate indigenous religions which said that we had no right to push nature aside, we developed new religions that justified this domination. We created the idea that God said we were above nature and had a right to use it as we see fit. This delusional, reality-ignoring idea is a foundation of modern economic and political systems. It is a main, if not the main, flawed idea driving humanity's unsustainable, destructive, suicidal actions.

The rise of the intellect over intuition created the need for religion. Intuition understands our connection to everything. It needs no explanation because it resides in the reality of oneness and unity. However, the intellect or conscious mind cannot fully understand our connection to everything. Fear and discomfort, often caused by lack of understanding about our place in the cosmos, make the mind vulnerable to simplified, irrational explanations. Religions provide these simplified explanations. As discussed in the Well-Being of Society section, religions are attempts to explain something that ultimately is incomprehensible to the conscious human mind. Therefore, all religions logically should be seen only as symbolic of something that is real, but cannot be fully articulated or understood consciously.

As humans and humanity overall evolve to conscious unity, we will rely more on intuition. This will tell us beyond the shadow of a doubt that we are interconnected parts of one whole system. We will use our conscious minds as they were meant to be used – as the servants of deeper, infinite wisdom. In other words, intuition provides the higher guidance and the conscious mind figures out how to get the job done. Once we reach this stage of development, we will manifest the same high level of cooperation and sophistication seen in nature because we will be acting on the same implied infinite intelligence that guides nature.

Currently, the conscious mind or intellect often is seen as the highest authority in humans. We frequently think that the human mind is the highest level of intelligence on Earth. This of course is ridiculous. One only has to look at the technology of the simplest of nature's creations, such as a blade of grass, to see an essentially infinitely higher level of implied intelligence than anything that has ever occurred in a conscious human mind. In this sense, the conscious human mind is the lowest level of intelligence on this planet. Every other life form implicitly is connected to and guided by the infinite wisdom and intelligence of nature. But placing the intellect above the intuitive disconnected the conscious human mind from this infinite intelligence. The conscious mind's necessarily narrowed focus makes it unable to fully understand nearly everything.

When we allow the servant (conscious mind/intellect) to act like the master, religion often is needed. The mind seeks explanations because it does not fully understand reality. Religions provide these simplified explanations. To motivate behavior that developers of religions considered to be good, the carrot and stick of heaven and hell often are used. Religions frequently essentially say, if you obey our rules, God will reward you after you die. But if you disobey, you will be punished for eternity.

These are simplified, human-created ideas. They will not be needed once we reach a higher level of development and consciousness. When we attain conscious unity, our minds will assume their proper roles as the servants of infinite wisdom. The mind will not need simplified explanations for infinity. It will trust what is known in the heart at the intuitive level. Religious exhortations to treat others kindly will not be needed because this information is known in the heart. The heart or intuitive always will guide the mind to treat others with kindness, love and respect because we all are parts of one interconnected system.

Intuition will guide individuals to focus on the present moment (or live for today as John Lennon says). As we are guided by the wisdom of nature, we will manifest the brilliance and beauty of nature in human society. There are no countries or money in nature. Nature is organized into local, largely self-sustaining communities. As humanity displays the same intelligence as that seen in nature, we also mostly will be decentralized into nearly independent communities and regions, with some actions being managed at a higher or global level when it is logical to do so.

As we follow our hearts (i.e. wisdom of nature), we will take only what is needed from nature and help our fellow humans, because we ultimately will be helping ourselves. The society described by John Lennon where humans share the world and have no possessions routinely occurs in nature, and was widely done among indigenous societies. People use things as long as they need them, and then let them go. There is little or no sense of "I own this". Instead, there is more of a sense that we are owned by nature. As our consciousness evolves to unity, systems thinking will become automatic. We will implement the many system changes discussed in this book. By taking only what we need, not wanting to own things, sharing and helping others, greed, hunger and poverty will be eliminated from human society.

Some people might say that this is utopian and unattainable. This perspective reflects myopia and the unsophistication of humanity. The preceding ideas simply describe what already exists all around us in nature and in our bodies. The idea that we cannot achieve what nature already does, when we are part of nature, is not rational. It is far more irrational to assume that we can continue to do what we are doing now. Nature will not allow us to grossly violate the laws of nature with impunity. Change absolutely is coming. It is irrational and utopian to think otherwise.

By following intuitive guidance and fully expressing who we are in the present moment, we will reach our highest joy and potential, individually and collectively. We largely will not be focused on the past or future because the present will be highly satisfying Heaven on Earth. We will not worry about a good or bad afterlife. The afterlife will take care of itself. As we create Heaven on Earth here and now, Heaven will occur in the afterlife, if an afterlife exists.

The Heaven on Earth described in John Lennon's song *Imagine* might seem utopian and unattainable. But all he is doing is describing what already exists in nature. We are part of nature. Therefore, we have the potential to live as John Lennon describes. As noted, the utopian idea is that we can continue living as we are now, massively violating the laws of reality and nature. This is a fantasy. It absolutely will not occur.

However, Heaven on Earth as John Lennon describes it not only is attainable. It is our destiny. Why? Because we have free will. Therefore, if we can freely choose our destiny, why would we choose anything less than the best we can be. Why would we choose to not display the infinite cooperation, sophistication, beauty and implied love seen in nature when we have the power to attain this outcome.

We are many steps away from reaching our fullest potential and creating Heaven on Earth. The consciousness of separation still pervades humanity. This produces widespread senses of fear and inadequacy. It drives competition, suffering, hoarding and many other problems in human society. We still have lots of work and consciousness raising to do. But we are near a turning point. Billions of people are suffering physically and psychologically on this planet. Pain is a great driver of change. We are near the point of collectively saying enough is enough.

Our flawed ideas and systems have enabled small groups of wealthy or powerful people to dominate and abuse the vast majority of citizens since the agricultural revolution. This cycle of authoritarianism, oppression and abuse is nearing its end. As discussed above, once We the People unite (in the US, other countries and around the world), we can establish true democratic government. As this occurs, we will use our collective wealth and power to equally and fairly protect and benefit all citizens. This ending of authoritarianism and establishing of true democracy is a major step toward creating Heaven on Earth.

Relying more on intuitive wisdom is the ultimate action needed to manifest the wisdom of nature in human society, and thereby create Heaven on Earth. However, there also is much work to do on the intellectual level. This book emphasizes the need for a Second Enlightenment. Like our Founders did in the 1700s during the first Enlightenment, we must use rational, objective thinking to see through vested interest deceptions and work together in our vast areas of common interest.

Religion is one of the most important areas where greater rational, enlightened thinking is needed. As discussed in the Well-Being of Society section, religions often compel people to blindly believe unprovable, dogmatic ideas. These ideas frequently pit believers against nonbelievers. They create in-groups and out-groups. These divisive religious ideas have caused vast suffering throughout human history, and continue to do so today. Dogmatic religious ideas that pit humans against each other only can be believed through the complete absence of rational thought (i.e. blind faith).

As discussed in the Rule of Dumb section, it is ridiculous to assume that God or some type of loving creator would pit different groups of humans against each other by giving them different versions of God. All versions of God (i.e. religions) were developed by humans. Applying rational thought shows the absurdity of fighting over differing opinions about God. This is exactly what a loving God would not want us to do. Our Founders applied rational thought to religion. We should do the same. As discussed in the Population section, George Washington, Benjamin Franklin, John Adams, Thomas Jefferson and James Madison did not believe in religious dogma. They believed in religious principles that are common to all religions, such as treating others with kindness, love and respect.

Our world no longer is divided into geographically dispersed tribes, as it was when the Bible and other old religious books were written. We now are one interconnected people on this planet. We need a new belief system that reflects this reality. We of course should respect different cultural and religious ideas. But these ideas must not be allowed to divide us. In a new global belief system, there would be no more out-groups. We all are part of one in-group – humanity. We all deserve to be treated with kindness, love and respect. This is the primary commandment of essentially all religions.

Our Founders and other great leaders shared this view. Benjamin Franklin said, "What is serving God? Tis doing good to Man."[250] Abraham Lincoln believed in God. But he did not belong to any church or believe in religious dogma or superstition. When asked about his religion, he said, "When I do good, I feel good. When I do bad, I feel bad. That's my religion."[251]

The Freemasons and Twelve Step programs further illustrate the focus on doing good in society and not allowing religious views to divide us. Many of the Founders were Freemasons. The Freemasons are focused on benefiting society. Within the Freemasons, people with different religious views agree that God exists and that their view of God compels them to do good in society. They are not required to adopt the same view of God. As discussed in the Twelve Step Programs section, the Twelve Steps are based on Christian principles, such as being kind to others and living a life of service. But there is no religious dogma. Members of Twelve Step groups are encouraged to develop their own conception of a higher power.

These programs and quotes from our greatest leaders illustrate the type of rational, enlightened thinking that must pervade society if we are to reach our fullest potential and achieve sustainability and real prosperity. We must act like the one people that we already are in reality by respecting others' views and treating them with kindness, love and respect. Religions can be highly useful and beneficial when they encourage us to do this. But religions block Heaven on Earth when they pit us against each other.

Ultimately, as John Lennon said, no religions will be needed amongst humanity. Religion is a uniquely human phenomenon. There are no Christian, Jewish, Muslim, Buddhist or Hindu cells in the human body or nature. The components of nature, except for humans, are directly guided by infinite wisdom. One could refer to this implied intelligence that guides nature as God. But ultimately labels are irrelevant. The key issue is accessing and utilizing intuitive wisdom, regardless of what label is placed on it.

The consciousness of separation often causes humans to feel alone and isolated in the world. Religions provide an intellectual explanation for our connection to everything. But as we rely on our intuitive wisdom more (which also could be called the inner word of God), we no longer will need intellectual explanations of God. The mind does not need explanations when the heart is in direct contact with God. People do not need religious books or leaders to tell them what God wants. They have direct contact within. God (or intuitive wisdom) will guide them in the present moment. Following intuitive wisdom will produce the most successful and satisfying life, in large part by putting people in harmony with others.

The need for God arose from the consciousness of separation. Other creatures do not think about God. But they create essentially infinitely higher levels of cooperation, coordination and sophistication. We do not need to think about God either. As we do what intuitive wisdom (or the wisdom of nature or word of God) guides us to do in the present moment, we will reach our fullest potential and achieve true, long-term prosperity, as nature already does.

Conscious unity means that we have the ability to reflect on our oneness. As part of following our hearts, we might explore different ideas, simply because it is fun or interesting to do so. As noted, religions ultimately would not be needed when we are guided by the wisdom of nature. Religions are needed for the mind that is not connected to the heart. Once connected, the mind taps into infinite wisdom and religions become unnecessary.

However, on our way to conscious unity, religions could play useful and interesting roles. But to do this, religious ideas often would need to become more rational and reality-based. For example, the idea of God being separate from humans is disempowering, harmful and incorrect. Based on conventional understandings of God, everything emanates from God. The energy of God pervades and sustains everything. From this perspective, we are not separate from God. Also, people can hear God (or intuitive wisdom) in their hearts. If we hear God within, then God is not separate from us from this perspective either. In reality, we are parts of one larger interconnected system. From this perspective also, we are not separate from God.

Perceptions of separation from God result from limited perspective or illusion. The individual mind steeped in separation consciousness often feels alone and isolated in the world. It feels separate from God and all else. But this is an illusion. As we expand our conscious awareness to unity, we recognize that we literally are parts of one larger system. At this highest level of consciousness, our awareness expands out to embrace everything. When we shift our identity out to this level, we attain God consciousness. We recognize that we (the broader we that includes everything) ultimately are God (i.e. all that is). However, while we are in human bodies, we understand that we are consciously exploring an infinitesimally small part of all that is. This awareness promotes the humility needed to follow one's heart without having to fully understand everything intellectually.

As religious ideas become more reality-based, we will recognize that we are not separate from nature. God is not somewhere else, apart from nature. We will once again see the Divine in nature, as indigenous people did long ago, and as our Founders and other Deists did in the 1700s. When this occurs, religions will become much more rational and reality-based. Rather than compelling us to degrade life support systems (by ignorantly saying we are above and separate from nature), they will encourage us to revere nature as the sustenance of our lives. When this occurs, religions will be strongly supporting the attainment of Heaven on Earth and true, long-term prosperity.

A key part of the Second Enlightenment involves honoring and utilizing intuitive wisdom far more extensively. Rational thought shows the immensely greater wisdom all around us. It is highly rational to seek to employ this infinite resource in one's life. As discussed, the label placed on intuitive wisdom ultimately is irrelevant. If some people discern and follow intuitive wisdom more effectively by thinking of it as the word of God, then religion is effective in these cases. However, religion is ineffective or harmful when blind faith in dogma blocks intuitive wisdom (or the word of God heard within).

Another major component of the second Enlightenment is increasing cooperation in society. It also is highly rational to seek to emulate the vastly greater level of cooperation seen in nature. As discussed extensively, elevating the status of wisdom and cooperation in human society naturally will elevate the status of women, because women innately manifest greater cooperation and wisdom than men. The lower status of women in the world reflects the imbalance between power and wisdom. Destructive power emanating from fear and the consciousness of separation literally are destroying our world. Power must be guided by wisdom. Our world is out of balance with power over wisdom and men over women. We must elevate wisdom and women to achieve balance in the world. Achieving true equality between women and men is a major and necessary component of reaching our fullest potential and creating Heaven on Earth.

Another necessary component is humility. Albert Einstein said, "My religion consists of a humble admiration of the illimitable superior spirit who reveals himself in the slight details we are able to perceive with our frail and feeble minds. That deeply emotional conviction of the presence of a superior reasoning power, which is revealed in the incomprehensible universe, forms my idea of God. I cannot imagine a God who rewards and punishes the objects of his creation, whose purposes are modeled after our own – a God, in short, who is but a reflection of human frailty. It is enough for me to contemplate the mystery of conscious life perpetuating itself through all eternity, to reflect upon the marvelous structure of the universe which we can dimly perceive and to try humbly to comprehend even an infinitesimal part of the intelligence manifested in Nature."[252]

If one of the most brilliant people to ever live on this planet felt humble in the face of the virtually infinitely greater intelligence of nature, we all should feel at least as humble, if not much more so. Humility will help to place the conscious mind or intellect in its proper role as the servant of infinite wisdom heard within all of us.

Albert Einstein also encouraged us to broaden our perspective and think systemically. He said, "A human being is part of a whole, called by us the 'Universe,' a part limited in time and space. He experiences himself, his thoughts and feelings, as something separated from the rest – a kind of optical delusion of his consciousness. This delusion is a kind of prison for us, restricting us to our personal desires and to affection for a few persons nearest us. Our task must be to free ourselves from this prison by widening our circles of compassion to embrace all living creatures and the whole of nature in its beauty."[253]

Humility and systems thinking open our minds to new information and possibilities. Albert Einstein's humility and big picture view of the world almost certainly played a major role in his ability to greatly expand humanity's understanding of reality.

Albert Einstein's encouragement to expand our compassion to all living creatures applies to all life, including humans. It illustrates another major component of reaching our fullest potential and creating Heaven on Earth – ending discrimination. Nelson Mandela said, "No one is born hating another person because of the color of his skin, or his background, or his religion... People must learn to hate, and if they can learn to hate, they can be taught to love, for love comes more naturally to the human heart than its opposite."[254]

Discrimination against people who are different is a product of the fear-filled consciousness of separation. In reality, every person on this planet is absolutely equal and endowed with the exact same natural rights to life, liberty and the pursuit of happiness. Rational thought shows that it is ridiculous to judge someone based on their religion or the color of their skin. Intuitive wisdom tells us that every person on this planet is our equal sister or brother. People usually do not judge others based on the color of their hair or eyes. As rational thought and intuitive wisdom increase in human society, we no longer will judge people based on the color of their skin or anything else. We will do what Jesus modeled for us – equally honor and respect every person.

Christian dogma says that Jesus came here to save us. But this is a disempowering view. A more empowering one is that Jesus modeled the power that we all have to change our lives, follow our inner wisdom and manifest love and beauty in the world. In Christian dogma, individuals externalize their power to Jesus. They believe Jesus or God is needed to 'save' them. But Jesus modeled empowerment, not disempowerment. He showed us what we all could do. We do not need to be 'saved' by some external entity. We have free will. Our lives depend on our own actions. No one can save us expect ourselves. To reach our fullest potential and achieve Heaven on Earth, we must let go of disempowering ideas that project or externalize our power onto Jesus, churches that claim to be God's representatives, or any other person or organization.

This illustrates another critical component of the Second Enlightenment and reaching our fullest potential – effective leadership. Throughout our largely authoritarian human history since the agricultural revolution, people often looked up to a few leaders. We frequently externalized our power onto them. But in true democracy, the ultimate leaders are We the People. As we stop giving our power and authority away to others, we will demand new types of leaders. Politicians and other leaders will be seen as servants. Their 100 percent focus will be on equally serving all citizens. Arrogant, boastful leaders who seek to puff up their egos, resumes and bank accounts will be replaced with wise, humble leaders, like Presidents Washington and Lincoln, who truly are focused on serving and maximizing the well-being of society.

At the individual level, an important part of reaching our fullest potential and manifesting the wisdom of nature in human society involves going on outer and especially inner journeys. Traveling and seeing other cultures opens people's minds and reveals the great beauty and diversity of our world. While traveling is beneficial and fun, going on inner journeys is even more important. The beautiful song *America* by Simon and Garfunkel indicates the importance of inner and outer journeys. In the song, a young man and woman are enjoying themselves while traveling and exploring America. But at night, while riding on a bus, the man says to his sleeping girlfriend that he's lost, empty and aching inside, and he doesn't know why.

This indicates a common human experience. Everything seems to be going well on the outside. But inside, people often feel empty, alone, sad and confused. As discussed in the Advertising, Media and Culture section, people frequently seek to fill their emptiness with busy lives, addictions and other distractions. But this usually does not work because the problem is inside, not outside. Therefore, an inside solution is needed. Going on an inner journey and exploring who one authentically is requires courage. Many people greatly resist this inner journey and work. They often distract themselves with nearly constant cyberworld and other activities.

This resistance to exploring the inner world has been shown in many studies. In one study, people of different ages and backgrounds were given a choice between sitting alone in a room and doing nothing for several minutes, or giving themselves a mild, but painful shock by pressing a button. Two-thirds of the men and one-quarter of the women chose to shock themselves rather than sit quietly doing nothing.[255]

This indicates why going on an inner journey requires courage. In today's busy, electronically-intense world, people's minds frequently are occupied or distracted. Pausing and contemplating one's inner world can seem boring, off-putting or frightening. But this work is essential for many people, especially those who, like in the song *America*, are empty and aching inside.

As discussed in the Life Satisfaction, Twelve Step Programs and other sections, there are many ways to explore one's inner world, fill inner emptiness, satisfy inner yearning, and experience truly fulfilling lives. These include meditating, participating in self-help groups, working with psychotherapists, reading personal growth books, writing in journals, and honestly and openly speaking with friends and family about inner issues.

Beginning the inner journey by getting honest with oneself often is difficult. But the benefits can be immense. People frequently uncover disempowering beliefs, replace them with empowering ones, discover their true passions and life purpose, refocus their lives on these passions, and thereby reach their highest potential and create the most successful and satisfying lives. As people proceed deeply on their inner journey, often through meditation, they frequently discover a very high level of bliss and serenity. They tangibly experience the reality of unity. Unity is not an intellectual theory. It is profoundly experienced reality. One knows that there ultimately is no separation with other people and the environment. This produces a strong sense of love and compassion for others.

However, this deep experience of unity is not necessary to achieve a truly successful and satisfying life. Even the inner journey is not needed for everyone. People who are naturally kind to others often attain rich, full lives without ever seriously contemplating their inner world. Their natural inclination to be kind and willing to help others makes the inner work unnecessary. They already naturally have what many people seek on the inner journey. Regardless of their beliefs about unity or oneness, they act as if they are one with others, and thereby achieve fulfilling and successful lives. This, in a sense, is like the unconscious unity of nature. People seem to automatically cooperate and treat others kindly, and thereby create fulfilling lives. As humanity overall evolves to conscious unity, cooperating and treating others kindly will become the natural, automatic action.

Another major aspect of reaching our fullest potential and creating Heaven on Earth at the individual level involves spending time in nature. As discussed in the Life Satisfaction section, we evolved from nature. It is our true home. Our lives literally are sustained by nature. If God exists, nature is the hand of God sustaining us. Myopic ideas and systems are causing us to rapidly degrade our life support systems. A whole system perspective shows that Native Americans had essentially infinitely more accurate, sophisticated and sustainable ideas about the human role in nature. They revered and protected nature. They saw the damage that our flawed thinking was causing long ago.

A Native American chief, Chief Seattle, gave a speech about this in 1854. While the translation is not fully known, many Native Americans agree that Chief Seattle's speech contained words like the following. Implicitly speaking to white settlers, Chief Seattle said, "Will you teach your children what we have taught our children? That the Earth is our mother? What befalls the Earth befalls all the sons of the Earth. This we know: the Earth does not belong to man, man belongs to the Earth. All things are connected like the blood that unites us all. Man did not weave the web of life, he is merely a strand in it. Whatever he does to the web, he does to himself... We love this Earth as a newborn loves its mother's heartbeat. So, if we sell you our land, love it as we have loved it. Care for it, as we have cared for it. Hold in your mind the memory of the land as it is when you receive it. Preserve the land for all children, and love it, as God loves us. As we are part of the land, you too are part of the land. This earth is precious to us. It is also precious to you. One thing we know - there is only one God. No man, be he Red man or White man, can be apart. We are all brothers after all."[256]

The Native American people understood unity with nature. Their ideas and respect for nature would have allowed humans to survive over the very long term on Earth. But our myopic and irrational ideas are quickly (and of course unintentionally) killing us by destroying our life support systems. That is why Native American and similar indigenous ideas essentially are infinitely more sophisticated than our own.

To reach our fullest potential and achieve sustainability and real prosperity, we must reestablish this indigenous wisdom and respect for nature in human society. Our myopic religious ideas often took God out of nature. These ideas implied that it was acceptable to degrade or push aside nature because we will be going to a better place – an afterlife in Heaven (if we blindly obey dogma).

The Divine, or wisdom of the universe, is transcendent. It is everywhere, especially in nature. Turning off electronic gadgets and other distractions and spending time in nature can be tremendously uplifting and empowering. Nature is a beautiful place to go on the inner journey. People can be cradled in the body (or as many Native Americans would say, Mother) that created and sustains us. It often is easier to directly perceive the reality of our unity with everything when we are in nature. Being in nature facilitates adopting a whole system perspective. It can inspire us to protect our life support systems and all life.

Another important part of reaching our fullest potential and creating Heaven on Earth involves art and music. These areas go beyond the intellect. Art and music often affect people on deep emotional, noncognitive levels. They show that there is much more to humans than the rational, intellectual mind. Music in particular often stirs emotions, such as love, passion and euphoria. It indicates that there is an energetic or vibratory aspect of humans. As discussed in the Meditation and Metaphysics section, some spiritual ideas and scientific theories say that matter is an illusion. Everything is energy vibrating at different frequencies. In this sense, raising our level of consciousness, for example from separation to unity, might involve raising our frequency. Love probably is a very high, perhaps the highest, frequency.

Reaching our fullest potential and creating Heaven on Earth involves increasing love in society, including self-love. The consciousness of separation, disempowering advertising, competitive grading in schools, and many other factors produce widespread senses of inadequacy, fear and isolation in society. Our competitive, materialistic, divisive culture often establishes irrational and arbitrary standards about what it means to be a successful, admirable, valuable person. The overwhelming emotional message of advertising is that people are not good enough without the advertised products. Our disempowering culture creates a shadow side in nearly everyone. We are made to feel ashamed or inadequate about certain aspects of ourselves because we do not live up to some arbitrary cultural or social standard.

To reach our fullest potential, we must end these ridiculous characterizations of what it means to be a successful human. We must put an end to the inadequacy that results from separation consciousness and culture. People are hobbled when they do not accept themselves for who they are. It creates negative emotions. Maintaining a shadow side (parts that we are ashamed of and do not want to show the world) puts up psychic barriers. It makes people inauthentic and causes them to hide their real selves.

As we move from separation to unity consciousness, we will learn to accept all aspects of ourselves. As discussed in the Life Satisfaction section, this does not mean that people accept negative behavior and do not try to change it. Paradoxically, as one accepts all parts of themself, changing negative aspects and behaviors often becomes easier. Self-condemnation frequently locks addiction and other harmful aspects in place. It creates negative emotions, which then often are suppressed with addictions and other harmful actions. As we evolve to unity consciousness, we will unconditionally accept all aspects of ourselves and others. Again, this does not mean condoning negative behavior. Harmful actions must be prohibited. But as people are accepted and treated with love, honor and respect, negative behavior naturally will decline greatly. Lack of love and respect during childhood frequently is the root cause of negative behavior.

When we unconditionally love and accept ourselves and others, we will take down our psychic barriers. ESP experiments often show that some people can communicate with telepathy. Messages pass from one mind to another with no verbal or physical communication. Apparently, ideas are communicated energetically, perhaps through some type of frequency, similar to how electronic devices communicate. At a much more advanced stage of human development, we might regularly communicate telepathically. But the mechanism probably would be more accurately described as telempathy. As we unconditionally love ourselves and others, our senses of shame and inadequacy are removed. Psychic barriers come down. The frequency of love and empathy facilitates nonverbal, telempathic communication.

Music probably already does something like this. Why does music make people feel good? Probably because it triggers or aligns with some higher frequency within us, such as love. The Woodstock concert in the summer of 1969 provides a beautiful example of music helping to create Heaven on Earth. As discussed in the Crime section, about 400,000 mostly young people attended the three-day concert in Bethel, New York. There were virtually no acts of violence at the concert. Instead, there was widespread peace, love and acceptance of differences.

This was a difficult time in the US. Through the draft, young men were being forced to fight in a war that appeared to have far more to do with helping defense companies make more money than protecting national security. Our young men were being killed and maimed apparently mainly to protect shareholder returns. There was a deep desire among many people to end the war and achieve peace.

The beautiful music of Woodstock helped to unite the people and raise their consciousness to a higher, more peaceful and loving level. Conditions at the concert often were uncomfortable. But many attendees treasure it as a once-in-a-lifetime experience. It seems that, for a brief time, hundreds of thousands of people were able to unite and create Heaven on Earth.

Barbara Hamilton, a Woodstock attendee, said, "I remember looking around and seeing all the different people. And I was thinking, Oh My God! All these people are different; every race, religion, background, everything and yet we are all, not the same, but connected together as one. It didn't matter what differences there were, people were just smiling and being nice to each other. I remember thinking, All you need is love... its about having compassion for one another. It was about the possibilities of getting all these different kinds of people together and proving that there was another way of living peacefully versus the falling apart life that was outside of Woodstock; the chaos of war and fighting... There was something beautiful, natural, and easy at Woodstock; and it was all these reasons that said to me that everything I had ever believed in was happening right then and there. And I felt that I had to carry this in my heart forever."[257]

Joan Baez sang one of the most beautiful songs at the concert, *We Shall Overcome*. (The video can be seen on YouTube.) *We Shall Overcome* often was sung at labor, civil rights and peace rallies. The beautiful and moving song is about having courage and faith that we will overcome adversity and live in peace. Overcoming in the song sometimes is seen as defeating people who oppress others, such as management oppressing labor, whites oppressing African Americans, men oppressing women, or proponents of war oppressing proponents of peace.

But another way of interpreting the song is that we are not overcoming oppressive people. We are overcoming oppressive, myopic ideas and levels of consciousness. Our flawed, myopic ideas often compel well-meaning people to take actions that harm society. These people are not the enemy. We mainly are oppressed by myopia and the illusion of separation. Fighting each other disempowers us. To overcome the true enemies of humanity, we must work together.

The 1960s and early 1970s were a time of social change and living in new ways. Christianity, as it was practiced in the time of Christ, saw a resurgence in many areas. True Christianity (i.e. loving, accepting, not judging and helping other people) was lived at Woodstock. This is what reaching our fullest potential and creating Heaven on Earth looks like – moving from the individual to the whole system perspective, raising our consciousness from separation to unity, living according to the natural laws and religious principles upon which our country was established – treating others with kindness, love and respect, helping the needy, and protecting the environment and all life.

We citizens of the United States are truly blessed to have had such wonderful and wise Founders. Quotes from President Washington's Farewell Address show the great affection he had for his country and the desire to see us prosper. Implicitly speaking to current and future citizens, he said, " [I wish that] Heaven may continue to you the choicest tokens of its beneficence; that your union and brotherly affection may be perpetual; that the free constitution, which is the work of your hands, may be sacredly maintained; that its administration in every department may be stamped with wisdom and virtue; that, in fine, the happiness of the people of these States, under the auspices of liberty, may be made complete by so careful a preservation and so prudent a use of this blessing as will acquire to them the glory of recommending it to the applause, the affection, and adoption of every nation which is yet a stranger to it."

Near the end of his Farewell Address, President Washington said, "In offering to you, my countrymen, these counsels of an old and affectionate friend, I dare not hope they will make the strong and lasting impression I could wish; that they will control the usual current of the passions, or prevent our nation from running the course, which has hitherto marked the destiny of nations. But, if I may even flatter myself that they may be productive of some partial benefit, some occasional good; that they may now and then recur to moderate the fury of party spirit, to warn against the mischiefs of foreign intrigue, to guard against the impostures of pretended patriotism; this hope will be a full recompense for the solicitude [concern] for your welfare, by which they have been dictated."[258]

George Washington, Benjamin Franklin, John Adams, Thomas Jefferson, James Madison, James Wilson and other leading Founders sought to establish true democracy for We the People that would be a shining light for the rest the world. As discussed in the We the People section, vested interests have suppressed democracy for nearly all of US history. We do not have to tolerate this any longer. We have the power to establish true democracy and be the shining light that our Founders intended.

George Washington said, "It should be the highest ambition of every American to extend his views beyond himself, and to bear in mind that his conduct will not only affect himself, his country, and his immediate posterity; but that its influence may be co-extensive with the world, and stamp political happiness or misery on ages yet unborn."[259] President Washington encouraged us to move beyond our individual and even national interests. He encouraged us to protect all of human society, especially future generations.

The most important reason to unite and create true, long-term prosperity is for our children and future generations. They take priority over us. We never should take any action that inhibits the ability of future generations to survive and prosper. Love and protection of our children is the most sacred and important obligation of humanity.

Let this love for children inspire us. They are the reason why we must change now. We should create Heaven on Earth, not so much for ourselves, but for them, the people who will come after us. Happiness does not result from selfishly seeking happiness. It is a byproduct of taking right actions and living a life of service. The most important right actions are caring for the needy, ending suffering on Earth, and protecting our children and future generations. Working to attain these goals will produce the most deeply meaningful and satisfying lives.

Equality, fairness, cooperation, sustainability and widespread prosperity are fundamental operating principles and laws of nature. Nature does not allow small groups to amass vast resources while the large majority suffers. Economic and political leaders who concentrate wealth and suppress democracy are good people who mean well. The vast majority of these leaders probably do not like operating in systems that put their own well-being in conflict with society's. We are smart enough to figure out how to evolve our systems into forms that remove these conflicts – forms where companies, business leaders and politicians prosper by benefiting, not degrading society.

Compliance with equality, fairness and other laws of nature is inevitable. This is our destiny. Our limited perspective might make it difficult to see how we could attain this. But we have the ability to expand our perspective out to the whole system. We have access to the wisdom of nature through our hearts. By making our minds the servants of deep, infinite wisdom, we will fulfill our destiny – achieving sustainability and real prosperity.

We are proud of our Founders for their selfless devotion to future generations. Let us make our children and future generations proud of us. Let us stand up, work together and create Heaven on Earth. As John Lennon said in *Imagine*, let us create a world where we all live as one.

APPENDIX – WHOLE SYSTEM BOOK TABLE OF CONTENTS

Global System Change
A Whole System Approach to
Achieving Sustainability and Real Prosperity

Table of Contents

support as humans
8. Learn from Indigenous and other proven effective cultures and models
9. Give priority to science and unbiased experts
10. Ensure effective, trustworthy government
11. Fully employ sustainable technologies, practices, ideas and lifestyles
12. Be in nature
13. Cooperate

Nature's Ability to Support Life
Climate Change
    Scientific Consensus
    Climate Change Problems
        Temperature
        Carbon Dioxide
        Temperature-Carbon Dioxide Correlation
        Methane
        Sea Level
        Oceans
        Glaciers and Ice Sheets
        Forests
        Biodiversity
        Storms and Droughts
        Public Health
        Climate Acceleration and Point of No Return
        Hydrogen Sulfide
        Insurance Losses
        National Security
    Climate Change Deceptions
        Small temperature change equals small impact
        Correlation Versus Causation
        Temperature Variations
        Climate Models
        Natural Versus Human Causes
        Europe may have been warmer in the past
        Carbon dioxide is not a pollutant
        As a small component of the atmosphere, carbon dioxide will have a small impact on climate
        Doubling carbon dioxide only would cause 1 °C of warming
        One Wrong Equals All Wrong
        Biased/Illogical Characterization
        Meteorologists Versus Climatologists
        Reducing greenhouse gas emissions will hurt the economy
        Humans should adapt to climate change rather than

Putting the How Before the What
Necessary Trade-Off
Adequate safety testing is too expensive
Safe chemicals are too expensive
Restricting chemicals will eliminate important services
Restricting chemicals will cost jobs
Restricting chemicals will hurt the economy
Company research protects society
Deceptive Independent Research
Government, laws and regulations protect society
Government safety claims are trustworthy
Full disclosure might unnecessarily alarm citizens
Job rotation between business and government does not hurt society
The court system protects society
Millions of potential lawsuits
All lawsuits are frivolous
Many people use chemicals with no ill effects
Lobbying and Media Campaigns
Conspiracy Theory
Rule of Dumb
Chemical Solutions
Implement Fair Capitalism
Adequate Safety Testing
Effective Laws and Regulations
Sustainable Chemistry
National Health Policy Based on Prevention
Limit Deceptive Corporate Communications
Full Disclosure
Raise Public Awareness
Support NGOs
Societal Actions
Individual Actions
Genetic Engineering
Regulations and Safety Testing
Genetic Engineering Problems
Human Health Impacts
Bovine Growth Hormone
Contamination
Economic Impacts
Increasing Herbicide Resistance
Growing Pest Resistance
Failure to Increase Crop Yields
Glyphosate Impacts
Fish and Animal Contamination

Pharmaceutical Crop Contamination
Gene-Editing
Synthetic Biology

Genetic Engineering Deceptions
Extensive research shows that GE crops are safe
GE food is the same as regular food
Millions of people eat GE foods with no ill effects
Widespread consumption of GE foods means that the public accepts them
Labeling GE foods would unnecessarily alarm citizens
GE is needed to address hunger and other problems
GE crops help farmers
Rush to Market
Patenting GMO's benefits humanity
Gloom and Doom
Opposing GE is anti-science

Genetic Engineering Solutions
Eliminate Limited Liability
Adequate Safety Testing
Restrict GE use when risks are large and uncontrollable
Require Labeling
Limit Corporate Communications
Emulate Nature

Nanotechnology
Oceans
Pollution
Sewage
Plastic Waste
Dead Zones
Bottom Trawling
Collapsing Fisheries
Jellyfish
Dolphins and Whales
Aquaculture
Development and Other Activities

Freshwater
Air
Land
Agriculture
Topsoil
Grasslands
Wetlands
Forests
Africa

Restrict Prescription of Psychiatric Drugs
Restrict Drug Company Marketing
Restrict Psychiatric Drug use among Children and Teenagers
Restrict Compulsory Psychiatric Drug Use
Require Long-term, Independent Drug Research
Hold Drug Companies Fully Responsible
Restrict Off-Label Drug Use
Emphasize Psychotherapy
Effectively Address Addictive and Compulsive Behavior
Consider Spiritual Solutions
Establish Support Networks
Expand Parent Support and Training
Research and Expand Alternative Treatments
Incentivize Recovery, Not Treatment
Encourage Following Intuitive Wisdom
Encourage Service and Activism
Promote Rational Thought, Not Skepticism
Face Negative Emotions
Encourage Meditation
Empower People

Higher Education
Rapid Tuition Growth
High Student Debt
Declining Class Mobility
Bloated University Administrations
Expanding For-Profit Colleges
Expanding Online Education
Business Control of University Research
Suppression of Professors
Suppression of Critical Thinking
Objectivism and Atlas Shrugged
Libertarianism
Limited Job Opportunities for Graduates
Unfair Student Debt Terms
Higher Education Solutions

Education Solutions
Clarify Purpose
Clarify Method
Teach Systems Thinking and Intuitive Wisdom
Teach Critical Thinking
Whole System Strategy
End Business Control of Education

ENDNOTES

[1] Robert D. Atkinson et al, *Worse Than the Great Depression: What Experts Are Missing About American Manufacturing Decline*, The Information Technology & Innovation Foundation, March 2012.

[2] *Sustainable Investing*, USB Research Focus, July 2013.

[3] Bill Saporito, *Making Good, Plus a Profit*, Time Magazine, March 23, 2015

[4] Robert Reich, *Robert Reich on America's Economic U-Turn and How to Move Forward Again*, www.AlterNet.org, March 10, 2014.

[5] David DeGraw, *Peak Inequality: The .01 percent And The Impoverishment Of Society*, www.DavidDeGraw.org, Accessed August 25, 2014.

[6] Thom Hartman, *Is America Going to Be the Flintstones or the Jetsons?*, www.AlterNet.org, February 18, 2014.

[7] Paul Buchheit, *Tax Avoidance On the Rise: It's Twice the Amount of Social Security and Medicare*, www.NationOfChange.org, January 7, 2013.

[8] Richard Eskow, *Wall Street-Backed Organization Blasts Rising American Populism and Elizabeth Warren*, Campaign for America's Future, December 4, 2013.

[9] Paul Buchheit, *5 Depressing Ways That one percent's Huge Profits Have Broken the Back of America*, www.AlterNet.org, October 6, 2013.

[10] Joseph E. Stiglitz, *A Tax System Stacked Against the 99 Percent*, New York Times, April 14, 2013.

[11] Same as above.

[12] Lori Wallach, *NAFTA at 20: One Million U.S. Jobs Lost, Higher Income Inequality*, Huffington Post, January 6, 2014.

[13] George Monbiot, *A Full-Frontal Assault on Democracy in Europe and the United States*, The Guardian, November 5, 2013.

[14] Simon Davis-Cohen, *Why Corporate 'Negative Speech Rights' Is as Dangerous as Corporate Free Speech*, www.AlterNet.org, June 18, 2014.

[15] Robert Reich, *Be Very Afraid: The American Economy Is Cannibalizing Itself, and We the People Are Going to Pay a Huge Price*, www.RobertReich.org, November 3, 2013.

[16] Les Leopold, *The Finance Industry Is Gorging Itself on Your Future—The Trend Lines Will Blow You Away*, www.AlterNet.org, December 31, 2014.

[17] Same as above.

[18] Robert Reich, *What's Really Destroying the American Middle Class*, www.RobertReich.org, September 29, 2014.

[19] Paul Rosenberg, *10 Things You Might Not Know About Poverty*, www.AlterNet.org, January 8, 2014.

[20] CJ Werleman, *The Decline of Liberalism Threatens Secularism in America*, www.AlterNet.org, August 26, 2014.

[21] Paul Rosenberg, *10 Things You Might Not Know About Poverty*, www.AlterNet.org, January 8, 2014.

[22] David DeGraw, *Peak Inequality: The .01 percent And The Impoverishment Of Society*, www.DavidDeGraw.org, Accessed August 25, 2014.

[23] Paul Buchheit, *5 Extreme Acts of Greed that Screw the American People*, www.AlterNet.org, June 15, 2014.
[24] Paul Buchheit, *3 Ways the Super-Rich Suck Wealth out of the Rest of Us*, www.AlterNet.org, December 8, 2013.
[25] David DeGraw, *Peak Inequality: The .01 percent And The Impoverishment Of Society*, www.DavidDeGraw.org, Accessed August 25, 2014.
[26] Same as above.
[27] Lynn Stuart Parramore, *3 Things That Make Libertarian Heads Explode*, www.AlterNet.org, March 10, 2014.
[28] Paul Buchheit, *Overwhelming Evidence that Half of America is In or Near Poverty*, www.AlterNet.org, March 23, 2104.
[29] Tami Luhby, *America's middle class: Poorer than you think*, www.CNN.com, June 11, 2014.
[30] Les Leopold, *You're Likely to Be a Lot Poorer Than You Were a Few Years Ago—And It's All By Design*, www.AlterNet.org, December 5, 2014.
[31] Natalie Shure, *.1 percent of America Now Controls 22 percent of Wealth: The Wealth Gap Has Killed the Middle Class*, www.AlterNet.org, November 12, 2014.
[32] Annalyn Kurtz, *7 setbacks for the middle class*, www.CNN.com, January 24, 2014.
[33] Paul Buchheit, *Super Bowl for the Rich: Upper-Class 91, Middle-Class 9*, www.AlterNet.org, January 25, 2015.
[34] Robert Reich, *3 Biggest Lies Corporate Lobbyists Will Use to Push Lower Corporate Taxes*, www.RobertReich.org, August 5, 2013.
[35] Paul Buchheit, *Super Bowl for the Rich: Upper-Class 91, Middle-Class 9*, www.AlterNet.org, January 25, 2015.
[36] Tom Hartman and Sam Sacks, *How America Is Turning into a Third World Nation In Four Easy Steps*, www.ThomHartmann.com, November 10, 2012.
[37] Same as above.
[38] Les Leopold, *The Finance Industry Is Gorging Itself on Your Future—The Trend Lines Will Blow You Away*, www.AlterNet.org, December 31, 2014.
[39] Robert Reich, *What's Really Destroying the American Middle Class*, www.RobertReich.org, September 29, 2014.
[40] Same as above.
[41] Tom Hartman and Sam Sacks, *How America Is Turning into a Third World Nation In Four Easy Steps*, www.ThomHartmann.com, November 10, 2012.
[42] Same as above.
[43] Same as above.
[44] Alex Henderson, *10 Economic Trends that Spell Doom for America's Workers*, www.AlterNet.org, November 7, 2014.
[45] CJ Werleman, *The Decline of Liberalism Threatens Secularism in America*, www.AlterNet.org, August 26, 2014.
[46] Chris Isidore, *More of the jobless are giving up on finding work*, www.CNN.com, January 10, 2014.

[47] Jodie Gummow, *70 percent of Americans Not in the Labor Force Are Under 55 Years Old*, www.AlterNet.org, March 6, 2014.

[48] Joseph Stiglitz, *The People Who Break the Rules Have Raked in Huge Profits and Wealth and It's Sickening Our Politics*, www.AlterNet.org, September 11, 2013.

[49] David DeGraw, *Peak Inequality: The .01 percent And The Impoverishment Of Society*, www.DavidDeGraw.org, Accessed August 25, 2014.

[50] Same as above.

[51] Paul Buchheit, *5 Depressing Ways That one percent's Huge Profits Have Broken the Back of America*, www.AlterNet.org, October 6, 2013.

[52] Joe McKendrick, *Half of all U.S. jobs will be automated, but what opportunities will be created?*, www.SmartPlanet.com, September 13, 2013.

[53] Mary Kay Henry, *The True Meaning of Labor Day*, www.AlterNet.org, August 30, 2014.

[54] Robert Reich, *US Companies Take Advantage of American Perks, Go Abroad*, www.RobertReich.org, July 29, 2014.

[55] Paul Buchheit, *3 Facts that Poverty-Deniers Don't Want to Hear*, www.AlterNet.org, August 3, 2014.

[56] David DeGraw, *Peak Inequality: The .01 percent And The Impoverishment Of Society*, www.DavidDeGraw.org, Accessed August 25, 2014.

[57] Same as above.

[58] Same as above.

[59] Same as above.

[60] Same as above.

[61] Same as above.

[62] Robert Reich, *Why the Republican Strategy to Set Working Class Whites Against the Poor is Backfiring*, www.AlterNet.org, January 10, 2014.

[63] Paul Buchheit, *Super Bowl for the Rich: Upper-Class 91, Middle-Class 9*, www.AlterNet.org, January 25, 2015.

[64] Paul Buchheit, *3 Facts that Poverty-Deniers Don't Want to Hear*, www.AlterNet.org, August 3, 2014.

[65] Christopher Matthews, *Nearly Half of America Lives Paycheck-to-Paycheck*, www.TIME.com, January 30, 2014.

[66] Hadley Malcolm, *A third of Americans delinquent on debt*, USA Today, July 29, 2014.

[67] Allison Linn, *Millennials hit 30: It's the economy, not us*, www.NBCnews.com, February 1, 2014.

[68] *Millennials earn 20% less than Boomers did at same stage of life*, www.USAtoday.com, January 13, 2017.

[69] Lynn Stuart Parramore, *Cost of Raising Child to 18 Soars Over $245,000*, www.AlterNet.org, August 19, 2014.

[70] Gregory Wallace, *Child care costs more than college*, www.CNN.com, December 4, 2014.

[71] Les Leopold, *We've Got a Billionaire Bailout Society—And the 99 percent May Never Recover From It In Our Lifetimes*, www.AlterNet.org, September 12, 2013.

[72] Same as above.

[73] Meteor Blades, *Nearly 300,000 Veterans Have Lost Out on Jobless Compensation Because of the Disdainful House GOP*, Daily Kos, June 28, 2014.

[74] Chauncey DeVega, *The Sick Ayn Randian War Against Everyone Who Isn't Rich*, www.AlterNet.org, September 26, 2013.

[75] *Snapshot of Homelessness*, www.EndHomelessness.org, Accessed August 3, 2014.

[76] Blake Ellis, *Student homelessness hits another record high*, www.CNN.com, September 22, 2014.

[77] Evelyn Nieves, *No Solutions: Laws to Make Everything About Homelessness Illegal Have Increased Dramatically*, www.AlterNet.org, July 19, 2014.

[78] Evelyn Nieves, *The United States Is Cruel, Inhuman and Degrading to the Poor, U.N. Report Charges*, www.AlterNet.org, March 31, 2014.

[79] Joshua Holland, *Political Polarization Hits New Extremes as Republicans Move to Far Right*, www. BillMoyers.com, June 15, 2014.

[80] George Scialabba, *How Bad Is It?*, www.TheNewIndquiry.com, May 26, 2012.

[81] Marian Currinder et al, No good options for Boehner, www.CNN.com, October 1, 2013.

[82] Kevin Zeese et al, *These Americans Are Fighting for an Actual, Legitimate Democracy, By and For the People*, www.AlterNet.org, April 18, 2014.

[83] Robert Reich, *American Democracy Is Diseased*, www.RobertReich.org, August 20, 2014.

[84] Kevin Zeese et al, *These Americans Are Fighting for an Actual, Legitimate Democracy, By and For the People*, www.AlterNet.org, April 18, 2014.

[85] Richard Eskow, *Wall Street-Backed Organization Blasts Rising American Populism and Elizabeth Warren*, Campaign for America's Future, December 4, 2013.

[86] Chauncey DeVega, *The Sick Ayn Randian War Against Everyone Who Isn't Rich*, www.AlterNet.org, September 26, 2013.

[87] Heather Digby Parton, *The Shameful Racism of Southern Conservatives: They Just Don't Want Minorities to Vote*, www.AlterNet.org, September 13, 2014.

[88] Richard Wolf, *Supreme Court blocks Wisconsin's voter ID law*, USA Today, October 9, 2014.

[89] Ashley Berrang, *2012 Election Turnout Dips Below 2008 and 2004 Levels: Number Of Eligible Voters Increases By Eight Million, Five Million Fewer Votes Cast*, www.BipartisanPolicy.org, November 8, 2012.

[90] CJ Werleman, *How Hyper-Religious Political Stunts by Republicans Keep Voters Captive to Corporate Ideology*, www.AlterNet.org, March 3, 2014.

[91] Same as above.

[92] Robert Reich, *Why the Republican Strategy to Set Working Class Whites Against the Poor is Backfiring*, www.AlterNet.org, January 10, 2014.

[93] Paul Buchheit, *3 Facts that Poverty-Deniers Don't Want to Hear*, www.AlterNet.org, August 3, 2014.

[94] Chris Hedges, *Totalitarianism, American Style*, www.AlterNet.org, September 22, 2014.

[95] Same as above.

[96] Same as above.

[97] Don Hazen, *The Retirement Crisis Is Upon Us*, www.AlterNet.org, January 7, 2014.

[98] Nari Rhee, PhD, *The Retirement Savings Crisis: Is It Worse Than We Think?*, National Institute on Retirement Security, June 2013.

[99] Don Hazen, *The Retirement Crisis Is Upon Us*, www.AlterNet.org, January 7, 2014.

[100] Same as above.

[101] Same as above.

[102] Virginia P. Reno, *What's Next for Social Security?*, National Academy of Social Insurance, October 2013.

[103] Paul Buchheit, *5 Extreme Acts of Greed that Screw the American People*, www.AlterNet.org, June 15, 2014.

[104] Constantine Von Hoffman, *Financial firms fight rule that would put client interests first*, www.CBSnews.com, June 24, 2014.

[105] Janet Allon, *Krugman on the Other Surprising Obama Success Story No One Is Talking About*, www.AlterNet.org, August 4, 2014.

[106] Travis Gettys, *Bernie Sanders: Destroy the Big Banks Before the Big Banks Destroy You*, www.AlterNet.org, December 17, 2014.

[107] David Sirota, *There Is a Vast Oligarch Conspiracy Afoot to Destroy the Retirement Plans of Millions of Workers*, www.AlterNet.org, October 10, 2013.

[108] Same as above.

[109] Michael Hudson, *How Wall Street and Its Democratic Allies Are Waging War Against Pension Funds*, www.AlterNet.org, January 5, 2015.

[110] Same as above.

[111] Same as above.

[112] Lynn Stuart Parramore, *Shocking Picture of What Life Will Look Like When You Can't Afford to Retire*, www.AlterNet.org, August 25, 2014.

[113] Sonali Kolhatkar, *How Wealthy Elites Are Hijacking Democracy All Over the World*, www.Truthdig.com, May 30, 2014.

[114] Amy Goodman et al, *Police Worldwide Criminalize Dissent, Assert New Powers in Crackdown on Protests*, www.DemocracyNow.org, October 10, 2013.

[115] *Working For the Few, Political Capture and Economic Inequality*, Oxfam, January 20, 2014.

[116] Same as above.

[117] *Inequality 'will fuel upheavals,' says WEF*, Business Day Live, January 20, 2014.

[118] Paul Buchheit, *3 Ways the Super-Rich Suck Wealth out of the Rest of Us*, www.AlterNet.org, December 8, 2013.

[119] *Working For the Few, Political Capture and Economic Inequality*, Oxfam, January 20, 2014.

[120] Shan Li, *Global unemployment jumped to nearly 202 million last year*, www.LAtimes.com, January 20, 2014.

[121] *Inequality 'will fuel upheavals,' says WEF*, Business Day Live, January 20, 2014.

[122] *Costs of economic growth have 'outweighted benefits'*, www.SciDev.net, July 19, 2013.

[123] Zaid Jilani, *Someone Crunched the Numbers on What the Bankers Did to the Greeks, and the Results Will Blow You Away*, www.AlterNet.org, March 26, 2015

[124] CJ Werleman, *Global Rankings Study Depicts an America in Warp Speed Decline*, www.AlterNet.org, April 8, 2014.

[125] George Scialabba, *How Bad Is It?*, www.TheNewIndquiry.com, May 26, 2012.

[126] *40 Maps That Will Help You Make Sense of the World*, www.TwistedSifter.com, August 13, 2013.

[127] Sam Pizzigati, *The Surprising Reason Americans Are Far Less Healthy Than Other People in Developed Nations*, www.AlterNet.org, August 20, 2013.

[128] Thom Hartmann, *The Corporate Right-Wing Agenda Is Driving Thousands of Americans to Attempt Suicide*, www.AlterNet.org, August 3, 2013.

[129] *The Suicide Crisis*, USA Today, October 9, 2014.

[130] David Sirota, *Comcast's Worst Nightmare: How Tennessee Could Save America's Internet*, www.AlterNet.org, July 18, 2014.

[131] George Scialabba, *How Bad Is It?*, www.TheNewIndquiry.com, May 26, 2012.

[132] Nafeez Ahmed, *Nasa-funded study: industrial civilisation headed for 'irreversible collapse'?*, The Guardian, March 14, 2014.

[133] George Scialabba, *How Bad Is It?*, www.TheNewIndquiry.com, May 26, 2012.

[134] Jessica Derschowitz, *Taylor Swift sings for young cancer patient*, www.CBSnews.com, August 5, 2014.

[135] Timothy Rapp, *5-Year-Old Cancer Survivor Scores TD at Browns Camp*, www.BleacherReport.com, August 4, 2014.

[136] David Seligman et.al., *Your Job Contract or Cellphone Agreement May Contain Language That Can Ruin Your Life*, www.AlterNet.org, November 7, 2014.

[137] Brendan Fischer, *How Scott Walker Showed Just How Wrong the Supreme Court Was on Citizens United*, www.AlterNet.org, September 16, 2016.

[138] Same as above.

[139] Same as above.

[140] David Morris, *Should Large Nations Split into Small Nations?*, www.AlterNet.org, September 12, 2014.

[141] Steven Rosenfeld, *Nation's Top Civil Rights Lawyers Say Discriminatory Jim Crow Voting Laws Abound*, www.AlterNet.org, August 6, 2014.

[142] *How Did We Get the Principle of Equal State Sovereignty (in the Shelby County Case)?*, Constitutional Law Prof Blog, www.LawProfessors.com, June 28, 2013.

[143] Ed Kilgore, *Throwing Away the Umbrella*, Washington Monthly, June 25, 2013.

[144] Ian Millhiser, *If The Supreme Court Reads This Study, It Could End Partisan Gerrymandering Forever*, www.ThinkProgressl.org, December 1, 2014.

[145] Same as above.

[146] *Policy Basics: Where Do Our Federal Tax Dollars Go?*, Center on Budget and Policy Priorities, March 4, 2016.

[147] Howard Gleckman, *Individual Income Taxes May Soon Generate Half of All Federal Tax Revenue*, www.Forbes.com, February 6, 2010.

[148] Paul Buchheit, *Tax Avoidance On the Rise: It's Twice the Amount of Social Security and Medicare*, www.NationOfChange.org, January 7, 2013.

[149] Same as above.

[150] Les Leopold, *The Finance Industry Is Gorging Itself on Your Future—The Trend Lines Will Blow You Away*, www.AlterNet.org, December 31, 2014.

[151] Les Leopold, *We've Got a Billionaire Bailout Society—And the 99 percent May Never Recover From It In Our Lifetimes*, www.AlterNet.org, September 12, 2013.

[152] Valerie Wilson, *North Carolina Cuts to Jobless Benefits Did Not Help Workers*, www.AlterNet.org, August 11, 2014.

[153] April M. Short, *Tennessee Drug Tests Welfare Applicants, Finds Just 1 Person Using Drugs*, www.AlterNet.org, August 8, 2014.

[154] Lynn Stuart Parramore, *5 Reasons to Consider a No-Strings-Attached, Basic Income for All Americans*, www.AlterNet.org, March 17, 2014.

[155] Same as above.

[156] Same as above.

[157] Same as above.

[158] David DeGraw, *Peak Inequality: The .01 percent And The Impoverishment Of Society*, www.DavidDeGraw.org, Accessed August 25, 2014.

[159] Same as above.

[160] Same as above.

[161] Lynn Stuart Parramore, *How the New Monopoly Capitalism Will Crush You to Smithereens*, www.AlterNet.org, August 14, 2014.

[162] Same as above.

[163] Nathan Bomey, *Dow Chemical, DuPont reach deal on merger*, USA Today, December 11, 2015.

[164] Lynn Stuart Parramore, *How the New Monopoly Capitalism Will Crush You to Smithereens*, www.AlterNet.org, August 14, 2014.

[165] Ellen Dannin, *How One State Protects Taxpayers From Privatization Pitfalls*, www.TruthOut.org, November 14, 2013.

[166] Marcin Gerwin et al, *Do We Really Need Economic Growth?*, www.Resilience.org, December 9, 2013.

167 *GDP – US, Inflation*, www.MeasuringWorth.com, Accessed December 11, 2015.
168 Andrew M. Allison et al, *The Real Thomas Jefferson*, National Center for Constitutional Studies, 2008, Page 197.
169 Andrew M. Allison et al, *The Real Thomas Jefferson*, National Center for Constitutional Studies, 2008, Page 163.
170 Same as above.
171 Andrew M. Allison et al, *The Real Thomas Jefferson*, National Center for Constitutional Studies, 2008, Page 207.
172 Andrew M. Allison et al, *The Real Thomas Jefferson*, National Center for Constitutional Studies, 2008, Page 162.
173 Andrew M. Allison et al, *The Real Thomas Jefferson*, National Center for Constitutional Studies, 2008, Page 167.
174 Same as above.
175 Andrew M. Allison et al, *The Real Thomas Jefferson*, National Center for Constitutional Studies, 2008, Page 168.
176 Andrea Wulf, *Founding Gardeners*, Vintage Books, 2011, Page 61.
177 Andrea Wulf, *Founding Gardeners*, Vintage Books, 2011, Page 85.
178 James O'Toole, *Americans pay more for slower Internet*, www.CNN.com, October 31, 2014.
179 Same as above.
180 Jim Hightower, *4 Ways Amazon's Ruthless Practices Are Crushing Local Economies*, www.AlterNet.org, September 25, 2014.
181 Alison Flood, *New Amazon terms amount to 'assisted suicide' for book industry, experts claim*, The Guardian, June 25, 2104.
182 Jim Hightower, *4 Ways Amazon's Ruthless Practices Are Crushing Local Economies*, www.AlterNet.org, September 25, 2014.
183 Same as above.
184 Same as above.
185 Alexander Smith, *North Korea expands prison camp where inmates dig own graves: Amnesty International*, NBC News, December 5, 2013.
186 Harris Wofford et al, *50 Years Later, JFK's Vision of Enduring World Peace Eclipsed by Focus on Assassination*, www.AlterNet.org, March 19, 2014.
187 Same as above.
188 Same as above.
189 Same as above.
190 *Former President Dwight D. Eisenhower speaks with CBS News' Walter Cronkite on the 20th Anniversary of D-Day on June 6, 1964*, www.CBSnews.com, June 6, 2014.
191 Harris Wofford et al, *50 Years Later, JFK's Vision of Enduring World Peace Eclipsed by Focus on Assassination*, www.AlterNet.org, March 19, 2014.
192 Michael Meurer, *Americans Are 110 Times More Likely to Die from Contaminated Food Than Terrorism*, www.Truth-Out.org, September 17, 2013.
193 Thomas Jefferson, www.USCPublicDiplomacy.org, Accessed September 7, 2014.

[194] William Peters, *A More Perfect Union: The Making of the United States Constitution*, Page 27, Crown Publishers, 1987.

[195] David DeGraw, *How the Ultra-Rich .01 percent Have Sucked Up Even More of America's Wealth Than You Think*, www.AlterNet.org, August 22, 2014.

[196] Dale Carnegie, *Lincoln, The Unknown*, Dale Carnegie & Associates, Page 98, 1932.

[197] Same as above.

[198] Thomas Frank, *Airline profits soar yet no relief for passengers*, www.USAtoday.com, January 27, 2015.

[199] Same as above.

[200] Paul Rosenberg, *Why Conservatives Win: George Lakoff Explains Why Framing Is Important and What Democrats Must Learn*, www.AlterNet.org, December 8, 2014.

[201] Rem Rieder, *The political news bubble*, www.USAtoday.com, October 21, 2014.

[202] Travis Gettys, *Fox News more wrong than ever: New Politifact review finds pundits spewing mostly lies*, www.RawStory.com, January 28, 2015.

[203] Ian Millhiser, *If You Want To Understand What's Happened To The Supreme Court, You Need To Listen To Rand Paul*, www.ThinkProgress.org, January 16, 2015.

[204] Same as above.

[205] William Astore, *War Is the New Normal: 7 Deadly Reasons Why America's Wars Persist*, www.TomDispatch.com, February 1, 2015.

[206] Luke Brinker, *This Conservative Anti-Tax Utopia Is Imploding*, www.AlterNet.org, April 1, 2015

[207] Thom Harmann, *Free Trade Deals Have Devastated the U.S.: Now Obama Pushes Through Biggest One Yet*, www.AlterNet.org, February 5, 2015.

[208] Same as above.

[209] Same as above.

[210] Same as above.

[211] Allegra Kirkland, *5 Most Insane Facts About Maternity Leave in the U.S.*, www.AlterNet.org, February 6, 2015.

[212] Nicole Pelletiere, 5-Year-Old Girl Paralyzed From Backbend Vows to Overcome Injury, www.ABCnews.com, March 14, 2016.

[213] Denis Campbell et al, *NHS is the world's best healthcare system, report says*, The Guardian, June 17, 2014.

[214] Thom Hartmann, *The Republicans Are Ruthless and Relentless in Their Drive to Push Down Wages*, www.AlterNet.org, March 8, 2015.

[215] Same as above.

[216] Same as above.

[217] Paul Buchheit, *How to Become a Conservative in Four Embarrassing Steps*, www.AlterNet.org, March 8, 2015.

[218] Same as above.

[219] Nicole Pelletiere, *50 bikers escort bullied boy to first day of middle school*, www.ABCnews.com, August 4, 2017.

[220] Paul Buchheit, *How to Become a Conservative in Four Embarrassing Steps*, www.AlterNet.org, March 8, 2015.

[221] Henry Gass, *Can Florida prepare for climate change without saying the words?*, www.CSmonitor.com, March 9, 2015.

[222] Paul Buchheit, *How to Become a Conservative in Four Embarrassing Steps*, www.AlterNet.org, March 8, 2015.

[223] Same as above.

[224] Gabriel Arana, *Fox News Doesn't Care If Bill O'Reilly Is A Liar*, www.HuffingtonPost.com, March 5, 2015.

[225] Andrew Rafferty, *Poll: Whites and Republicans Rank as Angriest Americans*, NBC News, January 3, 2016.

[226] Youssef El Gingihy, *How the NHS is being dismantled in 10 easy steps*, www.Independent.co.uk, August 27, 2015.

[227] Andrea Wulf, *Founding Gardners*, Vintage Books, 2011, Page 115.

[228] CJ Werleman, *The Decline of Liberalism Threatens Secularism in America*, www.AlterNet.org, August 26, 2014.

[229] Valerie Tarico, *6 Ways Religion Does More Bad Than Good*, www.AlterNet.org, November 12, 2014.

[230] Same as above.

[231] Same as above.

[232] Kelly McPherson et al, *The History of Sex*, The History Channel, 1999.

[233] Valerie Tarico, *6 Ways Religion Does More Bad Than Good*, www.AlterNet.org, November 12, 2014.

[234] CJ Werleman, *The Decline of Liberalism Threatens Secularism in America*, www.AlterNet.org, August 26, 2014.

[235] Thom Hartmann, One Simple Way to Save American Democracy: Get Serious About Taxing the Mega-Rich, www.AlterNet.org, March 6, 2015.

[236] Same as above.

[237] Same as above.

[238] Same as above.

[239] David Morris, *Inside the Major Political Fight for Broadband Internet That's Brewing Across America*, www.AlterNet.org, March 9, 2015.

[240] Claire Moser, *The Quiet Plan To Sell Off America's National Forests*, www.ThinkProgress.org, March 16, 2015.

[241] Robert Creamer, *GOPs Traitorous Letter to Iran: Breathtaking Attempt to Sabotage U.S. Foreign Policy, Stampede U.S. Into War*, The Huffington Post, March 10, 2015.

[242] Katia Hetter, *Get happy in the world's happiest countries*, www.CNN.com, March 20, 2015.

[243] Alex Henderson, *9 Reasons Why America Is a Terrible Place to Raise Kids*, www.AlterNet.org, March 11, 2015.

[244] Raj Raghunathan, *How to Deal with Highly Negative People*, www.AlterNet.org, December 17, 2014.

[245] Emily Esfahani Smith, *Masters of Love*, The Atlantic, June 12, 2014.

[246] Raj Raghunathan, *The Art of Complimenting and Criticizing*, Psychology Today, July 11, 2012.

[247] Raj Raghunathan, *How to Deal with Highly Negative People*, www.AlterNet.org, December 17, 2014.

[248] Stephen R. Covey, *The Seven Habits of Highly Effective People*, Free Press, 1989.

[249] Thomas G. Fiffer, *6 Ways 'Tough Guys' Are Actually Weak*, www.AlterNet.org, January 14, 2015.

[250] *The Quotable Franklin*, www.UShistory.org, Accessed April 3, 2015.

[251] Dale Carnegie, *Lincoln the Unknown*, Dale Carnegie & Associates, Page 75, 1932.

[252] *Albert Einstein and Religion*, www.Deism.com, Accessed April 3, 2015.

[253] *Einstein on Being Human*, www.LiberatorMagazine.com, Accessed April 3, 2015.

[254] Tracy Connor, *Nelson Mandela dead at 95*, www.NBCnews.com, December 5, 2013.

[255] Tanya Lewis, *Men prefer painful shocks to gadget-free alone time*, www.CBSnews.com, July 3, 2014.

[256] *Chief Seattle's Speech*, www.CSNU.edu, Accessed April 3, 2015.

[257] *Then and Now: An Interview with Barbara Hamilton*, www.Woodstock-Festival.tumblr.com, October 9, 2013.

[258] George Washington, *Farewell Address*, 1796.

[259] George Washington, letter to the Legislature of Pennsylvania, September 5, 1789.

INDEX

www.ingramcontent.com/pod-product-compliance
Lightning Source LLC
Chambersburg PA
CBHW060315200326
41519CB00011BA/1730